Praise for *Make Love Work*

'Nic Beets has written an excellent book that pulls no punches about what it takes to make a long-term intimate relationship *really* work for both partners.

You'll deepen your journey by learning from Nic's many years of personal and professional experience. If you want a more satisfying relationship without having to seek therapy, this book can take you far. And if you are considering therapy, read this book first. You'll save time and money.

In fact, this book is so good, many couple therapists can profit and learn from it.'
— **Dr Ellyn Bader**, co-founder of the Couples Institute and co-creator of the Developmental Model of Couple Therapy

'Whether you are single or in a new or established relationship, Nic Beets offers many ways to deepen your understanding of yourself and your partner and grow a more intimate, satisfying relationship. While sparing no punches in highlighting the real work of relating, he empathically confronts the challenges and encourages the reader to take the necessary risks to grow true emotional and sexual intimacy.

Nic's therapy on a page shows every reader how to take control of their relationship, one step at a time.'
— **Paula Dennan**, clinical psychologist and director at Sex Therapy NZ

MAKE LOVE WORK

A practical guide to relationship success

Nic Beets
Clinical psychologist, Relationshipwork

ALLEN&UNWIN
SYDNEY·MELBOURNE·AUCKLAND·LONDON

First published in 2023

Allen & Unwin
Level 2, 10 College Hill, Freemans Bay
Auckland 1011, New Zealand
+64 (9) 377 3800
auckland@allenandunwin.com
www.allenandunwin.co.nz

83 Alexander Street
Crows Nest NSW 2065, Australia
+61 (2) 8425 0100

A catalogue record for this book is available from the National Library
of New Zealand.

ISBN 978 1 98854 792 3

Design and diagrams by Megan van Staden
Set in Garamond 10/15
Printed and bound in Australia by the Opus Group

1 3 5 7 9 10 8 6 4 2

To Ryan & Elena
In hope for a better future

Contents

Acknowledgements

Kāhore taku toa i te toa takitahi, he toa takitini
We cannot succeed without the support of those around us

This book rests on three pillars. The first is the love of my life — my partner in work, family and fun, Verity Thom. Thanks for your love, patience, support, care, hard work, clinical wisdom, willingness, courage and faith.

The second pillar is all the clients who have taught me so much. Thanks for your bravery and determination. Any confidence I have about my insight into the inner workings of people and relationships is due to your trust and vulnerability. This book is an attempt to pay forward what I have gained from you.

The final pillar is the input from many skilled psychologists and therapists who have supported, nurtured and challenged me in my practice. I have been blessed to learn from some amazing practitioners over the years.

TRAINERS AND MENTORS IN COUPLE THERAPY
Drs Ellyn Bader and Pete Pearson (Developmental Model)
Drs David Schnarch and Ruth Morehouse (Crucible Approach)

SUPERVISORS	PEER SUPERVISORS
Dr Ruth Jackson	Paula Dennan
Johnella Bird	Dr Ally Waite
Dr Lynley Stenhouse	Verity Thom
David Carter	Marieke Pastor
Dr Ruth Morehouse	Marijke Batenburg
Dr Mary Miller	

Huge thanks to Michelle Hurley for commissioning the book and making wise suggestions throughout. To Leanne McGregor and the rest of the team at Allen & Unwin, my gratitude for making the mysterious business of publishing so welcoming and straightforward for a novice author. Deep appreciation to Teresa McIntyre, whose sympathetic editing made this a much better book and whose wit and warmth made the process a delight.

I also want to acknowledge three early readers who helped me with key sections of this book. Ngā mihi nui ki a koe for helping me out, Jill Butterworth, Adrienne Bartle and Verity Thom.

Author's notes

**ACKNOWLEDGING THOSE WHO ARE
LARGELY LEFT OUT OF THIS BOOK**

In this day and age, I think it is unacceptable to erase the experience of whole groups of people by using language and examples that deny their existence.

At the same time, this book is a reflection on my own clinical practice, where the vast majority of my clients have been cis-gendered, heterosexual and monogamous. I do not want to pretend to expertise that I do not have. However, this means that various groups of people have little or no representation in this book.

For example, trans people don't appear in the text, as I have no experience working with them. Likewise, aromantic and asexual people. The book is written on the assumption that readers are seeking romantic and sexual relationships, and I acknowledge that this is not everyone's desire or preference. Everyone I have worked with has had a strong identification with a sex, so intersex people are also absent here.

I do work with same-sex couples, so I do refer to that experience, but my experience is limited. I don't believe that my work is in any way authoritative regarding the relationships of people in the LGTBQIA+ community and I acknowledge that there is a lot of heteronormative language and assumption in my writing.

I have also worked with many couples who are ethically non-monogamous and so they also make an appearance in this text. However, the book has a distinct bias towards people trying to maintain a monogamous relationship because that represents the bulk of my practice. As such, there is a huge emphasis on couples in this book and it contains assumptions that some people in the CNM (consensual non-monogamous) community may not identify with.

I have worked with people of many different cultures, ethnicities and classes, and I have attempted to represent that diversity in the examples I offer. I hope I have done justice to the culture and values of the people from backgrounds different to my own.

This book is about love in long-term, committed relationships. People who are dating and still in the 'honeymoon' stage of relationship don't really appear. If you're single or dating, this book offers you a road map for the path ahead but doesn't speak to where you are at right now.

A NOTE ON THE EXAMPLES IN THIS BOOK

One more group who are left out of the book are my actual clients. I finish each chapter in the book with a story of a couple that illustrates crucial points. In these and all the other examples in the text, I use the literary device of writing as if they were real clients, but all the people and stories are fictional. If you are an ex-client and think you recognise yourself here, I assure you that it's a coincidence or an unconscious resonance. However, the issues and dynamics of the stories I tell are authentic, rooted in a composite of the many couples I have seen in my decades of practice.

Introduction

Whāia te mātauranga hei oranga mō koutou
Seek after learning for the sake of your well-being

Keeping love alive and intimate over the long term is a challenge. It requires hard work and dedication. For some people, the effort seems minimal compared with the rewards. For others, the cost in struggle and pain is too high and they would rather be alone or in a distant, non-intimate relationship.

Although I write this book as a professional, the contents are intensely personal. For me, making love work is not an academic or intellectual interest. I have been working on loving the same person well for over four decades. At times, I struggle to be open and intimate with her. Sometimes I find it hard to be civil to her. That's a reflection on myself, not on her. Verity is a gifted therapist and someone that people find easy to talk to. She has many friends who love her dearly. She is open, caring, reliable and kind. My passion for couple therapy has been fuelled by a hunger to be able to offer her the kind of love and relationship she deserves, and I desire.

This book is a summary of what I have learned so far in that journey. My hope is that it will inspire you to look deeper into yourself and aim higher for your relationship. That in having a deep understanding of the interpersonal dynamics of relationships, you will find insight into how love and intimacy work, and tools to help you deepen and refine your relationship. It's not an easy road, but it is the path to some of the greatest rewards and most profound joy that you can experience.

How to use this book

The first thing I need to stress is that this is a book about building an *equal partnership*. Most of the techniques and suggestions in this book are *not* suitable if you are not physically or emotionally safe in your relationship. If you can't speak your mind without fearing harm to yourself or people or things you love, then Chapter 19 is the only part of the book that applies to you. If someone would rather hurt you than look inside at themselves, there's not much you can do about that except attend to your own safety.

I encourage you to read the book interactively. Read with a highlighter or pen in your hand. Mark the passages that reflect your experience, that confuse you, or that you don't agree with.

I would be amazed if everything in here fits for you exactly — take what works for you, and leave what doesn't. At the same time, I invite you to let the book challenge some of your existing ideas and push your understanding of yourself and relationships in new directions.

Once you get past the theory in the first section, most chapters offer you exercises. As with any self-help book, the more you *do* what is suggested, rather than read about it, the greater benefit you will get.

Do share this book with your partner — invite them to journey with you deep into what makes relationships tick. Ideally, buy them their own copy so they don't have to deal with your highlights and dog-ears! If they are not a reader, talk to them about what strikes you as you read it. Push past your fear of being misunderstood or getting a negative reaction, and talk about the sections that put your experience into words or explain something you have always wondered about. Talk, too, about the bits that don't make sense or fit for you. See if you can engage their interest in understanding you *and* themselves to make a better future for the two of you.

If your partner won't engage, then find someone else who's interested to discuss the book with. There's nothing like trying to explain concepts to someone else to really consolidate your learning.

If you want to get a feel for what any chapter is about, flick to the end of it. The last section is always the story of a couple that illustrates the main themes of the chapter, and this is followed by a summary of the key points in the chapter.

To help those of you who like to dip in and out of a book, where I refer to a concept mentioned elsewhere, I try to give you the relevant chapter number so you can hunt it out if the meaning is not obvious from the current context.

The book is organised into five parts:

- Part One lays out crucial understandings that you'll need to make sense of the rest of the book. If you like to dip in and out, I encourage you to read the first three chapters to begin with. They lay out the core concepts from which the rest of the book operates. If your relationship is in crisis, you may want to start with Chapter 4. It offers some suggestions you can apply if your relationship needs urgent care. One of the tools in that chapter (Time Out) is referred to many times throughout the book.

- Part Two offers you three 'lenses' or ways of thinking about how relationships work — neurobiology, developmental stages and attachment theory. If you like theory and different ways of looking at the same thing, you'll love this part — it explores these three different theoretical approaches that we weave together in the Developmental Model that I practise.

- Part Three is focused on strategies to improve the way you operate in relationship — this contains many practical exercises for you to explore. If you want to skip the theory and get into 'How do I make things better?', this is the part for you. The first two chapters offer exercises and ideas you can work on by yourself; the next three chapters are more for you and your partner to work on together.

- Part Four examines five areas where couples commonly struggle with their differences: boundaries, 'who does what', sex, money and parenting. If there is a particular issue you are struggling with, you may want to go straight to the specific chapter devoted to that topic.

- Part Five explores three types of major crisis that can have impacts on relationships: infidelity, abuse and severe losses. If you have experienced infidelity, major losses or feel unsafe in your relationship, then these chapters are where you may want to head after reading the first three chapters of Part One. There will be ideas in these specialist chapters that are applicable to everyone. For example, while infidelity may not be an issue in your relationship, the discussion in that chapter about the relationship contract may still be of interest to you.

Take your time on this journey. There's a lot to digest in this book — be patient and gentle with yourself as you take it in and make it your own.

PART ONE

THE REALITIES OF RELATIONSHIP

In the first three chapters, I give you some crucial background information about how people and relationships work. The reality seems to be very different from what most of my clients expect. There's not much in the practical 'try this' variety here, but it's information that you need to get your head around to be able to use the rest of the book.

The fourth chapter in Part One offers some tools and approaches that you can apply immediately if you feel that your relationship is in crisis.

Chapter 1
Home truths about relationships

What you know about relationships, and yourself, is probably wrong

Misinformation has become a hot topic in recent years as we realise how social media is reflecting some of the worst aspects of human nature. It's something I have been talking about with my clients for decades — about how our modern, Western culture is full of ideas about relationships that are misleading, unhelpful and, sometimes, just plain wrong.

This chapter will try to correct some of the key misinformation that I see confusing and misleading people when they try to understand themselves and what's happening in their long-term, intimate relationships.

Before I begin, though, here's a little quiz you can do to check out where your beliefs and assumptions sit.

QUIZ: HOW DO YOU THINK RELATIONSHIPS WORK?

In the following table are 17 sets of statements about relationships, with pairs of statements labelled A and B. For each number, put a tick or cross beside the ideas that best reflect your beliefs about how relationships work. It's probably pretty obvious what I believe, but try to be as honest with yourself as possible.

	A	**B**
1	☐ Relationships should get easier over time. If your relationship gets harder or more challenging, there is something wrong with it.	☐ Relationships don't start out strong; they start out easy. You build strength by dealing with the inevitable challenges.
2	☐ The longer you have been with someone, the easier it should be to be intimate, open and vulnerable with them because you know each other better.	☐ Intimacy, openness and vulnerability get harder the longer you've been with someone, because their opinion of you becomes increasingly important to you as you invest more in the relationship.
3	☐ Intimacy begins with kindness and caring.	☐ Intimacy starts with your relationship with yourself — you can't share what you aren't aware of.
4	☐ If you don't feel close and comfortable with your partner, it's a warning sign.	☐ Great relationships don't feel close and comfortable all the time.
5	☐ If you feel uncomfortable (e.g. distanced, frustrated or anxious), then there is something wrong with your relationship.	☐ Uncomfortable feelings (e.g. of distance, frustration or anxiety) are expected in relationships and are not necessarily a sign that anything is going wrong.
6	☐ Closeness and intimacy are the same things, and you should aim to feel close to your partner all the time.	☐ Closeness is not the same thing as intimacy, and trying to be close all the time can get in the way of intimacy.
7	☐ Maintaining intimacy and closeness means you shouldn't rock the boat by bringing up differences.	☐ Intimacy requires noticing and dealing with differences. This can create a temporary sense of distance.

8	☐	If you disagree, then that's damaging to intimacy. Conflict means there's a problem, and you need to get rid of that conflict as quickly as possible.	☐	If you are being intimate, disagreement is inevitable — you are two different people. The challenge is to do the conflict well by taking responsibility for your behaviour and making sure it reflects your values and goals.
9	☐	Your partner's job is to make you feel good, especially about yourself. If they don't like or approve of you all the time, that means they don't love you.	☐	It's not your partner's job to make you feel okay about yourself — that's your job. It's hard to be honest (intimate) if you need your partner to like and approve of you all the time.
10	☐	It's foolish to bring up with your partner things that you know will be difficult or upsetting. Especially if you've tried once and got nowhere.	☐	Loving is risky — you have to be brave. Raise things that bother you, and persist if you don't get it sorted the first time. Tolerate the discomfort.
11	☐	You've got to go along to get along. It's all small stuff, so don't sweat it. Just give your partner what they want and have a peaceful home.	☐	'Keeping the peace' doesn't work. Have your conflicts sooner rather than later. The longer you leave things, the more resentment and misunderstanding build.
12	☐	It's always far better to say nothing than to be angry or upset with your partner. Even better, just give them what they want to be happy.	☐	Withdrawing and shutting off or 'pleasing' and giving in to 'keep the peace' are just as unhelpful and limiting to a relationship as flinging your anger, anxiety or other feelings at your partner.

13	☐ If you don't push for what you want, your partner will take advantage of you. You've got to stand up for yourself and not get pushed around.	☐ Dominating, bullying or coercing your partner to give you what you want will leave you feeling very lonely and unloved in the long run.
14	☐ If your partner upsets you, that's their responsibility. When they make you feel hurt or sad or angry, they always have to be the one to apologise and make up.	☐ It's your job to sort out bad habits (like appeasing, dominating or shutting down) that you came into the relationship with, not your partner's job to stop triggering them (though it is in their interest to attempt not to activate them).
15	☐ Most relationship problems are about communication. If we could just communicate better, everything would be fine.	☐ Communication skills are not the most important thing. Self-awareness and self-control (i.e. maturity) are more important than being a good talker.
16	☐ If you can justify what you did, then it was the right thing to do.	☐ Being able to justify what you did doesn't mean it was right, helpful or intimate.
17	☐ The way to improve the relationship is to tell your partner what they are doing that's hurtful or wrong or unhelpful.	☐ You have to work on yourself harder than you work on your partner.

- If you ticked more of column A than column B, congratulations: you are normal! You're going to love this book because it's full of new ideas that have the potential to transform your relationship and your life.
- If you ticked more of column B than column A, you must have read too many self-help books or something. You'll love this book because it will confirm and extend what you already know about relationships.
- If you ticked the same number of columns A and B, you cheated or missed one because that's not mathematically possible.

Assuming you ticked some of column A in that quick quiz, let's look at the likely origin of these sorts of notions about relationships.

I blame the troubadours

The romantic myths that pervade contemporary society undermine our ability to think clearly about relationships. One of the strongest threads in this web of lies is that if you find the 'right' person to partner with, joining your lives together is easy. 'Love conquers all.' Selling this fantasy to wealthy women stuck in the oppressive, exploitative business arrangements that constituted medieval marriages kept many travelling musicians, known as troubadours, employed. Good for them; maybe not so good for us.

This fantasy causes so much unnecessary distress, leading people to believe that if their relationship is challenging or uncomfortable, there must be something wrong with them, or their relationship, or both. As you read, I encourage you to hold on to the notion that **relationships are supposed to challenge and change us**. They help us improve at owning our faults, managing our emotions, and becoming more mature. The cost is surrendering some of our autonomy and accepting that experiencing discomfort is a necessary part of being in a relationship.

An accompanying romantic notion is that if you find the 'right' partner, your love is ageless, changeless. Our songs and stories push this notion, yet it is not what we experience. As we each grow and evolve as individuals and our circumstances change, the nature, meaning and intensity of love changes, too.

Are you stuck in stage one?

In contrast to the romantic fantasy of perfect, unchanging love, we can break the broad scope of relationship change into five stages (details in Chapter 2). Contemporary Western culture is obsessed with the first stage, the 'honeymoon' stage (formally known as the 'Symbiotic' or 'Bonding' stage). In love relationships, a range of chemical responses supports the bonding process.[1] These 'love drugs' make it easy for us to minimise differences and overlook each other's faults. The good feelings they engender fuel the fantasy of a perfect match who will meet our emotional needs without us risking the vulnerability of asking for what we want. We can stay in this stage for months, even a couple of years, until the drugs wear off and we have to start recognising reality and dealing with our differences.

This shift out of the honeymoon phase is entirely necessary and predictable. Yet, movies and TV shows, books and podcasts don't generally acknowledge this; instead, they tell us that love should always be easy and feel fabulous. The implication is that if your relationship isn't like that, there's something wrong with it (or with you). Our fixation on the delights of the honeymoon stage offers no preparation for the next phase, formally called 'Differentiating'. Here we focus on learning to accept and deal with our differences. This stage focuses on developing a culture within the relationship that allows us to disagree without harming each other and, eventually, to negotiate our way to an equitable resolution — one that both of us can freely accept.

Being conflicted about conflict

We are always in a relationship with someone different from us, so there will always need to be ways to deal with our differences. In my dictionary, 'dealing with differences' is a synonym for 'conflict'. Few of us have had good modelling and training for dealing with conflict well. Some of us are as reasonable as a cornered possum when disagreeing. Others are terrified of engaging in conflict and avoid it altogether, which leaves the management of differences to our unconscious processes (the automatic decisions our brain makes without us actively thinking about them) — frequently resulting in alarming consequences downstream. So, as you read, you may need to keep reminding yourself that some conflict is normal, necessary and inevitable.

Most of us automatically think that conflict means a battle between incompatible wishes or points of view that is always a threat to the relationship. It requires conscious effort to manage our anxiety and realise that conflict is a necessary part of a relationship and can contribute to personal growth and intimacy.

Nothing is either good or bad, but thinking makes it so

The meaning we put on things will change our subjective experience of them. This is vital to be aware of when considering your partner's behaviour. Consider the sentence 'When are you going back to the gym?' One person might take this as a gentle reminder of a goal they set themselves; the meaning they make of it is that their partner listened to them and is trying to support them. Another person may take it as their partner implying they are fat (and therefore ugly); the meaning *they* make is that their partner is shaming them, deliberately choosing to say something hurtful.

Our past experience often causes us to filter or distort the meaning of our partner's behaviour. For example, if I had grown up in a family where I was always told that what I was doing was wrong and never told when I was doing well, I would expect to hear criticism and would struggle to hear appreciation. It is a crucial part of self-awareness to recognise when and why these kinds of biases come into play.

A small disclaimer: I am talking here about the impact of your thinking and attitude on your subjective experience. At the moment, many popular change agents are selling the notion that you can 'manifest' anything you want in your life if you just think about it correctly. I do not believe that objective reality is that amenable to influence. For relationships, there is some behaviour that you simply shouldn't put up with, and no amount of changing your attitude will make it mean anything constructive.

Closeness is not intimacy; isolation is not independence

Many people, including therapists, use the words 'closeness' and 'intimacy' as if they were interchangeable. Likewise, a lot of people confuse emotional isolation with 'independence'. In thinking about relationships, it's helpful to separate these things.

Contemporary culture doesn't prepare us for the fact that intimacy is often uncomfortable. Intimacy ('into me see') requires challenging, revealing, effortful and even scary interactions. Closeness is all warm and cuddly and nice and friendly. Intimacy needs to include a lot more than just closeness. Closeness is about keeping things sweet to easily be in the same space; this is nice sometimes, but very limiting if it's the only way you can relate.

Some people avoid the discomfort of intimacy by insisting on their 'independence', when what they are really doing is avoiding the vulnerability that is a necessary part of showing their partner who they really are. True independence is when you can know and share what you think and feel and still have room to hear how it is for your partner.

Intimacy needs to include learning about yourself, growing and struggling with the less-than-ideal aspects of yourself *and* sharing that with your partner. This type of intimacy is not always pleasant, but it is necessary to stay truly connected.

Many people in relationships think this way: If I want to keep you close, I will avoid saying the things that I fear will 'rock the boat' or push you away. On the other hand, if I'm trying to avoid looking at or admitting my faults and limitations, I will avoid talking about subjects where we differ. I will also avoid mentioning those aspects of myself that I think you will reject, or that I don't like or am ashamed of, and tell myself I am 'independent'. If this forms the bulk of our relationship, then our closeness will lack depth because we avoid genuinely knowing each other.

In my view, the only closeness worth having flows from doing the work of intimacy. Likewise, the only independence worth the name is when you are honest to yourself and your partner about who you are, how you operate, what you want, etc., so that you can maintain your selfhood in the face of your partner being different from you.

Couples who avoid conflict are prone to overdoing closeness. Focusing on closeness is delightful at times (e.g. if you are having a special dinner together), but if you do it too much, your relationship becomes stagnant or false. By not airing your honest thoughts and feelings, you will likely feel resentful, ignored or misunderstood. You will probably feel blocked out, unimportant and frustrated, unless you are too cut off from yourself to notice.

Couples who fight or bicker are, obviously, less avoidant of upset.

People who are fierce in their pursuit of 'independence' will frequently seek improvement in the relationship by trying to make *their partner* change; which, of course, drives their partner further away. They are seeking connection, but they lack the self-awareness and self-mastery to resolve the issues in a way that builds intimacy.

In my practice, I encourage people to think the following way: If I aim for intimacy, in the sense of sharing what's truly going on for me, I'm going to be very aware of my connection to you, and yet we aren't always going to feel close. You aren't always going to like what I say. You might not even like some things about who I am. But at least you will know what's going on with me and will have a chance to deal with it. Our differences will be out in the open, and we can work through them. The payoff is that the more fully I can bring myself into the relationship, the greater chance I have of feeling accepted and truly loved for who I am.

The paradox of change

Most people who come for therapy or pick up a book like this are looking for ways to fix or change their partner. Even people who know that 'it takes two to tango' and 'you have to work on yourself' are usually focused on what their partner is doing that hurts, frustrates or confuses them, and are blind to or minimising the impact of their behaviour on their partner.

There is a paradox in the business of trying to change yourself or your situation. The more you can see where you have room for improvement, and the more you can accept and acknowledge your part in things not going as you would like, then the more power you have to make the changes that you want happen.

There are limits to this. Some people are stuck in cycles of self-blame and self-doubt, and the last thing they need to do is talk more about their failings. In that case, the room for improvement lies in their willingness to value and assert themselves.

If you want to get the most out of this book, I encourage you to focus on how it applies to *you* rather than your partner (although do, by all means, get them reading it and reflecting on themselves, too). Be prepared to consider that there is more going on for you, that you are not as in charge of yourself as you have previously thought. That attitude of humility and curiosity is essential if you want to learn to do things differently.

Accept that you, like all of us, have significant blind spots

One of the most important messages I have for you is that you are probably not as self-aware, not as accurate in your judgement about yourself, as you would like to think. This blind spot is true for all of us and is one way we cope with life. It wouldn't be a significant problem for most of us if we lived alone. But we are wired for connection, and if you are reading this book then relationships are clearly important to you.

By definition, our blind spots are impossible for us to see directly. But there are exercises we can do to highlight the limitations that our blind spots impose on our vision — you can *infer* what you do not see about yourself. If you pay close attention, the repetitive nature of difficulties with your partner will give you information about what you are missing about yourself. Think about how often you find yourself doing things in your relationship that you don't like or that you know are unhelpful. Maybe even things that you promised yourself you would stop doing, like being aggressive, avoiding topics, yelling, giving in, putting your partner down, winding your partner up, complaining ineffectually, withdrawing, appeasing, nagging or stonewalling. If you continue doing things that you know don't work or have vowed to stop, then this should alert you to the fact that you are *not* sufficiently on to yourself (self-aware).

Great relationships are intimate relationships. Neither closeness nor sex is what creates that connection. Intimacy is rooted in self-awareness, self-mastery and appreciation of difference.

Here's what this kind of intimacy looks like in practice:

- I reveal myself 'warts and all', including the things I don't like about myself or I fear you won't like or accept.
- I'm willing to learn about myself, including about the places where I need to change and grow.

- I can tolerate that you are different from me, and don't take that inevitable reality as critical of me or diminishing you.
- I stay open and responsive but not reactive. I know how to settle myself down if you challenge my view of myself, and I don't panic if things are difficult between us.

Doing all this takes work, patience and the ability to hang in there when it's scary. However, the intimacy in a relationship can only be as good as the state of the two people in it. If you want a solid, deep connection with your partner, you must first have a solid and deep relationship with yourself. The foundation of real intimacy is to **work on yourself, not your partner**.

How much of yourself you bring into the relationship is limited to things you are both aware of *and* willing to admit about yourself. If you aren't aware of it, you can't share it with your partner. If you can't admit it to yourself, you won't be sharing it with your partner either. Things you aren't aware of will still impact on your partner (and they are likely to be telling you about them!). As I said before, your partner's complaints can be the starting point for increased self-awareness and intimacy if you are willing to try and learn.

For that to happen, you have to be willing to admit that some of what you do isn't helpful. More bluntly, you must stop trying to keep yourself invulnerable by pretending that you have yourself sorted. Recognise what your 'hot button' topics are — the things that make you reactive — and work out how to stay centred when those buttons get pressed.

Try to develop true humility, which is as much the opposite of putting yourself down as it is of puffing yourself up. Learn to talk about your assets and liabilities, strengths and weaknesses, capabilities and insecurities. If you dare to share yourself fully and freely with your partner, you will learn what it is to be *truly* known, accepted and loved for who you are.

Every relationship is cross-cultural

One blind spot many of us have is around the fact that our partner grew up in a different culture from us — this encompasses family culture, relationship culture, ethnic and religious culture, and more. We often behave as if 'normal' is somehow objective rather than a product of environment and circumstance. Of course, this is not likely to be the case if you grew up in provincial Aotearoa and your partner grew up in central Guangzhou. Couples like this often know that their understanding of what's usual will need some negotiating. But most of us don't operate like that.

In my opinion, the family you grow up in determines what you consider 'normal'. You may be from the same ethnic, religious and geographical communities as your partner. Still, the chances are their family did all sorts of crucial things very differently from yours — from how the parents responded to a child's distress to their behaviour around conflict, sexuality or relationships with extended family.

If you are not consistently mindful of this fact, it's likely that you will be frequently blindsided by how your partner behaves. Even worse, if you are unthinkingly assuming that your 'normal' is universal, then you will talk to your partner as if their 'normal' is strange, inferior or just plain wrong. This is what is known as 'picking a fight'. Have the humility to recognise that what you know and believe is limited, and that one of the reasons to be with a partner is that they bring new, engaging, challenging ideas and understandings into your life. If you're wise, you will let your partner take you to places you would never go by yourself; sometimes literally (like a vacation spot you would never book), but certainly emotionally and culturally.

As I mentioned earlier, I will finish each chapter in the book with the story of a couple that illustrates crucial points. All the people and stories are fictional, but the dynamics are authentic, rooted in a composite of the many issues I have seen in my practice.

FIONA & KEHU

These two Kiwis had a delightfully romantic 'falling in love' story. They were both on their OE in London in their early twenties when they attended a party held by mutual friends. He thought she was drop-dead gorgeous and lively and couldn't quite believe that she was interested in him. She thought he was hunky and confident in an understated way. She was impressed that he was able to pursue his career in London, and thought he was very mature compared with the other guys she knew. They hit it off immediately, spending the whole night talking together, culminating in passionate sex in the early morning light.

Very quickly, their free time began to revolve around their relationship. They were both into the clubbing and Ecstasy scene and had enormous fun dancing the night away on the weekends and nursing each other through the Tuesday blues. While Fiona only had temporary work, Kehu worked as a lawyer on a good salary, so money was not a problem. After they had been dating for about six weeks, Fiona moved in when one of Kehu's flatmates left. They altered their plans so they could vacation in Europe together, and coordinated their return to Aotearoa so they could travel through Southeast Asia for five months on the way. By the time they got home, they had been inseparable for two years and had seldom had a cross word. Both of them believed that they had found their soulmate.

However, once Fiona and Kehu returned to Auckland, reality began to bite in a big way. They got a flat together and found work, but things were much less fun. Kehu felt he needed to be very committed to get ahead in his career, working long hours and socialising with his colleagues. Fiona found herself doing the bulk of the domestic labour and felt frustrated at his lack of energy to go out with her. Without being able to put words to it, she felt increasingly vulnerable and dependent on Kehu. She feared that she needed him but he didn't need her.

They began to have conflicts around him not keeping his word about when he was coming home, not wanting to spend time with her, and her 'nagging' him and 'not being supportive'. Kehu began to find more and more reasons to avoid coming home and began to drink more heavily after work, making him vulnerable to angry outbursts. Fiona became unhappy and passive-aggressive as she silently nursed her fear that Kehu had fallen out of love with her even as she tried harder to please him and 'make him happy'. Neither knew why things had got so bad so quickly, and both hated the fights and the bickering. Three years after their return from overseas, they sought couple therapy at Fiona's insistence.

As a first step to developing a more robust intimacy, we began by helping them make sense of why they had ended up in this cycle of conflict.

Kehu had grown up with a father who was quick to point out fault but never offered praise. As someone who had escaped the poverty/welfare trap of his alcoholic parents by sheer determination, Kehu's father saw the world as a hostile and dangerous place, and that his job was to toughen up his kids to survive in it. The shadow of racism hung over his view of himself and his kids. Out of his fear of fulfilling a racist stereotype, he would warn Kehu 'Don't you be a lazy Hori!' Kehu's mother was much softer but she always deferred to her husband, so he was the dominant force in Kehu's learning about himself. I helped Kehu understand that his upbringing had left him with a deep-seated fear of failure rooted in a belief that he was 'not good enough'. While those insecurities had driven him to perform at a high level in anything he had taken on in work or sport, they also led him to avoid any situation where he didn't believe he could excel. His insecurities were a constant torment, so when he wasn't busy he had a strong need to use alcohol and other drugs as an escape. Fiona's growing unhappiness made him feel like he was failing at an important task. Failing like this was intensely painful for him, yet at the same time he was bewildered that she was taking personally what he believed were just the demands of his job.

Fiona's mother, a ground-breaking corporate executive, was the dominant figure in her family. With her father also having a successful career in finance, Fiona had a life with 'every advantage'. She went to all the best schools, attended any class she cared to, etc. However, the emotional reality for Fiona and her sisters was feeling like they were somewhat unwelcome and frustrating appendages to their mother's busy life. Fiona reported times when her mother was very attentive to her — but those were the exception rather than the rule, and usually because Fiona had done something well. Given that her older sister was an academic star and her younger sister a sporting success, Fiona often felt like she didn't matter. It became clear that Fiona's sense of feeling unimportant to Kehu was a continuation of how she had felt throughout her upbringing.

Talking about these aspects of their upbringing was painful for both Kehu and Fiona. Still, it helped them make sense of their emotions, and evoked care as they began to have an intimate appreciation of their partner's struggles. They became able to approach their conflicts and upsets with much more understanding and compassion as they realised that their partner was struggling with old (largely unconscious) fears and beliefs. Until now, each of them had taken the other's competent appearance to mean that their partner was entirely in charge of themselves, so any problematic behaviour was conscious and deliberate.

The next step in building their self-awareness and intimacy focused on recognising where they needed to grow to make the relationship work better. For Fiona, taking this kind of responsibility involved learning to value and assert herself clearly. She did not find this easy; just identifying what she really thought and felt was a struggle. She was frustrated at finding herself continuing to please and appease Kehu. She could see that she feared his disapproval just like she had with her mother.

Fiona developed self-talk to reassure herself that 'conflict is normal' and 'I'm allowed to feel what I feel and want what I want'. She also found that if she was able to be clear about the positive outcome she was looking for (e.g. 'I'm bringing this up because it's making me withdraw from you, and I want to feel close to you instead'), that gave her confidence that she was doing the right thing. Rather delightfully, she found her mother to be a good source of coaching in being assertive without being aggressive. Her mother's constructive support brought the two closer together than they had been since Fiona was very young.

Kehu's learning was in the opposite direction. Rather than assertion, he had to learn to be more open to influence. He had to recognise that every expression of difference was not an attack or a criticism. He also had to realise that while backing his judgement could be a strength (especially at work), doing it compulsively was rooted in insecurity. Instead, he learned that being open to other ideas about how to do things was a sign of confidence, and built connection.

It was a revelation to Kehu how much his fear of failure was driving him. He realised he was in danger of developing an alcohol problem and began to substitute exercise to manage his stress. In talking with Fiona, he often needed to call a Time Out (see Chapter 4) to give him time to work out what to do rather than being defensive or combative. Keeping his focus on things like 'What kind of man/partner do I want to be?' and 'How can I be caring here?' gave him good guidance about where to take things. He was surprised at how much closer he felt to Fiona after having these 'difficult talks'.

Once they were both managing their respective insecurities, they still had the work of dealing with their differences. Topics like the boundaries around Kehu's work hours and the division of domestic labour remained tricky to discuss. But they managed to do so with a lot more goodwill. As they became more skilful at having these intimate conversations, the quality *of their closeness improved. Their sex life became more passionate, and they started to have more fun together again. Both of them began to feel a lot better about themselves and, rightly, had a sense of pride in what they were accomplishing in their relationship.*

Key points from Chapter 1

1. You live in a society that bombards you with misinformation about how relationships work. A lot of what you believe is probably incorrect.
2. Your partner is different from you, and dealing with your differences and learning to do conflict without harming your relationship is essential.
3. Intimacy is a vulnerable and challenging state, not to be confused with the more comfortable state of closeness. We have to do the hard work of building and maintaining intimacy if we want to enjoy the closeness.
4. You almost certainly have blind spots about your behaviour that will undermine the intimacy and security of your relationship.
5. Recognising that you will benefit from growing and learning about yourself, being open to feedback, and learning how to give feedback tactfully, are core relationship skills.
6. Whatever you grew up with is 'normal' to you, yet your partner grew up in a different family culture from yours; so expect that there will be a lot of work to do in determining what is 'normal' for your relationship and family.

Chapter 2
People in relationships need to grow

Intimacy gets harder the longer you've been together

As I discussed in Chapter 1, the conventional romantic myth implies that once you've found the 'right' partner, then the longer you are together, the better you will know each other — so the easier the relationship will be.

Yet this is not how it works in practice. That story overlooks that the longer you are together, the more important you become to each other, emotionally and practically. The more important your partner is, the bigger deal it is to risk their disapproval or rejection. If some random person you meet in a shop tells you 'You're stupid', it might annoy or upset you but it probably won't shake you to your core. But if your long-term partner says the same (and means it), it's much more likely to challenge your sense of yourself, more likely to really hurt, and more likely to make you reactive.

Every time we disagree with our significant other, a part of our brain goes: Is this going to break us up? The more our lives are bound up with our partner, by shared experiences, shared property, shared friends, and especially shared children, the more frightening any disagreement has the potential to be. Many people who separate after a long-term relationship can relate to the notion of starting your life over again. So the longer you have been together, the more likely it is that the self-protective part of your brain treats any notion of the relationship ending as 'life-threatening'. This is why we can become as scared and dangerous as a cornered possum at the slightest disagreement, acting reflexively from the 'fight or flight' part of our brain.

One of my mentors, Dr David Schnarch, coined the phrase

'Marriage is a people-growing machine' to describe how long-term, committed relationships present us with a stark choice.[1] We can either mature and learn to be less reactive, or lose everything we have invested in the relationship. He argued that this seemingly unfair choice is an evolutionary force driving us to become more adaptive as a species. Although looking around the world today, I'm not sure it's working!

Growth means taking your insecurities on before they destroy your relationship

The cliche is that opposites attract. When I ask people 'What attracted you to your partner in the beginning?', the answer I usually get is a list of how the other person is different from them. Even if we are attracted to someone because of apparent similarities, we will be very different people with many points of contrast. Inevitably these differences lead to disagreement and conflict.

Dealing with differences is tricky because we are all significantly influenced by our own deep insecurities (e.g. we will be abandoned or overwhelmed, we are unimportant or unwanted, we're not good enough or too much to handle, etc.). These unconscious fears consistently shape our behaviour, especially with people who are important to us.

To make matters worse, dealing with these differences is harder because of the internal tension between two of our hard-wired systems: on the one hand our need for connection, and on the other our need for autonomy (independence). The biological drive to feel important to others and to belong invites us to compromise and please significant people. At the same time, the drive to feel in charge of our own destiny invites us to be self-centred and hustle for what we want, even at the expense of those we love. As societies and individuals, each of us must find a way to balance these forces.

Growing and maturing as an individual involves finding that balance, as well as tolerating the discomfort of challenging our insecurities and the restrictions they place on us. This is hard, unpleasant work; arguably the most challenging thing we will ever have to face outside of the unexpected trauma and tragedies that life can sometimes throw at us.

The good news is that this growth prevents our relationships from becoming stale and predictable. Esther Perel puts it rather charmingly when she says:

> *In the west today most people are going to have two or three marriages, two or three committed relationships in their adult life. It's just that some of us are going to do it with the same person.*[2]

Understandably, we don't see the long-term benefits ahead of time and tend to avoid this challenging and painful work. Instead, following our society's script, we look to our partner to validate and reassure us that we're okay as we are. Developmentally, however, healthy independence needs to come before we can sustain healthy *inter*dependence.

The danger is that the more we depend on our partner's approval and validation to feel okay, the more it makes our sense of self (our identity) dependent on our partner's behaviour and responses. This dependency, in turn, makes it more likely that we will present a heavily edited self to our partner. The unconscious logic goes like this: I will avoid true intimacy and hide thoughts, feelings and desires that I expect will earn your displeasure or disapproval.

Two predictable negative consequences flow from this over-reliance on our partner's approval. Firstly, we can't feel truly loved if we know that we are managing how we present ourselves to our significant other. We think: I *know* that you don't realise what I'm like inside, so when you say you love me, I know for a fact that I can't trust it.

Secondly, relying on your partner's validation to feel okay about yourself means that your sense of worth depends on their moods, choices and facial expressions. Your thinking will go like this: I feel utterly at your mercy, vulnerable and out of control of my life and psyche. Given this, it is almost inevitable that I will try to control what you do to regain some sense of power in my own life. So I will complain or cajole, dominate or seduce, appease or manipulate, trying to ensure that you keep giving me the approving strokes I need.

In this situation, part of securing your partner's approval involves pressuring them, subtly and blatantly, to accommodate your insecurities. You are likely to react negatively if they challenge the limits you have unconsciously set for yourself: If I don't believe I can get what I want from you, I will try to create distance (emotionally and, sometimes, physically) between us so I can minimise your impact on me. So I will shut down and withdraw, or get very busy (with work, the kids, my hobbies, my church, etc.), leaving both of us feeling lonely and unloved.

Although many people prop up their self-worth by feeling superior to their partner, the reality is that we tend to mate with people who have a similar level of self-awareness and tolerance for vulnerability. If your partner struggles with intimacy, you are likely to have a comparable struggle, even if your self-protective strategies look different. With both of you doing this, your relationship is stuck in what David Schnarch calls 'the tyranny of the lowest common denominator'.[3]

If this sounds bad, it's because it is. There are a lot of bad relationships out there. So if you want to shift the odds in your favour, you must embrace a general 'growth and learning' approach to relationships and life. And regarding relationships, there are some particular skills you need to learn and a specific order in which you typically acquire them — as described in the next section.

The stages of growth

Another couple of my mentors, Drs Ellyn Bader and Pete Pearson, suggested that the stages of maturing that people go through in committed relationships are similar to those that Margaret Mahler observed in infants.[4] Their Developmental Model of Couple Therapy (the one I base my practice on and train other therapists in) suggests that there are five broad stages of development. We can get stuck at any one of these stages and not progress.

Of course, there are exceptions to this process. Cultures where elders arrange the marriages of young people don't rely on the randomness of 'falling in love', and so will have a slightly different (arguably more realistic) initial stage. In contemporary Western society, many couples become friends before they 'fall' for each other. Likewise, people get together at different ages and life stages, and their prior experience and personal maturity will influence how they progress through these stages. A couple getting together in their fifties may not need to spend a lot of time on the Exploration stage if they have both had successful lives before getting together.[5]

Exceptions aside, I have found that this notion of crucial

developmental tasks we each need to personally accomplish if our relationship is to thrive has real value when it comes to understanding my relationship and those of my clients.

Stage one: Bonding

This is the 'honeymoon' or 'symbiotic' phase: 'I don't know where I end and you begin', especially emotionally. A hallmark of this stage is minimising difference, alongside an expectation of, and emphasis on, **similarity**: 'Oh wow, you like (insert movie / book / place / music / food), too?!'

Typically lasting a few months to two years, this stage focuses on forming a sense of connection and commitment. It's also known as the Symbiotic stage, which refers to how an infant and a caregiver form one functional unit where, ideally, the child's needs are met by the adult (without the child being able to express them). Most people call it the 'honeymoon' phase — a reference to the sweetness of feelings it engenders, which is usually because we are high on naturally produced 'love drugs'. Typically our systems are flooded with chemicals that make us feel both horny (testosterone and oestrogen) and on top of the world (dopamine and norepinephrine).[6] This is something we have evolved to do: to keep the species going, our biology tricks us into a somewhat distorted view of our partner and our relationship.

This cocktail of feel-good chemicals makes it easy to be brave (it deactivates our amygdala,[7] the trigger for our self-protective reflexes) and to ignore our differences. We are full of joy and wonder at the places where we match or fit well together, usually overestimating how many of these there are and how significant they are. If you've been straight around people who are high on drugs, you know exactly how that looks.

I am not suggesting for a moment these feelings are 'fake'. They are authentic in the way that all of our experience is the result of chemical processes. It's just that they are not sustainable, and nor are they based on a complete picture of each other or the relationship. The intensity of this stage wouldn't be a problem if our society were saner about love and relationships.

Sadly, we tend to idealise this temporary phase, which miseducates us to believe that this is what 'real love' looks like, and that if our relationship doesn't keep feeling like this forever, there is something wrong with us or our relationship. This miseducation encourages us to stay stuck in the first stage of development and blinds us to the necessity of further growth and change. Modern culture teaches us that the natural, inevitable decline in how easy it is to feel good with our partner means that we are 'falling out of love' or have 'communication problems' or are 'growing apart'.

If the relationship stalls in this stage, it can turn to 'sour symbiosis', also known as 'enmeshment' or 'being fused'. If we haven't moved on, then difference feels intolerable and threatening. Noticing differences creates significant reactions, or damaging avoidance with nothing getting resolved.

BEING STUCK IN STAGE ONE: 'HOSTILE DEPENDENT'

If we try to hold on to the sweetness of the honeymoon stage, things are inevitably going to go sour. Some of us will become increasingly hurt and angry with our partner for not automatically knowing what we need and want: 'If you loved me, you'd know what I need.' Others will be frustrated with their significant other for creating problems in their life just by being a different person.

The term 'hostile dependent' refers to the fact that what we are angry about are the inevitable challenges of being emotionally dependent on another human being (more on this in Chapter 7). This anger harms trust and respect in the relationship, and usually kicks off a vicious cycle of increasing conflict and decreasing goodwill: The more I am hurt, disappointed or frustrated by you for being different from me and not meeting my needs without me having to ask and negotiate, the angrier I will get. The angrier I get, the less likely it is that you will give me what I want.

BEING STUCK IN STAGE ONE: 'CONFLICT AVOIDANT'

Other people will suppress all sense of hurt and frustration, minimising or dismissing all conflicts and doing everything they can to avoid 'rocking the boat' by raising differences or disagreements. While this makes for a much quieter home, nothing gets resolved. Needs and desires that we don't express aren't going to be satisfied. In the long run, this leaves people feeling disengaged, lonely, misunderstood and, ultimately, unloved.

To feel loved, we have to be known and seen; yet in avoiding all conflicts, we hide large parts of ourselves, so being known and seen is simply impossible. While less drama-filled than the 'hostile dependent' situation, 'conflict avoidant' couples are no more effective in building a lasting, reliable, intimate relationship.

Ideally, the Bonding stage lasts a year or two before we start to engage in the challenging tasks of the Differentiating stage (described next). But many couples never take that challenge and stay stuck in Bonding forever. Verity and I managed a good 20 years of being severely conflict-avoidant before we started to take the risk of engaging with our differences. Having both grown up heavily enmeshed with a self-involved parent, we were well-practised at appeasing others and it was 'normal' for us not to have our emotional needs met. Everyone praised us for having such a 'good' relationship, but we were just storing up trouble for later.

If our society were wiser about relationships, we would realise that having differences is normal and inevitable, and we would just get on with the business of dealing with them. That's the next stage of development.

Stage two: Differentiating

Here the emphasis is on **difference**, particularly on learning how to deal with differences well. This involves developing the skills to work through disagreements in ways that don't harm our intimacy and connection, but instead enhance it. Achieving this requires learning how to explore and negotiate differences, and learning to manage the anxieties that conflict inevitably creates. You could also look at it as learning how to be true to yourself while simultaneously making room for your partner to be themselves — staying connected to your partner, even when it's tough.

Just as a child comes to realise and adapt to the fact that they are a separate being from their caregiver, partners must work out how to be their own person while remaining connected to each other.

The term Differentiation was first used by the pioneering family therapist Dr Murray Bowen, who defined it as 'The ability to be in emotional contact with others yet still autonomous in one's own emotional functioning'.[8] A key aspect of doing this is continuing to be caring (or at least decent) when we have disagreements and differences.

People very frequently see their relationship as being 'in trouble' when one person tries to deal with differences and get them resolved. Frequently the other person sees this as betrayal, as changing the rules of the relationship, or simply as an attack on them. To be fair, people trying to grow in this way are sometimes unskilful in how they bring up differences and try to resolve disagreements, making it easy for their partners to mistake their intentions.

Like most things, Differentiating gets harder the longer you put it off. The longer we have stayed in the Bonding stage, the more entrenched are our usual ways of dealing with disagreement (through avoidance or hostility). This makes it more likely that our partner will react badly when we try to do something different.

Staying calm in conflict is something most of us need to *learn* how to do. Being able to know what you think, feel and want, while at the same time staying connected to the other person and caring about *their* thoughts, feelings and desires, is quite the juggling act.

Differentiating involves a complex set of skills that we tend acquire in roughly this order:

1. Developing the ability to self-reflect; to notice and accept your own thoughts, feelings, wants and desires.
2. Developing the ability to *express* those thoughts, feelings, wants and desires. This requires tolerating the risk of exposing 'who you (really) are'.
3. Developing awareness of your partner as separate and different. Often, people may initially respond to this as a threat. For example: I see your different opinion as a criticism of me; or, I see you wanting something different than I do as meaning that I will miss out.
4. Developing an increasing ability to listen, hear and respond to differences. Exploring the differences with curiosity and openness

and clear boundaries — caring about both your partner *and* yourself.

5. Developing the ability to create an environment in the relationship that supports desired changes. For example, negotiating in good faith, being able to compromise on an issue without compromising your selfhood, knowing when you can afford to be generous and when you can't, and being creative in finding solutions rather than sticking to first positions.

Ideally, during our upbringing our parents model all of these skills through how they relate to us as we develop an independent sense of ourselves. However, many of us did not get the opportunity to acquire these skills during childhood and adolescence. For example, if my parents couldn't tolerate me being upset or angry, I would have learned to suppress my emotions early, probably before I could talk. In that case, I would enter any adult relationship with a severely limited ability to know what I feel (Skill 1 in the list on the previous page). If I grew up in a home or school environment that emphasised competition — 'You're either a winner or a loser' — then the notion of exploring differences to create 'win–win' solutions (Skill 4) is going to be utterly foreign to me. I could end up with the same difficulty if I had a parent who was utterly selfless and self-sacrificing.

If you haven't come from an ideal family (and who does?), then you will have to learn these skills 'on the job' in order to be able to deal with differences, disagreements and conflicts. Being unable to acquire these skills is what causes most people to seek help from a relationship therapist.

Learning how to stay in a caring connection with your partner when you disagree, when they are pressuring you for what they want, or when they are standing in the way of what *you* want, is tricky. It is doubly so for couples who have been stuck in 'sour symbiosis' for years or even decades. Yet this is essential to make your relationship bearable and harness the benefits of being a team.

When you build an ideal team for work or sport, you want people with different strengths — the 'big picture' people and the 'detail-focused' people; attackers and defenders. Their differences are a strength of the team. That can be true of your relationship, too, but only if you and your partner appreciate and value what the other brings to the table. Differentiating is the key to being able to do that.

Typically, we have lost a bit of ourselves in the early stages of a relationship — in the intensity of the Bonding stage and the emotional demands of the Differentiating stage. Once we can explore, negotiate and harness our differences, then, developmentally, it is time for each of us to use that ability to reclaim a stronger sense of self.

Stage three: Exploration

Also known as the Practising stage, this involves using your Differentiation skills to 'do your own thing' *without* losing contact with your partner. Moving away from being solely focused on each other, this stage emphasises **self-development**.

Here is how this feels: With the skills to disagree and negotiate in place, I can 'do my own thing' without undermining the relationship. I can reclaim my independent sense of myself and what's important to me, explore who I am in the wider world, without too great a cost to you. I can put energy into developing my selfhood, my projects and priorities (be they careers, other friends, children, hobbies or whatever) in a way that feeds me and builds my sense of self. I use my Differentiation skills to explore whether our relationship has the time, energy, money and talent to provide what I desire. Where there is conflict between our desires, we can negotiate this in a way that is considerate of both of us. If I want the benefits of being in a relationship, I have to trade off some of my freedom (autonomy). But if I am Differentiated, and hence am open and fair with you, then everything I do has your full knowledge and support.

Not everyone who talks about needing to 'do my own thing' is at this developmental stage. Many people do their own thing *without* having the necessary Differentiation skills in place. Many people like this (especially men, in my experience) see the sacrifice of freedom required to maintain equity in a relationship as a *burden* placed on them by their partner, rather than as a consequence of the choice they made to be in a committed relationship. They can then use this blaming stance to justify making unilateral decisions and hiding their actions from their partner. Self-centred actions like this undermine trust and respect and keep these people stuck in ineffective ways of dealing with differences.

In contrast, people who act with empathy about the impact of their choices on their partner, those who consider and consult, are truly free to develop themselves and enrich their relationship as they do so.

Stage four: Reconnection

Sometimes labelled with the French word 'Rapprochement', this stage emphasises **relationship development**. Once people have developed their independent sense of self, they bring the energy, knowledge and other resources from their personal development back into the partnership.

This Reconnection stage is typically seen in middle age — where personal identity is more secure and the need to accomplish personal goals becomes less urgent. People take an active role in supporting their partner's development as an individual. This stage is often characterised by back-and-forth patterns of deeper intimacy and engagement, as the demands of external responsibilities take people out of the relationship. Then they come back in to renew and restore themselves.

Stage five: Synergy

The hallmark of the final stage in relational development is comfortable interdependence. If you are in this stage, you can be fully yourself and still very connected and generous to your partner. The emphasis is on **continuing to develop across the board, as individuals, as a team and out into broader systems**.

From the outside, this final stage can look somewhat similar to the Bonding stage. Partners are frequently attentive and affectionate to each other, generous, accommodating and tender. This coincidence may be why our society thinks that you can stay all 'loved up' throughout your relationship. However, this time the comfortable closeness is not the result of 'love drugs', illusion and ignorance, but of hard-won knowledge of self and other and how you work as a team. The relationship has a strong sense of equity, even though there may be very different roles. This is accompanied by an unquestioned valuing, supporting and honouring of each other.

Where their circumstances allow, people in this stage often wish to work together to give to extended family, the wider community, and society as a whole. As people who have learned all the lessons that a long-term partnership has to teach, others see people in this stage as mature, wise and reliable; the elders that every culture needs and smart people respect.

We don't all start our growth journey from the same place

I want to finish this chapter with a word of caution. Learning how to be the kind of person who can have a successful long-term, intimate relationship is a big mountain to climb. Along the way there are many ups and downs, requiring bravery and persistence. We all face similar dangers — anyone can be swept off the mountain by some avalanche of external circumstances (e.g. illnesses, injuries, losses). Yet, although we all have to climb the same mountain, the journey is different for each of us.

Some people come from mountain-climbing families. They have athletic genetics and all the right gear. They start their journey by being helicoptered in (by Secure Attachment [see Chapter 7] and healthy Differentiation in their upbringing) to a base camp halfway up the mountain. They still have an arduous climb ahead, but they are well equipped and well rested.

Also, these people will have guides: a network of friends and family with solid long-term relationships who have climbed the mountain already. This network can advise them on the best route and where the pitfalls are. They will also provide emotional support when the going gets tough and reassure them that the climb *is* possible and the journey *is* worth the effort. No one can climb your mountain for you, but this kind of support makes it much more do-able.

By contrast, other people come from families who have never left the coast, who don't believe that the mountain exists, let alone have an opinion on whether it is climbable. They grew up in families marked by deprivation, chaos, indifference or abuse. Relationships with caregivers were dominated by the adults' impulses and reactivity rather than the child's needs. These brave explorers set off from the coast with no gear, no accurate maps, and to words of scepticism and doubt. Their peers and elders feel threatened by their attempt to do better for themselves, and may actively try to undermine or sabotage them. They must travel countless miles alone, wading through swamps and bashing through jungle, all uphill, before they even get to base camp. Often they are exhausted and ill when they get there; in no fit shape, either health- or equipment-wise, to tackle a serious peak.

These people may need to rest and recuperate, get together the right gear, etc., before they can consider tackling the summit. They may even be delighted with the view from base camp and believe it enough of an achievement to have reached the mountain and proved the doubters wrong.

So be careful when considering your journey to improving your relationship — don't compare your progress with that of others. Be realistic about where you began your journey, how your upbringing has equipped you, and how much support you have or haven't had along the way. No one but you knows what it's taken and what it means to be where you are.

GINA & STU

Stu loves Gina's calmness and reliability — they create a sense of safety, and her enjoyment of his quirks makes him feel acceptable. His relationship with her starkly contrasts with the chaos and neediness he experienced with his mother. For her part, Gina values Stu's free-spiritedness and lack of conventionality. He shows her a different side of life from the narrow focus on achieving within social norms that marked her childhood.

Gina's upbringing was very focused on achievement and the practicalities of life. While they were all successful in a conventional sense, the whole family danced around the unacknowledged tyranny of their mother's anger. Meanwhile, Stu grew up in a home thrown into chaos by his father's drinking and his mother's erraticness. The eldest child, he was drawn into trying to care for his mother, especially from the age of 11 when his parents separated, and his mother struggled to cope emotionally and financially.

Gina and Stu were in their sixties with three grown-up children when

I met them. They described having a delightful and passionate beginning to their relationship. They lived together happily for three years before deciding to start a family. However, with the challenges of family life, the comfort very quickly went out of their relationship. They had never developed a satisfactory way of resolving disagreements.

Any discussion that started going into deeper, more vulnerable emotional territory was quickly diverted, by unconscious mutual agreement, on to practical and functional matters, punctuated by occasional outbursts of rage from Gina. Devoted to their kids, they kept sweeping their differences under the carpet; each of them became increasingly hurt and resentful. Gina felt unappreciated and unsupported in her role as the primary earner, and Stu felt he was not good enough for her and became increasingly fearful of her aggression.

By the time the children left home, Gina and Stu felt that things were incredibly tense between them, and they were leading very separate lives. The easy intimacy of their early years together seemed to belong to two different people.

Stu's insecurities focused on feeling unworthy and unsafe. He had tried to care for his mother using the resources of a child, but inevitably failed. He couldn't prevent her suffering, and formed an unconscious belief that he was 'not good enough' and 'inadequate'. The chaos of his home also left him untrusting of things going well and, fearing that bad things were always just about to happen, he firmly believed that 'I'm not safe'.

Given her family's massive emphasis on achievement, it is not surprising that Gina's insecurities focused on feeling unimportant and unacceptable unless she met others' expectations. Driven in all areas of her life, Gina could never believe that she had done enough or allow herself to relax. She dismissed vulnerable feelings of fatigue or overwhelm as 'weakness', and was extremely puzzled as to why she was so unhappy when things had gone so well in her life.

Gina had very little capacity for validating herself. While outwardly presenting as a highly successful professional, she constantly sought reassurance from Stu about her worth. This was unconscious on her part, so she never acknowledged it, but when she wasn't getting support in the ways she needed, she would fly into a rage. In the short term this was successful in getting Stu to appease her, but over time it damaged his trust in her and made him withdraw more and more.

Avoidance was Stu's way of coping with their differences. When the children were at home he threw himself into the nurturing role, which allowed him to feel valuable and safe without being vulnerable. Gina also benefitted from this focus, getting her unacknowledged dependency needs met through Stu's role as nurturer. However, as the kids grew up, Stu put more energy into his importing business (which until then had been a side-line to his role as a parent) in a vain attempt to prove himself more worthy by making a greater financial contribution. While outwardly encouraging Stu's business aspirations, Gina became increasingly hurt and angry in response to his focus being elsewhere.

Both were feeling unconsciously stifled by the unspoken insecurities and needs of the other. They both responded by creating increasing distance from each other to retain their sense of autonomy. People frequently refer to this self-protective distancing as 'growing apart' or 'falling out of love'.

Gina went the 'hostile dependent' route, becoming increasingly resentful of her emotional dependency on Stu and punishing him for not making her feel good, important and valuable. Stu used the 'conflict avoidant' strategy to cope with their unresolved differences. He defused Gina's anger and always put the family's needs ahead of his own. The cost of all this self-sacrifice was him becoming slowly more resentful and losing respect for Gina. Being capable and well-resourced people, they managed to make their relationship work on this basis for 30 years by the time I met them.

After all that time, it was challenging and painful for Gina to start the Differentiation process by insisting they go to couple therapy; this effectively meant acknowledging that she had insecurities and vulnerable feelings. Her upbringing at home and her elite private school made such admissions shameful. She was initially very blaming of Stu, and minimising and justifying of her own behaviour. For his part, Stu was well aware of his distressed feelings but terrified of sharing them with Gina. His upbringing had taught him to cope on his own, and that burdening those you love with your problems was the worst thing in the world.

Once Gina and Stu got their heads and hearts around the notion of Differentiating, they made rapid progress. Stu was amazed to discover that being more open and direct with Gina drew her towards him (sometimes, admittedly, after a scary initial negative reaction). She reported feeling increased respect and desire for Stu as he took a more solid shape in the relationship.

Stu, in turn, was drawn to Gina's increased vulnerability. It felt very different from the anxious and indirect demands for reassurance she had offered him previously. With her greater self-awareness, she was much less likely to evoke the spectre of his needy mother, so he found it easier to feel sexually attracted to her, much to her delight.

Once Stu and Gina had greater self-awareness and trust in their ability to sort out their differences, they naturally moved on to the Exploration stage. They could have a good series of conversations about Stu's business. Gina realised that this was an opportunity for Stu to step out from her shadow and experience wider world success after his years as a caregiver.

Rather than feeling unconsciously abandoned or threatened, she became supportive and turned down a promotion so that she had enough energy to keep the household running. Meanwhile, Stu realised that it was okay for him to want things for himself and that no one else was suffering if he pursued something important to himself in a considerate way.

This was when Gina and Stu stopped coming to see me. People in the last two stages of development usually don't need couple therapy unless they are under unusual stress.

Key points from Chapter 2

1. The longer you've been with someone, the more challenging and scary intimacy becomes.
2. We have to learn to validate ourselves to keep our relationships safe and stable.
3. A committed relationship is an opportunity to grow and become a more mature person.
4. There are five stages that people have to grow through to build the capacity for a successful long-term relationship: Bonding, Differentiating, Exploration, Reconnection and Synergy.
5. Most relationships get stuck at the second stage — learning to deal with differences and conflict while staying connected to their partner.
6. Life is not fair — some people start out equipped with very little of the knowledge, skills or experience necessary to make love work over the long term. But they can still acquire them.

Chapter 3
Why it's so scary and hard

Does it have to be such hard work?

Last year, I was taken to task by a colleague for insisting that relationships had to be hard work. That was not her experience — and I am delighted for her and all those who post articles online saying that love should be easy. Those people are never going to need to come to me for help.

I am privileged to have several lifelong friends with whom I have shared the ups and downs of life, career and family. Many have been with the same partner for 30 years or more. When I look around my friends and acquaintances, I see they all have challenges and struggles in their relationships, just as Verity and I have had in ours.

One explanation comes from Attachment Theory (see Chapter 7 for a discussion of this). The proportion of the population with a history of Insecure Attachment is 40% to 50%.[1] That's a lot of people! So, while maybe it's not like this for everyone, this book is for those who find the business of maintaining a long-term relationship a struggle, at times confusing and at others exquisitely painful, and, sometimes, full of joy and wonder.

A crucial part of explaining why there is so much challenge in maintaining a relationship is rooted in the anatomy of our brain. Even Securely Attached people are at the mercy of our species' evolutionary history and its influence on our biology.

Get to know your amygdala and how it operates

You probably already know that you have hard-wired reflexes that act to keep you alive and safe in the face of threats. You are programmed to protect yourself. Another way to say the same thing is that evolution rewards anxiety and reactivity.

Imagine a hominid (an early human) on the African savannah 100,000 years ago. They notice the grass moving and muse, 'I wonder what moved the grass? Was it the wind or an animal?' That particular hominid is *not* our ancestor; they got eaten by the proto-lion that was in the grass. Our ancestor is the hominid who, the moment the grass moved, panicked and fled without any time for conscious thought. You can see from this that evolution favours over-reaction.

The part of our brain that decides to activate our 'fight or flight' response is called the amygdala, and there are four things about the way it works that have profound implications for relationships. Although we don't fully understand how the brain works, we do know enough to help you stop being so hurt by what happens in your relationship. I encourage you to wrap your head around this science, as it can be very liberating.

Firstly, the amygdala 'is able to detect possible threats in the visual environment at ultra-fast time scales'[2] — that is one of its primary jobs. It gets signals from our senses and processes that information way before and much faster than the thinking and reasoning part of our brain (the frontal lobes of the neocortex).

Secondly, the amygdala changes how our body works when it detects a threat. You may already know that it pulls blood away from our digestive system and pumps it into the large muscle groups, so that we are ready to fight or flee. Fewer people are aware that, under threat, the amygdala also pulls blood away from the frontal lobes and the hippocampus (which is vital for memory). This so-called 'amygdala hijack'[3] means that we cannot think rationally or reasonably when we feel threatened, and that our memories are unreliable when we are stressed.

Thirdly, the amygdala focuses on individual survival — its job is to keep us alive. I celebrate that humans can be altruistic, cooperative, generous and self-sacrificing. For me, that side of human nature is a big part of what makes life worth living. But that is *not* our amygdala's business: it is solely out for Number One. So any response from our amygdala is likely to be personally protective and relationship-destructive. Even seemingly positive things (like appeasing or staying quiet) can damage trust, connection and intimacy as much as someone getting angry or critical. It just takes longer for the effects to show up.

If the amygdala limited itself to keeping us physically safe, it would probably not be a problem in most relationships. This brings me to my fourth point — it doesn't. Sadly and problematically, the amygdala does not distinguish between threats to our physical safety and threats to our psychological and emotional safety.

Recent advances in brain imaging allow us to see that 'severe social pain impacts the (brain) in a similar way as physical injury'.[4] So if you fear that your partner is trying to hurt you, your amygdala will react the same way whether they use their fists or their words. Please note that I am *not* saying that these two things are as bad as each other — just that our automatic defences react to both in the same way.

Our five self-protective impulses (the 'Five Fs')

Although it's common to talk about the 'fight or flight' response, recent research around trauma[5] suggests that our amygdala-driven self-protective impulses come in five flavours. When our amygdala detects a threat, it can instantly direct you to any of these:

1. Dominate your partner (a.k.a. FIGHT) — and not only with aggression. You can also dominate with pleading, eagerness, anxiety, sadness, etc. By emotionally dominating the space, you leave no room for what your partner wants; instead, you *make* them do what you need to reduce your anxiety (e.g. shut up, back off, have sex, agree with, go along with, or reassure you). You get your way for the moment, but the cost is high in terms of your partner's trust in you and respect for you.

2. Submit to your partner (FAWN or FRIEND) — do what you think they want, to please them and stop the pressure for you to be different (i.e. appease them). If this is a frequent response, you usually end up being unconsciously resentful the whole time. Sadly, although you may believe that you are being very attentive to your partner, it won't feel that way to them. Your primary relationship in this mode is **with your anxiety**, not with your loved one. To make matters worse, what you think they want is often not what they need. By abandoning yourself, you can both end up feeling alone in the relationship.

3. Shut down around your partner (FREEZE) — put up the shutters and withdraw emotionally. Sometimes this feels like a real 'deer in the headlights' freeze (some identify this as a separate 'flood' response, as in being 'flooded' with emotion); at other times, we just put up an emotional wall to hide behind. A lot of us tell ourselves that we are 'keeping the peace', but our lack of engaged response will, over time, leave our partner feeling abandoned and alone. And again it neglects our own healthy dependency needs.

4. Comply out of fear and/or collapse (FLOP or FATIGUE). If we feel particularly defeated, trapped or threatened, we may become drained and lethargic, complying with any suggestions our partner makes but being completely disengaged. It can include some forms of dissociation (being disconnected from thoughts, feelings or identity). This is more common if we have a history of trauma, either within or before our current relationship. We struggle to believe that we can have any impact, and our interactions with our partner are empty of emotion, leaving us both feeling isolated in the relationship.

5. Withdraw physically from your partner (FLEE) — into work, children, friends, hobbies, church, sport, alcohol and other drugs, gambling, compulsive use of porn or even an affair. We find a space away from our partner where we can connect with what we think and want without the pressure of their presence, expectations, desires and needs. We will often blame the demands of our obligations rather than recognise that we are pre-emptively protecting ourselves from relationship stress.

Like every other human being, you can do all five. You probably tend to use one or two of these more frequently than the others. If you don't recognise and accept that you automatically protect yourself like this, you are making your life and, especially, your partner's a lot more difficult.

The Five Fs don't work

Although the purpose of these five impulses is self-protection, they are destructive to your close relationships and risk alienating you from someone very important to you; this puts you at greater emotional risk. Sadly, only your frontal lobes, the reasoning part of your brain, are capable of appreciating this fact.

It can be hard on your ego and self-image to accept that you are doing destructive things to your relationship. Especially if you have a substantial investment in 'being good' or 'being nice', in 'getting it right' or 'it's not my fault'. It's worth noting that appeasing, pleasing and accommodating people can find it extremely challenging to recognise that all that effort and self-sacrifice is making the relationship worse, not better.

Part of why I focus on the biology of this behaviour is to emphasise that having these self-protective impulses is normal, human and inevitable — not some character flaw. Character comes into play in your willingness to admit this to yourself and those you love.

What do I do instead?

In some ways, most of this book attempts to answer this question. More specifically, Chapter 5 is devoted to strategies for managing your neurobiology. Here, let me give you a brief answer, on the understanding that there is much more to be said.

As I mentioned above, the question of character only comes in when we reflect on how we manage these impulses: Do I accept that I have them, and that, sometimes, they are in charge of my behaviour? If you can stop yourself acting on those impulses and instead give yourself time to engage your frontal lobes (perhaps by taking a Time Out — see Chapter 4), then you may be able to do things like:

- Respond in a way that takes care of your partner and yourself.
- Acknowledge how it is for your partner *before* you talk about what's going on with you.
- Recognise and take responsibility for how you have hurt, let down or frustrated your partner, while still holding on to the things that are important to you.
- Stay connected and caring, even if there isn't an obvious solution to your disagreements or problems.
- Accept that things may take time and effort to resolve in a way that works for you both.

Unfortunately, few of us had parents or caregivers who modelled this level of maturity and responsibility. Typically, we learn to justify and excuse our behaviour, and focus on what it is about our partners that we find difficult, unfair or hurtful.

The deadly seduction of justification

Just because you *feel* justified, this doesn't mean you are right! We all automatically justify what we do, whether good or bad. We *must* assume that our behaviour makes sense — the alternative would be pretty crazy! However, the sense that we make depends on what we know about ourselves at the time, and we don't always have all the facts.

For fun, let me illustrate with a report by Sigmund Freud, the 'father of modern psychology'. Freud reported that a doctor called Bernheim hypnotised a man and gave a post-hypnotic suggestion to put up an umbrella inside the house. When asked why he was doing this, the man immediately invented a justification — 'I want to see if the umbrella is working' — and it proved difficult to persuade him otherwise.[6]

We do the same thing in our relationships all the time. But there, the consequences are less amusing. Let's say I am reactive to my partner (e.g. I dominate, submit or withdraw) because they have triggered one of my insecurities. Most of us justify the domination, submission or withdrawal based on our partner's behaviour (i.e. I blame them). Even if I behave in ways that contradict my beliefs and values about the kind of relationship I want or what I think is acceptable behaviour, I justify my behaviour to myself and to my partner. Typical examples would be: 'I don't listen to you because you never listen to me', 'I have to yell like this because it is the only way to get through to you', or 'I have to tiptoe around you like this because if I don't you get so angry'.

While believing my justifications may help me feel better in the short term, this won't allow me to break the cycle of misunderstanding, fighting and distance. To do that, I have to do three things:

1. First, I must **stop justifying** my reactive behaviour, whatever form it takes, and accept that it's harmful to my relationship.
2. Then I have to look beyond my justifications and **understand the fears, anxieties and insecurities** that make me reactive.

3. Then I have to learn to **manage these fears, anxieties and insecurities** without doing things that go against my values or against what is best for the kind of relationship I want to live in.

Breaking the habit of destructive self-justification is hard, but it is crucial to building a successful and enjoyable relationship.

We all have insecurities

This section is a bit technical about how our psyches seem to work. It makes sense of a *lot* of puzzling behaviour, though, so I encourage you to try to get your head around it.

Firstly, we need to accept that we are all, regardless of age, still influenced by things we learned in our upbringing. Some of that learning was conscious, some of it was helpful, some of it was unconscious, and some of it was very unhelpful.

If the events you lived through when young were extreme (like abuse, gross neglect, war or other trauma), then it is pretty easy to accept that those events shaped you. I liken them to a mighty hammer smashing the rock of your childhood safety and security.

However, a rock can also be carved into fantastic shapes by the dripping of water over time. If your childhood was comparatively uneventful, if you think of it as 'normal', then it may be hard to recognise how it shaped you. The long-term effects of, for example, your mother's coldness, your father's demandingness, your peers' teasing, or your school's blaming of you for its failures can be hard to accept when you know that you had a 'pretty good' childhood.

Often it is the lack of emotional validation from parents that shapes us. This is tricky, because the absence of something doesn't create memories you can recall. This lack of memory tends to lead to people blaming themselves for behaviour that was a response to their parents not being well attuned to their needs. For example, many people are proud of their 'self-reliance' or independence when they are actually phobic about vulnerability and intimacy because no one noticed or responded effectively when they struggled emotionally in childhood.

We call our childhood and adolescence our 'formative years' with good reason. Our brains are not fully formed until our mid-twenties or later. So we do a lot of our learning about ourselves and how the world works with child brains that operate differently from adult brains.

Younger children don't have the equipment in their brains to see or understand the context in which things happen to them. They also struggle to see things from another's point of view. A tragic consequence of these limitations is that children tend to believe that everything that happens around them is *about them*; even that they are the cause.

I vividly remember a successful businesswoman in her forties telling me, in all seriousness, that her parents broke up when she was seven because she broke a vase. That was how it seemed to her seven-year-old brain. What was fascinating was that she had never questioned this explanation in the subsequent decades. It didn't take much enquiry from me for her to realise that there had to be other reasons for her parents' separation — but until she engaged her adult brain about it, she continued to carry guilt and shame.

So kids experience themselves as the centre of the universe. If Mum is unhappy or Dad is angry, in a child's understanding that says something about them. It is entirely appropriate that they are Symbiotic or un-Differentiated.

As a result, we all leave childhood with what I call insecurities (a.k.a. 'shame'), fears or beliefs about ourselves that are global, persistent and, usually, wholly inaccurate. The lively girl born into a quiet and contained family whose energy makes her parents fear that she's 'wilful' or 'naughty' develops a belief that 'I'm difficult, I'm a problem'. The boy who feels 'bad', 'weak' or 'unacceptable' for having perfectly normal feelings because his parents routinely deflected, distracted or looked displeased when he showed any negative emotion. The girl with one unpredictably angry parent, another who is anxiously appeasing and an older sister who seeks attention by aggravating their father grows up knowing that 'I'm not safe'. The bright boy with dyslexia whose parents accept the school's assessment of him as 'slow', and won't complain even when his teacher shames him in front of his class, comes to believe, not surprisingly, that 'I'm stupid and worthless'.

Whatever you grow up with is 'normal'. It's your normal because it's what you know. Another client who sticks in my mind is the woman who didn't think it was significant that, in his rages, her father used to drag her up the stairs by her ankles. She was confident that she'd had a 'good' childhood, and those events had no significance to her present-day lack of assertion in her relationship.

Not everyone is oblivious to their insecurities. Some of us may be well aware of a struggle within ourselves. We say things like 'I've always felt inadequate', or 'I don't have much trust in humanity'. Whether or not you are aware of them, you probably underestimate how big an influence your insecurities have on your behaviour today, especially with the most important people in your life.

Our insecurities motivate our defences

When someone extremely significant to you says or does something that confirms your insecurities, your amygdala will kick in. That's when you become self-protective and fall out of connection. These are what I call *reactive defences*.

There is another way our insecurities have a powerful influence on our lives. We also have *proactive defences*: we are motivated to try to prevent our shame from being triggered. Having your insecurities confirmed is the worst thing that can happen to you in day-to-day life (outside of trauma and tragedy).

So we become driven, irrational and off-balance in our need to prevent our worst fears coming true. The person who fears that they are 'not good enough' pushes to succeed at every endeavour and is crushed if they make the slightest mistake. The person who believes they are 'not important' ensures they are at the centre of everyone else's life. By anticipating others' needs and selflessly ensuring that those needs are met, they never manage to have a sense of 'self', and they end up resentful, martyred and unable to understand why their partner shows them so little care.

Again we will have justifications for how we operate, and it can be tough to see past them to what is pushing us around. There is more on how to identify and work with the impact of your insecurities in Chapter 8.

Move away from over-reliance on your partner's responses

Another reason why relationships can be so challenging lies in how we try to proactively use our relationship to protect our sense of self, and how this — paradoxically — makes us feel *less* safe and solid.

The self-disclosure and vulnerability of intimacy are much easier when met with acceptance, empathy and reciprocation from your partner. Here is how it looks: When I share intimately, the response I hope for from my partner is something like this:

- They show interest in how it is for me.
- They let me know that my feelings, thoughts and desires seem reasonable to them.
- They care about how it is for me.
- They have a sympathetic emotional response to my experience.
- They share that they feel that way, too, in similar situations.

This kind of validation of your experience and feelings usually makes you feel 'seen' and 'heard' and encourages the belief that you are acceptable, good enough, important, wanted and loved. Not surprisingly, this feels great and is something that all relationship theories encourage. It seems simple enough . . . but it isn't.

Remember, the more important someone is to you, then the more significant it is for you to receive their acceptance and validation. Likewise, the more important that person is to you, the greater the impact if they respond to your vulnerable sharing with defensiveness, dismissiveness or incomprehension. Consequently, the more important your partner is to you, the riskier it feels to self-disclose unless you know that what you share will be well received. This relationship between importance and vulnerability is why intimacy gets harder the longer you are together, and the more significant you are to each other.

This becomes particularly tricky when it comes to conflict. It plays out like this: When the topic I want to share is a difficulty I have with you, then the chances of you offering me an accepting and supportive response are very slim. If you're stressed or depressed or self-involved, it can be hard for me to be confident of getting a good reception, especially if I have had bad experiences with you in the past.

So, what do you do if there is vulnerable sharing you want to do and there's little hope of a validating response? The solution to this problem is realising that it is possible — indeed necessary — to be able to support and affirm *yourself*. To have enough trust in your own judgement, faith in your own worth, and belief in your good intentions that you can tell your partner important things about yourself that you expect they won't want to hear. To risk revealing yourself to them even when (*especially* when) you anticipate a negative response. Unlike situations when you get acceptance and validation from your partner, this may not feel so great at the time.

So, why would you do it? It's because there is a real danger to your relationship and your mental and emotional well-being if you *solely* depend on support and affirmation from your partner.

The danger of relying solely on your partner for affirmation

If you are dependent on your partner's validation in the way described, it leads you to attempt to make them responsible for you feeling better about yourself. In most cases, they are trying to do the same thing (i.e. using you to make them feel better about themselves). This leads to a predictable pattern of interaction:

I feel insecure about myself and seek validation from you

↓

Early in the relationship (i.e. in the Bonding
stage), I get this quite reliably

↓

You feel useful, wanted, powerful

↓

I feel better (i.e. validated), but dependent
on you to feel okay about myself

↓

I realise (maybe unconsciously) that I am at the
mercy of your choices and behaviour

↓

I make various attempts to secure my supply of validation (e.g. by
asking for reassurance, anxiously scanning you, or initiating sex)

↓

You (accurately) feel I am trying to control you

↓

At this point, the selfhood of both of us feels threatened

↓

The amygdala activates in both of us, and reactivity increases

↓

Both of us blame our distressed feelings on the other

↓

Decreased intimacy and respect poison the atmosphere
and continue to activate our respective insecurities

↓

But the only way I know to deal with my insecurities is to
seek validation from you, so the cycle starts again

If you recognise yourself in this pattern, you may wonder: 'Am I not supposed to care what my partner thinks about me? Should I not be hurt when they are unempathetic or unsupportive?' I am *not* saying those things. I *am* saying: 'Let your partner be an imperfect human being.' I'm saying that even the most wonderfully empathetic, loving partner will have bad days and weeks. They will have times when they are caught up in their own troubles and not readily available to be a support to you. Likewise, even the best partner will struggle when you have a complaint about them (and no one is perfect, so you will have your complaints!).

How self-validation works

In situations where you feel you need validation, if you don't want to set off the cycle described above, then you need to find a way to recognise and manage your insecurities, shame and defences. You need a way to validate your experiences, feelings and desires and feel okay about yourself, even when your partner can't or won't.

Here's how it can play out if you do that:

I notice I am becoming reactive or feel insecure about something

↓

I take my insecure feelings as a cue to stop
and look at what's going on in myself

↓

I recognise that some current event has triggered my insecurities

↓

I identify my insecurities as coming from
formative experiences (childhood)

↓

I recognise my insecurities as irrational, unhelpful and (usually) pre-dating this relationship (so they *can't* be your responsibility)

↓

I validate myself as normal and not shameful for
having insecurities and self-protective impulses

↓

I own my insecurities as my problem

↓

This allows me to share with you in a vulnerable way

↓

You can empathise without feeling responsible for my pain

↓

You feel useful but not controlled

↓

I feel seen and heard, supported but not dependent
on you to feel okay about myself

↓

Increased intimacy, respect and trust all round

Being able to validate yourself this way requires you to be sufficiently self-aware or 'on to yourself'. I encourage you to think this way: I need to take responsibility for myself (rather than justify my reactivity by blaming my partner), and act with integrity, according to my values. This will create respect and strengthen our relationship even when we are in conflict.

A wee point of clarification — nothing in this section denies our healthy dependence on our partners. Interdependence is a hallmark of adult Attachment relationships. The notion of becoming better at self-validation simply recognises that it is unrealistic to expect our partner to be 100% reliable and available to us at all times. Our healthy dependency on them can turn toxic if we do not have reasonable expectations of what they can and can't do for us.

Let me finish this chapter with a diagram that I use to illustrate the choice we face when something our partner does makes us feel anxious or threatened.

PARTNER DOES SOMETHING I EXPERIENCE AS ANXIETY-PROVOKING

↓

TRIGGERS MY INSECURITIES

↙   ↘

SELF-PROTECT
I get reactive and:
- Fight (dominate)
- Friend (submit)
- Flee (withdraw)
- Freeze (shut down)
- Flop (comply)

SELF-CARE
I stop and:
- Understand and accept my feelings
- Own my baggage
- Self-soothe (mentally and physically)

↓   ↓

DISCONNECT

ENGAGE INTIMATELY (VULNERABLY)

↓   ↓

Partner feels abandoned, attacked, etc.

Partner feels connected

LYNETTE & TOM

Lynette feels like Tom turns every discussion into a debate that he has to win. She believes she has 'done everything' for Tom yet can't get him to take her seriously, and is increasingly despairing about having a voice in the relationship. Lynette is not realising that her tone and approach are much more critical and frustrated than she believes. While crucially aware of how Tom protects himself, she has a blind spot about how and how much she is protecting herself. Pointing out Lynette's protective behaviour is not to say that Tom isn't defensive, but that is not something that Lynette can control. If Lynette can recognise that there are things **she** can change that **will** make a difference, then she has more options for exerting control in her life.

Tom and Lynette had themselves tied in knots when they came to see me after she'd discovered Tom's affair with an old colleague. Unusually, neither of them fell into the trap of justification. Unlike many people caught in an affair, Tom didn't use Lynette's behaviour to justify his breaking their contract. In our first session, when I explained our self-protective impulses, Tom could say 'I dominate with my emotions all the time.' He could see how he had driven Lynette away with his defensiveness and anxious reassurance-seeking, coupled with periods of shut-down when he was convinced that Lynette didn't want him. He was embarrassed to realise that he had created a self-fulfilling prophecy that allowed him to kid himself that he 'needed' his affair.

Similarly, despite her distress at discovering the affair, Lynette avoided going into a self-righteous tirade at Tom (which would have been pretty easy to justify). She recognised that her tendencies to appease, withdraw and shut down had reinforced Tom's insecurities. As much as Tom had let both of them down with his controlling and demanding behaviour, Lynette had also let both of them down by allowing Tom's insecurities to dominate their relationship. She had not been meeting him at an intimate level, either emotionally or sexually, for a long time. While that didn't excuse his infidelity, it did help her understand the context in which it had occurred. Furthermore, it helped her realise that there were things she could do that would make it less likely for this to happen again, which she found very reassuring.

Tom identified with the notion of validating yourself rather than looking to others for affirmation. Because of his selfish and abusive alcoholic parents, Tom had real insecurities about his worth and importance. In the

Bonding stage of the relationship, he felt hugely affirmed by Lynette's love and attention. For her part, growing up as the only child of a solo mum meant that Lynette had received great rewards for being attentive to her mother. The selflessness she had learned in that context made Tom feel like the centre of the universe in a way he had never experienced growing up, and it was great!

Tom felt bulletproof in the warmth of Lynette's love and support. At the same time, Lynette felt useful, powerful and deeply wanted. They had no doubt that they were a 'good match', and marriage and kids seemed natural and inevitable.

Moving out of the 'honeymoon' phase of the relationship, Tom unconsciously realised how dependent he was on Lynette's choices and behaviour. As the children's demands grew, Lynette had less time and energy to validate him. Tom's insecurities began to reassert themselves; he began to feel 'neglected', 'unimportant' and, his worst fear, 'not good enough' for Lynette.

Tom tried to get Lynette to return to the level of validation he had received early in the relationship — especially by talking about his distress (implying it was Lynette's fault) and trying to get Lynette to engage intimately, both in conversation and sexually. Sadly, all Lynette heard was complaint.

As a result of all Tom's efforts to get her to validate him, Lynette, understandably, started to feel controlled and unimportant. Feeling unimportant came from an unconscious sense that Tom didn't want her as a person; he only wanted what she could do for him, emotionally and sexually. To protect herself, she became increasingly distant and walled-off from Tom.

By this stage, the selfhood of both of them was under siege — Tom's by the withdrawal of validation and Lynette's by the threat of being controlled. The amygdala in each of their brains was activated by the mere presence of the other person, making their relationship increasingly volatile and reactive. Each of them blamed their growing distress on the other, and their trust and respect for each other started to nose-dive. The increasingly hostile atmosphere further activated their insecurities.

At this point, Tom felt justified in seeking validation from his former colleague, regardless of the potential harm it could do to his partner, kids and life in general.

To make sense of the carnage caused by his infidelity and to rebuild

Lynette's trust, Tom had to learn to self-validate. Before he could do that, he had to compassionately accept that he struggled to feel 'good enough' and that him feeling bad, inadequate or unwanted resulted from his upbringing, not what Lynette thought or wanted. Tom had to learn to recognise when those old insecurities were activated, which he described as 'feeling stink about myself', and use that as a cue to take care of himself. Although he found it difficult, once Tom realised that it was up to him, not Lynette, to make up for his crappy childhood, he began to treat himself more kindly. Drawing on his experience parenting his children, he worked out some key phrases to say to himself and things to do that helped him settle down.

At the same time, Lynette was working on believing in her inherent worth, being willing to speak out and take up more space in the relationship.

As Tom began to make himself vulnerable to Lynette, talking about 'struggling with feeling stink', she realised how important she really was to him. She responded to this clean and direct approach well. Lynette could ask helpful, clarifying questions and offer empathy without feeling like she was responsible for fixing things for him. It also helped that as she experimented with being more assertive and 'good selfish', she discovered that Tom was encouraging and supportive.

Lynette reported a sense of relief — 'like I've been let out of a prison I didn't even know I was in' — as she realised that there was room for her to be herself in the relationship. As Tom recognised the effectiveness of being self-aware and asking for help from a vulnerable place, he started to feel more and more in charge of his life and less and less under the influence of his parents' historical abuse of him.

Key points from Chapter 3

1. You are at the mercy of your neurobiology.
2. The more important your partner is to you, the easier it is for them to trigger an 'amygdala hijack' of your brain.
3. The way your amygdala tries to protect you works for physical threats but puts you at greater risk of emotional harm in relationships.
4. Justifying your self-protective behaviour (blaming your partner) harms trust and respect.
5. Owning your self-protective behaviour and its impact on your partner is a crucial aspect of intimacy.

6. 'Needing' your partner, being utterly dependent on their validation of you to feel okay about yourself, is a recipe for disaster.
7. For our relationship to be safe and stable, we have to learn when and how to validate and affirm ourselves when our partner can't or won't.

Chapter 4
Relationship first aid

First aid is immediate assistance — temporary solutions until more-thorough treatment is available. I've put this 'relationship first aid' chapter early in the book because, in my experience, people usually wait until things are at crisis point before they seek help.

In this chapter there are things you can do immediately that may settle down reactivity in the relationship and make it possible to deal with underlying issues. There are a bunch of 'Do this'-type scripts and tools that you can use immediately. The rationale behind them is covered in the rest of the book.

IF YOU ARE CONCERNED ABOUT YOUR SAFETY, GO STRAIGHT TO CHAPTER 19. The tools in this first-aid chapter assume that your safety is not at issue beyond you fearing that things might get unpleasant or emotionally painful.

What kind of crisis are you having: hostile or avoidant?

Generally, people get into relationship crises in two ways, depending on how they react to stress and threat.

- Some people become blaming, demanding, judgemental, aggressive and outward-focused. As I mentioned in Chapter 2, we call this strategy 'hostile dependent' because the hostility is about blaming your partner for you feeling vulnerable through having normal dependency needs. If you tend to protect yourself like this, then you will need to focus on the parts of this chapter about settling yourself down, soothing your hurts, and being more accepting of your partner's experience.

- Other people become shut down, avoidant, appeasing, compliant and focused more inwardly. Remember, the formal description of this strategy is 'conflict avoidant', as these people seem willing to do almost anything rather than deal with anxieties the differences in the relationship raise for them. Sometimes people in this situation will repress their thoughts and feelings for a time and then 'blow up' and become briefly aggressive or have an affair, to everyone's surprise and fright. They also tend to behave in passive-aggressive ways — making little comments or 'digs', forgetting to do things, denying their evident anger, making pointed 'jokes', etc. Although usually less dramatic in the short term, the conflict-avoidant strategy is just as destructive to relationships in the medium to long run as the hostile-dependent strategy. If this is you, then you will need to focus on the parts of this chapter about being more self-aware and bringing yourself more fully into the relationship, even at the risk of causing upset.

This chapter offers tools and approaches to address both kinds of relationship crisis.

Stop blaming and instead focus on what you can control

If you're hurt and angry, it's common to spend a lot of time thinking about what your partner has done or is doing to cause those feelings. The trouble with this is that you have very little control over your partner's behaviour. You need to put your energy where it might do some good — into yourself. Here are some pointers for the essential attitude to dig your relationship out of a crisis. The principal theme is: **aim to confront yourself, not your partner.**

- Focus on understanding and articulating your insecurities and anxieties — where they come from in your upbringing (i.e. your partner does not cause them) and how they drive your behaviour. Remember this is intimate sharing, not a command for your partner to stop triggering your insecurities.
- Focus on and talk about *your* unhelpful behaviour after every negative interaction, *not* your partner's.
- Talk to your partner about how you think *your* insecurities contribute to the negative patterns between you.

- Notice when you are getting worked up, and don't assume that your self-justification for this is accurate; instead, assume that your insecurities are being triggered.
- Practise tolerating your partner's reality, and show interest and concern for their experience (even if it's critical of you) rather than denial and minimisation.
- If you really must give your partner feedback, *first* talk about your part in the dynamic, *then* theirs. Don't dwell on your hurt feelings. Talk humbly (i.e. acknowledging it's your experience, *not* objective reality) and care-fully (full of care) about the behaviour of your partner's that you are struggling with, but do name it rather than let it poison your communication.
- Expect and be willing to tolerate hearing the same kind of feedback from your partner.
- If you can't work out your contribution to the dynamic, you can at least acknowledge this inability as a fault and be *genuinely* willing to hear your partner's suggestions about what your part is.

If some of this language is confusing or unfamiliar to you, look at Chapter 8 for a more detailed explanation.

Now, you would have to be a saint to be able to do all this perfectly. Much of this book aims to help you develop the self-awareness and self-control needed to build healthy relationship habits. I include this summary here more as an indicator of where to put your energy and what to aim for if things are in crisis.

The next section is one I will be referring to often in other chapters. It offers you a specific practice that is challenging to learn but will buy you time to put into place all my other good suggestions.

The most crucial exercise in the book: Time Out

Hostile-dependent relationships have a pattern of escalation and volatility, with one or both of you frequently getting very angry or shut down. If you can see that nothing productive comes from those interactions (there's an explanation of why this happens in Chapter 3), then an excellent way to stop having these hurtful clashes is by learning how to take a Time Out.

The same tool is helpful if you are a conflict-avoidant person, afraid that things will get out of hand. The two of you agreeing to use Time Out gives you a way to ensure that you can keep things safe and on-track. That can give you the confidence to take risks and 'rock the boat' without things getting out of hand.

Time Out intends to keep your relationship safe by giving you both a chance to settle yourselves. You mustn't use it to end or escape from difficult conversations. **The purpose of Time Out is to allow discussions to continue safely and productively.** If trust has been damaged, it may be understandably hard to believe that your partner will 'play fair' using Time Out. I encourage you to give it a go, however — do your best and see if the two of you can break the cycle of useless conflict or avoidance.

The first step to using this process successfully is to accept that we all get upset, anxious, overwhelmed, hurt or angry to the point where we can't think straight or act well. It's a normal, human thing. Stopping before you make things worse is one of the best tricks for making a relationship work. It's not a sign of personal or relationship failure to accept the need for this.

Before you need it, you *both* must agree that using Time Out is a good idea. An explicit agreement is crucial because you are giving your partner consent to interrupt any interaction, at any time, without explanation or justification. The logic may be obvious when you are calm, but when you are in the middle of something you may find it difficult to accept your partner abruptly pausing the conversation. Unless you are clear in your mind that this is a good idea that you have freely consented to, you are likely to interpret your significant other calling a Time Out as an aggressive move — but allowing yourself to see it that way will only escalate things. So think carefully about the implications of agreeing to use this tool. Try to imagine how it will feel in the moment, and make peace with the sense of 'unfairness', 'rudeness', 'dismissal', or whatever else might arise for you.

For this to work, you need to assume that if your partner calls a Time Out, they are doing it to try to look after the relationship. They are trying to *stay connected* to you, not run away from you. You may need to ignore how it feels and stick to this assumption. You can always review how the tool was used at a later date when you are both calm and centred.

EXERCISE 1: HOW TO USE TIME OUT

1. If you believe that the situation is becoming unproductive or destructive — stop! Don't make things worse.

2. Tell your partner you are taking a Time Out without explaining further. You are not asking — you are telling, because your partner has already agreed to you doing this. Say 'I need a Time Out. I'll be back in this many minutes', and leave.

   • Always use the phrase 'Time Out' — maybe even use the basketball 'T' symbol — so that there can be no misunderstanding that you are employing this tool (rather than avoiding the conversation). If you say something imprecise like 'Let's not do this' or even 'I need a break', your partner may misunderstand your intentions.

3. Don't tell your partner that *they* need a Time Out (even if it's true) — this will sound like blame and will likely rev things up, not calm them down.

4. Say clearly the time you want to resume talking. For simplicity, pick one of '5 minutes', '30 minutes', or 'the next practical opportunity' (which may be days away if your life is busy).

5. If it is your partner who is calling Time Out, you may be surprised and not understand why they are doing this. Don't ask for an explanation at this point — you can review it later once things have calmed down. Accept the Time Out call with good grace. You may feel hurt or offended if you see your partner calling Time Out as implied criticism or an attempt to avoid or silence you. *Don't let those feelings rule you.* Remember that Time Out is (a) something you have agreed to and (b) intended to keep you both safe.

6. Get space away from each other (e.g. in different rooms) for the shortest time practical to settle yourself or the situation.

   • Maybe this is just 5 minutes if you've caught it early.
   • If you or your partner is upset and your physiology is worked up (e.g. pulse over 100 beats per minute), then you will need to take 30 minutes to allow enough time for your body to settle down.
   • Sometimes this isn't practical. So your Time Out is until the next opportune time. For example, if it's late at night, talk tomorrow after work or when the kids are in bed. Whoever called the Time Out should set an alarm on their phone so that you don't forget!

7. It is vital that **both** of you use the Time Out to **settle yourself down**,

not wind yourself up. Even if you don't think you need it, use the time to reflect on how you have been behaving. See if you can bring fresh, constructive energy back to the conversation.

8. If you know you are agitated or distressed, do things that will calm your body, like deep breathing, going for a walk, or making a cuppa (see Chapter 5 for more suggestions). At the same time, do things that will calm your thinking. For example, remind yourself that this is someone you love, that they love you, that it's normal to get upset, and that nothing is going wrong when you disagree.

9. If you are the one who called the Time Out, **make sure** you come back and re-start the conversation at the time you said you would, with fresh energy and attitude. You mustn't avoid it because it's scary. Getting it wrong once can seriously damage trust.

10. Later, when you are both in a non-reactive space, review how using Time Out went. Be open to suggestions for ways you could have done it better, made it easier for your partner, how the timing went, etc.

Things go off-track quickly in a relationship. Becoming skilled and practised at using Time Out is a great way to buy you time to respond well and be the person you want to be. I encourage you to use it early and often to build safety.

Try this instead of blaming

Time Out allows you to stop and consider what you want to do. However, if you have been in the cycle of anger and blame, you may not know how to engage positively with your partner any more. Here's a checklist, courtesy of the Couples Institute, that gives you 20 examples of positive things you can do for your relationship.

EXERCISE 2: 20 POSITIVE THINGS

Pick one thing off this list that you don't do routinely and do it every day for a week. Then, the next week, pick another one. Do this for yourself, and don't worry whether your partner notices; just see how it makes *you* feel.

1. I told my partner something I appreciated about them.
2. I was able to repeat back (recap) what my partner said to me before I responded.
3. I used some appropriate humour (i.e. humour my partner *did* appreciate).
4. I used 'Time Out' to stop a situation from getting out of hand.
5. I was able to show caring for my partner's thoughts and feelings even though we were in conflict or the discussion was tense.
6. I went out of my way to do something nice for my partner.
7. I listened to difficult comments (e.g. complaints or criticism) and kept my cool.
8. I looked for something positive about my partner today and told them about it when I noticed something.
9. When I disagreed with something my partner said, I asked questions to try and understand their thinking instead of arguing with them.
10. When I felt I needed to solve a problem for someone else, I first asked if they wanted advice.
11. When my partner did something annoying, I took three relaxing breaths and then decided whether I needed to say anything about it.
12. I apologised to my partner for my part in a bad situation or conversation.
13. When I had negative thoughts about my partner, I shifted my focus to what I appreciate about them.
14. I used 'please' and 'thank you' in talking with my partner today.
15. I deliberately did something I knew my partner would value without them having to ask me.
16. I was able to keep my tone of voice positive during a difficult discussion.
17. I touched my partner in a way that communicated care or support.
18. I was genuinely curious about my partner's ideas and experiences – I asked them questions about how it is for them.
19. I was open with my partner about what I thought and wanted without being demanding.
20. When we disagreed, I thought about what the issue meant or symbolised to me and talked about that rather than just arguing to win.

When you have been focusing on your partner's failings and your own hurt, it can feel strange or false to behave positively. Don't let the weirdness put you off trying to move your relationship in the direction you want it to go. If you're sick of the negativity and fighting, try doing some of these positive things and see where it takes you. The longer or worse the negativity has been, the more persistent you will need to be.

If you're avoidant, you need to engage

If the way you protect yourself is more the conflict-avoidant style, it can be hard to understand how this is as damaging to your relationship as being hostile dependent. This is how I summarise the problem:

THE CONFLICT-AVOIDANT CONUNDRUM

If you feel unseen, it's hard to feel loved or
wanted or understood or known
BUT
If you really show yourself, the differences you inevitably have with
your partner will become apparent, and you will be in conflict
BUT
Conflict is scary, so you want to avoid the conflict
BUT
If you avoid the conflict and don't really show
yourself — you will remain unseen

Conflict-avoidant people tend to have quieter crises. 'I love my partner, but I'm not in love with them any more', or 'We're still good friends, but there's no spark'. As mentioned earlier, sometimes conflict-avoidant people suddenly explode, or have an affair, or do something else equally 'out of character' as their repressed needs suddenly erupt. Sometimes they become bitter and passive-aggressive.

If you are having that kind of crisis, often the first thing to do is talk with your partner about your pattern of avoidance in the relationship. Talk about how you don't talk — however strange or awkward that feels. Keep the focus on what *you* do or don't do, not your partner's behaviour (i.e. don't justify your avoidance).

Expect that sorting things out is going to take time. Going slowly is safer, so don't let your anxiety about conflict drive you to try to get out of difficult conversations in a hurry. Don't expect that you will get everything sorted in one conversation, either. Commit to a *process* of engaging.

The next exercise gives you a six-step process to start climbing out of a conflict-avoidant rut.

EXERCISE 3: HOW TO STOP AVOIDANCE AND INSTEAD ENGAGE

1. Sit down with a piece of paper or a screen, and reflect on the times you do amygdala-driven things. See if you can work out what these situations have in common. You might also want to note down your thoughts about the points below. Once you feel that you have your thinking clear, make a time to talk with your partner about concerns you have about the relationship.

2. Begin by acknowledging the good things about your relationship. For example, conflict-avoidant people tend to be nice, kind, caring and considerate (at least until they become resentful). If that's true of your partner, say so. If you believe it's true of yourself, talk about that still being important to you.

3. Talk about how afraid you are of ruining what you have, hurting your partner or damaging the relationship. From there, you can explore how those fears put you in danger of damaging the intimacy by not sharing yourself fully, by only sharing the positive things and avoiding the negative or difficult things.

4. Ask whether your partner understands what you are talking about, whether those concerns make sense, and whether they share them.

5. Assuming that your partner sees sense in it, suggest that you both experiment with trying to talk more openly about difficult things.

6. Discuss what would make this seem safe for each of you. Consider things like the timing (a particular time of day, or only at a scheduled time, so no one feels 'ambushed'), the location (in private so you don't feel exposed, or in public so that you're confident it won't escalate), or the content (only one topic at a time; start with more minor issues).

If one or both of you is concerned that you will make things worse by deliberately engaging around challenging topics, put the effort into learning to use Time Out, as described earlier in this chapter. Then you can be confident that if either of you feels hurt or overwhelmed, you can stop things immediately and they won't get out of control.

Bringing things up safely

If you have not been talking about things with your partner, especially if you come from a home where your family avoided difficult subjects, you may have no idea how to have this kind of conversation. In the next exercise I give you a step-by-step process for raising things you have been avoiding or have gone nowhere with. It's not the only way to do it, but if you follow these steps then it's likely to go well.

EXERCISE 4: HOW TO BRING UP A TOPIC THAT MAKES YOU UNCOMFORTABLE

1. Get your partner's consent to talk seriously: 'Hey, I'd like to talk about something that's bugging me. Is now a good time?' If now isn't a good time, accept that with good grace and make a time that does suit them.
2. To reassure your partner that you are not just being critical or negative, talk about the potential benefits of having this conversation: 'I want to bring something up that is making me irritable. I know you hate that, and I don't want to go on being like that. It's not about giving you a hard time; it's that I want to feel closer to you.'
3. If you are anxious about making the situation worse, saying the wrong thing or hurting your partner, then say something about that: 'Please bear with me if I do this badly. I've been afraid to bring this up because I know I tend to sound blaming, and I don't want to hurt you that way', or 'I'm hoping you can be patient with me; I find it really difficult knowing how to express myself.'
4. Ask your partner to hear you out before they respond, but make clear that you will listen to their thoughts on the matter.
5. Stick to one topic. If there are many things you haven't talked about,

you may need to arrange several different times to talk.

6. Try to be succinct — don't lecture your partner for ages. Deliver the key points quickly, so that you or your partner don't get stuck on the first thing and miss all the rest. If that's difficult for you to do, do some planning beforehand. Write down the key points you want to cover and keep this note by you to check against — but don't just read it out, as that is likely to come across as disconnected and uncaring.

7. If there is something you are asking your partner to do, then make sure that you are clear and detailed about what that is. 'I want you to pay me more attention' is vague and open to misinterpretation. Something like 'I would love it if, once a day, you could say something that shows appreciation for my work around the home' makes it much more likely that you'll get what you want.

8. Once you have stated your concerns (briefly!), thank your partner for listening. Their attention is a gift.

9. Now listen carefully to your partner's response. Look for what concerns them, and don't be upset or offended if it's different from your concerns.

10. Notice if they feel criticised, attacked or blamed, and do your best to reassure them that this isn't what you intend. If it seems that your partner is appeasing you (giving you what you asked for to keep the peace), then encourage them to consider if they have thought about it enough, especially whether what you want really works for *them*.

11. If you reach an agreement, repeat it so that it's clear that you both have the same understanding of what the deal is.

12. If you don't reach an immediate agreement, accept that and schedule time to talk again about it after you have both had time to reflect. Make sure you keep that appointment!

Getting good help — choosing a couple therapist

If things feel out of control, or you have tried everything in this book and still can't make it work, you may want to get some couple therapy. If it's a relationship issue, couple therapy is where I would recommend you start. There can be benefit in doing individual therapy if you are having difficulties in your relationship, but (as I discuss in the next section) there are limitations and risks to this.

Sadly, getting good help is not as easy as it should be. There is a shortage of well-trained counsellors, therapists and psychologists generally, and even more so when it comes to the speciality of working with couples. Make no mistake — it is a specialist field! Just as you wouldn't want your GP doing surgery on you (unless it's a real emergency and there's no other option), you should avoid letting a therapist who specialises in individual therapy do your couple therapy.

You will have to put in the work to find someone who is a couples specialist. Unfortunately, there is no regulation about how people advertise themselves in this area. If someone advertises that they do relationship therapy, this doesn't mean they have done much of it with two people in a session. Most individual therapy involves a lot of talking about relationships, but that's not the same as having two people in a therapy session and knowing how to work with them safely and powerfully.

Here are some useful questions to ask any therapist you are considering going to see for couple therapy:

- *How much of your caseload is couple therapy?* This is the critical question for finding yourself a specialist. If the proportion of clients they see is over 20% couples, then this is someone doing quite a bit of couple therapy who should have quite a bit of specialist knowledge (assuming they are adequately trained).
- *How long have you been seeing couples?* As a rule, the longer, the better. Therapy is one of those professions where experience makes a big difference to skill levels.
- *How much training have you had in couple therapy — how many hours or days over what period?* You want someone who has done more than four days (24 hours) of training, and it ideally should have been over a year or more, not just a single block course.

Therapy is a very personal business. Even though it can be hard to find a couples specialist, they must still be the right person for you and your partner. If after the first session, one or both of you doesn't feel like there was a good fit or doesn't feel listened to or understood, I suggest you try someone else. If it's not that clear but you have some concerns, maybe go back and have one more session, and raise your concerns with the therapist and see how they respond. If you don't get a good feeling, go elsewhere.

One positive that has come out of the COVID-19 pandemic is that many more therapists are working online, meaning that wherever you live, it is possible to access specialist help. However, the reality is that you may have to wait to see a specialist couple therapist — and that can be hard to do if it feels like an emergency. If there really is an emergency, then by all means take what you can get. But if at all possible, hold out until you find someone good.

Be wary of doing individual therapy for relationship issues

Many people contact us asking for individual therapy, saying either 'my partner won't come' or 'I need to work some things out for myself'. Usually, it's apparent within a few minutes that they are simply avoiding the stress of dealing with differences, and what they really need to do is couple therapy.

There *are* times when doing individual therapy is helpful for relationship problems. Most commonly, it's when you have clearly identified a difficulty of yours that pre-dates or is independent of your relationship. Suppose you are dealing with a history of abuse, addiction issues, clinical depression or anxiety, and haven't developed strategies to manage these. In that case, it may be appropriate to do some work to get them under control before you show up to work on the relationship.

In my opinion, if you are hoping to find a way for your relationship to continue, there is a real danger in doing individual therapy about difficulties you are having with your partner. Your personal therapist will only hear your side of the story, and they have an ethical duty to be there for you. That means that if you are blind to yourself or have a distorted view of your partner, it will be hard for an individual therapist to spot that. They may have an inkling, even ask you questions — but they can't tell you that you are being unfair, missing something critical or kidding yourself, the way a good couple therapist can (with compassion and care). Reinforcing your mistaken ideas is not going to improve your relationship.

It is common, for example, for people to experience their partner as 'controlling' when what is really controlling them is their anxiety and their inability to back themselves in a situation of healthy, appropriate conflict. An individual therapist empathising with your feeling of being controlled will do nothing to make your relationship a better place for you to live. And if you are too accommodating of someone behaving selfishly or unfairly, your therapist can only encourage you to stand up for yourself; they can't do anything to take on your partner's behaviour.

I know this because I have had some quite awkward conversations over the years when liaising with individual therapists. It quickly becomes apparent that they have developed a picture of their client or their client's partner that is at odds with the behaviour I see in my room with both of them present. The difference can be extreme. More than once I have seen a guy who was empathic and open in couple therapy being labelled a 'narcissist' by his partner's individual therapist (who had never met him).

So if you are having *relationship* difficulties, get *relationship* therapy. Get an independent view; a neutral 'referee' to help you determine what's going on. Have the humility to recognise that your perspective is likely to be distorted, and so is your partner's.

If your partner is refusing to come to therapy, consider the implications of this. Why are you willing to accept this stand? If the relationship is not working well for you, have you made it clear to your partner that the choice is between you ending the relationship or you both going to therapy? In my experience, many reluctant partners will come once they realise that you are serious.

Reluctant partners often fear being blamed. If they are selfish or exploitative, then this is a reasonable fear — but not a reason to allow them to keep behaving this way unchecked by avoiding being held accountable. If they are decent, well-intentioned people who are a bit lost and anxious, couple therapy is often a pleasant surprise for them, and they quickly come to value the new options it creates for them.

To illustrate this chapter, I'm telling two short stories — one of a hostile-dependent couple and one of a couple who are chronically conflict avoidant. In neither case are all their problems solved, but it shows how they each made the initial shift from 'stuck and hopeless' to 'seeing a way forward'.

JEN & MICK

Mick comes from a farming family where people never discussed feelings. He and his older brother were close to their parents, and particularly enjoyed helping their father out on the farm. A good sportsman, Mick flourished when he had to go away to boarding school for his high-school years from age 13. A bit of a 'man's man' with a bunch of good mates from his school days, he is a senior executive in a large agricultural business.

Jen's family was a lot more tempestuous. Between her mother's huge mood swings and violent rages and her father's alcohol-fuelled criticism and shaming, her early years were undermining and terrifying. When her parents separated, she was still on the outside as her father and step-mother concentrated on her younger half-siblings.

Jen and Mick met in their mid-thirties, and were pregnant within a year of meeting as Jen's biological clock was ticking. A second child followed within two years.

By the time they came to see me three years later, they had a well-established cycle of Mick closing down in the face of Jen's emotionality and Jen escalating to try to get a response out of him.

Getting them to use Time Out properly took many weeks of practice and coaching. When they finally had a way of using it that worked for them, they reported an instant transformation in their relationship. Once Jen had time to sort her feelings out, she was able to come back and apologise for her over-reaction and aggression and ask for what she wanted without being critical or blaming. Mick was able to own that he had not been following through on promises he'd made (i.e. he had been appeasing rather than engaging).

Following a couple of these productive 'post Time Out sort-outs', Mick started responding in a more engaged and proactive way. He felt relieved that they had a way to talk productively. Although he still wasn't very verbally demonstrative, he got on and organised things that Jen had wanted, and she felt heard and valued while he felt successful and hopeful for the first time in years.

LUNI & ALEKI

Luni and Aleki are New Zealand-born Samoans who have been together for 15 years since they met at university. They have three children, the youngest of whom started school about a year ago. They sought my help after Luni told Aleki she had feelings for another man at work, which was distressing to her.

Aleki grew up the youngest of six children in a family that valued fa'a Sāmoa (Samoan culture) and education in equal measure. Both his parents expected unquestioned obedience, and he grew up fearing and hating his parents' anger when they were upset by one of his siblings. In his teens, Aleki was a peacemaker in the family, and cherishes memories of being able to talk his siblings out of 'making a scene'. His older siblings teased him about being their parents' favourite, but he maintains that they could have had the same praise if they had made more effort to be pleasing.

Luni is the only child of a Samoan mother and a palagi (New Zealand European) father. Her father left when she was three, and she had limited contact with him as he moved away. She started helping her mother around the house from a very early age, as her mother had to work two jobs to make ends meet financially. Luni also worked hard at being a 'good girl' to avoid adding to her mother's stress.

Both Aleki and Luni's families approved of their relationship, and everything seemed to be going well. They waited until they both had good jobs before having kids, and Luni, who had done some part-time work while the kids were pre-schoolers, was easily able to return to full-time employment once the youngest was at school.

When they came to see me, neither of them could understand what had happened for Luni. It quickly became apparent that both of them were highly conflict avoidant, never directly expressing any disagreement or discontent. Luni had been increasingly dissatisfied with many aspects of their relationship since the kids were born, but she didn't know how to talk to Aleki about it. Her experience was that if she tried to raise a concern, he would deflect or minimise; if that didn't work, he'd shut down and withdraw for days, which she experienced as deliberate punishment. A big part of her attraction to her co-worker was how he listened to her and took her seriously.

Aleki had shut down once Luni told him about her fears of falling for this other man. It was hard to get him to look beyond his hurt and scared feelings to think about what was going on in the relationship. I encouraged him to recognise how brave and caring Luni had been to tell him about what was going on rather than pursuing the affair, and also to value the respect and trust it implied that she had for him.

I also encouraged them to see that by avoiding conflicts, they were missing out on knowing themselves and each other intimately. I got them doing a daily exercise to connect as soon as the kids were in bed — practising talking about how they felt about themselves and each other in the relationship.

Although this was stilted and clumsy at first, they both came to value their 'connect time'. After a few sessions of me drawing out Luni's discontents and them discovering that it was possible to talk about these things without harm, I asked them to make a weekly time to continue these conversations without me (using the guidelines in this chapter about bringing things up safely).

Four months after they first came to see me, Luni and Aleki were eager to report feeling more connected (intimate) and excited about their relationship than they had been for years. Both were aware of their ongoing tendency to avoid, and realised that they still had work to do sorting out roles and responsibilities in the family — but they were confident they would be able to handle it.

Key points from Chapter 4

1. Some people react to feeling vulnerable in a relationship by becoming angry, blaming, volatile and escalating ('hostile dependent'). Others react in the opposite direction and appease, please, shut down and withdraw ('conflict avoidant').
2. If the relationship is in crisis, these two sets of people need to do entirely different things.
3. Hostile-dependent people need to stop focusing on their partner and put their energy into becoming more self-aware and having better emotional management skills.
   - Learning how to disengage, calm down and then re-engage is a valuable first step, and the Time Out protocol offers a structured way to do this.
4. Conflict-avoidant people need to recognise how their avoidance is damaging the relationship, and find ways to manage their anxiety

so that they can have the necessary conversations about what they really feel, think and want.

- Taking the emotional risk to engage in a vulnerable and inclusive way is an urgent priority if your relationship is in crisis. Time Out may give you the confidence to risk talking honestly.

5. Individual therapy for relationship issues can make it more likely you will break up.

6. If you can't settle yourselves and engage constructively, get professional help from a specialist relationship therapist (not just any therapist).

PART TWO

THE THREE STRANDS OF RELATIONSHIP THEORY

In the Developmental Model of Couple Therapy,[1] we look at relationships from three perspectives or through three 'lenses'. Other approaches will emphasise one of these over the others, while in this model we believe that they are complementary and there are things to be learned and acted upon from each perspective. In the three chapters that follow, I explain each of the three lenses and suggest some strategies that flow from thinking about yourself from each perspective. This is where the 'here's something you could try' part of the book begins in earnest.

Chapter 5
Manage your neurobiology

Understanding your neurobiology is crucial

This chapter is one of the biggest in the book, for a simple reason. Recognising when we are being reactive, along with having the skills to do something to prevent or reduce that reactivity, is the backbone of making your relationship a good place to live. While there's still a lot we don't understand about our brains, there are some things we *do* know that are useful.

As I explained in Chapter 3, it's hard not to let your amygdala hijack your behaviour — that's why I ended the first part of the book with a chapter on 'first aid'. But even though it's hard, it is something you can get better at — and this is essential if you want your relationship to thrive.

You'll see that there are several places in this chapter where I suggest you write a list. That's because it's hard to remember what your 'wise self' wants to do when your amygdala is hijacking your brain. If you have your strategies written down (ideally on your cell phone so you can access them wherever you are), you can read them rather than trying to remember them. Just having the lists with you and knowing you can access them if you need them can be reassuring.

Also in Chapter 3, I outlined how the more important your partner is to you (which is usually equivalent to 'the longer you have been with them'), the more the self-protective part of your brain is likely to see them as a threat.

Most people who seek therapy arrive hoping that I will stop their partner from doing the things that trigger amygdala hijack. Some think they never do anything to upset their partner; many believe they only do unhelpful stuff in response to how their partner treats them. The initial part of therapy is an eye-opener for these clients.

If you're a typical person, like those clients are, you're not as self-aware or in control of your behaviour as you think. *Unless you accept this simple truth, you will always look in the wrong place for answers.* In particular, you will blame your partner for how you feel, which is a disempowering way to live.

There can be great relief in recognising that the cause of much of the distress in your life is, ironically, how you try to protect yourself from pain (especially the pain of having your worst fears about yourself confirmed). Paradoxically, accepting this allows you to be more empowered and in control of your life.

Nothing will change if someone continues to focus solely on what their partner is doing wrong. A fundamental truth of relationships is that you *cannot* control your partner. You have influence, but not control. This is true even if you are willing to be abusive and coercive — which is why abuse, coercion and violence tend to escalate.

The only person you have control over is **yourself**. If you and your partner are stuck in a cycle of unpleasant, distressing, hurtful or confusing behaviour, the most efficient and effective place to put your energy is in managing yourself. The path out of the frustration and hurt is through decreasing *your* reactivity, increasing *your* ability to regulate your responses, and being mindful of the meanings *you* impose on your partner's behaviour.

Decrease your reactivity

The sooner you get on to your limbic-system reflexes, the better it will be for you and your relationship. There are a couple of ways to try to catch your self-protective reactions before they are beyond your control.

ANTICIPATE TROUBLE BASED ON EXPERIENCE

People who have been in a relationship for a long time will often have a good idea of the topics and situations that tend to lead to an amygdala hijack. When you can see these patterns in your relationship, you can start to plan for them. You can think about what they represent and how you can care for yourself better, so you don't get hijacked.

This kind of proactive action can only be taken after you have gained hard-won experience. You have to be able to reflect on your part in exchanges that are challenging and work out what you needed at that moment — what would allow you to stay connected with yourself and your partner, rather than being at the mercy of your self-protective reflexes?

Like everything else, this approach works best if you both do it; but, as always, don't wait for your partner to get with the programme, and don't make improving *your* functioning in the relationship conditional on *them* doing the same.

EXERCISE 5: WHEN DO I USUALLY GET TRIGGERED?

Sit down with a piece of paper or a screen and reflect on the times you do amygdala-driven things, then see if you can notice what these situations have in common. It might be:

- A particular problem or set of issues that keeps recurring.
- A time of day, a time of the month.
- When you have been drinking or are tired; this is a prevalent one.
- When you are worried about or stressed by your job, kids or family.
- Some aspect of your partner's behaviour that you struggle to deal with calmly, such as their being late, telling you what to do, correcting you or not following through.

In all cases, but especially if it seems to be something about your partner, you need to find a way to make it about *you*. Keep the focus on yourself; don't fall into the trap of thinking 'If only my partner didn't do X, then I wouldn't get reactive.' Instead, accept that X will happen (unless it's violent or abusive — don't ever accept that!), and that it triggers you. Your partner is always going to challenge your sense of self. The more significant you let them be in your life, the easier it is for them to trigger your pre-existing insecurities.

Think about what their behaviour or this type of situation means to you. What do you believe it implies about you, or about how your partner feels or thinks about you? For example, 'Him being late triggers feelings of unimportance that I know I have had since my little sister was born', or 'Her correcting me evokes an old, familiar sense of being inadequate'.

Once you identify the common elements in what's happening, then think about what you need to put in place to avoid getting reactive. Don't forget the value of taking a Time Out (see Chapter 4) to buy yourself time to give a more considered response.

LEARN YOUR WARNING SIGNS AND ACT ON THEM

Obviously, you can't anticipate every difficult or triggering situation. So the other approach focuses on recognising as early as possible that you are heading towards self-protective mode. Despite how it may seem, an amygdala hijack is rarely an instantaneous response. The flow of blood to your frontal lobes takes time to stop.

Like a car rolling down a gentle slope, it's possible to stop your self-protective reflexes if you catch them early enough. Once they are rolling at full speed, they will flatten you (and your partner) if you get in the way.

The aim is to train yourself to recognise the earliest possible warning signs that your amygdala is trying to hijack you. Learn to identify these quickly, and work out what you need to do to stop your reactivity from escalating. Here are some suggestions of things to look for in three different places:

- **Your body**: muscle tension, flushing, churning gut, pulse rate up, tight chest, jaw clenching, chills, light-headedness, shakes, tingles . . .
- **Your behaviour**: shutting down, going stony-faced or silent, laughing inappropriately, moving away from your partner, pacing, tears, raised voice, 'little' (quiet or childish) voice, fist clenching, appeasing with touch or other care-taking . . .
- **Your thinking or language**: justifying, blaming, criticising, shaming, running down, worrying, appeasing, anxiously trying to please, blankness, silence . . .

EXERCISE 6: LEARN YOUR WARNING SIGNS

Write a list of what you think your warning signs are, and refine it every time you get reactive until you are confident that you know what they are. Keep trying to find the earliest possible indication that you are in danger of an amygdala hijack.

Strategies to manage your neurobiology

In the rest of this chapter, I will look at four different ways to approach managing your neurobiology. Two options expand on being proactive — trying to ensure that you are less likely to get triggered. Two look at being reactive — knowing what to do when you *are* triggered. In each case, I will offer some strategies that focus on your body, and others that focus on your thinking.

The logical place to begin is looking at what you can do to try to *prevent* getting reactive. Let's start with what you can do with your body (physiology).

Proactive body-based strategies

This section explores the notion of being in a 'fit state' for doing relationship safely. To explain what I mean by 'fit state', consider this: most parents quickly learn that tiring out their toddler is a recipe for tantrums and other challenging behaviour. Smart parents work hard to prevent getting their toddlers in that state. Yet those same adults are often surprised when they struggle to behave well when they are tired, overwhelmed, drunk or otherwise not in a fit state to do relationship.

So this section is about ensuring that you have the internal resources (e.g. energy or concentration) to manage yourself. Neglecting yourself makes you less able to regulate your emotional state, and more vulnerable to becoming reactive.

EXERCISE 7: HOW WELL AM I CARING FOR MY BODY?

Look at this list and mark all the items that describe your state in the past month.

I have been:

☐ Overloaded or over-committed — have more tasks than I can cope with
☐ Overworked — physically or emotionally exhausted (or both)
☐ Working harder, not smarter
☐ Burnt or burning out
☐ Unable to feel enthusiastic about things
☐ Full of resentment or feeling 'put upon'
☐ Significantly depressed — down, blue, unable to enjoy anything
☐ Significantly anxious — worried all the time, tense, uptight, controlling or frightened
☐ Frequently irritable or impatient
☐ Struggling to wind down at the end of the day
☐ Not exercising
☐ Not re-creating — not doing hobbies, etc., that I enjoy
☐ Not connecting with friends or whānau (family)
☐ Unable to find time for myself
☐ Eating poorly
☐ Breathing poorly
☐ Sleeping poorly
☐ Struggling with a major health condition
☐ Hormonally imbalanced
☐ Relying on coffee to get going or stay awake
☐ Using drugs (including alcohol / porn / food / shopping, etc.) to cope

This is a list that Verity and I devised, so it's not scientific. However, if you ticked more than a couple of these, I would have questions about whether you really have the time or energy to change things in your relationship. If you marked more than four, it's unrealistic to expect challenging situations in your relationship to go well.

It's not practical for me to work through all the remedies for everything on the list in Exercise 7. I will stick with the basics: sleep, breathing, exercise, eating and drinking. If your situation is so stressful that you can't get these sorted, you must expect that your relationship won't go well.

SLEEP

Let's begin with sleep. Sleep deprivation is routinely used as torture. We have signs beside our rural roads saying 'Tired? Pull over', because driving when fatigued is as dangerous as drink-driving. Maybe you have learned to share the driving on long trips, and to pull over and have a nap if you need to when you're on your own. Well, running a relationship is *way* more complicated than anything you'll encounter when driving. You need to have your wits about you.

Whether you have a new baby, work shifts, have insomnia, or are in the middle of a crucial online gaming campaign, you must find ways to get enough sleep to function. Exactly how much is very personal; you will need to experiment. While you're doing this, be honest with yourself about your mood, patience and energy for tasks.

Napping can make a massive difference if you have broken night-time sleep. If we are short of sleep, our body will make efficient use of even a short nap to help restore itself. For example, someone who typically needs seven hours of sleep but only gets four hours because of an unsettled baby can benefit significantly from 'napping when the baby naps', even if they get only two 20-minute naps. Those 40 minutes of sleep won't fully compensate for the lost four hours, but they will do a lot more good than if there had been an extra 40 minutes of sleep in the night.

Some people struggle with allowing themselves to nap. Being out of sync with the rest of the world's bio-rhythms is hard, and it's easy to fear being seen as 'lazy' or 'indulgent'. Don't let your insecurities about what other people may think (including the people inside your head who judge you) over-ride the realities of biological necessity.

BREATHING

The next essential function is breathing. Anxious or stressed people tend to take short, shallow breaths using their chest. Your body associates shallow breathing with stress and threat, and creates a feedback loop: you are more anxious, so you become more readily reactive; then things don't go as well for you, so you become more anxious . . .

If you are breathing in this shallow way, you are starving your brain and body of oxygen and will need to recapture a more effective, deep-breathing pattern. For a full, nourishing breath, your diaphragm needs to move down and push the contents of your belly out.

EXERCISE 8: DEEP BREATHING

If you don't know how to 'belly breathe', try this.

- Lie down and put one hand flat on the middle of your chest and the other just above your belly button.
- Breathe naturally, and notice how much your hands are moving. Your bottom hand should rise and fall much more than your top hand.
- If this doesn't come naturally to you, you will need to practise. Do this exercise for 5 to 10 minutes at a time, three or more times a day, to entrench the new habit. Once you have the feeling of it, you can do it sitting or standing.

EXERCISE

If I don't exercise regularly, I get depressed. Although it took me years to accept that fact, once I did, it made getting regular exercise relatively easy for me — I hate being depressed, so that's a powerful incentive for me to pull on my shoes and go for a walk. You may not have such a direct relationship between your mood and exercise, but you do have one.

Do you say 'I know I should exercise, but . . .'? You'll already know that exercise has lots of health benefits. But did you know that, apart from sleep, it's the only way your body can process stress hormones? So if you're under pressure and aren't exercising, you will keep your body more stressed for longer.

To look after yourself, you don't have to be a triathlete or a gym bunny. As with sleep, everyone has to find their own way to a healthy activity level. The key is finding reasons to move your body that make sense and are intrinsically rewarding for you. For example, you may love walking in nature, while your neighbour likes walking on a treadmill so they can take in the news. You may hate to 'exercise', but love gardening. If you know yoga works for you but can't get to a class, don't forget all the wonderful online options for doing yoga (or qigong or tai chi, or whatever takes your fancy). Even 10 minutes a day is beneficial.

However you find your exercise, some is better than none. Regular is more important than big. Do what works for you. Do it out of kindness and care for yourself, not because you are 'bad' if you don't.

EXERCISE 9: DOING EXERCISE AS SELF-CARE

If you know you would benefit from more exercise, pick one thing that you suspect you might enjoy, or at least tolerate, if you did it for 10 minutes. Commit to trying to do it daily at the same time.

EATING AND DRINKING

A final fundamental is what we put in our bodies. Interestingly, I sometimes find it's what people *aren't* putting in their bodies that causes them to be 'unfit'. We joke about being 'hangry', but it is a fact that low blood sugar and dehydration affect our cognitive functioning and ability to manage our emotions. A related issue is where you are using food as comfort and subjecting your body to big swings in blood sugar levels.

The other big one is when we put mood-altering substances into our bodies. Did you know that coffee mimics the physiological effects of anxiety? So being 'wired' on caffeine will make it harder for you to stay calm and centred.

However, the most common problem with what we put in our bodies is to do with drugs, especially alcohol. I'm not against drugs — like most people, I enjoy altering my consciousness. But it's my experience that if you are under the influence, you are not in a fit state to do the work of intimacy.

Among my clients, alcohol is the big problem. And you don't have to feel 'drunk' to be badly affected. So let me take this opportunity to stress how foolish it is to try to deal with relationship issues after you have been drinking. I know it loosens you up and gives you 'liquid courage' to say difficult things. That might work well sometimes. But it's playing Russian roulette to enter into challenging conversations with your frontal lobes already disabled.

I have worked with many couples who found that their terrible fights miraculously disappeared once they learned not to talk about serious matters when drinking. Having had a few stiff drinks is an excellent reason to take a 'Time Out' that lasts until the 'next practical opportunity' (see Chapter 4).

I'm glad that our national hysteria against marijuana is slowly subsiding. It's objectively a much less harmful drug than alcohol; however, that doesn't mean it can't harm your relationship. If you are a chronic stoner, you may not believe that it matters whether you have had a puff or not. But let me assure you that it *does* make a difference, and that if you get stoned daily you are almost certainly self-medicating. That means there is some emotional stuff going on that you (and your relationship) would benefit from learning how to deal with straight.

Here I also need to acknowledge the historical and recent research into using drugs (particularly MDMA) to enhance relationships. All I can say is that those studies involved the support of trained professionals and carefully controlled conditions. The attitude to drugs is changing for the better in our culture, and research on the therapeutic use of various 'recreational' drugs is continuing. There are some interesting preliminary results, but from where I sit, the jury is still out on its long-term value for couples.

Obviously, you might need to look at many more items on the checklist in Exercise 7; I don't have space here to address them all. However, I do want to address the source of stress that, in my experience, underlies many of them. I want to emphasise that this section is very much about those of us who are privileged, wealthy, and free enough to have choices. People struggling to put food on the table or keep a roof over their heads are understandably stressed, and there's not much they can do about that. The next section is not about that kind of stress.

You can't have it all

In many of the middle-class couples I see, the root of people being unfit for relationship comes from having unrealistic expectations of themselves or what's necessary for their lives. In my 30 years of practice, our society has become notably more unkind to human beings. The emphasis on financial 'success' at the cost of humanity and connection, of business 'success' at the expense of workers' welfare, takes a real toll on relationships.

Often people have material goals that seem laudable ('house, bach and boat' or 'retire by 50'), but they do a poor job of calculating the present-day costs of achieving those goals. If you ruin your relationship or emotionally neglect your children to achieve your financial goals, I suggest that you are guilty of bad accounting practices. The costs are not just emotional; divorce is expensive. Starting again with half the assets is not a good way to get ahead.

The reason for such poor accounting is that those financial goals are often driven by insecurity. The classic case is having an unconscious need to 'prove' yourself worthy by 'succeeding' financially. So many people tell me they are doing it 'for the family'. Yet a bigger house or a private-school education does not make your children happier or more secure if it comes at the cost of having a consistently grumpy or unavailable parent. Your kids are only young once, and for a surprisingly short time. When I dig deeper with driven clients, I typically find a kid still trying to win his father's approval, or one trying to show a teacher who shamed her that she's not 'dumb'.

So consider that there may be more going on in your material goals than you think. A big warning sign is when your partner says something like 'I don't need us to have that much money to be happy.' Even if your partner isn't complaining, do some meticulous cost accounting that factors in the 'intangibles' like relationship time, family time, emotional energy and overall well-being. Don't buy what our consumer culture sells without thinking hard about whether it's truly the best for you and your loved ones.

I will leave the discussion of how to get yourself 'fit' for relationship there. Please be honest with yourself (and your partner) about what state you are in, and have realistic expectations of your capabilities. You can't have it all, and you need to work out what you really want and put your energy there.

Proactive brain-based strategies

Even if you are caring for your body reasonably well, what is happening between your ears can undermine how available you are for your relationship. Many suggestions from throughout the book could fit in this section, but I will stick to the one core idea here.

It's all about **attitude** — how you are 'framing up' the picture of your relationship. How you experience the world is the result of what happens *and* the meaning you make of it. You can't control what happens, but its meaning is much more under your control than most people think.

If you are walking around thinking 'He doesn't love me' or 'She's never satisfied', that will affect how you interpret the events in your relationship and how it feels to be in it. The challenge is to frame things in a way that not only allows you to get what you want but also makes it more likely to happen.

Let's say your partner is quite shut down. If instead of 'He doesn't love me', your framing is 'Growing up, he had to be self-reliant and keep his thoughts and feelings to himself', you are going to interpret and respond to your partner's shut-down in quite a different way. Remember, our brains automatically look for and attend to worst-case scenarios. That's a survival trait. But this whole section is about you not letting your biology dictate your choices.

Of course, there's no one-size-fits-all answer. You need to work out what attitudes and beliefs you carry that are setting you up for more distress and less emotional safety than you might otherwise have.

Identifying those unhelpful attitudes and beliefs can be difficult because they feel like facts unless we are mindful that they are not. Knowing what your core insecurities are is often a significant clue to how you filter or interpret your partner's behaviour. There's an explanation of how to learn about them in Chapter 8.

For now, let's focus on the kind of constructive attitude that is likely to get you what you want in your relationship.

EXERCISE 10: CULTIVATE A COMPASSIONATE AND HOPEFUL ATTITUDE

Look at this list of statements and mark the ones that resonate with you, that feel like they express something important about an attitude or intention you want to bring to your relationship. In particular, look for phrases that would help you stay calmer and more open when the going gets tough in your relationship.

Feel free to change the wording to make them fit you better.

☐ We are on the same team.

☐ Our differences are a resource if we use them right.

☐ I can't expect you to be perfect, because I'm not (nor is anyone else).

☐ In the big picture, our relationship and life together has a lot going for it.

☐ I'm allowed to have a voice in our relationship, and so are you.

☐ We have worked things out before and will do again.

☐ It's okay to have disagreements.

☐ It's okay for things to be difficult and unpleasant sometimes.

☐ Hard emotional work never killed anyone.

☐ My insecurities (and yours) come from formative experiences I had no control over.

☐ A lot of the emotions you trigger in me often come from my past, not what you did.

☐ I am responsible for my behaviour, but my thoughts and feelings mostly just happen.

In the space below, write some more phrases that reflect *who* and *how* you want to be in your relationship. To be helpful, they need to be phrases that you genuinely believe to be true. Be positive and encouraging, but not unrealistic.

_____

_____

_____

_____

_____

_____

Now take both the phrases you have ticked and the ones you have added and write them up on your phone. Look at this list daily (at least), and keep adding, subtracting and changing it as you try to use these attitudes in your life. Notice which ones help in challenging situations, and which aren't relevant or impactful. Do some give you a lift, and others just seem like words? Keep fiddling with the list until you feel like you are getting the messages that are vital to feeling good about yourself and your relationship.

The narrative running inside your head about yourself, your partner and your relationship will have a significant effect on what it's like to be in your relationship. Make sure that those stories are as helpful as you can realistically make them.

Reactive strategies: take charge of your biology

If you have a list of situations where you get triggered (Exercise 5) and warning signs that your self-protective system is swinging into gear (Exercise 6), the challenge is to work out what you can do in those situations that is more effective than what you have been doing.

No matter how 'fit' you are for relationship, no matter how constructive your thinking about the relationship is, you are still human, so there will be times when your amygdala unhelpfully tries to take over. The next two sections suggest what you can do then.

It is essential to explore the options thoroughly, because everyone needs a range of responses for different situations. There are a *lot* of strategies we can use, so we have to determine individually what suits us. What works for your friend may not work for you, and vice versa.

Make sure that your toolkit covers both *working with your body directly* (physiological approaches) and *looking at how you think about things* (cognitive approaches).

Covering all of the possible strategies would require a book three times this size, so what follows will give you an idea of the kinds of things that work for various people. Not all of these strategies will work for you; maybe none of them will. Do your research and find some that *do* work for you.

Here's a tip for success in making the shift to feeling empowered in your relationship: Anytime you find yourself dwelling on something your partner has done wrong, use it as a prompt to go and find a new self-soothing technique for you to try.

'IN THE MOMENT' BODY-BASED STRATEGIES

When you feel yourself getting upset, what works for you to calm your system down? If you don't know, then I urge you to find out, and find as many options as you can. Note that if you are in the middle of a conversation with your partner, you may need to take a Time Out (see Chapter 4) to get the space to employ these strategies.

Here are some of the strategies that I would typically explore with a client, in no particular order.

- Remember what I said above about how fundamental breathing is to our physiology? There's a reason why 'Take a deep breath' is the advice offered when people are stressed — it works! Especially if you take several slow breaths where the out-breath is longer than the in-breath (e.g. 'in for a count of 4, out for a count of 5'). Make sure you are breathing in and out through your nose. This kind of measured nose-breathing activates the 'rest and digest' part of our nervous system (the ventral vagus nerve), which you can think of as the opposite of the 'fight or flight' reflex.[1]
- Interestingly, singing, humming and even gargling also activate the 'rest and digest' reflex.[2] There are other ways to initiate it — cold water on your face or your whole body is pretty reliable. You can also achieve the same effect by holding a bag of ice to your face and neck.[3] Of course, some people find a long hot bath or shower a better way to calm themselves.
- If your muscles feel tight or shaky, tensing them up and then releasing them can help your body relax. For example, pull your shoulders up towards your ears as high as you can, and then let them drop, trying to open your chest.
- Some people calm themselves by becoming still, turning inwards, and focusing down. Some have an object or animal they can focus on that they find comforting. Others need to move — pacing the room, dancing or going for a run. Going outside and being able to

focus on the far distance can also work to activate the vagus nerve.

- Some people find solitude helps them settle; others need to talk out their upset (with someone who doesn't upset them further).

- Receiving caring touch is settling for most people. Surprisingly, this is something you can do for yourself. If you are focused and intentional, you can offer yourself comforting touch. For example, putting your hand over your heart, hugging yourself or stroking your arms or thighs, and feeling the warmth of your hands as kindness you are offering yourself.[4] It might seem weird, but give it a go and see if it works for you.

EXERCISE 11: BUILD A LIST OF WAYS TO SETTLE YOUR PHYSIOLOGY

The danger here is that you read this page and then do nothing with the information. I *strongly* encourage you to interact with this information.

Write a list on your phone of what you think works for you to settle your body down when you are getting stressed, angry, hurt, or otherwise upset. Make sure you include things you already know about that aren't mentioned above.

If you are trying new things, it's wise to experiment when you are *not* upset and see what might be effective when you are in danger of an amygdala hijack. Keep reflecting on your list, removing things that don't work and adding new ones to try. And remember to *use* the list when you are getting stressed or upset.

'IN THE MOMENT' BRAIN-BASED STRATEGIES

If you have managed to catch yourself before your amygdala has entirely hijacked you, you may still have the cognitive capacity (brain power) to stop your self-protective 'stinking thinking' and instead focus on a strategy that takes you where you want to go. Remember, you may need to take a Time Out (Chapter 4) to give yourself the space to shift your attitude.

A backbone to these strategies is recognising fearful assumptions, self-protective impulses and negative thinking, and naming them as such. Accept your perceptions and feelings, but don't treat them like 'facts'. For example, just because you feel attacked this does *not* mean your partner intends to hurt you. Be humble about your perceptions and your reflexive (automatic) assessment of the situation.

If it's obvious that your partner is triggered, don't use that as a justification for your own reactive self-protection. Accept that for the moment, they are not available to you. Be kind to yourself, settle your physiology, acknowledge and soothe your hurts. Then remind yourself that because your partner is so distressed, it would be ideal if you could be more settled and solid than them right now.

Reflect on the distorted, unhelpful self-talk you usually do when you feel hurt or upset with your partner. Check your thinking for blaming, excuses and justifications, self-blame, 'poor me', and so on. Look at the bigger picture of the relationship, what you know of your partner's intentions and your own integrity. Notice whether your usual indignation, self-blame, self-denigration, righteous anger, etc., take you where you want to go, serve your self-interest and your self-respect. (They won't.)

EXERCISE 12: BUILD A STRONG SENSE OF THE BIG PICTURE

A tool that helps many people is thinking about what I call the Big Picture. So often, the things we get upset over are specific, of-the-moment events. We get tunnel vision about what our partner just said and lose all contact with the many good things about them and our relationship.

The Big Picture is a realistic summary of the overall situation in the relationship, with all the history factored in but emphasising what's **hopeful**. It's going to be different for everyone, but typically has these elements:

- Recognition that we are both imperfect humans trying to do our best.
- Reflection on the strengths of the relationship.
- Acknowledgement of positive shared history.
- Statement about current intentions.

I encourage you to have a go at writing your version of the Big Picture and keep refining it until it feels accurate and powerful.

Here are a couple of examples of how people have written up their Big Picture:

- Evan (whom you'll meet at the end of the chapter) had this on his phone to look at when he felt hurt or intimidated by Angela: 'Ang is the most important person in my life. I love her, and I know she loves me. We have been through a lot together and been good for each other. We are getting better at not hurting each other when we're scared, but we're human, and both of us sometimes forget.'
- This one is by someone in a conflict-avoidant relationship: 'Even though Frank and I have become distant, we have a lot of good shared history. I know that when I feel alone, it's usually because one or both of us are protecting ourselves. Frank hasn't actually ever abandoned me. He has hung in there, doing his best all along. We are learning new skills and have had moments of real intimacy lately. It's hard for me to trust and be open, but I will keep taking risks, so we get more of the good times.'

If your relationship has been toxic and abusive from day one, you may struggle to write a positive Big Picture. But even when the relationship has been bad, if you are both trying to change things then you may find a way to summarise things that helps you settle yourself. For example, 'Even though my partner has been abusive in the past, he has responded well to me standing up for myself and is willing to take himself on and work with me to build a better relationship.'

A helpful exercise is devising your own credible, values-based self-talk to settle yourself down. Again, this is something to write down so you can read it when you are losing perspective, getting tunnel-visioned about some momentary hurt or frustration.

EXERCISE 13: DEVELOP A LIST OF CENTRING PHRASES

Try thinking about what a good and wise friend would say to you when you are upset. Here are some helpful questions you can ask yourself to get started:

- *Am I acting in service of my goals and aspirations? Am I being the person I want to be? Is what I'm doing going to take me to a place I want to go?* The key here is to focus on your behaviour, regardless of what your partner is doing. If you want to be in a loving relationship, are you behaving lovingly? If you desire a calm home, are you behaving in a way that encourages serenity in yourself and your partner?
- *Have I become blinkered? Is my focus too narrow?* If you fixate on winning an argument or making a point about something trivial, you are way off-course. Remind yourself of what is important. You are talking with a person with whom you share a commitment, a life, a home and maybe a family. When you are calm and centred, do you believe this is a relationship of love and care? Hold on to what you know when you are not triggered.
- *What's really going on for me? Why am I being so reactive? What's making it hard for me to settle myself?* The more you know about your insecurities and defences and where they come from in your upbringing, the easier it is for you to see how much and how often you are reacting to your partner out of your own shame and hurt.

Over time, if you keep answering these questions honestly, you will build up a repertoire of self-talk that will help settle you down when you get upset or triggered. To get the most benefit out of this, gather a list of the phrases or sentences that are effective in keeping you centred and being who you want to be when a situation is becoming stressful for you.

Grounding

If you're particularly anxious or worked up, you may need to do something to cut across your self-protective thinking. Pulling you out of your fears and negative assumptions and into the present moment is called 'grounding', and, as always, it's a matter of finding a way to do it that works for you.

Many grounding exercises encourage you to be mindful of your sensations in the moment. A commonly used one gets you to focus on each of your senses in turn. This is the classic grounding exercise called the '5-4-3-2-1 Technique'. It's a great thing to do if you have taken a Time Out (Chapter 4) because you are about to lose it. Talking out loud to yourself may feel foolish, but it's an integral part of the process — it changes how your brain is processing.

5-4-3-2-1 TECHNIQUE

Start by slowly listing, *out loud*, five things you can see, taking time to give attention to each one. Then do the same for four things you can touch (maybe even go and touch them and notice how each one feels different as you name it out loud), then three things you can hear, two things you can smell, and one thing you can taste (even if it's just the sourness of the coffee you had two hours ago).

That's just one of the many ways you can ground yourself. Here are a few more you can experiment with:

- If you are near a freezer, try getting an ice cube and holding it in your hand, and notice the sensations and how they change as it melts. Don't worry; it can feel slightly painful, but it won't hurt you. Or go to a sink, run the cold water over your hands, and notice how it feels.
- If you have ever learned a song or poem, reciting it can be an excellent way to shift your thinking out of a distressed rut. Even saying the alphabet backwards can work.
- If you have someone in your life (living or dead, human or animal) who has been a powerful source of comfort or support to you, bring them to mind. If you can visualise, try to picture them as clearly as you can, looking at you with an expression of kindness and care.
- Likewise, if there was a place or an occasion that was very positive for you (like a really relaxing holiday, or being in your grandparents' house), try to bring it to mind as vividly as possible. Try to remember as much detail as you can about the place (what it looked like, sounded like, smelled like, the temperature, etc.), and what it felt like within you to be there.

EXERCISE 14: EXPERIMENT AND LEARN WAYS TO GROUND YOURSELF

Try the grounding exercises in this section. Choose three that you think will work for you. Commit to using them the next time you are distressed.

Notice what is effective and what isn't. If none of them works for you, then google 'grounding techniques' and find some more to try. Make sure you have two or three that work for you.

Building up a repertoire of strategies to manage your reflexive impulses to protect yourself is something that takes time and persistence. If you've had little training or modelling of this kind of self-regulation in your upbringing, it will feel weird, false or unnatural. It's still an excellent idea — being in charge of yourself is the bedrock of making your relationship as good as it can be.

Connecting with your emotions

As I said earlier, we can't control the thoughts and feelings that arise in us — only how we respond to them. However, if we want to be able to choose our responses, we need to be aware of our feelings. When we ignore, suppress or deny our emotions, they will affect our behaviour without us having any conscious choice about their impact. So if you don't want to react in unconscious, indirect, passive-aggressive or out-of-control ways, you need to have good skills in connecting with your emotions.

EXERCISE 15: RECOGNISE YOUR PRIMARY EMOTIONS

You don't have to make 'getting in touch with your feelings' complicated. All of us have certain core emotional responses. I find it helpful to think about six 'primary' emotions:

- Three 'negative' emotions — Sad, Angry, Scared.
- Three 'positive' emotions — Joyful, Curious, Powerful.

If you don't know what you are feeling, ask yourself: 'Is it positive or negative?' If you can answer that, then try to pick one of the three primary emotions that best fits what you can feel in your body.

The aim is to be aware of the emotions you are feeling without them controlling your behaviour. Here's a strategy for making the best use of your feelings.

EXERCISE 16: MANAGE YOUR EMOTIONS MINDFULLY

1. *Notice and allow your emotions.* Be aware of the emotion(s) and attend to where you feel them in your body. Emotions are sensations — don't turn them into thoughts. So notice 'I'm feeling tight across my chest' or 'I'm feeling my guts churning'. Direct your attention to those sensations (most of us tend to avoid focusing on uncomfortable feelings).

2. *Give the emotion(s) a name.* The name may be obvious, and you can simply say to yourself 'This is frustration' or 'I'm feeling anxiety'. If it's not apparent, guess, then ask yourself if your guess is correct. 'Am I feeling anxious right now?' Usually, you will feel a sense of whether that's right or not. If you find this difficult, you can pick from the list of primary emotions in Exercise 15.

3. *Accept your emotions — don't try to control them.* You can't stop them, so don't deny them. Breathe into the sensations and allow them to be. They might get stronger. You might get shaky or cry. That's okay; you're allowed to feel! Acknowledge and accept that they're there without judging them. All emotions have useful information for you, though sometimes what that is can be hard to determine. (Of course, if you are in public and don't want to be emotional, that's different — but make sure you come back and explore your feelings if you have to pack them away.)

4. *Remind yourself that emotions come and go. Let the feeling exist and trust that it will leave.* Even if it feels overwhelming or never-ending, it is a fact of your physiology that this emotion will pass. According to neuroscientist Dr Jill Bolte Taylor, an emotion's chemical part lasts only

about 90 seconds. 'After that, if you continue to feel fear, anger, and so on, you need to look at the thoughts that you're thinking that are re-stimulating the circuitry.'[5] The briefness of the emotional impulse is particularly significant for those of us who struggle with being aggressive. Momentary anger is not responsible for lengthy tirades.

5. *Check if your perceptions created your feelings.* If your emotion is prompting you towards self-protection, enquire about your thinking and interpretations: 'What triggered me?', 'Am I making assumptions?', 'How much is this about how I am interpreting things?'. Often, the initial emotion we feel is not the important one to discuss.

6. *Use your values, aspirations and standards to guide your behaviour.* Accepting your feelings doesn't mean that you act on them without thinking. Make sure that what you *do* reflects who you want to be. If you want to build connection with your partner, then the way you share your emotions needs to be vulnerable and intimate (as opposed to blaming or defensive). There is a vast difference between saying 'You made me angry. You're so inconsiderate' and 'It took me a minute to work out what to say. I wanted to be angry with you, but I realised I felt hurt. I doubt you meant to do this, but forgetting to send that parcel triggered my feelings of being unimportant.' Which do you think is more likely to build a connection with your partner?

Have a plan of what to do

Once you have some notion of your warning signs and some strategies for how to manage yourself when you recognise them, I recommend writing down a clear plan for what you are going to do once you realise you are feeling threatened or overwhelmed. Do this ahead of time when you are calm and centred. You may need to work on building resources and skills to make your plan effective.

EXERCISE 17: MAKE A PLAN FOR WHEN YOU FEEL THREATENED, STRESSED OR OVERWHELMED

In making a plan, start with the broad-brush stuff and work your way to specifics. Begin by thinking about the general scope of your situation:

- What values are in play here for me?
- What are my goals for situations where there is a disagreement between us?

Once you have a sense of those things, start exploring what attitudes and behaviour will best serve those values and goals. For example:

- 'Treating you as an ally'
- 'Being curious and asking questions about what this issue means to you'
- 'Being assertive about what I'm thinking and feeling'
- 'Using reflective listening'
- 'Using a friendly tone'
- 'Using affectionate touch'.

Here's an example of a plan; obviously, the details will differ for you.

1. Take a Time Out if I haven't caught things soon enough.
2. Otherwise, say something like 'This is getting into tricky territory for me, so I want to go slow because I don't want to be reactive. I'm not saying you've done anything wrong; I'm just feeling anxious.'
3. Breathe (!), move, and ground myself using 5-4-3-2-1.
4. Remind myself: 'This is my partner, who is on my side, who loves and cares about me. We are just exploring a difference, and that's okay.'
5. Remember that our relationship is more important than the issue. Focus on HOW I talk to you and treat you.
6. Ask questions about why you feel the way you do about this issue, and try to listen and show care about how it is for you. Trust that you will do the same for me, even if you can't right now.
7. Make sure I talk about what the issue means to me in a vulnerable way, especially without trying to 'win' or to protect myself.

EVAN & ANGELA

Evan had very little sense of his own reactivity when he first came to see me. He felt like he was always on the back foot, could never win, could never get it right. From his point of view, Angela was the reactive one, 'always' upset, angry or critical of him.

Evan came from a family who dealt with the drowning of his younger brother when Evan was five by suppressing and avoiding emotions. As a result, he disconnected from his internal processing. The notion that his appeasement, avoidance, withdrawal and shutting down was just as emotionally driven as Angela's expressiveness was quite shocking. Together, we discovered that his parents' grief-stricken state meant that Evan was emotionally alone growing up, and developed an unconscious belief that he was unimportant and unworthy.

As he grew up, Evan kept his unconscious fears about his worth and importance at bay by trying to 'prove' himself, leading to success in sports and at school. By the time he and Angela came to see me, the focus was on his earning power. As well as taking any overtime he could get, he spent all weekend adding an extension to their home with a view to selling it and making a profit. He often worked late into the night and rarely had more than six hours of sleep. He reported that if he went to bed earlier, he 'just lies there thinking about all the things that need doing'. He felt free to dismiss or minimise any complaints from Angela about his irritability and emotional unavailability because he believed he was doing all this 'for the family', and he privately thought she was just an unreasonable, overly emotional woman.

It took some blunt talking from me to get Evan to see that his behaviour was destroying the lynchpin of his family (i.e. his relationship with Angela). Eventually, he could see that rather than 'securing the family's future', his ineffective attempts to manage his insecurities were in danger of obliterating their future. Once he accepted this, he started trying to get more sleep. He struggled to retrain his rhythms, and used medication for a few nights to begin the process. Once he got enough sleep, however, he was noticeably more available to the therapy and the relationship.

From there, Evan was more open to recognising and talking about the vulnerable emotions under his irritation and impatience. It was initially a bit depressing for him to realise how much he feared being unimportant and not good enough.

As Evan started to see how much the thoughts and feelings he'd been ignoring and suppressing affected him, there was a lot for him to work on cognitively. There were two key places where he needed an 'attitude adjustment'. The first was towards himself, finding ways to challenge the need to 'prove' his worth, and instead be more accepting and affirming of his worth based on who he was rather than what he did. For Evan, like so many, the notion that you can separate those two things was a radical idea.

The second area was his attitude towards Angela and emotional expression in general. As we unpacked the sexism implicit in his ignoring what she said when upset, it became clear how strongly he believed in conventional notions of manhood like being the 'strong, silent type', and that he unconsciously viewed men as superior. He was rather appalled at himself as we explored how much his internal dialogue dismissed Angela's experience as unimportant, 'silly', or 'over-emotional'.

To be fair, Angela had become increasingly exaggerated in her claims and manner in a vain attempt to get Evan to engage with her, so she had been unwittingly fuelling his beliefs. Growing up as one of four girls, the family culture was 'She who shouts loudest, wins'. In hindsight, Angela could see that her mother was overwhelmed and emotionally unavailable, and that she and her sisters were competing for her limited energy and attention. Angela recognised that she had taken on the belief that 'I don't matter' — constantly feeling second-best or unimportant compared with her sisters.

They each developed key phrases that they wrote down on their phones and repeatedly read throughout the day. Evan talked about it as 'reprogramming my brain'; although there was no quick fix, he reported after a couple of months of working on this that he was much better at switching off his brain at night, and Angela said she felt like he was much more reachable when she did raise a concern. Evan reported that he thought Ang had become gentler and kinder in how she approached him.

When Evan and Angela began exploring the notion of 'predictable trouble spots', they quickly agreed that Angela interrupting when Evan was in the middle of a task was a risky time; another was when either of them was tired. Because Evan was doing jobs in the evenings so often, there was a frequent 'double whammy' of them both being tired, but Angela needing some input from Evan and going out to the extension to get an answer, frequently with frustrating results.

There were several practical steps they took to deal with this. Evan began checking in with Angela before disappearing off to the extension. Angela started keeping a notebook of stuff she wanted to talk to Evan about, so she wasn't afraid she would forget it. They also instituted Evan taking a break to help put the kids to bed and (if that went well) taking time to have a cuppa with Angela.

Angela had difficulty identifying warning signs in her body, though she did get to recognise 'flushing' and 'tightness in my chest'. However, she could readily identify familiar thoughts like 'He doesn't care about me' and 'I don't matter'. Accompanying these was a sense of indignation — a critical cue for her.

Evan's early warning signs included tension in his shoulders and jaw, going silent and thoughts like 'Here we go again' and 'Nothing is ever good enough'. Although he could identify these reasonably easily, it took many weeks of persistent reminding on my part before he acted on them and took a 5-minute Time Out. He was frustrated that the first time he did this, the conversation didn't go much better after returning. We worked out that he didn't know how to settle himself once he had got defensive or irritable. Eventually, Evan found three things that seemed to help. The first was to go and splash some cold water on his face — he said that seemed to help him 'snap out of it'. The second was some deep breaths, especially if he could go outside. The third was that moving, walking around, seemed to help him settle down.

Angela, on the other hand, responded well to warm water. Taking a hot shower or, even better, a bath calmed and soothed her. She found deep breathing hard, but if she put her hand on her belly, that seemed to work. I encouraged her to offer comfort with her hand and focus on being compassionate and kind towards her upset, which also seemed to help her settle.

Angela found the 5-4-3-2-1 Technique good at cutting across her distress when she could feel herself getting worked up. It was hard to remember to do it, but when she did, she always felt like she did a much better job of communicating with Evan.

In terms of developing ways of thinking that would help him stay constructive, the list that Evan had on his phone included things like:

- 'I don't want to let Connor's death define my life.'
- 'I'm okay as I am; I don't have to prove myself all the time.'
- 'My family is more important than this reno.'
- 'Ang wants to connect with me; she's not trying to annoy me.'
- 'Ang has things to teach me about being in touch with my feelings.'

Ang's had things like:

- 'Ev loves me and is doing his best.'
- 'Ev has shown me many times how much I matter to him.'
- 'I don't need to shout to be heard.'
- 'I'm not a lost middle child — I'm a grown-ass woman.'
- 'Be smart, not aggressive.'
- 'What would Nana do?'

The other thing that worked for Angela was holding the image of her grandmother in her mind (and her heart). Nana was someone who Angela had always found to be calm and kind, and available to her. She said that imagining her Nana worked in two ways. Not only was her presence comforting, but she was also someone Angela wanted to imitate. In dealing with Evan (and the kids), that last question on her list, 'What would Nana do?' often helped her make good choices.

The thing that amazed them was how much better the atmosphere was in the house when each of them focused hard on managing their own distress. Evan commented it was 'like night and day' compared with what they were doing before.

Key points from Chapter 5

1. You can *influence* your partner, but it's only yourself you have *control* over.
2. You can learn warning signs that you are in danger of an 'amygdala hijack'.
3. The state of your body has a significant influence on how easy it is to stay in control of yourself — make sure you're fit to be in relationship.
4. It's wise to have a range of ways to calm your body when you get distressed. These take experimentation and practice to develop.
5. The stories you tell yourself about your partner, your relationship, and yourself greatly influence how the relationship goes. Make sure your narrative is serving you well.
6. Write yourself a clear plan of what to do if you start to go into self-protective mode.

Chapter 6
Dealing with difference[1]

A great marriage is not when the 'perfect couple' comes together.
It is when an imperfect couple learns to enjoy their differences.
— Dave Meurer[2]

Pain can be healthy

The second 'lens' to use in your relationship is that of the Developmental Model stages. Most relationships run into trouble when people need to transition from the Bonding stage to the Differentiating stage (see Chapter 2). For some of us, this is our first attempt at being ourselves while staying connected and caring. We didn't get the opportunity to Differentiate in a healthy way growing up, because our parents couldn't handle us being different from them (or their expectations of us).

Even if we did get some practice with our parents, doing it with your life partner is challenging. Learning how to be loving to both your partner and yourself simultaneously requires many different skill-sets: self-awareness, emotional regulation, self-expression, enquiry, empathy, delay of gratification and more are all needed.

To deal with our differences effectively, we must accept that a healthy intimate relationship is sometimes uncomfortable. We must stand against the dangerous misinformation that tells us discomfort means 'something going wrong'.

There's an analogy here with physical pain. We associate pain with injury, and rightly go out of our way to avoid pain. If we feel pain, we assume there is a problem and try to fix it. However, if you are training for a sport and need to build or maintain muscle, you learn that specific aches and pains — certain kinds of discomfort — are a sign that you are training well. It is the same with emotional pain. Not all of it is good, but some is, and you need to learn the look and feel of healthy discomfort.

You can see this clearly if you consider, and redefine, what is meant by the words 'closeness' and 'intimacy'.

Intimacy vs closeness: learning to tolerate vulnerability

In Chapter 1, I discussed the value of using the words 'closeness' and 'intimacy' to point to very different aspects of relationship. In my training with David Schnarch and Ruth Morehouse, I learned to think of **closeness** as focusing on areas of similarity and predictability, so that both partners are confident things will go smoothly and companionably. Most of us are hoping our relationship will feel warm and cuddly and nice and friendly all the time, especially if we equate discomfort with something being wrong.

Attempting to stay free of all emotional pain requires avoiding areas of vulnerability and challenge, so as to create an atmosphere of comfort and ease. It's about keeping things sweet in order to be easily in the same space, which is nice — but very limiting if it's the only way you can relate.

Feeling close and comfortable is a desirable state, but it's important not to see it as the *only* way to be connected. To be sustainable in the long term, robust intimacy *must* accompany and support closeness. I encourage you to see closeness as the payoff for doing the work of intimacy or the reward for risking healthy vulnerability.

You can think of **intimacy** as revealing those aspects of yourself that lie beneath your public presentation. Being fond of a bad pun, I tell my clients that you can spell intimacy as 'into-me-see'. In most cases, allowing your partner to see what is happening underneath makes you feel vulnerable. A working definition of vulnerability is 'sharing something my partner could use to hurt me'. It's understandable if that feels like an unwise thing to do! Sharing vulnerably will be particularly challenging for you if you have had prior experiences of abuse of trust (e.g. parents shaming you for your feelings, or a partner who was persistently 'gaslighting' you, i.e. making you doubt yourself — more on this in Chapter 19).

Another way that intimacy is challenging and uncomfortable is that it will frequently reveal or highlight your differences and disagreements. It works like this: When I tell you what I genuinely think, feel and want, and it turns out we are on the same wavelength, that feels wonderful and shifts very quickly into an experience of profound closeness and a sense of connection. However, some of what I say will inevitably be different from what you think, feel and want. Indeed, some of what I think and feel may express dissatisfaction with you or the relationship. At this point, our intimacy has highlighted difference at the level of things that are significant to me, and this is likely to feel very uncomfortable.

When we encounter conflict at this intimate level, it creates an enormous sense of vulnerability. This is what activates our limbic system and triggers our self-protective impulses (see Chapter 3). A key to dealing with differences well is learning to recognise these impulses as 'ancient history' and not letting them determine our behaviour. Instead, we need to learn how to act in service of our values and goals.

In sum, by this definition, the level of intimacy we can achieve in our relationship depends on our ability to tolerate vulnerability. To willingly enter into challenging, revealing, effortful and even scary interactions. Let me stress again: *this is not a bad thing.*

The dangers of avoiding conflict

I talked briefly in Chapters 2 and 4 about conflict-avoidant people. While knowing how to create and maintain a sense of closeness is an important relationship skill, some people and some couples make it the be-all and end-all of their relationship. If you and your partner 'never fight' and focus on 'keeping the peace', even when important things are at stake, you probably fit this category. Of course, in some couples you have one person who dominates and the other who is endlessly appeasing and accommodating, so there is only one person avoiding conflict.

The trouble is that there is a lot of social support for behaving this way. If you never upset each other, your relationship is unlikely to upset your friends, who will show appreciation for that. If you are always 'nice' and never assertive with each other, people will likely tell you what a great relationship you have.

Your friends are not doing you any favours, though. If you never risk the discomfort of honesty, the vulnerability of intimacy, then any closeness you have will lack depth because you are avoiding genuinely knowing each other. Over time, it will get harder and harder to feel close because there will be so many unexpressed thoughts, feelings and wants that you are carrying.

Pete Pearson from the Couples Institute puts it this way:

> *All significant growth comes from disagreements, dissatisfaction with the current status or a striving to make things better. Paradoxically, accepting that conflict produces growth and learning to manage inevitable disagreements is the key to more harmonious relationships.*[3]

If you want your relationship to flourish, and to grow as a human being, you must recognise when you are avoiding opportunities for intimacy because you fear the discomfort it entails. It is much harder to realise that we are in our limbic brain and being reactive when we are pleasing and appeasing, or quiet and withdrawn, than when we are shouting and screaming and throwing things. Sadly, because of the intense anxiety that underpins self-protective behaviour, couples where both partners are conflict-avoidant can go on like this for decades.

So, don't dismiss the suggestions in this chapter because 'we don't fight'. You may need to take a Time Out (see Chapter 4) to wrestle down the fear preventing you from being open and honest, just as much as another person needs it to wrestle down the fear that's making them aggressive or demanding.

A word on 'independence'

Mainstream, Euro-centric colonial culture in places like Aotearoa and Australia increasingly places emphasis on the individual and has a long history of fetishising self-sufficiency, especially for men. (It is not a coincidence that the 'great New Zealand novel' I grew up with was *Man Alone*.)

In my experience, when people (including increasing numbers of women) proudly assert their 'independence' or 'self-sufficiency', they are usually pointing to avoidance of vulnerability and a denial of the reality of their nature as social animals with dependency needs. Feeling unsafe and untrusting, they keep their true selves hidden and invulnerable. (This style of relating can also be a hallmark of Avoidant Attachment — see Chapter 7.) If this has been a norm in their upbringing, they will be unaware that any other way of operating is possible. They will react virulently against the natural discomfort of intimacy, the vulnerability that is necessary to 'show you who I really am'. They regard invitations to open up as suspicious and pathological (deeply unhealthy). Vulnerability equates with weakness, and many people will tell you so as if it were an unquestionable fact.

As the work of vulnerability researcher Brené Brown shows us, in fact the reverse is true: tolerating vulnerability is necessary and requires significant courage and emotional strength. Brené Brown says: 'Experiencing vulnerability isn't a choice — the only choice we have is how we're going to respond when we are confronted with uncertainty, risk and emotional exposure.'[4]

I think of our society's over-emphasis on self-sufficiency as 'pseudo-independence'. Its hallmark is a brittle rigidity masking the fear of vulnerability and dependence. True independence requires an acceptance of the inevitability of vulnerability and dependence in human relationships.

From that tolerance for the realities of intimacy flows the ability to be confident in the validity of what you think, feel and want *while* being connected to your partner and engaging with what they think, feel and want. To be able to 'think my own thoughts' while still being open to theirs . . . True independence is when you can know and share what you think and feel and still have room to hear how it is for your partner. (Not coincidentally, this is also a definition of Differentiation; see Chapter 2).

A word on 'selflessness'

In Chapter 1, I talked about cultural differences in how we resolve the tension between autonomy and connection (our need to be in charge of our lives versus our need to belong). Some people are encouraged to focus on becoming masters of their destinies. Others are encouraged to focus on the needs of other people to make the collective work.

Many families train their girls to be pleasing and accommodating while excusing the self-centredness of their brothers with 'boys will be boys' and viewing it as 'independence'. (Note there is a fuller discussion of 'good' and 'bad' selflessness in Chapter 10.) This inequity persists because changing it would require the parents to model something different. For many couples, that seems too steep a hill to climb (although, happily, increasing numbers of women in hetero relationships are pushing for it). It is worth noting that while this scenario can arise due to family members taking traditional gender roles, it can also be a consequence of Preoccupied Attachment (see Chapter 7). Sadly, this means that if you are a woman in our society with a Preoccupied Attachment style, you get a double dose!

Highlighting the dangers of excessive selflessness is not to decry generosity, willingness to compromise or the selflessness required to be a good parent. However, if the level of self-sacrifice in an intimate adult relationship becomes too high, it frequently results in a struggle to identify what you think, feel and desire — let alone to express that clearly and cleanly. To ask for what you want, to demand an equal say in the partnership, feels wrong, bad and selfish.

The impact on relationships of this level of selflessness is comparable to that of the rigid, pseudo-independence of the previous section. There is an avoidance of vulnerability, a hiding away of the true self in the inability (or unwillingness) to speak up. Partners are left in the dark about who you are, let alone how to give you what you want. Differences are driven underground to be dealt with unconsciously — with predictably bad results.

Differentiating happens in phases

Learning to deal with the anxiety raised by our differences is not a simple thing. Staying calm in conflict is something most of us need to *learn* how to do. Being able to know what you think, feel and want, while at the same time staying connected to your partner and caring about their thoughts, feelings and desires, is quite the juggling act. The good news here is that you can break the process of learning down into a series of steps — Exercise 18 takes you through this process.

EXERCISE 18: EXPLORING YOUR PHASE OF DIFFERENTIATION

Differentiation isn't something we learn how to do all at once. We tend to follow a typical path as we develop our ability to differentiate. You can break this process into five phases:

1. Developing the ability to **self-reflect**, to notice and accept my own thoughts, feelings, wants and desires.
2. Developing the ability to **express** those thoughts, feelings, wants and desires. This requires tolerating the risk of exposing 'who I (really) am'.
3. Developing **awareness of my partner** as separate and different. Initially, I may respond to this as a threat. For example, I see your different opinion as a criticism of me, or you wanting something different from what I want as meaning that I will miss out.
4. Developing an **increasing ability to listen, hear and respond** to differences. Exploring the differences with curiosity and openness and clear boundaries — caring about you *and* myself.
5. Developing the **ability to create an environment** in the relationship that supports desired changes. Negotiating in good faith, being able to compromise on an issue without compromising my selfhood, knowing when I can afford to be generous and when I can't, being creative in finding solutions rather than sticking to first positions, etc.

Think about how you deal with differences in your relationship. In which of these phases do you see yourself? You might want to focus on where you believe your *partner* is at, but try to keep your attention on how *you* operate.

Working through the phases outlined in Exercise 18 requires two complementary skill-sets: Differentiation of self (a.k.a. 'Individuation') and Differentiation from other (a.k.a. 'Empathy'). If you look at the list in Exercise 18, you will see it suggests that we need to acquire Self-Differentiation skills first.

MAKE LOVE WORK

Differentiation of self

To bring yourself into relationship with your partner, your first task is to know what's going on with you: 'You can't share if you aren't aware.' As I mentioned in Chapter 5, if you're not tracking what's going on with you, you're likely to be unconsciously looking to your partner to manage your deeper emotions and insecurities for you. That's part of what we mean when we talk about the Bonding stage of relationships being 'symbiotic'.

Even if you do have some sense of what's going on for you, you may feel it's not safe to share it. Usually this is rooted in a belief that sharing your inner thoughts and feelings will lead to conflict, rejection or pressure to conform. Working your way out of that pattern of avoidance requires taking risks and learning how to tolerate your partner's imperfect responses.

If all that seems a little vague and theoretical, Exercise 19 will allow you to identify where you are on your Self-Differentiation journey.

EXERCISE 19: EXPLORING YOUR LEVEL OF SELF-DIFFERENTIATION

Below is a typical example of how someone might progress towards becoming more Self-Differentiated.[5] It's not exactly a neat, linear progression. Some items are more about 'my relationship with myself'; some are about 'my anxieties about how you'll respond to me'. Nevertheless, read through them and see if you can identify roughly where you are in your development:

1. I never reflect on myself and mostly don't know what I think or feel.
2. I'm aware of my thoughts and feelings, but it doesn't cross my mind to share those with my partner.
3. I expect my partner to know what I think and feel without me having to say it.
4. I never ask for what I want because it feels too vulnerable — I expect a negative response.
5. I only express my feelings or desires in defensive or irritable ways.

6. I feel ready to explore my own desires more deeply and can see that I need to share them with my partner.
7. I share a little of what's going on for me or bothering me, despite my fear.
8. I ask for support sometimes on issues that matter to me.
9. I feel curious to know parts of myself that are yet undiscovered, and accept that my knowledge of myself is incomplete.
10. I trust that my partner can tolerate my concerns and wants to know me better.
11. I risk saying what I think and feel, and hold on to my perspective in the face of our differences.
12. I proactively initiate discussions and activities that are challenging but healthy for me and us.

Once you have identified where you are at, this list gives you pointers about the next steps for you. For example, let's say you recognise yourself in no. 5: 'I only express my feelings or desires in defensive or irritable ways.' This suggests that the next things you can work on (no. 6) are connecting more deeply with what you want and recognising the value in sharing that with your partner. You can even look one step further and see that the action step might be asking for support around something important to you.

Note: It can be disheartening to look at this list and realise that you are only at no. 2 or 3. But being aware of the path ahead allows you to take heart from knowing it's just a series of steps you can do one at a time.

THE VALUES AND LIMITATIONS OF INDIVIDUAL THERAPY

At this point, I want to say a word about the value of individual therapy in this process of Differentiation of self. I've done a bunch of personal therapy in my life, and when I have found the right person, the therapy has been hugely valuable. Good one-to-one therapy can be a great place to learn about yourself and build a stronger sense of connection with the thoughts, feelings and desires that populate your inner world.

Individual psychotherapy should help you understand how your 'normal' was shaped by your formative years, your insecurities and motivations, your values and priorities. Ideally, it will also help you be more aware of your defences, triggers and your less-than-desirable ways of operating. You can hopefully see how all of that will contribute to you moving through the phases of Differentiating listed in Exercise 19.

So I am very supportive of people doing their personal 'Differentiation of self' work in individual therapy. However, be aware that individual therapy has a particular danger with respect to couple issues. If you are spending a lot of energy on connecting with yourself and growing, leaving your partner behind is a real danger. You may develop a much more self-aware and considered (and considerate) way of relating. But if your partner is not engaged in comparable growth work, they will not have the awareness and skills to meet your new desires and expectations.

Individual therapy is also not as useful in helping you do the 'Differentiation from other' part. Without direct access to your partner, an individual therapist is limited in their ability to coach you on how to connect with your significant other. Without seeing how they behave and how you interpret and respond, a therapist has to be very tentative in their suggestions about what's going on with your partner.

Be very wary of an individual therapist who 'diagnoses' your partner without meeting them. While it is appropriate, and sometimes life-saving, for a therapist to help you identify if the behaviour you report is unfair or abusive, they only have your side of the story to work with. A good therapist will have the humility to recognise that.

Differentiating from other

The bottom line is that learning how to Other-Differentiate is something you can only do in relationship with an Attachment figure (see Chapter 7 if that's an unfamiliar term). For most of us, that means we can only do this kind of learning in relationship with our partner and close family.

As I mentioned earlier in talking about 'independence', our society increasingly encourages us to be self-focused, to look out for number one. Hopefully it is clear that this attitude does not offer a sound basis for a loving and intimate relationship. However, neither does a romantic fantasy of endless self-sacrifice.

The challenge of Other-Differentiation is to accept and even welcome your partner's different reality and ideas; to feel empathy without getting lost in their experience; to show interest and care without abandoning yourself. Exercise 20 will allow you to track where you are at, and identify what your next steps are, in your journey towards Other-Differentiation.

EXERCISE 20: EXPLORING YOUR LEVEL OF OTHER-DIFFERENTIATION

As for Self-Differentiation (see Exercise 19), there is a reasonably predictable progression in our ability to Other-Differentiate. Look at this list of items and, once again, see if you can identify your level of personal development.

1. It never occurs to me to think about what my partner is feeling or experiencing.
2. I assume I know what my partner wants based on what I want.
3. I spend most of my time focused on what I want and am not getting.
4. I get easily distressed and threatened by how different my partner is from me.
5. If my partner raises a grievance I take it personally and react defensively.
6. I can sometimes be curious about my partner's perspective and ask questions.
7. If I need time (e.g. a Time Out) to calm down, I continue the discussion afterwards, showing interest in my partner's point of view.
8. I can mostly manage my reactivity and stay calm and really listen to my partner.
9. I can put myself in my partner's shoes and identify with their experience.
10. I notice when I have hurt my partner and know how to repair things quickly.
11. I spontaneously do things that I know will help my partner feel more loved, valued and appreciated.
12. I am genuinely interested in learning from my partner's experience in order to be a better person and a better team player.

Use the list to try to identify where you are and what might be the next steps for you. As with Self-Differentiation, these steps are not strictly sequential, but each points to an aspect of learning to hold yourself in relationship to a significant other.

For example, suppose that you can sometimes manage to show curiosity about your partner's perspective (no. 6 in the list). In that case, you might profit from working on increasing how much you can do that by using Time Out (Chapter 4) and coming back to what they were saying, with a view to getting to no. 8 — where you can mostly hang in there with them, whatever they are saying.

It's complicated, learning to be aware of and share yourself with someone of enormous importance to you *and* learning how to show care, interest in and support for them. This process of Differentiating is at the heart of our struggles in relationship, and much of what follows in later chapters will add to your understanding of how to do it well.

SIMONE & GAVIN

Simone is the youngest of three girls in her family, and she also has a brother five years younger. She always felt like the 'ugly duckling' compared with her older sisters and struggled to feel 'good enough' by comparison. This self-appraisal would have surprised Simone's parents, who were very encouraging of her (and her siblings) — putting time in to support her academic, sporting and social interests. Her family was also part of a sprawling network of whānau (extended family) relationships on both sides of the family. Simone was encouraged to form friendships with her cousins and, as she grew up, developed confidants among them and even one of her aunties. Simone never had to 'test' her worth or popularity by making friends with strangers. Among the women of the family, there was a lot of discussion of emotions and people's internal states and, frankly, quite a lot of gossip about the wider family.

Gavin grew up in a family that was very task-focused. His parents were very actively involved in the children's activities (coaching, managing, fund-raising), creating a lot of community connection. There was significant emphasis on sport and on keeping busy. There was also a strong understanding in the family that emotional subjects were not to be discussed, especially with anyone outside the immediate nuclear family.

When Simone initiated conversations about how she felt about things or — worse — enquired about his feelings and desires, Gavin felt intensely uncomfortable. He dealt with this by saying very little (Simone: 'I'm lucky if I get a grunt out of him') and shifting the conversation back to the safe area of the practical world as quickly as possible. Because the men in her whānau were not a lot different, Simone was pretty accepting of Gavin's avoidance of this sort of intimacy.

Gavin's default setting was to submit and appease; 'Anything for the quiet life' was his motto. If he couldn't please Simone, he would disappear into his hobbies and hope she would settle down. With his upbringing, he couldn't see the point of engaging to disagree with her. If she confronted him and demanded that he engage on some difficult or emotional topic, he would comply but would frequently fail to follow through with whatever he had agreed to.

Simone tended to dominate the relationship with her emotions. She saw this as a virtue: 'I'm an open book'. When she was really frustrated with Gavin, Simone would withdraw into a sulk, but that tended to be only for a brief period. She was able to use her female friends (cousins) to give her the emotional support she craved.

Intuitively, Simone knew that sex was a big part of the glue that kept them together. She felt important and wanted by Gavin when they made love, and he was always more open and tender after sex. She enjoyed sex and was often the one to initiate it. So it was a big deal for her when Gavin started to show less interest in sex about seven years into their relationship. Although she knew he was stressed out by pressure at his workplace, including the threat of redundancy, Simone couldn't help wondering if it was because she was older, bigger, boring, etc. Of course, the more she tried to ask Gavin what was wrong, the more he retreated into himself and avoided sex. She took her fears to her auntie, who didn't do much to reassure her, encouraging her to put more effort into her appearance.

However, the problems in their sex life took a back seat when Gavin found out that Simone had been talking to her auntie about them. Gavin was shocked and felt exposed and that Simone had violated his privacy (i.e. his boundaries). Simone was bewildered and scared by his outrage and thought he was over-reacting and completely distorting what she had done.

Predictably, telling him that only made him angrier (and more hurt).

Without someone to step in and show them that neither of them had done anything wrong, that they had simply run into a place where they were culturally different, it's hard to see how Simone and Gavin were going to sort this out. Each would cling to what they believe was 'normal' and 'right'. Even if Simone agreed never to talk to her auntie again about their sex life, she would be complying under duress to avoid another upset — not because she believed that was where they should draw the boundary around their relationship. Meanwhile, Gavin would be even more guarded and shut-down with Simone now that he felt he couldn't trust her.

It was a real flip in their relationship's dynamic when Gavin's reactivity dominated their interactions following his discovery of Simone's intimate talks with her auntie. While this was very distressing for them both, it opened the door to them moving out of the Bonding stage and into a much more self-aware and vulnerable phase of their relationship.

That involved both of them letting go of their self-righteousness about the other's behaviour and looking closely at the anxieties and insecurities driving each of them. Simone had to explore her longstanding fears of being 'ugly' and 'less than' from her childhood comparisons with her older sisters. Gavin had to face his fear of failure and its origins in his family culture of doing (which he had internalised as 'you're only as good as your last game').

It was not easy for them to acknowledge the ongoing influence of these past events, but when they did, each began to be able to see the other with more compassionate eyes. Gavin opened up about his fears about his erectile dysfunction, which he had not talked to Simone about. It was a revelation to her that he feared she would think him less of a man — and she was smart enough to see how her fears about his judgement of her were equally without foundation and just a projection of her insecurities.

The notion that they were simply two different people with different ways of looking at things, different histories and different experiences (even of the same event) took time to get their heads around. As they understood this and developed their ability to tolerate the discomfort that came from intimately exploring their differences, they found themselves drawing closer again. They created a mutually acceptable boundary about what Simone could and couldn't say to her family. An unlooked-for bonus was that they found that talking more directly about what they wanted could extend to their sex life, making it more enjoyable and rewarding for both of them.

Key points from Chapter 6

1. Intimacy and closeness are not the same thing. You need to accept that intimacy is sometimes challenging and uncomfortable.
2. Don't confuse the avoidance of intimacy with 'independence' or 'being self-sufficient'. Intimacy requires tolerating vulnerability.
3. Don't confuse being caring, selfless and other-focused with being intimate. You need to show up to be known and connected with.
4. The sooner you deal with a difference, an upset, the better. Avoiding conflict is setting yourself up for worse trouble later on.
5. 'Sooner' doesn't mean 'reactively' — make sure that your frontal lobes are engaged before you raise a contentious issue.
6. Successful relationships depend on you Differentiating: being able to connect with and express yourself at the same time as showing interest and care for your partner.
7. You can only share if you are self-aware. Being connected to your thoughts, feelings, desires and values is essential to sharing yourself intimately with your partner.
8. When your partner shares intimately, their reality may be very challenging for you. Learn to tolerate it and, ideally, be curious about it.

Chapter 7
Attachment in adult relationships

The third 'lens' to use in your relationship is Attachment. If you're a parent, you may already be familiar with Attachment theory. Understanding how it applies to adults is complicated, but is valuable in making sense of some things in your relationship.

The core principle is that the relationship you had with your caregivers in the first 18 months of your life (yes, before you could even talk!) forms a **template**, a style of relating, that affects all your other serious relationships for the rest of your life.

It's important to understand that we talk about Attachment *style* for a reason. It's not 'personality' in the sense of a genetically inherited way of being; it's a style of relating that we learned very early.

So, although your infant Attachment style strongly influences your adult Attachment style, it is also affected by other influences and can be modified in adulthood. It is vital to understand and remember that you *can* learn to operate in a more secure style of relating as an adult even if that's not what you learned as a child.

The origins of Insecure and Secure Attachment

Before the pioneering work of John Bowlby and Mary Ainsworth,[1] people saw infants as blank, passive recipients of whatever their parents did to them. Bowlby's revolutionary insight was to suggest that, from birth, children are active participants in the relationship, learning strategies to secure as much parental care and support as possible.

Mary Ainsworth's genius was to come up with a way to assess something so complex in pre-verbal children. To summarise briefly, her 'Strange Situation Procedure' studied the meaning of behaviour that infants show on reuniting with their caregiver after being stressed.

The child is left alone for a short time in an unfamiliar environment. Researchers then assess how the child responds when its mother re-enters the room, looking for signs of 'secure' or 'insecure' Attachment.

Secure Attachment

Securely Attached children demonstrate confidence that their caregiver will respond to them in a way that is both *timely* (i.e. when the child needs it) and *attuned* (i.e. in a way that genuinely meets the child's needs). They learn this even though their caregivers are less than perfect. Every caregiver needs to know what the research suggests: that caregivers of Securely Attached infants only respond in an attuned way **about 30% of the time!**[2]

Put simply, secure kids have had enough experience to know that they can rely on their parents (or other caregivers). They will turn to their caregiver for comfort when distressed and allow that comfort to soothe them. This support makes them confident in moving away from their caregivers to explore the world, knowing that they can always 'return to base' if the world gets scary. Research suggests that close to 60% of the population is Securely Attached.[3]

Insecure Attachment styles

Insecure infants aren't confident that they can rely on their caregivers. For all sorts of reasons, the child's needs have not consistently been met in a timely and attuned way. Not being able to rely on caregivers trains kids to act in specific 'insecure' styles, depending on the type of learning history they have.

Bowlby and Ainsworth identified three styles of Insecure Attachment that have stood the test of time. Unfortunately, although the styles have remained the same, the number of names for them has proliferated. It is very confusing when writers use different words for the same thing; it drove me mad when I was first trying to learn about Attachment.

PREOCCUPIED (A.K.A. AMBIVALENT, RESISTANT, ANXIOUS) ATTACHMENT

These children have unpredictable caregiver relationships in their formative years, where attuned love and care are intermittent. Often they had a parent who was able to attune to them (to give the child what the child really wanted and needed), but who had other demands on them — perhaps as a result of poverty, a struggle with their own health (e.g. chronic illness or addiction), or demands of other family members (e.g. a terminally ill parent, or six other children).

The child ends up knowing what 'being well-cared for' feels like but can't trust that it will happen. This unreliability leads them to be anxiously uncertain about having their needs met. Consequently, they also become worried about their worth, importance and lovability. It also trains them to nervously scan for signs that their caregiver will or won't be there for them. The 'ambivalence' part shows in their behaviour under stress. Sometimes they can be very 'clingy' and reluctant to let the adult out of sight. At other times, they become quite angry and rejecting of their parent, even when the parent is trying to offer them comfort. The kid is saying, with reason: 'I don't trust this; I'm scared to get my hopes up. I'm frightened to rely on you.'

Adults with this Attachment style tend to be preoccupied with the relationship and hypervigilant about perceived threats or failings. People who 'play games' or become manipulative to get reassurance (e.g. choosing to over-react or provoke jealousy) tend to have this Attachment style. Another hallmark is powerful 'fears of abandonment', a person who looks so hard for evidence of abandonment that they will always find something to confirm their fears. Finding the evidence they are looking for usually results in a distress reaction (e.g. anger, criticism, withdrawal, pleading) that is demanding or frightening for their partner. This tends to make the partner want to distance themselves, thus creating a self-fulfilling prophecy. The research says that about 11% to 14% of the population is in this category.

AVOIDANT (A.K.A. DISMISSIVE) ATTACHMENT

Children who adopt this Attachment style often had all their physical needs met. They were reliably fed, clothed, housed, schooled, exercised, etc. However, they didn't get their *emotional needs* met in an attuned way.

Sometimes this was a result of benign neglect. Children left to their own devices often come to cherish their freedom, not realising that the price for it is learning to be unhealthily self-reliant, distancing or denying their Attachment needs.

For other children, their caregivers didn't know how to engage effectively with their emotional needs. They responded to pain with denial: 'Don't cry; you're not hurt.' They found curiosity annoying: 'You're driving me crazy with all these questions.' Poor attunement like this can also result from parents being overly intrusive — where the parent's behaviour is driven by their own feelings (e.g. anxiety about being a good parent) rather than the child's needs.

Before they can talk, these kids learn to keep their feelings to themselves and, indeed, soon learn to suppress their emotions, so even *they* don't have to deal with them. After they have grown up, these children are often told 'You were such a good kid. Never any bother.'

As adults, these people tend to over-emphasise autonomy and self-reliance — they can have an almost compulsive need to 'be their own person'. Intimacy is enjoyable only if it doesn't threaten freedom and autonomy. They will frequently avoid intimacy and be dismissive of dependency needs in themselves and others. The kind of healthy interdependence that characterises secure Attachment seems stifling and controlling to them.

The vulnerability necessary to create real intimacy can seem very threatening and alien to an adult with an Avoidant Attachment style. Some will unconsciously do things to create distance in the relationship, like making unilateral decisions, being dismissive of or ignoring their partner, flirting with others, etc. Often they will focus on the faults and mistakes of their partner to create mental distance and justify their cut-off.

As with the Preoccupied Attachment style, this distancing also tends to create a self-fulfilling prophecy. Being shut off and avoidant invites their partner to try to 'dig deeper' or to 'break down' their self-protective armour. These attempts at getting them to be more vulnerable are typically experienced as invasive, and confirm their fears that the relationship threatens their autonomy and safety. The research suggests that over 25% of the population fit into this category.

DISORGANISED (A.K.A. FEARFUL-AVOIDANT) ATTACHMENT

These tend to be children whose caregivers were the source of threat — who were abusive or grossly neglectful. Children are wired to seek comfort and protection from a caregiver, so it is fundamentally confusing when that same person is the source of distress. In one sense, the Attachment system, which bonds us to others, conflicts with the self-protection system, which is trying to keep us alive.

These people tend to have quite erratic behaviour as children or adults, swinging from the Avoidant's disengagement to the Preoccupied's clinginess or anger in a short space, with little warning. Not surprisingly, they are challenging to be in relationship with as adults, tending to create chaos and confusion in their partners. It is one of life's bitter ironies that people who have a rough start find it hard to form healthy relationships. The lack of good modelling also makes them prone to choosing unreliable or even abusive partners, adding to their store of learning that Attachment is dangerous. The numbers of people who fall into this category are small, so research is not as clear about the proportion, but it's probably less than 3% of the population.

To finish this discussion of Insecure Attachment styles, a word of warning about a language trap that catches some of my clients. If you read about Attachment, you may come across the term 'Anxious' as a synonym for the Preoccupied or Ambivalent style. This implies that the other styles are not anxious, which is wrong and unhelpful.

It is especially problematic for couples. People with an Avoidant Attachment style usually see themselves as unemotional, unreactive and 'not anxious'. Often they feel superior to their partners who express emotion or show anxiety about the relationship. Yet, *all* Insecure Attachment styles are an attempt to deal with the anxiety raised by relationship stress. The reality is that someone with an Avoidant Attachment style is just as anxious about relationships as someone with a Preoccupied style; they are just better at hiding it, including from themselves.

The Attachment Grid

The following diagram summarises my core understandings of the different adult Attachment styles. I have tried to show how the different styles operate across the same five dimensions of relationship (refer to the bracketed numbers in the diagram, which relate to the five dimensions below):

1. Interactional style.
2. Impact of insecurities.
3. Management of vulnerability.
4. Emotional and relational style.
5. Boundary setting.

I have organised the diagram around two axes — how much attention and care we show to ourselves, and how much we show to others. Secure people do both, which highlights the overlap with well-Differentiated people.

One thing I like about a diagram like this is that it captures the idea that you can be anywhere in the quadrant that fits your attachment style. For example, you could be 'medium' on the 'Orientation to Self' axis, meaning that you are somewhat aware of and able to say what you think, feel and want. Yet because you are also very high in 'Orientation to Others' (i.e. you obsess about your partner), you end up in the top left corner of the 'Preoccupied/Ambivalent' quadrant.

ADULT ATTACHMENT STYLES

	HIGH ← *ORIENTATION TO SELF* → LOW	
HIGH ← ORIENTATION TO OTHERS → HIGH 		

	HIGH ← *ORIENTATION TO SELF* → LOW	
	Secure	**Preoccupied/Ambivalent**
	(1) is resilient in relationship — 'available'	(1) is visibly reactive — 'thin skin'
	(2) believes they are accepted and acceptable	(2) seeks validation and approval of others excessively
	(3) is able to tolerate vulnerability	(3) tries to reduce vulnerability by managing others
	(4) is empathic and responsive	(4) talks about feelings and relationship a lot (anxious engagement)
	(5) has clear and flexible boundaries	(5) has poor boundaries — abandons self ('bad selfless')
	Avoidant/Dismissive	**Fearful/Disorganised**
	(1) is dismissive of the need for others — 'invulnerable'	(1) is erratic in relationship — pulls close then pushes away
	(2) is compulsively self-reliant	(2) feels unworthy and mistrusts partner's intentions
	(3) avoids vulnerability by being emotionally isolated	(3) feels a constant sense of danger and vulnerability
	(4) does not notice or show emotions readily or talk about relationships	(4) has poor self-regulation of emotion; unpredictable
	(5) has rigid boundaries — inflexible ('bad selfish')	(5) has inconsistent, arbitrary boundaries

LOW ← ORIENTATION TO OTHERS → HIGH

Exercise 21 shows you how to identify your Attachment style.

EXERCISE 21: IDENTIFYING YOUR ATTACHMENT STYLE

Use the descriptions in the Attachment Grid diagram to identify where you sit on the grid. For most people, one set of statements will fit better than the others. If you don't immediately get a clear sense of where you fit, you might want to think about specific relationships. It's possible to have a very different infant Attachment style with different caregivers; that will mean you will have different adult Attachment styles in different situations.

Be as ruthlessly honest as you can about how you were parented and about how you operate when under relationship stress. You don't have to agree with every statement in a particular quadrant — the diagram is just a rough summary of complicated matters.

The politics of Attachment theory

I suggest you ignore this section unless you already know a bit about Attachment theory or care about theoretical perspectives. However, I want to address some strong beliefs about Attachment theory as these shape a lot of advice given to people about parenting and adult romantic relationships. This has become a highly political issue in relationship therapy, with some people asserting that we are doing harm if we don't stick to their interpretations of the theory. In particular, there is a strong emphasis on 'co-regulation' of distress and a de-emphasis or even dismissal of the importance of 'self-regulation'.

I believe it's essential to recognise that adult and infant Attachment dynamics are very different, even though they rely on the same underlying biological and psychological systems. I stress this because some people generalise directly from caregiver–infant studies to adult relationships, which results in some questionable expectations (more misinformation!) about how adult relationships are supposed to work. Typically this leads to the advice that adult partners should care for each other with the patience and responsibility of a parent for their child.

The infant–caregiver relationship is **hierarchical and dependent**. Although the theory holds that the child is an active participant in the relationship, the relationship is still primarily one-way. Adults give, and children take what is given, utterly dependent on their caregivers for their physical survival and, initially, for making psychological and emotional sense of the world. That complete dependence requires children to accept and adapt to whatever comes their way psychologically and emotionally.

In contrast, adult Attachment relationships are **reciprocal and interdependent**. As adults, we are capable of surviving on our own. The needs we want our partner to meet are authentic and very human, essential to the *quality* of our existence but not to our survival. Most of us are capable of feeding and clothing ourselves, and most of us don't die without love, sex or even companionship. So, outside of situations of abusive power and control, adults have a choice about what they accept at the psychological and emotional levels.

Furthermore, an adult Attachment relationship is one of mutual give and take. Our ability to give to our partner is influenced by the quality of our relationship and our capacity for self-regulation. Our ability to maintain an independent sense of ourselves, separate from what our partner chooses to do or how they see us, is central to our ability to be emotionally stable in the relationship.[4]

Realistic expectations of adult Attachment

Understanding our adult capacity for psychological and emotional independence (and the attendant ability to self-regulate) is crucial when dealing with differences. It plays out like this: When we disagree, expecting you always to remain caring and supportive of me is unreasonable. It's wonderful if you can, but no one can be a saint all the time. Sometimes you will be hurt and angry or confused and shut down. If our relationship is to remain stable when you are not immediately available, I need to have a solid sense of myself and how to look after myself.

The famous psychoanalyst Heinz Kohut put it beautifully: 'The mark of a good marriage is when only one of you goes crazy at a time.'[5]

Our capacity to care for ourselves develops alongside our capacity to rely on others for care. There is evidence that the ability to self-regulate (e.g. turning away when over-excited by parental gaze) develops by about three months, so this capacity is a factor even in infant Attachment,[6] one that some writers on parenting ignore.

Another massive difference in adult Attachment is that, unlike an infant, adults can seek care directly and explicitly, taking the guesswork out of caregiving. Of course, this can only happen if you have a clear sense of yourself and your desires. Furthermore, when your wishes and those of your partner differ, your partner will respond positively to your requests only if they are sufficiently self-aware and in control of themselves to tolerate you wanting something different from them. Thus Differentiation is an important factor in adult Attachment relationships.

People who remain stuck in the Bonding stage (see Chapter 2) still form Attachment relationships, but they are inherently unstable. The unrealistic, Symbiotic expectation that 'you should *know* what I want without me having to tell you' creates misunderstanding, confusion, hurt and anger. People trapped in Symbiosis unconsciously seek to be cared for in the same way as infants. This is inappropriate for an adult, and they are bound to be disappointed.

Realistic expectations are that, first and foremost, you need to be able to recognise and care for your own desires and needs, anxieties and insecurities so that you can bring them to your partner in a clean, clear and consensual way.

Emphasising our adult capacities is not to deny our emotional dependence and the attendant vulnerability on our partners in long-term, committed relationships. We do, and should, look to our partners to meet many of our emotional, psychological and practical needs. The co-regulation aspect of our relationship is also vital; our neurobiology means that we have impacts on each other's physiology.

While we are wired for connection and become emotionally and practically dependent on each other in long-term relationships, it's important not to lose sight of our choice and will. This book aims to help you learn about yourself so you can be there for your partner more effectively.

One way to understand this is to look at the difference between 'need' and 'want' in relationships.

Why 'I need you' is unromantic and not sexy

The romantic fantasy of relationship idealises what Helen Fisher called the 'temporary insanity' of love.[7] One particularly insidious aspect is how we glorify excessive dependency.

We know that being 'needy' is not a good thing. People who describe their partner as 'needy' are not being positive. They complain about pressure for affection, sex, attention, conversation, etc. Yet our society idealises the notion of *needing* your partner. 'I need you' is generally offered up in a movie or book as the ultimate declaration of love, the acme of romance. It is considered the height of passion to tell your partner you 'need' them, even that you will die without them. So why is it that so many people complain about it?

While it is important to accept our dependence on significant others, when we abandon ourselves or become reliant on our partner to the extent of 'needing' them, we are making our identity dependent on the choices and behaviour of another person. Being solely reliant on my partner to meet my needs means that essential aspects of my life are entirely at the mercy of my partner's choices, moods, whims and capabilities. If this is your model for love, it will lead to you feeling vulnerable and disempowered.

As well as disempowering yourself, using the language of 'I need', as opposed to 'I want', 'I desire' or 'I'd prefer', is very demanding of your partner. The implication is: 'I will suffer and even die (if we are being literal about it) without what I am requesting.' This is language appropriate to an infant–adult Attachment relationship but not an adult–adult one. This kind of language places your partner in a real bind. In my experience, people often use it in a manipulative way. It's an attempt not to allow your partner a choice about giving you what you want. The subtext is 'If you don't give me what I need, then you condemn me to suffering or death.'

This way of talking is typical of people stuck in the Bonding stage of development: 'I *need* you to be with me / have sex with me / tell me what's going on with you / share my hobby, etc.' The difference between 'wanting' and 'needing' gets lost in this way of talking. Yet the difference is crucial.

The following table spells out what I see as some of the implications of using *wanting* or *needing* as your frame of reference.

THE DIFFERENCE BETWEEN 'NEED' AND 'WANT'

	When you say: I NEED you	When you say: I WANT you
It's about:	excessive dependence	desire and choice
The implicit message is:	you have to	you are free to choose
Your partner feels like a:	thing	desirable person
It comes across as:	controlling	an invitation
The tone will feel:	needy	romantic (even sexy)
You will seem:	weak	strong
Which is usually seen as:	unappealing	attractive

Giving your partner a choice is an essential component of partnership — a crucial difference between an adult Attachment relationship and an infant one. I also believe it is a big part of what makes a relationship feel romantic: If I literally 'need' you, I can't choose you. So you will never feel chosen or wanted for yourself, only for the function you serve in my life. The sense of my partner *choosing* to love me and do nice things for me makes me feel special, wanted and desired. If they *have* to love me, then I am just another obligation on their chores list, which is about as romantic as cleaning the toilet.

What to do if you have an Insecure Attachment style

The research is clear that you can moderate or even change your Attachment style.[8] A frequent piece of advice is to try to partner with someone with a Secure style. This probably does work, but it's not a partnership I frequently see. In my experience, most Secure people have too much self-respect and empathy to tolerate the frustrating, self-defeating behaviour of the Insecurely Attached.

What I see is that we tend to partner with people who are roughly at a similar developmental stage, so we have a comparable capacity to tolerate intimacy. Sometimes one person will think they are a lot more 'evolved' or 'together' than their partner. For me, this usually means that their insecurities operate in a more hidden way, rather than that they are less insecure. It's usually people with the Avoidant style who think this, because (a) feeling superior is a common strategy for maintaining emotional distance, and (b) they hide their vulnerabilities from themselves. They are saying what they honestly believe; it's just that they are wrong.

So, most of us with Insecure Attachment styles will partner with each other. Given this, how *do* you change your Attachment style? In many ways, much of the advice on how to do this is of the 'fake it till you make it' kind. The commonly used phrase is 'act Secure'. This is a place where you need to use your thinking to over-ride your impulses and feelings. If you are Insecurely Attached, then, by definition, in the past you learned that you couldn't rely on people you love. That learning history tends to make your perception of your partner unreliable, and your 'natural' reactions counter-productive. Exercise 22 will help you learn how to 'act Secure'.

EXERCISE 22: 'ACTING SECURE'

There is no simple or quick way to change your Attachment style. However, it is possible to be quite specific about behaviours you can cultivate that will help. In this exercise we look in detail at four areas where Attachment goes awry and what 'acting Secure' looks like in each area.

Read through this exercise with a pencil or highlighter in your hand, and mark the bits that resonate for you. At the end, make a list of the 'acting Secure' behaviours you want to develop to improve your relationship.

1. Boundary confusion (I don't know where I end and you begin)

If you find yourself unable to stay positive when your partner is down, or stay calm when your partner is upset, this is 'emotional contagion'. It points to an inability to maintain your psychological boundaries (a.k.a. 'symbiosis', 'emotional fusion' and 'co-dependency'). There's a difference between showing empathy for your partner and feeling controlled by your partner's mood. In those of us who have an Avoidant style, boundary confusion also shows up when you have to withdraw from your partner if their mood is uncomfortable for you.

Flowing from that boundary confusion can be a strong tendency to appease, giving your partner what you think they want and ignoring what you want for yourself. You may tell yourself you are 'keeping the peace', but what you are really doing is acting as if your partner's wants and needs are more important than your own.

One frequent indicator that you have gone down that path is feeling resentful. Remember, in equal partnerships, resentment is usually a sign that you have not looked after yourself at some point in the past.

Another typical example is the expectation that your partner should be able to read your mind, to know what you want or feel without you telling them. That would only be possible if you were one person. And you're not.

These are warning signs that you need to work on your internal boundaries, your Self-Differentiation (a.k.a. Individuation). Acting secure in this case requires a conscious decision to try and keep your equilibrium, think your own thoughts, and maintain your own mood while still showing interest and care for your partner.

2. Distress over emotional distance (You're too distant / You're too close)

This comes in two forms depending on whether your Attachment style is Preoccupied or Avoidant. Sadly, if your style is **Disorganised**, you are likely to feel distress about too much and too little distance at different times. You will have to work on both of the strategies suggested here.

If you have a **Preoccupied** style, the distress will show up as 'separation anxiety' — intense anxiety when your partner is physically or psychologically distanced (e.g. shut-down or distracted). You may see yourself being 'clingy', have baseless fears about what your partner is doing when they are away from you, or know you are unreasonably demanding of your partner's time, attention or approval. Recognising that behaviour is your cue that fears and beliefs from your early Attachment history are influencing you.

In this case, acting Secure means first realising that the justifications you make for your behaviour are not necessarily valid. Secondly, acting

Secure means extending trust and faith in your partner's goodwill and desire to be there for you, and accepting that they are an imperfect human being who won't meet your needs perfectly but who wants to. Believe that if you don't make them 'bad' or 'wrong', they will probably be open to learning about how to give you what you need. Note: This only works if your expectations of them are reasonable, and you are doing your part in keeping yourself feeling safe and secure (by attending to your own physical and emotional needs).

If you have an **Avoidant** style, the distress over distance will show as you feeling overwhelmed — feeling intense anxiety when your partner draws close, physically or psychologically. If you are highly Avoidant, you won't allow yourself to feel the anxiety, and it will show up as distancing or avoiding behaviour. If you feel overwhelmed by your partner's expectations, smothered, angry, or find excuses to avoid your beloved, that's your cue that your Avoidant Attachment style is in play.

If you want to do something more constructive, more in line with Secure Attachment, you have to start by not getting caught up in your justifications for trying to create more emotional distance. Those of us with an Avoidant style are particularly prone to 'buying our own bullshit' — one of our distancing strategies is to see ourselves as right and others as wrong, so our tendency to believe our justifications is powerful.

Instead, we must remind ourselves that if we genuinely want less drama in our lives and the joys and benefits of a romantic partnership, then we have to be humble equals in the relationship. We must recognise that we have insecurities at play and an Attachment style that makes it hard for our partners to feel loved. We must remind ourselves that closeness and the vulnerability of intimacy are necessary and, ultimately, rewarding. We must stop making our partners 'wrong' for reminding us of our dependency needs, and take responsibility for them ourselves. That means being more proactive in talking about our inner lives and the relationship; prioritising time for being together, and not being resentful or reluctant when the relationship requires work.

3. Inability to self-soothe (At the mercy of my feelings)

If you feel like your emotions and mood are out of your control, or have had a lot of feedback that your reactions are extreme or disproportionate, that would be a sign that your ability to self-regulate needs work. Remember, if you have an Avoidant Attachment style, you must consider reactions like stonewalling, withdrawing or appeasing. Another sign is that you depend on external things to regulate your mood, such as alcohol or other drugs, food, exercise, shopping or sex. It also can show as a need to have (and keep having) success, achievement, status or wealth to feel okay about yourself.

In this situation, it's not your feelings that are the problem; it's that your *emotions* are driving you to behave in ways that negatively affect your well-being and relationship stability. We can't 'control' our feelings; they come and go (though how we *think* about things sure can influence our emotional response). What we can control is how we *act* based on our feelings. If we are focusing only on our emotions and show little regard for the impact of our behaviour on others, that's a choice with consequences. This maps on to having poor Self-Differentiation.

Acting Secure means accepting your feelings and emotional responses but being wise and caring, compassionate and considerate, in how you behave. You may need to work on your relationship with yourself, your self-worth and shame to be able to do this. If you grew up in an environment where the adults around you 'let it all hang out' and threw their emotions around, you might need to teach yourself some self-regulation strategies (see Chapters 5 and 9). If that seems impossible for you, that's an excellent reason to seek individual therapy. Self-regulation is a core life skill, and it's worth the investment.

4. Difficulties with self-activation (Don't know who I am or what I want)

To create a stable Attachment system, you must be 'present' in the relationship. You need to have, and share, a healthy sense of who you are and what you think, feel and desire. If you don't, you are unlikely to get what you want in your life. In addition, your significant other is likely to feel lonely or dissatisfied because they don't have a partner who is engaged, active and 'real'.

Warning signs that you are in this situation include always leaving it to your partner to take the lead, not having goals or desires for yourself, needing external reward or punishment to motivate yourself to do anything, or being vague or absent in conversation.

You will often need to work out what the history is in your upbringing that made it feel unsafe for you to 'show up' and have a self. Acting Secure, in this case, means showing up, being 'present', saying what you think, feel and want (including disagreeing with and challenging your partner), as well as demonstrating genuine interest in and care for them. Many of us learned early in life that 'being yourself' in this way means making yourself a target — for shaming, abuse, intrusiveness, neglect or disappointment. You may need to work out what you are afraid of and why before you can take the risks involved in being fully present in the relationship.

Having used Exercise 22 to identify where Insecure Attachment might be tripping you up, what can you do? Well, suppose that you behave as if you are Secure and your partner is trustworthy and reliable. By doing this, you are much more likely to act in ways that foster stability and security in the relationship. The next exercise offers four examples that will help.

EXERCISE 23: FOUR ABILITIES TO CULTIVATE FOR SECURE ATTACHMENT

Again, read through this exercise with a pencil or highlighter in your hand, and mark the things you need to work on. Add them to your list of 'acting Secure' behaviours from Exercise 22.

The co-editor of the *Handbook of Attachment*, Professor Jude Cassidy, identified four things you need to be able to do to give and receive an experience of secure Attachment in an adult Attachment relationship.[9]

1. The ability to seek care

When you're stressed, you need to be willing to take the risk of asking for help. Asking is risky because it requires trusting that your partner is responsive and available. Your partner is imperfect, and may not fulfil your request perfectly or even at all. So you have to risk disappointment.

You also have to believe in yourself as worthy of love and care. Some people had upbringings that make that difficult. They may need to work on healing that wound before they can bring themselves to reach out for support.

You need to be able to work out what you need and communicate it in a way that it's reasonable to expect your partner to understand. If you say 'You're such a cold fish. You never give me a hug', it's not reasonable to expect your partner to offer you a hug in response. Saying 'I'm so stressed. Would you give me a hug?' will work much better.

You also need to persist if you don't get what you want the first time you ask. Maybe your partner is distracted, or your request was not as clear as you thought. Secure people believe they are loved and worthy of love, so they are surprised when their requests aren't responded to and they enquire further.

2. The ability to give care

As I stressed earlier in the chapter, an adult Attachment relationship is a two-way street. A Secure Attachment relationship needs you to recognise when your partner is asking for care and to know what to do. Although it's not reasonable to expect you to mind-read, you do have to pay attention and see your partner's pain and distress as a cue to move in and engage, rather than distance and protect yourself. If their request is unclear to you, you must be willing to enquire and persist with patience.

As with adult–child Attachment, attunement is critical. Secure people can tolerate their partner's subjective reality being different from their own. You may not understand why something distresses your partner, but you can show care that they are distressed. This is especially necessary if it's something you have said or done that is distressing your partner. What's important to them may not be the same for you, but you can acknowledge the importance to them. What would help you may frustrate or hurt them. Have the humility to learn how to support your partner the way they need it, not the way you expect to give it.

3. The ability to maintain an autonomous self

Secure Attachment, like intimacy, requires knowing what you think, feel and want, and being able to share those things without getting defensive. Being able to regulate how you express your emotions is vital to maintaining a sense of security in the relationship. If you collapse into limbic-brain self-protective strategies under the pressure of the differences in your relationship, in that moment your primary relationship is with your anxiety, not with your partner. Your partner is then likely to feel unseen and uncared for.

In the same vein, it's essential for your partner's sense of safety and trust that you can take responsibility for your choices and actions. If you insist on blaming them for things they are not responsible for (like how you feel), you become unreliable and may damage trust irreparably.

4. The ability to negotiate closeness

We all have to deal with anxiety raised by difference, especially around how much closeness and intimacy we want at a given moment. Two people are often not automatically in sync and need to *negotiate* the level and nature of contact.

Even with infants, there is a negotiation about this: I mentioned earlier how tiny babies will turn away when they have had enough connection with a caregiver. You need to be responsive and attuned to your partner's desires, preferences and needs as well as your own. Where they differ, it is vital to show care for both of you in how you talk about the differences. Secure people accept that to make the relationship work, there needs to be discussion, negotiation, give and take, and delay of gratification. Many of us have learned to make the other 'wrong', even to shame them, when they want something different from us in the realm of closeness and intimacy. ('You're so clingy' vs 'You're a cold fish'. Or 'You're a sex addict' vs 'You're frigid'.)

Negotiating in good faith requires a lot of trust:

- Trust in yourself as worthy, fair and reasonable.
- Trust in others as reliable; they will meet my needs eventually.
- Trust that this relationship is solid and can withstand difference and disagreement.

This kind of trust is a hallmark of secure Attachment.

Secure Attachment and healthy intimacy are robust

When you bring yourself forward in the relationship and start acting based on who you really are and what you want and believe, you will likely end up in conflict with your partner. Secure Attachment doesn't create an absence of conflict; it simply means being less alarmed about difference and disagreement and being more likely to sort these out in a way that doesn't harm the relationship.

If your relationship already feels poised on a knife edge, this can feel like taking unnecessary risks, like pouring fuel on the flames. But the kinds of conflict you have when successfully holding on to yourself are a healthy form of intimate engagement — which is precisely what most relationships in trouble need.

Usually, when a relationship is distressed, couples avoid genuine engagement, and instead let their Insecure Attachment styles and self-protective behaviour (the Five Fs in Chapter 3) control their behaviour. You have disengaged exchanges or ritualised combat where no one is really listening or connected to the other. You might anxiously appease your partner, and kid yourself that you are being nice, considerate or respectful. You might anxiously over-ride or stonewall your partner, and kid yourself that you are standing up for yourself. But no growth comes from this kind of interaction, and its futility strengthens our frustration and despair. In contrast, if you:

- settle yourself down (self-regulate), manage your insecurities and defences well *and*
- say what's going on for you, what the issue is *about* for you (Self-Differentiate), *and*
- this provokes a strong response in you partner about what they think and feel, *and yet*
- both of you manage to behave well enough to allow the other person to stay in the conversation (Other-Differentiate), *and*
- you keep taking in what the other is saying . . .

then, all of a sudden, you are having an honest, engaged discussion about things that matter to you. Even if what you are talking about is apparently negative (like someone thinking they have to leave the relationship), this is a huge step forward for most couples.

If you hang in there with yourself and stay away from being reactive or defensive (by 'acting Secure'), you will likely start finding out about what is and isn't important to you. If you share that with your partner, then all of a sudden you are being intimate.

Remember, intimacy is learning about yourself in the presence of another ('into-me-see'). Don't equate intimacy with closeness; don't assume that it always has to feel good. Intimacy makes you vulnerable, which is rarely a comfortable feeling and can be awkward, embarrassing, scary or painful. It is more likely to happen during a healthy conflict than during a cuddle.

Understanding that conflict can be a healthy form of engagement that facilitates intimacy helps decrease anxiety and liberates us to take more risks in our relationship when courage is most needed. That's what Securely Attached people are willing to do, over and over again.

AMY & NIKAU

In my practice, it's common to find people with a Preoccupied Attachment style paired with someone whose style is Avoidant. The Preoccupied person is attracted to the Avoidant's solidness, stability and lack of drama. At the same time, the Avoidant delights in the Preoccupied's aliveness, openness and vulnerability. Once they get past the honeymoon stage, this sets up the classic 'Pursuer–Distancer'[10] dynamic that Amy and Nikau were experiencing.

They came to see me after Nikau suggested that they open up their relationship (specifically so he could have casual sex with other women). He believed that Amy was uninterested in sex, and while he wasn't willing to go without, he still loved Amy and their three kids. He didn't want to end the relationship, so this seemed like a logical solution.

Amy was shocked and, after giving the matter some thought, decided that given the problems in their relationship (of which sex was just one), now was not the time to experiment like this. Instead, she suggested they come to therapy.

It didn't take long to establish that Amy was frustrated by how little of himself Nikau shared and how minimal his emotional engagement was with her. She recounted years of feeling hurt by his dismissal or avoidance of her concerns. In typical Avoidant fashion, Nikau continued to dismiss her worries, saying he could see nothing wrong with the relationship other than they had 'mismatched libidos'.

There was an unspoken invitation for me as a man to join him in viewing Amy as a 'silly woman making a fuss'. As a result, Nikau was surprised when I suggested that he struck me as someone who was trained to ignore his feelings and that there was more going on than just 'horniness'.

Like many Avoidantly Attached people, Nikau didn't allow himself to acknowledge his hunger for intimacy and connection. Before they had children, Amy could meet those needs without any great effort on her part. Her Preoccupied Attachment style meant she was incredibly attentive to and accommodating of him, including sexually, for the first five years of their relationship. She particularly valued how relaxed and open Nikau seemed after they had made love.

Despite her best efforts, the demands of having three children under six stopped her from being able to make Nikau the centre of her life. Although simple fatigue was a factor, as Nikau became increasingly withdrawn and shut down from her, she became less willing to find the energy for sex. To make matters worse, her anxiety about his emotional cut-off made her more complaining and demanding — usually about him not doing his share of the domestic labour.

It was a revelation when I got them to understand that their fights about the washing and getting the kids ready for school were really about their struggle to believe they were emotionally safe in the relationship. Although Nikau was initially sceptical, he was smart enough to be open to trying some new things.

We explored their upbringings and the likely origins of their Attachment styles. Nikau was 'always self-sufficient' as the only boy with three sisters, and it was clear that the family praised him for 'never being any bother'. When we explored the notion of attunement, it became clear that he loved the distance his father kept and he found his mother over-attentive and 'fussy'.

I got the impression that both his parents were very busy (his mother worked part-time while running the household). Furthermore, his mother, as the primary parent, had a 'one size fits all' approach to parenting. Sadly, the strategies that worked for his sisters often didn't fit Nikau. Once his parents separated when he was 11, he was left to his own devices even more, and his 'independence' got the final boost when he went off to boarding school at 13, which he enjoyed immensely.

Amy grew up as the peacemaker in her family. Her father was aggressive and violent to their mother at irregular intervals. When he was settled, Amy was well cared for by her mother (and even her dad could be fun). But when her dad was stressing over work, finances or family troubles, Amy ended up caring for her mother and, from a very young age, was trying to build bridges between her parents. Her older sister attempted to fill the gap when her mother took to her bed (sometimes because she was injured, sometimes because the emotional abuse just shook her).

In her teens, Amy drew away from her mother, seeing her as 'weak', and invested heavily, firstly in her friendships with other girls and then in getting attention from boys. She reports having 'a lot of bad sex with a lot of bad guys' in an effort to feel wanted, worthwhile and connected. By the time she met Nikau in her mid-twenties, she was determined to make better choices about partners.

Once they understood how their Attachment styles fed their dynamic, Nikau and Amy began to see what they needed to do. It was not easy — changing life-long patterns never is. Initially, Nikau's acceptance of the need to be more open and vulnerable was strictly intellectual, as was Amy's recognition of the importance of her being more directly assertive. These moves created tremendous anxiety in each of them. However, they had some experiences in therapy they could draw on, and each began to see a change.

Nikau recognised that despite what he had been telling himself, he had been increasingly shut-down and passive-aggressive in retaliation for what he perceived as Amy 'withholding' sex. Once he accepted this, he started to engage more fully, both in the running of the household and in conversation with Amy. In particular, he began to be aware of and talk about his inner world, including when he felt lonely or unappreciated, which made Amy feel much more secure in her importance to him. At the same time, Amy began to behave like she was important, that her ideas and desires were worth sharing. It was strange to realise that she didn't need to justify and guilt-trip; just to ask.

A significant shift happened when she realised that one of the key places where she needed to be more assertive was around sex. The notion of sex for herself, for her own pleasure, was new to her and, to her surprise, *she discovered that when sex became about pleasing herself, rather than pleasing Nikau, she had enough energy for it. To his credit, Nikau was smart enough to recognise this was to his long-term benefit and was an active supporter of Amy's explorations.*

Key points from Chapter 7

1. Your infant Attachment style is a significant influence on how you behave in intimate adult relationships.
2. If you have an Insecure Attachment style, you will have predictable ways of relating that will make it harder to have a stable relationship.
3. You can change your Attachment style as an adult. You must learn to 'act Secure' and behave in ways that make relationships work better.
4. Don't confuse 'wanting' with 'needing' something in your relationship.
5. Understanding personal boundaries, healthy emotional distance, how to self-soothe and being present in the relationship are all part of 'acting Secure'.
6. Acting Secure shows up in our ability to both give and receive care.
7. Acting (or being) Secure is pivotal to being able to tolerate the discomfort and challenge of dealing with our inevitable differences.

PART THREE

BEING IN RELATIONSHIP

In these five chapters, we look at strategies to improve your self-awareness and take more control of how you behave. We look at how to translate that into being a good team member, and dealing with conflicts, and, finally, we look at some of the power and gender dynamics that can make those things hard to do.

Chapter 8
The influence of
your insecurities

The importance of self-awareness

In this chapter, I will try to put some practical meat on to the bones of rather vague concepts like 'being self-aware' and 'owning your stuff'. Let me begin by returning to my theme that the best way to improve your relationship is to change and grow to be the best you can be in the relationship. To change something, it's helpful to understand it first.

It is usual when your relationship is causing you pain to fixate on what your partner is doing (or failing to do) and, rightly, feel helpless to change things. It is equally unhelpful if you believe everything is your fault and never offer challenge or an alternative to your partner's way of doing things.

Neither of those stances will get you a stable and secure relationship, let alone an enjoyable or passionate one. In both cases, you overlook your role in keeping things stuck. I have previously said that you are likely to be at roughly the same level of development as your partner. So if their behaviour is 'out of whack', probably yours is also — and likely in a very different way to theirs.

Remember, while you can and do *influence* your partner, the only person you have *control* over is yourself. If you aren't focused there, if you are insufficiently self-aware, you will be exerting unconscious, reactive influences on your partner. Trust me: that will not bring you the kind of relationship you want to live in!

How our insecurities are formed

Hopefully, it is not a new idea that everyone has psychological and emotional 'baggage'. 'Insecurities' is the term I most often use. Other people use words like 'shame', 'negative core beliefs' or 'old stories'. All of them point to the fact that during our formative years, we develop some negative ideas about ourselves as well as (hopefully) some positive ones. This does not necessarily happen as a result of tragedy and trauma (though they certainly can, and do, shape you), but simply because life and caregivers are never perfect and kids are weird.

No big deal, you may be thinking. But the trouble is that when we are young, we don't have fully formed brains. This means kids can't see the big picture and can't see things from another's perspective, and it makes them self-centred. Their limited understanding also means that children have a simplistic view of cause and effect. In a literal sense, every child is at the centre of their personal story. Whatever happens is *because* of them.

Remember the intelligent, capable woman in Chapter 3 who sat in my office and told me that her parents had split up when she was seven *because she broke a vase*? She hadn't talked to people about this guilty secret she had carried all her life, so the child's thinking had gone unchallenged. Once we examined this idea, she could see that it was preposterous. But until she did, it influenced her view of herself and her history.

That is a minor example. The kinds of insecurities that shape your life are usually more extensive and more complicated; global beliefs or fears you form about yourself. One child may believe that their father's absence means 'I'm not important.' Another may explain their mother's angry outbursts by assuming 'I'm a problem.' A dyslexic child repeatedly shamed by teachers may well conclude 'I'm dumb.' A prevalent one is the child who turns their parents' anxious attempts to encourage growth and achievement into 'I'm not good enough.'

Sometimes the insecurities are more accurate. The eldest child with a lot of responsibility in a large family likely believes 'I'm responsible' — which often has the implication 'I'm unacceptable if things aren't perfect.' Or the child who grows up in a literal war zone will conclude 'I'm not safe.'

People who are still psychologically enmeshed with their family of origin will struggle to accept that what happened in their early years has shaped them. Many people feel it's disloyal to consider their caregivers as ever having done them harm, however inadvertently.

If they are praised and validated by their family, they don't want to question the way that system operates. They confuse reflecting on how they learned to operate in their childhood environment with 'blaming' or 'criticising' their parents. This is especially common for people with an Avoidant Attachment style (see Chapter 7) when it is the *absence* of something (e.g. emotional attunement) that is pivotal. They face a practical barrier to accepting the influence of their upbringing — you can't have a memory of something that never happened, so it is hard to recognise that this absence was significant.

Why accepting your insecurities is vital in relationships

If I can't convince a client that they, like every other human on the planet, have insecurities like those I've discussed, I typically suggest that they try a different therapist. That's how important I think insecurities are to changing how we operate in relationships.

The reason is two-fold. Firstly, our insecurities are frequently what we are trying to protect when we are being defensive in any fashion. They are driving most of our self-protective behaviour. One working definition of an insecurity is 'The type of fear or belief where having it confirmed is the worst, most painful thing that could happen to you in normal daily life' (of course, excepting traumas and tragedies).

Much of our behaviour is motivated by trying to prevent our insecurities from being confirmed. It goes like this: I fear 'I'm not good enough', so I focus on worldly success and neglect my partner to prove that I am worthwhile. I believe 'I'm not important', so I focus on being everyone's friend and am endlessly pleasing. I attempt to ensure that I am central in the life of everyone I know, although I am burning out and feeling used and unappreciated.

The second reason why accepting and understanding your insecurities is vital to improving your relationship is because of what happens when your insecurities seem confirmed by something your significant other says or does. That is usually what people are referring to when they say 'I got triggered.'

Having an Attachment figure confirm your insecurity is intensely painful. Examples might be your partner pointing out a mistake you made when you fear 'I'm inadequate', or them forgetting to do what you asked when you fear 'I don't matter'. If you don't understand your insecurities and where they come from, then you will blame your partner for that acute emotional pain.

Here is the crucial thing you need to understand. **Your partner is not responsible** for the pain you feel when they trigger your insecurities. They are simply causing you to connect with the pain you still carry from your upbringing. Much of the worst distress I see in relationships comes from people not understanding this fact. Blaming your significant other does nothing to address the cause of the pain — which lies within *you*, not them. Worse, blaming them makes it much less likely that they will offer the care and support you need in your distress.

Identifying your core insecurities

We can have many insecurities, but typically only a few drive most of our self-protective behaviour. You may already be well aware of yours; but if you aren't, here are some ideas for connecting with them.

You're looking for a global fear or belief about yourself that makes you feel extremely uncomfortable if you say it out loud. I suggest it needs to take the form of 'I am . . .', but, as you will see from my list of examples in Exercise 24, that's not essential.

A core insecurity may be something that when you are calm and centred you know isn't true, but you still have a lingering, subconscious fear that it *might* actually be true. Many successful people *know* they are good enough, but are nonetheless driven by an 'irrational' fear that they aren't.

EXERCISE 24: IDENTIFYING YOUR INSECURITIES

Below is a list of some of the common insecurities I have come across. It's not *all* the possibilities, by a long shot. Feel free to add to the list!

Read them OUT LOUD (that's important — we process things differently if we voice them). If one of the items makes you feel uncomfortable, it may be worth considering whether it's an insecurity that is affecting you. If one is 'sort of' right, try refining it — change the language or the emphasis until saying it about yourself makes you feel a bit sick. Getting exactly the right word or phrase seems to matter.

Write down the insecurities that resonate with you. Think about whether some have more impact than others, then put the list in order of impact. Keep referring to this list. See if you can recognise when these insecurities are influencing your behaviour.

I'm not important
I don't matter
I don't exist

I'm not good enough
I'm unacceptable
I'm useless
I'm not worthy/worthwhile

I'm not loved/lovable
I don't belong
I'm unwanted
I shouldn't exist

I'm inadequate
I'm bad
I'm wrong/defective

I'm alone (This is often secondary to something like 'I'm
    unlovable', i.e. 'There's a reason why I'm alone')
No one is ever there for me

I'm responsible (for things going well or for others' well-being — usually
    translates to 'I'm unacceptable/bad' the moment things aren't perfect)
It's my fault (if things go wrong)
I'm to blame

I'm not safe
The world is not safe
I'm helpless (i.e. 'I can't have an impact', maybe even 'I'm a victim')

Working backwards from your behaviour

If you can't immediately work out your core insecurities from Exercise 24, another way to connect with them is to infer them from your behaviour. Look at times when you do relationship-destructive things (i.e. limbic-system-driven self-protection), and then work backwards to see if you can identify what you were trying to protect or what got triggered.

Ellyn Bader and Pete Pearson of the Couples Institute have developed a deceptively simple way to identify the ineffective self-protective behaviour to target in your current relationship, and I've based Exercise 25 on it. The exercise contains a list of behaviours that people in relationships might do to protect themselves. It's in no particular order, and my clients and I have added items to the original list that Ellyn and Pete gave me. We call these *ineffective* self-protective behaviours, because if you are in an intimate relationship these behaviours put you at *greater* risk of emotional harm in the long run. They damage connection and trust, making your attachment relationship unstable and unsafe.

Here's a big tip. If you do only a couple of exercises from this book, make them the next two (they are effectively two stages of the same exercise)! After Time Out, learning to use your Ineffective Self-Protective Behaviours as cues to connect intimately makes the greatest difference to most people's relationships.

EXERCISE 25: IDENTIFYING YOUR INEFFECTIVE SELF-PROTECTIVE BEHAVIOURS

1. Look at the following list, and circle ALL of the behaviours you know you have EVER used (across all your relationships). There should be a lot of circles. The purpose is to highlight that you, like every other human on the planet, are capable of a variety of relationship-damaging behaviours.
2. This is not a scientifically validated instrument; it's just a list to act as a prompt, so make it your own. Add in any behaviour you do that isn't on the list. If the words on the list aren't accurate for you, change them.
3. Thinking about your *current* intimate relationship, put an 'X' next to the handful of behaviours that you currently do that are the most concerning to you — mark four to seven, *no more*. These may be the behaviours that

you do most frequently, or those that cause the most damage even though you don't do them that often (e.g. threatening to end the relationship).

Blame
Have to be right / dominate
Defensive
Name-calling
'Forget' to say or do things
Sulk or pout
Appease / keep the peace
Withdraw
Drink / drug too much
Deny
Intimidate
Keep secrets
Diagnose
Escape to work
Hide in a hobby
Complain to friends
Stonewall
Make fun of partner
Be sarcastic
Yell to drown partner out
Be judgemental
Criticise partner's family or friends
Walk out on partner
Tell partner what they feel
Lie or mislead
Get impatient
Attack
Comply grudgingly
Hold on to resentment / stew on things
Minimise / dismiss
Maximise (blow out of proportion)
Invalidate
Get stubborn

Use contempt
Bring in the kids
Try to guilt-trip partner
Belittle / shame partner
Interrupt
Nag
Be condescending
Try too hard to please
Compete with partner
Bring up old issues
Micromanage
Cry excessively
Close mind to partner
Reject
Change the subject
Distract
Put partner down / get personal
Dismiss partner
Criticise
Manipulate
Act superior
Give partner the silent treatment
Pick a small detail to challenge
Deflect blame onto partner
Talk *at* partner, *not with*
Keep busy (avoid engaging)
Buy things / shopping / spending
Talking / answering for partner
Negative 'non-verbals'
Baiting (antagonise to get a reaction)
'Move on', then blow up later
Lengthy explanations
Make assumptions and act on them

The aim is for you to end up with no more than seven behaviours to track.

To get the most out of this exercise, put your list on your phone and *review it at the end of each day.* Take the time to reflect on how much and how often you have been ineffectively protecting yourself.

Once you are familiar with the ways you typically 'shoot yourself in the foot' with your significant other, the next exercise shows you how to use these ineffective strategies as a cue to do something different and more constructive. If you want to feel in charge of your life and reduce the influence of your insecurities, I strongly suggest you *make this a daily practice*. Once you are familiar with the task, it doesn't take long, and the rewards are immense.

EXERCISE 26: USING INEFFECTIVE SELF-PROTECTIVE BEHAVIOUR AS A PROMPT TO CHALLENGE YOUR INSECURITIES

Once you have reviewed your list of ineffective self-protective behaviours (see Exercise 25) and identified which ones you have done today, I suggest that you take these four steps:

1. Be compassionately accepting that you do these things

Resist shaming or beating up on yourself about them. Shame will make it harder for you to own the behaviour to your partner. Instead, remind yourself that being reflexively self-protective is part of our human nature — everyone has an amygdala!

This compassionate stance will also allow you to be less hurt or threatened when your partner protects themself in a similar reflexive way.

2. Talk to your partner about what you have seen yourself doing on this list

Name it and own it without justification. Apologise, if the behaviour warrants that. Your aim is to rebuild the connection damaged by your self-protective behaviour.

One way to do this is to talk with concern about the impact and consequences for your partner. Suggest what you imagine those consequences to be, and then listen and show care for your partner's experience.

NOTE: If your partner is doing this exercise and trying to guess the consequences of their protective behaviour, don't correct them harshly if they don't get it right. Appreciate and acknowledge their effort to empathise, then modify or update so that they have accurate information.

3. Use your behaviour as a cue to think about what's motivating your need for protection

It might be something to do with having your core insecurities triggered or confirmed. It might be that you were trying to prevent that from happening. Remember that you may have more than one insecurity in operation. Recognise that the situation evoked or triggered some old pain. Be curious. Ask yourself 'Why did I feel the need to protect myself?'

Avoid the trap of blaming something your partner did (or failed to do). Focus on what meaning *you* made of the situation and what that connects to in your psychological make-up. Often we can think about this most easily by thinking about what conditions from our upbringing it reminds us of. For example, 'If I experience my partner being disapproving of me, I can recognise that because I grew up with very critical parents, I always expect criticism and disapproval. And if I look hard enough for it, I will find it' (even when it's not there — this is what therapists call 'projection').

4. Take care of that part of you that felt in need of protection

It is helpful for everyone to have a set of self-care behaviours that work for them (see Chapter 5 for suggestions). Try to respond to the underlying distress like you are the best friend in the world. For example: If I was connecting with my parents' disapproval, I might put my hand on my heart with a deliberately caring touch and tell myself 'You really are okay just as you are. You don't have to be perfect to heal your parents' pain.' I might make myself a cup of tea. I might go for a run. I might watch a favourite TV show to distract and reward myself.

Most people I give this exercise to don't do it; it is normal to avoid looking at our unhelpful behaviour. Those who *do* do it learn a lot about themselves. If they follow through, own their behaviour to their partner and repair the damage to the relationship daily, they find that the trust and respect in their relationship improve by leaps and bounds.

Because owning your behaviour is difficult, here is another exercise from Ellyn Bader and Pete Pearson of the Couples Institute you can use. This one gives you a structured way to use your ineffective self-protective behaviour as a starting point for increasing intimacy in your relationship.

EXERCISE 27: EMPOWERING YOURSELF THROUGH TAKING RESPONSIBILITY

Fill in the blanks below, then use it as a script to talk with your partner. Warn them first that you want to talk about something challenging for you. Maybe explain that you are trying to do better at recognising and owning when you are being difficult or unhelpful. Make it clear that they don't have to do anything other than listen with an open mind and heart.

However, your partner may want to correct your guesses about the impact on them (positive and negative). I would encourage you to value that intimate information, acknowledge it, and then press on with the next step in the exercise.

If you complete these eight sentences with sufficient self-awareness and honesty, you should end up with a good picture of behaviour that you need to 'own' to your partner, and the language you need to do it cleanly.

1. When I do (name an ineffective self-protective behaviour):

   _____

   _____

2. I know it is a problem for you (my partner) because I notice that you (describe their reaction using neutral, non-blaming language):

   _____

   _____

3. I assume that if I continue doing it, the negative consequences for you will be (guess how it makes them feel about you, themselves and the relationship):

   _____

   _____

4. And the negative consequences for me will be (describe where you typically end up after you have reacted this way and your partner has responded):

_____

_____

5. Yet, part of me has trouble eliminating this attitude/behaviour because (**this is the intimate bit**: talk about yourself, not your partner. Think about how this may have been learned or conditioned in your upbringing, how you are using it to protect you or to relieve pain, etc.):

    _____

    _____

6. I believe that if I stop this behaviour, the positive effect on you would be (imagine how it would be for them if you did something more constructive):

    _____

    _____

7. And I might even benefit personally if I stop doing this because (it's vital you know what the payoff is for you; note it down):

    _____

    _____

8. Therefore, one step I will take toward changing this is (be as specific as you can about what you will do *instead* of reflexively protecting yourself):

    _____

    _____

Insecurities affect your perception of reality

As well as driving a lot of our self-protective behaviour, our insecurities also impact our relationship by biasing or distorting our perception:

- If I unconsciously fear I'm unimportant, I will take your forgetfulness as a sign of not mattering to you (rather than you being over-stretched or having ADHD).
- If I fundamentally believe that I'm not safe, I will anxiously scan everything you do for threat or hostile intent and am very likely to see it, even when it's not there.

Not being able to rely on your own perception is challenging. It's doubly difficult if we had formative experiences that we had to negotiate on our own when we were young (because our caregivers were unsafe or unavailable) or, worse, if we grew up in an environment that invalidated us. If we never had anyone else to rely on but ourselves, it can feel crazy-making to be told 'You can't necessarily trust your own judgement.'

However, it's possible to use a strategy that allows you to recognise that your insecurities likely affect how you see things without abandoning yourself.

As discussed in Chapter 5, there is usually a set of very familiar emotions and bodily sensations that we experience when our insecurities are activated. Recognising those can allow us to go 'Okay, probably triggered — can't trust my judgement right now. Need to Time Out and take care of myself.'

Another strategy that seems to work is to assume that you're wrong *every* time it feels like your partner is being unkind, uncaring or whatever. If you act on that assumption, you'll be able to engage with your partner more openly. If it does turn out that your initial sense was accurate (e.g. your partner *was* being unkind), you can deal with that later. But if you have begun in a less self-protective fashion, you will deal with it more effectively.

Working on your insecurities — the key to happiness

Clients often ask me 'Can you get rid of your insecurities?' A reasonable question, given how painful they are. Sadly, the short answer is 'No.' Ideas so profoundly established in your formative years remain interwoven in your adult identity.

The long answer is that while you can never be free of core insecurities, you *can* change the amount of influence they are having on your life. You can shift them from being something you organise your life around to thoughts that occur sometimes but which you don't take seriously. Another way of saying this is that you can turn them into old wounds that still niggle when you bump them but don't stop you from living your life how you want to.

EXERCISE 28: REDUCING THE INFLUENCE OF INSECURITIES

Here is a five-step process for challenging your insecurities. I strongly encourage you to take your time with this exercise. **In many ways, it is the heart of the book**. Each step will require considerable thought and effort. In laying it out like this, I am trying to make it clear and straightforward; that is not the same as easy or quick.

1. Remind yourself of the historical reasons why you have these fears or beliefs about yourself

Review the events that were going on in your childhood and adolescence that led to you forming these ideas. Maybe write them down. You must recognise that circumstances *beyond your control* created your insecurities in your formative years. You didn't choose to think or feel this way about yourself; you were just coping as best you could with situations not of your making. You don't have to be angry, blaming or judgemental about the adults involved in those situations, but you must place responsibility where it belongs.

2. Make sure that you are kind and compassionate to yourself about the impact of those insecurities

This is particularly important if the circumstances that created your insecurities were not dramatic or out of the ordinary; if you had an 'okay' or even a 'good' childhood. If you say things like 'That wasn't a big deal' or 'Other people had it much worse', you are minimising and denying your reality. Usually, you are implicitly saying that there is something wrong with you that such 'trivial' or 'unimportant' events had such an effect on you.

It's even worse if you are hostile or judgemental to yourself for having the insecurities you do: 'I shouldn't feel like this' or 'It's just silly'. Typically, that way of speaking to yourself will have its origins in your upbringing — it will mirror how caregivers or other significant people spoke to or treated you. Being harsh, judgemental, impatient or uncaring about yourself will worsen your insecurities. Talking to yourself in those ways affirms your negative beliefs about yourself and your place in the world.

3. Combat the shame your insecurities create by being open about them and the self-protective behaviour they generate

Examples of self-protective behaviour include being defensive when you fear you aren't good enough; or trying too hard and being insincere when you fear you aren't important enough. Talk about these insecurities with trustworthy people as a way to normalise this part of your humanity. To quote leading shame researcher Brené Brown: 'Shame hates it when we reach out and tell our story. It hates having words wrapped around it — it can't survive being shared. Shame loves secrecy . . . When we bury our story, the shame metastasises.'[1]

4. Show interest and care about how your behaviour (including your filtering or interpreting) has affected your partner

Being able to do this is usually very dependent on doing the first three things. If you can accept that you are allowed to be human and have insecurities and make mistakes, it's easier to hear how you have hurt someone you love.

5. Decide what you need to do in response to any particular situation where your insecurities have been in play

This may involve things like:

- apologising
- making amends
- asking to revisit a discussion in the light of new understanding
- planning to prevent future upsets and misunderstandings.

As I said at the start of Exercise 28, this is not a quick process. You may have a moment of insight into your insecurities and how they have been operating in your life, and that can be important; even life-changing. However, benefiting from that insight requires *behaviour change*. Altering the behaviours and attitudes influenced by your core insecurities means changing habits and reflexes that are established and operating throughout your life. In most cases, the only way that will happen is through diligent, conscientious work over many months and years.

DEB & HANK

In her younger years, Deb grew up in a rural area with a typical taciturn dairy-farmer dad: 'He was a bit selfish, really.' Her mum was a teacher at Deb's small local school. 'She was always there for us, but wouldn't stand any nonsense'. Deb was somewhat in the shadow of her sister Karla, who was four years older — Deb was always a bit too young to keep up with what Karla was doing. Then, when Deb was 11, Karla was severely brain-injured in a motorbike accident on the family farm.

Needing more care than could be provided at home, Karla had to be placed in a facility many hours away. This meant that most weekends Deb's mother was absent for one day and sometimes both. Deb went with her occasionally, but most often stayed to help her dad on the farm, including cooking for them both. She admitted that she found visiting someone in a wheelchair with the cognitive abilities of a three-year-old both incredibly stressful and tedious. Deb reported that while her mum became more distant as she struggled to adjust and accept Karla's situation, her dad became much more open and demonstrative with her. Karla eventually died when Deb was at university.

Hank was the eldest of four from a family whose circumstances changed a lot over his childhood. His dad went from being a digger-driver to the owner of a large contracting business by the time Hank was 10. They moved four times in that period, each time to better neighbourhoods and bigger houses. However, this also meant moving schools, so Hank was always the 'new kid' and became very self-reliant. His parents' messages about being the 'big boy' of the family reinforced his self-sufficiency. His father's long hours at work, including on the weekends, meant that Hank took on a lot of responsibility around the house and property, especially with the family's final move to a lifestyle block on the city fringe. Though he got recognition for his hard work, there was not a lot of praise, with his parents tending to focus on what he could do to improve things.

Given their work ethic, it's not surprising that both Deb and Hank were successful in their careers early on. They each had a house before they met in their late twenties. When they came to see me in their early forties, they had two sons, a thriving business, and one house in the city and another in the country near a beach.

They were self-aware enough to know that their respective complaints about feeling neglected were very typical, but this didn't stop them from having unpleasant, repetitive fights. Deb believed that Hank was using the demands of the business to avoid her, including sexually. She was resentful at being cast into the role of mother and housekeeper when she was legally an equal director of the business. Hank couldn't understand Deb's fuss; being at home with the kids was her choice, and she used to work crazy hours, too, before the kids. He felt that her criticism was punitive and controlling, and she was ungrateful about his work to maintain their lifestyle.

As two Avoidantly Attached people, neither of them was very comfortable talking vulnerably, and they had both been content with a less verbally intimate relationship than many. This avoidance meant that it took a long time for the pressures that might push them into Differentiating to emerge.

It was a slow process getting the couple to accept that there was more going on here than arguments about sex and work hours. Hank, in particular, always tried to shift the conversation on to practicalities and tangible things, even when asked repeatedly about his thoughts and feelings.

Using the ineffective behaviours checklist as a starting point, we explored what was happening when each protected themselves. We discovered that Deb had a hefty dose of 'I'm responsible' with the attendant 'I'm wrong and bad' if others were upset or displeased. She connected this with an unconscious decision to 'make up for' the loss of her sister. Deb also identified a belief that she was 'the ugly one', being quite strongly built and hirsute from quite a young age due to a slight hormone imbalance. She realised that this was a big part of why she was so hurt when Hank reported being too tired for sex — it touched on her fears of being unattractive.

Hank struggled to own his ineffective self-protective behaviour. In exploring why that was so, it became clear that he desperately feared failure. Tracking the origins of this fear, we discovered that despite his litany of successes, he still unconsciously believed the 'not good enough' message he had internalised from his parents. This was hard for him to accept, because Hank was renowned in his working world for his confidence. Eventually he could see that his confidence was a way to compensate for and protect himself from the underlying fear of failure.

Once Deb and Hank each had these building blocks of self-understanding, the work shifted to using their ineffective self-protective behaviour as a cue to try to be more intimate. Using the structure of the 'Empowering yourself through taking responsibility' exercise was necessary, as both of them tended to minimise the impact of their behaviour on the other unless they marched themselves through the implications.

Working diligently through these exercises in this chapter rekindled their trust and respect for each other. They started to have regular business meetings that encompassed planning for **all** their joint endeavours. Deb commented that 'there must be something to all this vulnerability stuff' when Hank responded positively to her suggestion that they also schedule time during the working day (when the boys were at school) for sex!

Key points from Chapter 8

1. Everyone has deep and powerful insecurities formed in childhood that drive a lot of our relationship-damaging self-protective behaviour.
2. If you aren't tracking these insecurities consciously, they are influencing you unconsciously. This always has negative impacts on your relationship.
3. Insecurities filter our perception. We attend to and believe things that support them, and ignore or discount things that challenge them.
4. The ways you typically protect yourself are a vital clue to when your insecurities are triggered.
5. It's empowering to take responsibility for your self-protective behaviour (i.e. stopping blaming your partner when you behave unhelpfully).
6. You can't get rid of your insecurities, but you can stop them from being central to your life. This takes diligent and brave effort over time.

Chapter 9
Work on yourself

Integrity as your compass

Our society idealises those who are 'driven' without acknowledging the cost of being unrelentingly chased by your insecurities. People who damage their health and happiness by making lots of money, or self-sacrificing to the point of ill-health, are lauded as role models. If compensating for or avoiding your insecurities has been a powerful force in your life, it can be hard to imagine a life that doesn't operate this way.

An alternative is *moving towards your values and aspirations* rather than running away from your fears and insecurities. Work out what is truly important to you and who you really want to be. Not what you *think* you should want and do, but what *actually fits* you. This is at the heart of my understanding of 'integrity'.

If your behaviour does not align with your values, you may need to reflect on whether they genuinely *are* your values. I have worked with many people who say that their family comes first, but who have pursued paid work in a way that destroyed their connection with their family through neglect, absence and self-centredness. Usually, they rationalised that what they were doing was for the 'family's financial security', but in many cases even that was compromised once the parents' relationship broke down. (Note that I am talking about people with a choice, not people forced to work that way by poverty.)

I have also seen many people who say that their family comes first, but who have persistently remained focused on, and frustrated by, their partner's behaviour as the source of their well-being and happiness; they are refusing to take real responsibility for their own lives and are making everyone miserable in the process.

Yet others say that family comes first, but they project their insecurities onto their children and make the kids' lives miserable.

Driving your children to fit a particular mould is no more life-enhancing than driving yourself.

In all of these cases, insecurities about their worth were driving these people, but their shame meant they couldn't recognise and own their insecurities in a vulnerable way. Thinking about your integrity is not something most of us were trained to do, so Exercise 29 offers one way to go about it.

EXERCISE 29: A QUESTION OF INTEGRITY

Here's a pivotal question that I encourage you to reflect on regularly. If you feel uncomfortable or bad about something you're doing, it's crucial that you check in with this. But asking yourself this question when life is rolling along without drama is also valuable. So many of us pour energy into doing what's familiar, what's expected or what we think we should do, and never notice how far off-track we are going.

'Does what I am doing fit with who I want to be?'

You can also ask:

'Is what I am doing taking me where I want to go?' or
'Am I being the person (or partner or parent
    or friend) that I aspire to be?' or
'Does this support my values and goals?'

Here's an example of Exercise 29 in practice: When my partner doesn't do something they promised to do, it is understandable that I might feel some irritation, even anger. If being close to my family is a strong value for me and having harmony in my home is an important goal, then shouting at my partner will not take me where I want to go. If closeness were my only goal, I could achieve it by saying nothing. Yet I may also value honesty and the goal of being open with each other. Saying nothing about my upset is lying by omission. How do I maintain my integrity and act on both of these goals? This focus invites me to find a way to be open and honest that doesn't destroy the harmony of the home and the sense of our family being close.

Other people will try to give you a road map of how to behave; most religions and philosophies try to do this. However, their map is not your territory. Ultimately, you are on your own journey. Their maps may be a useful *reference*, especially if the terrain looks similar. Your integrity is more like a compass than a map. Your values point in a direction that you want to go. At any stage, you can check with your compass: 'Am I heading in the right direction?' You might end up at a dead-end and have to retrace your steps and find a way around an obstacle, but you will never be totally lost.

Feeling vulnerable vs being vulnerable

The Merriam-Webster dictionary defines vulnerable as 'capable of being physically or emotionally wounded; open to attack or damage'. Understandably, many of us work hard to avoid feeling vulnerable. Why would you want to leave yourself open to being wounded or attacked?

You will choose to make yourself vulnerable if you believe that the rewards are worth it. Emotional vulnerability is an essential part of intimacy and feeling truly loved. We all have ways we reflexively protect ourselves from emotional hurt. For example, you might be smiley and pleasing (so you don't offer any threat), or you might be stony-faced and grumpy (so you look tough and dangerous). You are hiding your deeper thoughts, feelings and desires from view so that people can't use them to manipulate or hurt you with them. You *feel* vulnerable, so you act defensively.

Remember, the more important someone is to you, the easier it is for you to feel hurt by them. When a stranger ignores, rejects or attacks you, that's bad enough; but when an Attachment figure does, the pain is so much worse. That pain causes your amygdala to see your loved one as a threat. In a committed relationship, you organise your life around an Attachment figure. A rupture in that relationship threatens not just your feelings but also your living arrangements, your financial security, and your connection with your children (if you have them).

So when your partner is upset, insincere, grumpy or withdrawn, you may **feel** very vulnerable to hurt. The instinctive response is to protect yourself. But when you put up your defences, you sever your connection with your partner. As we explored in the previous chapter, this is an ineffective way to try to protect yourself. It destabilises the Attachment relationship, making you much more open to significant hurt in the long run.

To maintain your connection, you must accept your vulnerability to your significant other rather than fight it. **Being** vulnerable is part of acting with integrity. Consciously sharing what's happening inside you *does* give your partner information they could use to hurt you. It's a risk. But you are far better to take that risk and find out whether your partner can meet you, as well as whether you can look after yourself when your partner is unavailable.

Being vulnerable requires being Differentiated — knowing and showing how it is for you at the same time as being accepting of and interested in how it is for your partner. **Being** vulnerable also requires effective management of your neurobiology, i.e. good self-regulation. The impulse to protect yourself will arise and require managing. Remember, tolerating vulnerability is a hallmark of those who are Securely Attached. If you're just 'acting Secure', then learning how to **be** vulnerable, rather than focusing on the anxiety of how vulnerable you **feel**, is a crucial component. Exercise 30 offers you a structured pathway to being vulnerable with your partner.

EXERCISE 30: A SCRIPT FOR BEING VULNERABLE

Here is a step-by-step guide for how to respond when you feel vulnerable or hurt.

I feel **VULNERABLE** (maybe because I have been hurt)
↓
Triggers reflexive impulse to self-protect or
act out, distract, feel numb, etc.
↓
Recognise the impulse for what it is, allow self to feel the
VULNERABILITY and *don't let yourself act impulsively*

↓

Go slow and self-soothe — attend to **VULNERABLE** or hurt feelings
(may include reaching out to friends and other supports)

↓

Organise your thinking — maybe write some notes, or practise
talking out loud to yourself or a friend, so that you have clear,
non-judgemental language to describe what's going on for you

↓

Be **VULNERABLE**
Open up to partner about the original **VULNERABLE**
or hurt feelings (use non-blaming descriptions)

↓

Compassionately *explore and discuss* the **VULNERABILITY**,
focusing on the meanings you make, your interpretations and
insecurities (not the same as justifying self-protective behaviour)

↓

Be sure to talk about how much **VULNERABILITY** *and hurt are from
your upbringing rather than focusing on what your partner did*

Know the difference between an excuse and an explanation

When you have made a mistake, got something wrong, or behaved in
ways that are hurtful to your partner, you often end up talking about
why you behaved that way. The most common way to do this is to try
to **excuse** and justify your behaviour. For example, 'I only shouted at
you because you were rude.' Usually, this is an attempt to minimise
your responsibility; your 'why' typically focuses on your partner's
behaviour and how it has affected you.

That focus on what your partner did to 'cause' your behaviour
usually comes because you struggle to feel okay about yourself.
Recognising and accepting that 'I got it wrong' can feel devastating,
like you are confirming what a terrible person you are. For example,
you might unconsciously fear that 'I am like my domineering father
when I am aggressive. That's unbearable for me, so I blame you.'

In those moments when you are making excuses for yourself, you are more in relationship with your insecurities than with your partner. Your distress at the triggering of your fears about yourself makes it hard for you to recognise, let alone accept and respond to, the impact of your behaviour on your significant other.

Your excuses will frustrate them and make them feel uncared for and unseen. These excuses will damage their trust in you, and, because trust is foundational to safety, will make them more likely to become reactive (i.e. use one of the Five Fs).

Explanations tend to come from a very different place and attitude. Here is how they work: When I accept that I have done something unhelpful or hurtful, I will acknowledge that *without justification*. I will take responsibility for my behaviour and focus first on repairing my connection with you; things like apologising, recognising the impact on you, and doing what I can to make things right. 'Sorry, I came on way too strong there. I didn't need to shout like that. That must have been scary for you.'

Somewhere in that process, it is likely to be useful for you to understand *why* you acted in ways that were contrary to your values and against your intention to be loving, kind, supportive, etc. Your focus will be on yourself, your insecurities, your upbringing and training around intimacy, and your present circumstances.

Working out what was going on inside you, why you interpreted your partner's behaviour the way you did, is essential for making effective plans around acting differently next time something like this happens. It becomes an opportunity for intimate reflection and connection that helps both of you understand what makes you 'tick'. It's also a chance for both of you to show some compassion for what drives you to be self-protective.

When you offer this kind of in-depth, self-exploratory *explanation* of why you did something unhelpful, your partner will find it much easier to believe any assurances you make about not doing it again. It allows you to offer specific plans for how you will deal with that type of situation in the future. It becomes an example of intimate, vulnerable communication that builds trust and respect. Processing upsets in this way is a vital plank in building a relationship that appeals to both of you.

So next time you do something to your partner that *you* don't like, make sure to focus on taking responsibility and repairing the relationship before worrying about *why* you did it. Avoid making excuses; instead, find an in-depth and self-aware explanation that will help you change your behaviour and help your partner to trust and respect you.

Turning distress into intimacy

In relationship, it is possible to do more than just manage your self-protective impulses and emotions. You can also use those feelings to prompt interactions with your partner that build trust, respect and intimacy. When you are upset and still manage to stay connected with and caring for your partner, that goes a long way to making your relationship a safe place where both of you can thrive.

When you feel the impulse to use the Five Fs (see Chapter 3), the trick is to stop yourself self-protecting and instead become reflective. Ask yourself: What made me get reactive? Why am I feeling the need to defend myself?

The aim is to answer those questions based on what you know about yourself, especially your insecurities, shame, fears or negative beliefs about yourself. They usually have a part to play when you become reactive to your partner. If you can talk about these things openly, you are likely to draw your partner towards you instead of pushing them away by being reactive. There's a detailed description of how to do this in Chapter 8.

For example, 'When you were upset that I had forgotten to put the rubbish out like I had promised, I had a big reaction inside myself. I had to really battle with myself not to get defensive, but I realised it's another example of my struggle with perfectionism. Even though I know it's not true intellectually, I still feel that if I make a mistake I am unacceptable, wrong and bad. I know how much I have made you feel wrong and bad by being defensive in the past, and I want you to know that I'm working on not doing that, but it is a real struggle for me.'

Of course, sometimes we won't catch ourselves in time, and we will Fight, Freeze, Flee, Friend or Flop. When we have calmed down, however, we can still turn this situation into one of intimacy; it just takes more work. Exercise 31 shows you one way to achieve this.

EXERCISE 31: A SCRIPT FOR TURNING AN UPSET INTO AN INTIMATE CONNECTION

1. Start by apologising in a general way for your self-protective behaviour

'I'm sorry I've been so grumpy / withdrawn / resentful / passive-aggressive', 'I'm sorry I said I was okay with X, and then I wasn't.'

Beginning with an apology shows that you want to be conciliatory and take responsibility for your behaviour.

2. Next, name the insecurity that is driving your unhelpful behaviour

'I'm struggling with feeling . . . (name your insecurity).' For example: 'not good enough', 'no one is there for me', 'I'm not important', 'I'm not safe'.

Naming an insecurity signals to your partner that you own your insecure feelings as the driver of the difficult interaction (instead of blaming your partner).

3. Then go on to talk about your behaviour, naming the unhelpful aspect

'Because I'm struggling with that insecurity, I . . . (name the ineffective protective behaviour(s) you have been doing in detail).' For example: 'have withdrawn from you', 'appeased you and then reneged', 'tried to make you wrong so I could feel right', 'got angry to try and shut you down'.

4. Once you have owned your self-protective behaviour, express some empathy

'I imagine that made you feel . . . (name the likely impact on your partner of your behaviour).' For example: 'under attack', 'abandoned', 'not cared for', 'unimportant', 'like you're the enemy'.

Then invite your partner to tell you if you got that right; if you didn't, listen and show care as they tell you what the actual impact was on them.

Take as much time as necessary to restore the goodwill, to undo the damage you did to your connection with your self-protective behaviour.

5. Finish up by suggesting a way forward that might make a difference in the future

'I'd like to try that again, and this time I will . . . (name the new behaviour).'
For example: 'stay in the conversation', 'tell you what I think at the time', 'listen to what you have to say with interest and respect'.

Make sure you listen to and engage with your partner's response.

Connecting with positive aspirations, not negative emotions

When things are getting tense or tricky with your partner, it can be easy to get 'tunnel vision' — focusing only on what's unpleasant. When we're caught up in our negative feelings of frustration, anxiety, hurt or impatience, we lose sight of our 'Big Picture' (see Chapter 5); and then we do or say things to protect ourselves in the short term that will undermine our relationship in the long term. Here's a writing exercise that can help you break the pattern of being driven by your emotions.

EXERCISE 32: BUILDING A PICTURE OF THE LIFE YOU WANT

Pick a time when you are calm and centred, and have a moment to yourself. This exercise is easier to do on a computer, but you can also do it with pen and paper. To begin with, don't censor yourself — just write whatever comes to mind without judgement or even a lot of thought.

1. Write down all your hopes and aspirations for your relationship (and your family together, if that's relevant). Try to look beyond the pragmatic and material, like 'being mortgage-free by 50'. Think instead about your values and ways of being, e.g. 'feeling loved and safe' or 'well-connected with my kids'. Try to answer these questions:

- Who do I want to be in this relationship?
- How do I want to be in this relationship?
- What do I believe I am trying to accomplish in this relationship?
- Where do I want this relationship to take me?

Keep your focus on *yourself* rather than how you want your partner to be. These are *your* aspirations. Set this writing aside and let it percolate — add things to it if more come to mind.

2. When you next have another block of calm and centred time, sit down and review what you have written. Consider whether you have missed anything you know is significant to you. Then see if you can work out the rough order of priority of all these things you aspire to in your life. Turn it into a list with the most important items at the top.

3. Now pick the top few items (three to five of them is a good number), and write them into your phone or on a card you can keep in your wallet or purse. Above them, write something like this: 'This is what I am in this relationship for; this is who I want to be.'

4. Anytime you get caught up in your negative feelings, getting into 'tunnel vision', take two deep breaths, taking slightly longer to exhale, and then pull out your list and ask yourself this question: 'How do I best serve these aspirations right now?'

5. You can also do this as a daily practice — reflect on the list at a regular time each day and deliberately commit yourself to these goals and values. Say something like this to yourself: '*This* is who I want to be and how I want to be in my relationship.'

What about when it's your partner who's being reactive?

It's frustrating when your partner's reaction to something you did or said seems out of proportion or, worse, incomprehensible. A typical response is to try to show them why what they are doing is wrong. This usually doesn't work very well — especially if they are triggered. Exercise 33 gives you an alternative strategy you can try.

EXERCISE 33: ENGAGING WITH A REACTIVE PARTNER

If your partner is reactive, remember that this is because they feel unsafe (even if they are being aggressive). The aim is to offer them responses that reassure them and help them re-engage their frontal lobes. If you want to be effective, you have to care about *that* more than proving that you were right or they were wrong.

1. Show interest and care in their experience, rather than being defensive or immediately trying to correct their 'mistake'.
2. Ask about how what you said or did 'landed' with your partner (i.e. how they interpreted it, what it meant to them). Be willing to *listen* to their experience of the interaction. Treat it with respect, and show empathy for their experience.
3. Only then, try to give them information that will help correct their perception — i.e. clarify what your intention was, how you were trying to come across.
4. If your partner insists on their own interpretation or perception, you can:
   - Be open to the possibility that it is *you* who is mistaken. In particular, are there feelings you have about this issue or situation that you weren't consciously aware of (e.g. hurt or resentment) that nevertheless came across to your partner?
   - Take a Time Out (Chapter 4), and both of you reflect on whether there is more going on here than you have been aware of so far.
   - Ask that your partner accept your intentions as the basis for the interaction to go forward. This sidesteps the issue of whose perception is accurate.
   - Talk *vulnerably* (not accusingly) about the impact of their refusal to accept your good intentions. For example, 'When you insist that you know better than I do what I meant, it reminds me of being unable to talk to my mother.'

No strategy will work 100% of the time if your partner is triggered, but talking in the way demonstrated in Exercise 33 makes it much more likely that you can bring your partner back into relationship with you and, eventually, have your reality acknowledged.

How you treat yourself dictates how you treat others

If you are lashing out or being irritable with your loved ones, it's often a sign that you aren't taking care of yourself. Most discussion about self-care focuses on the external world: the need for rest, pleasure, etc. There is less written about what might be called 'internal self-care' — how we treat ourselves in our own minds.

If you struggle to believe that you are worthy, acceptable, important, safe or good enough, it's almost impossible to put yourself first and do all those admirable self-care behaviours. Many of us internalised a lack of self-worth during our childhoods, even if we can't point to especially negative experiences. Remember, kids' brains are weird, and kids tend to take way too much responsibility for things that are not their fault.

Building self-worth usually begins by simply accepting who you are and what you feel. Too often, we are critical and judgemental of our responses to situations. We say 'I shouldn't let that get to me' or 'I should be able to do better', not realising that we are invalidating ourselves. We are trying to motivate ourselves, but all we do is undermine our self-belief. Treating ourselves as worthy means allowing ourselves to be less than perfect and to have less than 'ideal' emotional responses.

Internal self-care means responding compassionately to our own distress, saying to ourselves things like 'Ouch, that really hurt', 'That was really difficult', or 'I felt overwhelmed and didn't know how to respond'. If we behave in ways that don't fit with who we want to be, we need to get curious, not judgemental: 'I don't like how I spoke then; what got in the way of me being patient?'

If we can see and accept that we were hurt, overwhelmed, ashamed, etc., the next step in 'acting as if we are worthy' is responding to those emotions. If your child or a good friend were hurt or overwhelmed, you (hopefully) wouldn't ignore this or tell them to 'get over it' (though many of us were parented that way). Instead, you would give them a hug or other soothing touch, reassure them that they'll be okay, tell them you are there for them, and ask them what they need right now. These are all things you can do for yourself (yes, you can hug yourself!) — if you believe you deserve it.

Building this kind of relationship with yourself is challenging, especially for men in our society. The macho 'take a concrete pill' attitude has much to do with the appalling rates of domestic violence and suicide in this country. Acknowledging your vulnerability and being kind to yourself are generally equated with weakness and self-indulgence. But in fact, it's the opposite — it takes real strength to face and accept your emotions and insecurities. It takes courage and discipline to manage them rather than letting them manage you.

It also takes hard work. Determining what kinds of self-care work for you takes a lot of experimenting. You will likely have to try many variations to find the right words to say to yourself and the behaviour that you find comforting and soothing. Persisting with the project of building your self-worth is often challenging because you don't usually see immediate results. It's one of those situations where we need to remember the words of the great New Zealand sage Rachel Hunter: 'It won't happen overnight, but it will happen.'

JULES & LEON

Leon was sick of Jules complaining and erupting: 'Nothing I ever do is enough for her.' Over time he had become increasingly contemptuous and dismissive of any issue she brought up. In recent times, Leon had shut down and thrown himself into work, largely abandoning the running of the house and the parenting of their three kids to Jules during the week. He'd also given up on having a sex life with Jules and contented himself with masturbating to porn when he was horny. On weekends, he was heavily involved in the kids' sports, did chores outside the house, and usually cooked a meal. He wasn't happy, but protected himself from feeling any distress by keeping busy and telling himself 'we are lucky in so many ways'.

Jules found it much harder to settle for such a distant relationship, and was increasingly frustrated and unhappy. This was not what she had expected. Jules felt incredibly lonely in her marriage, and it did nothing for her hope for things to change to hear that all her woman friends felt much the same. She kept trying to 'be positive' and maintain a civil atmosphere in the home for the kids. Still, her resentment and frustration at Leon's emotional disengagement and hostility had become unmanageable. Her increasingly frequent angry eruptions at Leon only made her feel worse about herself, her partner and her situation.

We began by trying to get clear on what was really important to both of them. This was pretty straightforward for Jules. She wanted a loving and harmonious home for their kids. Fighting had dominated her childhood — initially between her parents, leading up to and following their separation when she was nine. By the time of the divorce, her older siblings were all having loud and explosive conflicts with their parents and each other. It horrified her that she was beginning to replicate this pattern with her children.

Leon initially struggled to talk in a deep and vulnerable way — 'I just want Jules to get off my case' was not a statement of integrity. However, as I kept probing, it became clear that the notion of 'success' was essential to him. He felt he had 'been given every opportunity' growing up, being sent by his farming parents to a prestigious boarding school. He felt a lot of responsibility to make use of the advantages he had and to give his children the same opportunities. He hadn't thought much about what 'success' meant, apart from 'getting a good job and making good money'. Reluctantly, Leon acknowledged that in those terms, he had succeeded. The fact that he was far from content or satisfied led to him opening up about feeling like a failure (his biggest fear) in terms of his relationship with Jules.

This vulnerability from Leon was a revelation for Jules, who had come to believe that he didn't like her, let alone care what she thought about him. Realising how vulnerable he felt whenever he was home turned her view of her world upside down. Suddenly she had an explanation, not an excuse, for so much of the behaviour that frustrated her. Leon wasn't lazy — he was just avoiding a situation where he believed he couldn't win. Jules was also honest enough to recognise that her insecurities about not mattering, and the anxious and controlling behaviour they drove, had created a self-fulfilling prophecy, driving Leon away from her.

From this point, things took a different turn. They each used this conversation as a touchstone and began to learn how to repair the relationship by being more self-aware. Leon found it particularly helpful to use the script in this chapter for turning upset into intimacy. Initially, he feared it would come across as 'fake' when he went through it with Jules. However, she was delighted; both at what he said and that he was willing to do something he found so challenging. More than any declaration of love, it showed her how important she was to him.

Once she realised that she did matter to Leon, Jules found it a lot easier to keep her focus on who and how she wanted to be instead of what she feared she was.

It took a lot of work for the couple to learn how to disagree without things going off the rails. Leon found it hard to change his way of working (and his workplace's expectations of him), and this remained a point of tension. However, when he was calm, he could acknowledge that Jules's complaints about his commitment to work (and how little was left over for her and the kids) were valid — and a good prompt for him to get on top of his fear of failure.

Key points from Chapter 9

1. It's vital to be guided by your values and priorities, not your insecurities and self-protective impulses.
2. Intimacy depends on your ability to tolerate being vulnerable.
3. You can learn to use upsets and disagreements as opportunities for intimacy.
4. You can learn how to respond skilfully (and vulnerably) when you believe your partner is over-reacting.
5. It's your job to work out how to care for yourself, both practically and in how you talk to yourself.

Chapter 10
Be a team player

If you have been processing everything in this book so far, you will hopefully have:

- An understanding of relationships that goes beyond the conventions of mainstream culture.
- A recognition of the need for growth and change, and the stages that relationships typically move through.
- A sense of why relationships are so challenging, including how your neurobiology supports survival rather than love.
- An acceptance that dealing with difference well is essential, and that conflict is an inevitable part of a relationship.
- A notion of how Attachment works, and maybe what your predominant Attachment style is.
- Some notion of your insecurities, where they come from, and the typical 'ineffective self-protective behaviour' they drive.

Until now, you could have done much of the work alone, without involving your partner. This chapter is about how to be in relationship, especially working together in challenging conditions. I'm going to talk a bit about teamwork in general, and then more specifically about different ways to operate better as a team in different situations.

Don't make your partner the problem

At the beginning of your relationship, many of the things about your partner that appealed to you were probably about how they are different from you: 'She was so lively (and I'm a contained person)' or 'He was so steady and calm (and I get upset easily)'.

Even if you see yourselves as very similar, you are two different people who will sometimes disagree. You will approach things in diverse ways and have a different sense of how to prioritise your shared values. This is inevitable, and part of what keeps a relationship fresh and rewarding *if* you handle it right.

As we discussed in Chapter 6, dealing with difference is a challenge. The more important your partner is to you, the harder it is to tolerate their point of view without getting anxious — fearing rejection by someone you are Attached to. And when you get fearful, you get reflexively self-protective. Like every human, you get hijacked by your amygdala and lose touch with your wise self.

In self-protective mode, a common trap you may fall into is blaming your partner for creating the anxiety and tension you feel when you disagree, rather than accepting it as a natural and inevitable aspect of a partnership. You get hurt, angry or scared that they don't automatically see things your way. You unconsciously define the 'problem' as 'them and their beliefs'. You make them 'bad' and 'wrong' simply for being themselves. In doing this, you invite them into a competition with you about who is right and who is wrong.

Often, your partner disagreeing with you will evoke your insecurities, triggering feelings of being unacceptable, unimportant, bad, wrong, unwanted, not good enough, etc. As we explored in Chapter 8, if you are not mindful then you will blame those feelings on your partner's opinions, rather than on the baggage you have brought into the relationship. Even worse, you are likely to be angry or hurt that they 'made' you feel like that when they have actually done nothing wrong.

The kinder, and more constructive, alternative is to define the 'problem' as 'we are different people, and we differ on how to approach this issue'. We need to come from a place that says, 'You have valid thoughts and feelings on this issue, and so do I. We need to find a way forward that works for *both* of us.'

In the moment, this may create uncertainty. The outcome is not guaranteed. You have to be open to the possibility that you may not get things your way, that you may have to learn, grow and adapt. Resolving your differences may require a very different solution than your original ideas. While tolerating that uncertainty takes work, in the long run this is much less effortful than having endless unresolved conflicts that poison the atmosphere of the relationship.

If you value each other's differences, they can become a strength of the relationship. You will make much better decisions by taking account of both points of view. You will learn about yourself and each other and, ultimately, feel like a real team who can deal with whatever life throws at you.

TEAM: Together, Each Achieves More

The notion that the whole is greater than the sum of its parts is central to teamwork as it applies to couples. A powerful and effective team is created by accepting, valuing and utilising what each team member brings.

As I said in Chapter 2, if you are constructing a team, you want different abilities and strengths. In sports, you need attackers and defenders; in a work project, you need 'big-picture' and 'detail-focused' thinkers. If you value, respect and utilise the differences in the team, you will get the best results. However, if the teammates are competing, telling each other 'your way is wrong and my way is right', the outcome will be suboptimal. If one person dominates, you are wasting everyone else's time and energy. It would be better to let them do it by themselves.

As I write this chapter, it is the day before my first ever waka ama (outrigger canoe) race. When I began training, one of the first things I learned is that the speed of the waka depends primarily on team-work, not the strength of individual team members. Six beefcakes who can't work with each other will get beaten every time by six skinny guys who have their timing and teamwork sorted. As well as valuing each other's contribution, teamwork requires constructing a culture of how we fit our different strengths and abilities together.

Working well together doesn't just magically happen. In all teams, it takes time and effort to work out who will do what. You must juggle preferences and needs, abilities and opportunities, strengths and weaknesses. In long-term committed relationships, you must learn to utilise disagreements and conflicts as opportunities to build the team through deepening intimacy. Couples need to hang in there, and realise that nothing terrible is happening if all that is still a work in progress.

Reliability leads to trust

Trust is the bedrock of long-term relationships. Trust is something built by experience over time. There's no great mystery to this: you earn your partner's trust by being **reliable**.

Reliability is essential at times when the world is scary. In stormy seas, it's crucial to be able to rely on the people in your boat. It can be helpful to think about reliability in your relationship in two ways: practical and emotional.

The practical realm is about *doing*. Do you follow through on your promises? Can I rely on you to do what you say you will do, to be where you say you will be? Can I trust you not to do what you say you won't? Are you a person of your word? If you are forgetful, overwhelmed, or let other things get in the way of your commitments to me, what does that say about my importance to you?

The emotional side is more about *knowing* you will stay engaged with me, even if my emotions are challenging for you (e.g. because I am upset or angry). Will you listen to me saying difficult things? Will you care about how it is for me as well as yourself?

When times are tough, it stresses everyone at the same time. When you feel anxious or overwhelmed, that's when you want your partner to be there for you. But in tough times, they will likely struggle just as much as you. That's when your ability to be reliable is most needed and most valuable.

Owning your mistakes and failings is crucial to building a good sense of team.

If you struggle with being 'wrong' or accepting you made a mistake, you will likely erode trust by reflexively describing events in ways that make you look blameless. You will damage your partner's trust and respect for you if you say things like 'I didn't say that', 'I didn't mean that', 'You misunderstood me', or 'You should have known'. Worse, if they believe you, you will damage their trust in themselves. That's called undermining someone, and is one of the ugliest things you can do in a relationship.

Being reliable is not the same as being pleasant or pleasing. Sometimes being reliable means saying what you honestly think or want, even though you know your partner thinks or wants something different.

Making good trouble

Some people have no problem bringing up problems and complaints. There are significant cultural differences in this. If you come from a family or culture that avoids talking about things directly, you may need to learn how to value this skill.

Bringing up troubling issues, things you expect to disagree on, is tricky. Most of us had either no training or bad modelling from our parents about bringing up challenging topics well. So we do it poorly and then build up a history with our partners of fighting, withdrawal, counter-accusations, or other unpleasantness where nothing gets resolved. Unsurprisingly, we conclude that there is little point in bringing up these kinds of issues. And we suffer in silence.

Yet if you are dissatisfied, hurt or frustrated, that will affect your relationship whether you say something about it or not. By saying nothing, you risk poisoning the connection with your unexpressed feelings (resentment, hurt, rejection, loneliness, etc.).

Bringing up challenging topics is 'making trouble' in the relationship, but it is possible to do this so that the 'trouble' is productive. In my experience, *much* more severe harm is done to relationships by people avoiding talking about things that are important to them than is caused by people who bring something up intending to sort it out productively.

A key tactic for making 'good trouble' is to talk about *your experience*, **not** your partner's behaviour, motivations or intentions. If you need to reference an interaction, describe what happened neutrally. 'When you were on my case about the shopping' implies things about your partner's intent. 'When you pointed out that I had forgotten to do the shopping' describes what happened without any speculation about your partner's intentions or emotions. Describing things in neutral language is a skill that is worth learning!

You can then talk about *your* subjective experience — what it is like being you in that situation. Aim to be intimate, vulnerable and revealing, *not* to be right. You *can* talk about what you thought your partner intended, so long as you do so in a way that owns that it's a guess: 'I felt like I was a failure, that you were disappointed in me and angry with me.'

Another aspect of this is seeing past your initial self-protective response, which usually involves secondary emotions like blame, judgement, anger and criticism directed at your partner or yourself. Instead, talk about the more vulnerable primary emotions: 'I felt about seven years old, and all I knew how to do to protect myself from feeling that little and vulnerable was to get angry and blaming.'

The more you can 'own your stuff' — your contribution to the cyclical pattern of interactions between you — the more your partner is likely to be able to hear what you have to say about their impact on you.

It's also important to signal clearly by your tone and manner that, firstly, you see your partner as an ally you are trying to work *with*, not an enemy or competitor you are working *against*. Secondly, that you are open to hearing their experience and what this issue means to them.

Making 'good trouble' requires skills that you only get from practice. But the reward for the work is a stronger connection, greater intimacy and the joy of being truly known by your partner.

Good selfishness and bad selflessness

Let me continue to challenge the language we use in relationships; moving on from 'trouble', let's consider the words 'selfish' and 'selfless'. As I mentioned in Chapters 2 and 6, in every kind of relationship you are in, there is tension between your need for autonomy (being in charge of your own life) and your need for connection (staying in and supporting the functioning of the relationship). Different cultures have different norms about how to balance those needs.

One way to think about this is by looking at the words 'selfish' and 'selfless'. In English, 'selfish' has negative connotations and 'selfless' has positive ones. That's unhelpful when we're trying to think about how people behave in relationships. If you write off *all* self-centred behaviour as 'bad', you pathologise people who are being appropriately authentic. On the other hand, if you idealise all selflessness as 'good', then you end up sanctioning people who are being inauthentic.

Verity and I tried for ages to find words that would capture the nuances of the healthy self-interest that helps relationships flourish. In the end, we settled on talking about 'good selfishness' and 'bad selfishness'. Likewise, we talk about 'bad selflessness' and 'good selflessness'. These nuances are valuable as you evaluate your contribution to the team.

'Bad selfishness' is what most people think of when they say 'selfish' — caring only about yourself and not other people. Not worrying about or even considering the impact of your behaviour on others is the epitome of 'bad selfish'. This kind of behaviour is a relationship-killer. Sadly, our modern culture's emphasis on the individual and competition, and de-emphasis on the collective and cooperation, normalise a level of 'bad selfishness'. This is particularly true for men in our society; in my experience, it is far more common to see the man in a heterosexual (hetero) relationship behave this way than the woman. Conventional (toxic) masculinity identifies caring with vulnerability and vulnerability with weakness, and treats them all as a threat to male identity.

Think back to Chapters 2 and 6 and what you learned about Differentiation. Remember that Self-Differentiation requires knowing and being able to share what you think, feel and want, even when you are aware it may cause difficulty for your partner or your relationship. That's what I call being 'good selfish'; being fully present in the relationship — sharing all of who you are.

As discussed in the previous section, that may cause trouble for your partner and heighten differences and disagreements. *There is nothing wrong with that.* Remember, that's a necessary part of relationship and a potential path to intimacy. It also allows your partner to see and know you for who you really are. Ideally, that will please your partner — because they love you for who you are, not how you present yourself. It will also make them more secure because they can feel confident that they know what you think, feel and want. Being honest and open enough — good selfish enough — to make 'good trouble' will reassure them that they can trust that they are getting the full story.

One place to see how being 'good selfish' works is during sex. In this context, it means: I know where I'm at and what I am in the mood for, and I am upfront in my communication, so you don't have to guess. If both of us can be 'good selfish', then sex is likely to be much more straightforward, relaxed and pleasurable. Of course, you might be in a different place and want different things than I do. So then we have a healthy, intimate disagreement. Done with goodwill, both of us being 'good selfish' tends to spark energy and passion.

'Good selflessness' is the generosity and kindness that makes the world go round. Being thoughtful and giving to others is a great way to enhance relationships. Indeed, being with someone who puts energy into supporting and caring for you both is a big reason to be in a relationship.

'Bad selflessness' is when you give to others at too great a cost to yourself. Often it is marked by giving with strings attached rather than freely and generously; this usually means expecting praise or reciprocal giving. People who practise 'bad selflessness' typically become resentful and, ultimately, bitter.

There is a substantial gender split in how our society trains us regarding selflessness. Girls are taught to be pleasing, accommodating and 'nice'. There is still a strong expectation that women will be of service. In most families, there is a default assumption that if there is unpaid care (e.g. for children, the elderly and the differently abled), the women will do it. So many women end up caring for not only their own elderly parents but also their male partner's.

'Bad selflessness' is where you deny your selfhood. You neglect or disregard your own needs, and self-sacrifice to a degree that is bad for your emotional, mental or physical health. Your background may teach you that this is a good thing and that your partner will benefit. In my experience, it doesn't work out that way.

It requires two selves (two people able to Self-Differentiate) to make a healthy, equal partnership. When you are 'bad selfless', you effectively abandon your significant other because you are not fully present in the relationship. The chances are that you are in a closer relationship with your 'shoulds' than with yourself. If your partner cares about you, it will frustrate them not to know what you want or how to please you.

Many people will praise and reward you for being 'bad selfless'. Some will be those who struggle to have a self. Others are people who love to take: family members who enjoy your generosity without reciprocating, employers who delight in your productivity without paying you properly and, of course, partners who *love* having things their own way.

In the face of all that societal pressure, turning towards being 'good selfish' and making 'good trouble' can be tough. Even if you recognise the value of it, working out what is 'good selfish' rather than 'bad selfish' is a judgement call. You may get it wrong sometimes, especially at first. But if you want to be truly known, to be sure that you are loved for who you are, not just what you do, then you had better learn. (Exercise 34, below, will help you do this; and Exercise 47 in Chapter 12 offers a different perspective on what the alternatives to 'bad selfishness' and 'bad selflessness' are.)

Use resentment wisely

Resentment is the displeasure or anger you feel at being mistreated or forced to accept something you don't like. If you are in a hierarchical situation (like an employee of a large firm) where many things happen that are out of your control, resentment is an appropriate response.

In a partnership of equals, I encourage you to see the emotion of resentment as a cue that, somewhere in the past, you haven't looked after yourself well enough. Usually, it means you haven't been assertive enough or persistent enough in establishing boundaries with your partner. You've put your partner's feelings ahead of yours to the point where it's not okay for you. That's an example of being 'bad selfless'.

Blaming your partner for when you feel resentful is understandable, but leaves you powerless. The more empowering response is to review your past behaviour and work out what you could have done differently to avoid ending up like this. It may not be too late to start being more 'good selfish' and less 'bad selfless'. If you're anxious about becoming 'bad selfish', then the following exercise will help you be confident that you aren't going too far down that path.

EXERCISE 34: LEARNING HOW TO BE 'GOOD SELFISH' SAFELY

Use this three-stage checklist any time you are anxious about making things worse by being 'good selfish' or if you worry that you tend to be 'bad selfish'.

1. Self-confront (Note: this is the part most of us get wrong or skip over lightly)

Ask yourself:

- Have you honestly done your best in this situation? Have you acted from the best in you — your values and goals; your robust, hopeful self?
- Are you kidding yourself about your motives, actions or the effects of your behaviour?
- Are you aware of tracking and owning your insecurities and reactive behaviour? (If you are not admitting them to your partner, you are *not* owning them.)
- Are your actions based on a view of yourself and of others as capable and resourceful?
- Have you genuinely considered other points of view? Are you willing to take them into account, even if you don't agree with or understand them?
- Are you open to changing your mind or discovering you were wrong?
- Are you keeping to agreements that you have made?
- Are you behaving according to your ideals of generosity, love and caring?

If — *and only if* — you are clear about your integrity in this situation, then:

2. Self-validate

Remind yourself that:

- You have really thought it through and are doing what you believe to be best.
- Being true to yourself is the most likely way to achieve a good outcome for everyone (remember, this applies to your partner, too!).
- You are willing to listen and take account of your partner's point of view.
- You have to know and respect yourself to stay in honest connection with someone.
- You are willing to own up and deal with the consequences if you are wrong.
- This is supposed to feel scary — it's not wrong if you feel anxious.

Once you are clear with yourself about what you are doing, then you may still need to manage your anxiety.

3. Self-soothe

You can:

- Check your breathing — make sure it is slow and even (you can learn techniques for doing this if you don't know how).
- Check your thinking — make sure it is constructive and hopeful. Notice, especially, what fearful or negative thoughts you have about the other person's reaction and work out a constructive response to each of these.
- If need be, take time to do something that calms or centres you — go for a walk or run, take a bath, chat with a friend, make or mend something . . .
- If appropriate, make concrete plans about how to carry through the action you have identified. Prepare for positive and negative receptions — how will you remain calm and clear if the worst happens?
- When you engage with your partner, keep doing all these things. If you can't keep your anxiety under control and you're becoming reactive, break off (Time Out; Chapter 4) for as short a time as it takes to calm yourself down — the briefer, the better. Make it clear when you will resume the conversation.

Dealing with past hurts — the epitome of teamwork

If you have been 'bad selfless' a lot in your relationship, you may have a store of situations where you feel let down or hurt by your partner. Even if you have been quite 'good selfish', you can still have unresolved issues. If, on the other hand, your style has been 'bad selfish', expect your partner to have a backlog of resentment that needs sorting.

I am all in favour of letting go of the past. Couples should let bygones be bygones and 'move on' as much as possible. *However*, if you are experiencing vivid memories and strong feelings about something that happened — it could be last week *or* ten years ago — then this is not just 'in the past'. It is actively affecting your relationship in the present and needs to be dealt with as soon as possible.

One of the essential paradoxes of intimate partnership is that even when our significant other is the person who has distressed us, we still look to them for help. The best way to heal past hurts is for your partner to be the one to give you care, support and empathy as you process them. Although challenging to negotiate, this is how you want your relationship to operate.

Many of us find it difficult to be supportive in that situation. If your partner is talking about a situation where, in their experience, what you did was thoughtless, unfair, selfish or cruel, you may struggle to accept it. Often it is hard to believe that the hurt you did to your partner is as bad as the pain you feel they are causing you by discussing their historical grievance.

The picture they are painting of you hurts your pride or self-image, and you want to reject it. Typically, you will minimise or justify your behaviour. You might try to prove that it was your partner's fault, or do something else that undermines or dismisses their experience. This will compound the past hurt and ensure that it stays alive in your relationship, forever unresolved between you.

The alternative is to place your partner's well-being above your ego, to accept their subjective experience as authentic and valid, and acknowledge how it was for them. It goes like this: I can show interest and care about your perception, even if my experience differs. Even better, I can show empathy by acknowledging that it makes sense how your subjective experience affected you.

If you are hurt by your partner's words or actions and tell them about it, and they respond like this, *it makes a difference*. It signals to your brain that you are both in a different time and place, that things have indeed 'moved on'. Human beings process hurts by 'getting them out' — by talking or writing about them. When you can do this in the presence of a caring other, who validates your experience, it will frequently shift how heavily this past event weighs on your heart and mind. And true healing can occur when the caring other is the person who was the source of your pain.

Make time for team talks

All of this work to ensure that your relationship runs harmoniously takes time. If you don't have children, you may get away with allowing these conversations to happen spontaneously. However, if your life is so busy that you never get around to having these conversations, you need to schedule them.

I'm not much of a planner (Verity will probably choke on her tea at this understatement), but once I had kids I accepted the necessity. Life got crazy. I soon learned 'If it's not in my diary, it probably isn't going to happen.' While most couples who don't have children can organise and coordinate their life together without getting too formal, in my experience the relentless demands of parenting young children, plus juggling the rest of your lives, mean that parents need to have regular meetings.

If that sounds horribly like work, it is. It takes work to make a relationship go well, and even more work if the relationship is the management team for a complex and many-faceted business like a family.

Team talks can be powerful. When I watch rugby, I am often astonished at how much a good coach can turn a team around in the half-time talk. In a rugby team, however, there is a designated boss. In an equal partnership, we need some agreements around how team talks happen. What I suggest in Exercise 35 is quite formal and, not coincidentally, may remind some people of organising a team meeting at work.

EXERCISE 35: A ROUGH STRUCTURE FOR TEAM TALKS

This exercise outlines how to have a team talk about anything.

1. The first thing to do is to put time aside. In most couples, many vital conversations occur with one person (the person initiating the conversation) being well prepared, having spent quite some time building up to raising a complex topic. This can result in the other person feeling ambushed or wrong-footed. Often, their initial startlement

either creates reluctance or their partner interprets it as such. This does not lead to good outcomes. It's safer to make an appointment with each other. I strongly suggest having time set aside on a regular (weekly or fortnightly) basis, when you can be reasonably confident you won't be interrupted for at least an hour (ideally for two hours).

2. Make sure to agree that this is time for business — to get things done. Remember to aim for intimacy, not closeness. It's a time to learn and grow, accepting that things might get uncomfortable and difficult sometimes. If you end up with nothing to discuss, you might renegotiate the time to be more relaxed and close.

3. If there are topics you know you want to talk with your partner about, tell them ahead of time. This way they have a chance to warm up to them, too. Yes, I *am* suggesting that this meeting has an agenda!

4. Don't let your fear and anxiety make you appeasing, guarded (withdrawn) or hostile. Think about what you are trying to achieve with this meeting. A decision? Connection through getting on the same page? Understanding yourself? Understanding your partner? Make sure you bring an attitude and behaviour that supports your intention.

5. State and keep repeating your positive intention. For example, 'I want to talk about how we discipline Sam because I know we have differences, and to me it seems like it's creating distance between us, and I'd like us to be closer,' or 'I've been under a lot of stress with my mother's illness, and I know I've been taking it out on you, and I really want to hear how it's been for you, so you don't feel so pushed away by me.'

6. In the same vein, talk about the Big Picture, your goals (see Chapter 5) — how you want your family and your relationship to operate and the atmosphere you are trying to create. In maintaining your boundaries, focus on what you *do* want more than what you *don't*. Remember that your relationship is simply, at root, *how* you talk to each other and *how* you treat each other.

7. Talk about your limitations, failings and insecurities, and how these negatively affect your partner before (and more than) you complain about your partner's behaviour.

8. If things get reactive, **stop**. Stop sooner rather than later. Take a Time Out (Chapter 4) and use it to reorganise your thinking and attitude. Then come back and have another go.

9. If the conversation derails completely, use it as an opportunity to learn

about yourself and what you need to do differently to get what you want in this relationship. Schedule a time to review, and come back with ideas about what *you* could have done differently.

10. Remember to be kind to yourself about failings and mistakes, but also remember that it's *not* kind to yourself to avoid doing what you need to do, such as having anxiety-provoking team talks with your partner.

'Levelling up' your team talks

To avoid confusion, and have the kind of connection you want, sometimes it can be constructive to think about what 'level' or 'depth' your relationship discussions are at. I suggest you talk about three levels or types of conversation.

1. THE 'CONTENT' LEVEL

The first level is the most simple, straightforward kind of talk — where the focus is *on the topic*. Often called the 'content' level, it's a helpful way to share information and ideas; for example, a discussion about whether we should try to take a holiday this winter.

- One person says: 'It would be good for us to have time away together. You need a break from work and chores. The kids would love a week of uninterrupted "Dad time".'
- The other says: 'Taking a week off at that time isn't going to help me. Work and chores will just pile up. I'd much rather go when the weather is more reliable.'
- You've now both put your thoughts on the table to begin the process of exploring.

'Simple and straightforward' doesn't mean that resolving these kinds of differences is easy. This level of conversation encompasses the critical issues of 'who's responsible for what?' and 'is the division of labour fair?' This is a question for all couples, but is urgent for people with children. In Chapter 14, I stress the need for parents of young kids to prioritise — do what you can and let go of the rest. But who gets to decide what the priorities are?

If, say, you are a professional person coming home from work unexpectedly late, you have made a unilateral decision that the needs of your job were more of a priority than the needs of your partner or family. That's not teamwork; that's dictatorship. Your partner has been given no choice and simply must function without the help they expected. They will have to reorganise their plans and let go of some things they thought they were going to get done.

Ideally, all significant choices are explored and negotiated ahead of time. Maybe when you talk through your partner's concerns about taking a winter holiday, they can see that the chores they're worried about aren't that high a priority and that you have a point about their need for a break. Or maybe they can persuade you that now is not the right time and the two of you can plan a holiday at a different time.

2. THE 'PROCESS' OR 'META' LEVEL

If the discussion isn't going well or we want to deepen our connection, we can shift to discussing *how* we talk. This is often called the 'process' or 'meta' level.

Most people make the mistake of focusing on how their partner is speaking (i.e. complaining about their partner). This usually derails the conversation as your partner defends themself and you insist that they are being unhelpful.

It is far more productive to reflect on how *you* are talking — especially if you identify when you are doing something unhelpful. Typical examples would be arguing your point instead of listening and considering theirs, being hostile instead of compassionate, or staying silent and avoiding saying what you think.

Here are a couple of examples of this shift away from the content of the conversation on to the process:

- 'Sorry, honey, I'm anxious and just shooting down everything you say. You must feel like I'm not listening to you at all. I can hear how much you want to get away, and I don't mean to be annoying.'
- 'I can feel myself shutting down and stonewalling, and I don't want to do that. Give me five minutes to settle myself down and then let's keep talking about when is the best time for a holiday.'

3. THE 'MEANING' LEVEL

The deepest level of discussion is the one that often creates the greatest sense of intimacy because it involves vulnerable self-reflection. This is the 'meaning' level, where you ask yourself: 'Why does this matter to me? What is it about for me?' Often, this is initially subconscious — we aren't aware of it unless we stop and question ourselves.

There are frequently things going on for you that would not be obvious to your partner, so there is no way they could have considered them. For example:

- 'Having holidays is about feeling like I am free and succeeding, unlike my parents who were chained to a business that never quite made it.'
- 'I'm struggling with my imposter syndrome. I know it's silly, but I fear that if I take a week off work, they'll decide they can do without me.'

If you can go deep into yourself like this and work out what the issue is about for you, that often opens the door to creative, alternative solutions that are more acceptable to your partner.

Getting down to the 'meaning' level requires enough mental energy to stop and reflect. Sometimes life can conspire to make that difficult to achieve.

However, this process does not have to mean carving out hours of time for 'deep and meaningfuls'. You can reduce the need for significant chunks of time by committing to the following brief daily practice (Exercise 36) that helps you attune when you reconnect.

EXERCISE 36: RITUALS OF CONNECTION

Over decades of talking with couples, I have observed that the moment you come back together at the end of your separate work days is pivotal. It frequently sets the tone for the whole evening.

When you are both full of your busy days, it's so easy not to connect or to misconnect, to start your evening frustrating or hurting each other. If you have children, your reconnection typically coincides with the 'witching hour', when the kids are tired, hungry and need attention. Plus, there are all the practical demands of getting them fed, bathed and off to bed.

This is the most common time when a couple can benefit from developing what I call 'rituals of connection'. It's not the only time — for example, some people like to do it as they reconnect in the morning. The ritual is a deliberate, even formal, way of greeting each other that gives you a chance to feel seen and like you matter to your significant other.

1. Unless there is a genuine crisis, take two minutes to attend to your relationship, *despite all the other pressures on you*. One minute to get yourself organised — put down your bag, rinse and dry your hands, tell the kids you just need to stop and give Mum/Dad a hug. Then take one minute to connect. The essential communication is non-verbal, usually something like a hug, a kiss or a held gaze. It only needs to last a minute. You may need a bit of experimentation and practice to figure out what works for you both. The key is that you do it with a clear intent to **connect** with your partner and with *full concentration and focus*.

2. Aim to be fully present to the importance of this person in your life, your desire for them to be happy, and for you to have a good life together. Do your best to let that attitude show in how you greet them, look at them and touch them, even if you are stressed or tired. It's only one minute.

3. If you are coming home from work stressed out of your head, use the trip home to get yourself ready to greet your partner. If you are at home, then when you notice it's getting towards the time your partner usually arrives, orient yourself towards having that one minute prep time. You might ask your partner to text five minutes before they get home, so you have a chance to get organised.

You can also use a ritual like this when you say goodbye, and at any other time you see the necessity. Rituals grow in power the more you do them, so long as you practise them mindfully and with clear intention. If you use this tool to manage those tricky times of transition into and out of connection, you may find that they become a cornerstone for your relationship.

Exercise 36 offers one suggestion of a way and a time to connect. Happy couples develop their own ways and rhythms of making time for the relationship. If you aren't seeing those in your relationship, I encourage you to make time (!) to talk with your teammate about how you can work better as a team.

CASSIE & SHARON

Sharon and Cassie had a relationship centred around trying not to upset each other. Sharon came from a family that was outspoken and aggressive. You got what you wanted by shouting the loudest. She hated that environment and was desperate not to re-create it. In Cassie, she picked a partner who was the opposite. Cassie came from a strongly religious family that shamed children (girls especially) if they weren't quiet and compliant.

Yet after a few years of living together, Sharon started erupting in frustrated anger from time to time. She hated seeing herself behave like her bullying father and couldn't understand what was happening. The more she tried to get Cassie to engage, the more Cassie withdrew from her: 'I get louder and angrier because it's like talking to a stone, trying to get a response out of her.' Cassie responded, 'Sure, I shut down, but that's only because she goes on and on. Whatever I say just makes things worse.' Both were operating from very fearful scripts about conflict and needed to find a different way to deal with their differences.

We discussed how, to be a good team member, Sharon needed to work out new ways of behaving when she experienced Cassie as emotionally unavailable. She needed to shift from her 'ineffective self-protective behaviour' into 'making good trouble'. We began by exploring why Cassie's walling-off was so triggering for Sharon. It was ironic, because one of the reasons Sharon was so attracted to Cassie was for her calmness and solidity.

Although Sharon's family fought all the time, they were very engaged with each other. However, when displeased, Sharon's mother would go cold and withdrawn. This was a far worse punishment for Sharon than her father's rages, although they left their mark, too. When Cassie shut down, Sharon unconsciously connected with the feelings of being unlovable and unwanted that her mother's coldness used to evoke.

It was a struggle for Sharon to accept that these feelings belonged to her and her upbringing and were not Cassie's responsibility, and to recognise that no amount of love, attention or care from Cassie would heal her childhood wounding. Sharon's challenge was working out how to care for herself when something Cassie did activated her insecurities. Caring for herself might include asking Cassie for help, but she needed to do that in a vulnerable and humble manner, rather than the blaming and demanding way she had been. I stressed that this couldn't be her only strategy. Sharon needed to develop means of self-care that didn't rely on Cassie being available.

On the other side of the dynamic, Cassie needed to recognise how her conservative religious upbringing had trained her to hide. In trying hard to please her parents and meet their expectations around being a 'good girl', she quickly learned that her spontaneous, natural child self, with all its messy feelings, was unacceptable, even 'evil'. Young Cassie believed she was flawed because it was so difficult to be 'good' (yet, by all accounts, she was a well-behaved child). As her sexuality emerged in adolescence she had even more reason to hide her true self away. While she had moved away from her parents' religious beliefs, she still struggled with expressed emotions and conflict. She typically 'Froze' when Sharon became loud and agitated, and would say and do almost anything ('Flop') to try to pacify Sharon.

To contribute to the team, Cassie had to work out a way to bring herself, her feelings and her thoughts into the relationship. Learning how to be 'good selfish' and do her part in creating 'good trouble' required enormous courage as it went against everything she had learned growing up. At the same time, she learned to tolerate the discomfort of conflict and not collapse into feeling flawed or unacceptable when Sharon was hurt or angry.

Sharon realised that she had a lot of negative thoughts about Cassie and their relationship and was almost always anticipating hostility and rejection. This was colouring the interpretation she put on everything Cassie did. She started a list of things she knew to be true (when she was calm and centred):

- Cassie is on my side. She loves me and wants the best for me.
- Cassie is not my mum or my dad; she doesn't judge me the way they did.
- We are a great team — our differences are a strength.
- I'm going to feel hurt or scared, and it will be okay; I don't have to get fierce.
- I know I'm a good person and don't have to be defensive about it.

Sharon found that she needed to read this list and remind herself of these things several times a day for it to sink in. Over time, she found herself less reactive and defensive and more able to see Cassie's good intentions towards her.

Cassie and Sharon frequently had fights when they were planning outings, especially holidays. Sharon loved getting out into nature. For her, it represented freedom and expansiveness. Plus, camping trips were some of her fondest memories from her childhood; a time when the boisterousness of her family created good times, not least because they could get away from each other. Cassie found camping and tramping quite stressful; it was not part of her upbringing. Her family was very urban-based and church-focused. They saw fun and pleasure, spontaneity and freedom as pathways to selfishness and sin. Cassie valued how Sharon opened up the natural world for her, and they have had some lovely camping holidays and nature walks over the years. However, they would often fight at the planning stage.

Sharon was always looking for chances to get away and tended to spring ideas for trips on Cassie with great enthusiasm, often having done quite a lot of research about where it would be nice to go. When Cassie didn't immediately share her excitement, she got hurt, angry and critical. As time went on, Cassie came to dread these interactions and became even more paralysed in response.

In our discussions, Sharon realised that she needed to involve Cassie much sooner in the planning process, and also had to give Cassie time to manage her initial reflexive negative response. She also had to remind herself that she is loveable, does matter, and that Cassie not wanting precisely what she wants is not a rejection of her.

For her part, Cassie learned to say something positive first and then to ask for time to think about what she wanted. She recognised that at the moment she was faced with a suggestion from Sharon, she felt obliged to say 'yes'. She came to see that while this reflexive compliance was what her parents wanted, Sharon cared about what **she** wanted and only wanted her to say 'yes' if she meant it.

As each of them got a firmer handle on themselves and got used to talking vulnerably about what they wanted and how they protected themselves, things gradually got easier between them. Cassie put it beautifully when she said 'I've gone from worrying when Sharon was going to attack me next to knowing she's always got my back. I feel like I've come home for the first time in life.'

Key points from Chapter 10

1. Your partner is your ally, your teammate — don't treat them as a problem, even when you disagree.
2. Your differences are a resource for your relationship. They will make you stronger and more successful if you harness them.
3. Build trust by being reliable, both emotionally and practically.
4. A good teammate makes 'good trouble' — brings up difficult topics and situations, and engages with them.
5. You need to know the difference between 'good selfish' and 'bad selfish'. Ditto for 'good selfless' and 'bad selfless'.
6. Accepting that you have hurt your partner and hanging in there with them to heal that hurt is the essence of being a good teammate.

Chapter 11
Learn to do conflict well

'You can be "right" or you can be in relationship; pick one.' I first heard this challenging statement from Dr Stan Tatkin, who is an expert on Attachment relationships. It points to the fact that when we disagree with people there is more going on than winning the argument. Indeed, it suggests that arguing to win the battle can cost you the war.

This chapter is all about winning the war and keeping the battle in careful perspective. A lot of the chapter focuses on having the humility to accept that how you see things is not necessarily how they are.

Disagreement is an opportunity for intimacy

As I touched on in Chapter 9, if you do disagreement well, you can develop a stronger sense of yourself in close relationship with your loved one and help them really know you. At the same time, you can learn new and important things about them and demonstrate your care for and acceptance of them, even when they are different from you.

Remind yourself that having a disagreement is not a bad thing. As I stress throughout the book, disagreeing is necessary, inevitable and frequently uncomfortable, but there is nothing going wrong in your relationship if you happen to disagree. It can also help to remember that if something goes wrong, and the way you are handling the disagreement becomes frustrating, hurtful or simply ineffective, you can always come back and have another go.

Make sure you both believe that there is strength in diversity, as I discuss in Chapter 10. Also, make sure you understand how doing conflict well is essential for turning differences into an asset.

In approaching a situation where you know, or suspect, that you have a disagreement, the first thing to do is remind yourself that maintaining your connection, your sense of team, is **more important**

than whatever you are disagreeing about. Aim to stay intimate and make that a priority above resolving your conflict. It may seem slower, but if you take the time to care for your partner and the connection, it's a faster path to a resolution that *works for you both*. If you rush to 'resolve' things and don't attend to the relationship, the chances are you won't get a resolution that is effective in the long run.

- This means recognising that 'this needs to be an intimate talk', and beginning by exploring the *feelings and meanings* the issue raises.
- The moment one of you gets reactive, start paying attention to, and talking about, your insecurities and defences. Don't forget to take a Time Out (Chapter 4) if you need to.
- Shift from the CONTENT to the PROCESS (Chapter 10) and 'own your own stuff' (acknowledge and take responsibility for things you have done that protect you but hurt or frustrate your partner). If you don't, you'll never get far in your discussion. Although it may feel like you are 'off topic', you are on target with respect to your connection.

Here's how disagreements can lead to deeper intimacy. Imagine you and I are in conflict about where to live. If we 'fight' about it, as in I try to make you wrong and prove why I'm right, I will likely learn nothing about myself or you in this kind of process.

On the other hand, if we go slow and deep and explore what's going on, I might learn something. So, we talk about why you want to live in the country and why I want to live in the city. We explore what it means to each of us, what it represents for us, how it's connected to our dreams and aspirations, our identity and sense of self. As we explore like this, new understandings are likely to emerge. In trying to explain to you why being in the city is so important to me, I may learn things about myself I hadn't realised. If you do the same, I will be learning new things about you.

That's an intimate conversation. Exercise 37 will help you have this kind of conversation.

EXERCISE 37: KEEPING CONNECTED IN CONFLICT

1. The first thing to keep in mind is that you want to go slow and take your time:
   - so you don't mess up (by being reactive) *and*
   - because you want to get the most out of this intimate opportunity to learn more about yourself and your partner *and*
   - you want a resolution that is going to work long-term — a rushed, forced compromise or capitulation won't get you that.

2. As soon as you realise there's a significant disagreement, say something that makes it clear that you want to stay connected, that your relationship is more important than this issue: 'It looks like we disagree on this and we need to sort it out. I want to go slowly and carefully so neither of us gets hurt.'

3. Invite your partner to talk about what the issue is about and what it means to them. Repeat back what they said to be sure you heard it accurately.

4. Only then, talk about what the issue means to you. Focus on expressing your point of view, feelings and experience rather than trying to invalidate your partner's.

5. Unless there is an urgent deadline, be open to the idea of having several conversations to sort things out — don't get hung up on sorting it out now.

6. Don't try to come up with solutions until you have a handle on what the issue means to each of you. Be as creative as possible in trying to find a win–win solution; one that attends to what's significant about this issue for *both* of you.

7. The aim is to foster a spirit of working on the problem together, of you both being a team. Not win–lose or 'I'm right and you're wrong', but 'you have a valid perspective and so do I'.

8. Make sure you *really* accept that your partner is different from you, that they have a different reality from you (e.g. if they remember yesterday's conversation differently from you, it *doesn't* mean they are lying). If you can't understand their point of view, be curious rather than condemning. Let them be equally valid. If you can't hold that position — what stops you? What are you afraid could happen if you accept that your partner might have a point?

He said, she said: there is no such thing as reality

Implicit in 'dealing with difference' positively is an acceptance that *reality is always subjective*. It goes like this: when you and I have an interaction, you will experience it one way from your point of view, and I will experience it differently from mine. Much of the time those differences are trivial and unremarkable. But when we get into conflict, they can become huge issues if we aren't careful.

There *are* relationships where your partner is deliberately lying to or even 'gaslighting' you, but I am not talking about those here — see Chapter 19 for a discussion of those situations. Here I am talking about the normal differences in perception, interpretation and meaning-making that occur between people who are both doing their best and operating with goodwill and decency.

Before I realised what a useless waste of energy it was, I spent a lot of time trying to argue with Verity that her subjective experience of me was wrong and unfair. I have inherited from my mother an unfortunate tendency to look disapproving when my face is at rest (yes, men can suffer from 'bitchy resting face', too). As well as sometimes inadvertently terrifying my clients, what this means is that it is very easy for Verity to misunderstand what is going on with me.

So, we used to have this pattern when Verity raised an issue: I am sitting there feeling scared about saying the wrong thing, so I am slow to respond. Verity sees my grumpy face and my silence and concludes that I am frustrated or angry with her and starts getting defensive, explaining more about her point of view. I feel increasingly overwhelmed and anxious and end up saying something aggressive to stop her talking at me. She gets hurt; I get frustrated that I never got to say what I was thinking. We used to waste a lot of time trying to establish who was at fault.

It's hard to accept that your partner lives in a world that is radically different from yours. When we are talking about a shared experience, like our respective memories of a conversation, it can feel like your partner is lying or deliberately distorting reality when they report what they remember. Alternatively, you can feel like you are going crazy. The more emotionally dangerous the environment you grew up in, the more likely you are to draw those kinds of conclusions.

Here's the vital thinking: Unless I have powerful reasons to believe that you have hostile intent, I don't take personally the difference between your subjective reality and mine. I train myself to show curiosity and care about your lived experience and how it's different from mine. This is particularly true if we are having a disagreement.

The other side of this coin is that you can't assume that your partner is reading your intentions accurately. You may know that you were just asking a question because you were genuinely unsure whether the rubbish had been put out. Your partner doesn't know that. If they have a background of being criticised or fearing failure, or if there has been a lot of contention in your relationship over chores and responsibilities, then it's going to be easy for them to misinterpret the intention behind your question.

This is frustrating, but it's important that you don't take it personally. If your partner (or your relationship) has that kind of history and you want to avoid these kinds of misunderstandings, you may need to routinely spell out your intentions. If it's a recurring pattern, the two of you may need to sit down at a time when you are both calm and centred, and strategise about how to prevent such misunderstandings. Again, I must stress that although this seems like a lot of work, it is *reliably worthwhile in the long run.*

How upset undermines your memory

When it comes to the memory of discussions, things get even more complicated if one or both of you was upset or angry at the time.

As I discuss in Chapter 5, we know that when you get into certain states of fear or upset, your brain begins to work differently. In that state what you do is focused on *survival,* not the good of the relationship. The very fast-acting 'protect yourself at all costs' parts of your brain (limbic system) are running the show.

In Chapter 5 I talked about how when we feel threatened, there's less blood going to the 'think and be rational' parts of the brain (e.g. the pre-frontal cortex). Another important part of the brain, called the hippocampus, also goes offline when you get into a 'Five F' state. The hippocampus is the part of your brain that puts things *in context,* in terms of both time and space. It is essential for memory.

This means that when you try to recall what happened when you were distressed, you are *not* able to reliably put events in order, judge the time things took or when they happened, or even be sure where they took place. The bottom line is:

You can't trust your memory of things
that happen when you're upset.

This can be extremely challenging to accept. Our memories are fundamental; you can argue that they are the core of our sense of ourselves. And we are used to trusting our memories. And some of us are upset *a lot*.

But if you understand the science of your brain, you might be able to calm yourself down and realise that how you remember things isn't 'right' or 'reality' or 'truth' in any objective sense. It is your memory, but it is *normal* for your partner's memory to be different. It's challenging but vital to get your head around this.

Being true to yourself while allowing your partner to be a different person, with a different reality, is at the heart of making a relationship work. When there has been upset and distress, this is more essential than ever.

There are ways to bridge between two different realities, but they can only happen if you accept that your memory is not infallible. If you want to make things work, then staying in relationship and showing caring for your partner's experience, as well as your own, must be more important to you than being 'right' about what happened.

Correcting your partner's misinterpretations

It can be frustrating when your partner describes something you said or did in such a way that you feel misrepresented and misunderstood. When your partner doesn't see or understand you accurately, it is sometimes excruciating (especially if this echoes formative experiences in your life). You can feel very hurt or threatened.

The typical response is to dispute your partner's version of events, try to correct their view and assert what 'really happened' or what you 'really meant'. Sadly, this is rarely successful and typically leads to an unproductive conflict where you argue about 'the facts' of what happened and both of you are left feeling unsatisfied.

This way of responding is rooted in an unconscious assumption that your subjective experience is accurate and fair. This means, by extension, that your partner is being at best inaccurate and at worst unfair or even deceptive.

As discussed earlier in the chapter, one of the critical attitudes at the heart of a harmonious relationship is **accepting that all experience is subjective.** We each live inside our own head, interpreting and making meaning in ways that are not always accurate and are often under the influence of formative experiences in our early life.

Taking this attitude opens up a way to correct misinterpretations that *will* be effective. Exercise 38 helps you develop this effective approach.

EXERCISE 38: STAYING CONNECTED WHILE CHALLENGING MISINTERPRETATIONS

1. Acknowledge your partner's subjective experience as valid

Demonstrate that you accept that what they remember and how they interpreted things is the reality *they* lived. (Note that accepting the reality of their subjective experience is not the same as agreeing with it.)

The simplest way to demonstrate this acceptance is to repeat what they said in a tone and manner that indicates you acknowledge that this is how it was for them. Recapping in this way simply lets them know that you have heard them and are taking their experience seriously. For example: 'So you heard me saying I thought you weren't pulling your weight in the relationship, and that made you think I didn't respect or value you.'

2. If their experience sounds painful or difficult, show some care or empathy

This is especially important if you believe that your partner has misunderstood your intentions — meaning that they have suffered unnecessarily. 'I'm so sorry to hear you felt like that. It must be horrible to believe I judged you in that way.'

If you do these two things sincerely, your partner will probably feel heard and cared for. That creates an atmosphere where you can try to correct the misunderstanding.

3. In correcting misinterpretations, make sure you take responsibility for your part

If you said something in the heat of anger that doesn't reflect your considered opinion, own it before you explain why that's not what you truly believe. But don't deny you said it — that's gaslighting. If you said something that your partner took out of context, it is worth acknowledging this and, where appropriate, admitting that it was open to misinterpretation. This is particularly important if you said something that touched on your partner's insecurities.

If you have validated your partner's reality and owned your part in any misunderstanding, then you can say what you think and feel and have a reasonable expectation that your partner will hear and believe it. 'I am sorry that I implied you weren't pulling your weight. That's unfair and untrue. You do more than your fair share, and I know I am lucky to have someone so generous and supportive in my life.' If your upbringing involved many invalidating experiences, correcting painful misinterpretations in this way can be a powerful healing experience for you both.

Being 'logical' isn't always rational

One flavour of disputes over reality is where someone claims the high ground by saying they are being 'logical' or 'rational' or something similar. Many of us try hard to stay 'logical' or 'rational' when we are having a conversation, especially when we are disagreeing with someone. On the surface this looks like a good idea — we want decisions made on factual information, not vague feelings. But, as fans of *Star Trek* will know, this is a doomed enterprise (pun fully intended, with apologies).

What we usually achieve is the exact opposite of rational behaviour. When we talk in an 'unemotional' way, what we actually do is disown and deny the feelings that are the motivation for our opinion. Emotion researcher Karla McLaren[1] stresses that emotions are a fundamental part of our cognitive system. We can't think without feeling. To pretend otherwise is to fly in the face of facts — to be irrational. Although this is a problem in wider society, it is particularly tragic in intimate relationships.

When we present our ideas and opinions as if they were devoid of feeling, we are often trying to position ourselves as 'better' than our more visibly emotional partner. It is common to use the fact that someone has emotions about a topic as a reason to dismiss their opinion. There are several things wrong with this approach.

1. It is rooted in a competitive, 'win–lose' view of disagreements that is toxic to intimate relationships. If your partner feels strongly about something, that's an opportunity for intimacy, for knowing them better. Rather than being dismissive, be curious about why and what it means to them.

2. Kidding ourselves that we are emotionless obscures our motivation and deprives both us and our partner of crucial information necessary to make any valid conclusion. Being partially blind to what's going on inside you, to what things mean to you, does not improve the quality of your decision-making. When we are not looking at all the data, our choices are likely to be misguided.

3. An 'emotionless' presentation invites misunderstanding of our intention. In the absence of the necessary information, our partner is forced to guess where we are coming from. Because of the way human brains are wired, their guess is likely to be more negative or catastrophic than our actual position. This leads to their emotional response to us being off-kilter and confusing to us.

4. Most importantly for couple relationships, when we deny or suppress the emotional aspect of our being, we issue an unconscious invitation to our partner to take care of it for us. In my experience, it is a cultural norm in our society for men in hetero relationships to do this to their female partners, and for the women to willingly, even gleefully, accept it as their job. However, it is not just men who do it — I have seen the exact same dynamic with the genders reversed and also between two women. Outsourcing our emotional

well-being this way leaves us feeling unnecessarily vulnerable and out of control because we are *not* in charge of our own life. Our emotional well-being is in the hands of someone else. No matter how much they love us, they cannot know or give us exactly what we need. Frequently this results in us feeling frustrated and angry with them because of their inability to do an impossible job. This dynamic is a recipe for mutual hurt, and cannot be solved unless we *reclaim responsibility for our own emotional well-being.*

The truly rational approach is to accept that you, like every other human, are full of feelings, and that these represent important information that needs to be acknowledged and understood. As such, this needs to be part of what we think and talk about, especially when we disagree with someone else. When we talk about and take responsibility for our own emotions and show interest and care in those of our partner, then we are finally acting rationally in service of our goal of having a good relationship.

Talking in tricky territory

If you accept that having an intimate relationship means choosing to go into tricky territory — having interactions that are uncomfortable or even scary — then one way to reduce your anxiety is to have strategies that improve the likelihood of you ending up feeling close rather than distant.

The following five exercises will help you stay connected when you disagree.

EXERCISE 39: REFLECTIVE LISTENING

One way to slow things down and make them deeper and safer is to use reflective listening. The nuts and bolts of this are simple, but implementing them takes lots of practice.

- When your partner says something, instead of replying with your thoughts, take the time to 'reflect' what you heard. Say something like 'What I heard was . . .' then repeat back or summarise what you thought they said. End with 'Have I got that right?'

- Repeating back what you heard, *before* you respond, lets you check that you have accurately understood what your partner meant. If your partner corrects you, take that as a gift, not a criticism. They have just saved you from wasting time and energy on a misunderstanding.
- Recapping what you heard also gives you double the amount of time to consider how you want to respond. Even more importantly, it reassures your partner that you have listened to them, meaning that they are much more likely to be able to listen to you in turn.

This can be a hard discipline to apply, but it is amazingly effective if you are willing to put the effort in.

EXERCISE 40: SPELL OUT YOUR POSITIVE INTENTIONS; DON'T ASSUME TRUST

It is so easy to assume that your partner knows you mean them well. But remember, their amygdala doesn't care how much love and care you have shown them over the years. *Don't take that biological reality personally.* Just accept that if you say something that can be interpreted as a criticism, your partner's amygdala will react to protect them unless you have given it a good dose of reassurance first.

If you are saying things that are critical or demanding of your partner, spelling out the good outcomes you are seeking for the relationship can make it much easier for your partner to hear you. Here are a couple of examples:

- 'I really want us to work this through to a solution we both feel good about. So, I really want to hear what you have to say about this and I'm hoping you'll do the same for me.'
- 'I know I've been pretty unfriendly lately. I want to feel relaxed and close again. I'm upset about what happened on the weekend and I want to sort it out so I can have my best friend back.'

EXERCISE 41: THINK LONG-TERM AND BIG PICTURE

I hope I have already made it clear how much our self-protective impulses are focused on the short-term, often with little regard for the long-term consequences. As discussed in Chapter 5, it is up to our 'centred' selves, our frontal lobes, to make sure that we communicate in a way that supports our values and goals.

Let's imagine I am feeling exasperated because I have tried and tried to get you to stop doing something (like dropping your dirty clothes on the bedroom floor, or spending money on Lotto). In the heat of the moment, I shout something that captures the intensity of my frustration but that I don't really mean: 'It's worse than having a third child' or 'I'm done with this shit — I'm out of here.'

The problem is that those words will register and be interpreted by my partner through the filter of their experience and insecurities. To make matters worse, when we are angry, we will often unconsciously choose a 'dig' or criticism that connects with our partner's insecurities. We are feeling hurt by them, and we unconsciously hurt them back. These exchanges have the potential to do serious damage to trust and stability in the relationship.

It's hard to make yourself 'not do' something. Rather than trying to 'not say nasty things', it's better to try to focus on what you *do* want to do. I encourage you to put your energy into the Big Picture of your life and relationship (see Chapter 5). Exactly what this looks like will be different for everyone, but this example should illustrate what I mean:

- This is my partner, whom I love and care for. We are not in competition. We are a team trying to do something really difficult in joining our lives, raising a family and caring for our elderly parents together. I am not perfect and it's not reasonable to expect that they should be. I want to be kind and fair and patient with them, even if they are struggling to do the same. This is a situation I am finding challenging, but I want to keep it in proportion. Dirty clothes on the floor makes me feel uncared for, but it's not more important than our connection.

EXERCISE 42: MAKE SURE HOW YOU TALK AND ACT *HELPS* RATHER THAN *HINDERS*

Showing care for your partner in a challenging interaction is not the same as 'walking on eggshells' — which usually means being full of anxiety and trying to anticipate and manage your partner's responses. Being 'care-full' is about holding on to and expressing your care for your partner, even if you're having a difficult discussion. Remember that the non-verbal parts of communication (posture, facial expression, tone, manner, etc.) are the most powerful parts.

When you're in tricky territory, make a special effort to communicate your care and respect for your partner in *how* you talk to them. You can disagree with someone while still showing care for them. For example:

- 'Hey, I can get that it's really frustrating for you that I don't see it the way you do, but I don't at the moment. I'm really willing to talk with you more about it and am working hard to keep an open mind, so let's keep going.'

EXERCISE 43: STOP THE VICIOUS CYCLE

No matter how self-aware you are and how carefully you plan, difficult conversations are sometimes going to become frustrating, unproductive or hurtful. You and your partner are imperfect, like the rest of humanity, so things won't always go perfectly.

It's no good trying to keep going if one or both of you has been hijacked by your amygdala (see Chapter 5). Have a mechanism like 'Time Out' (Chapter 4) that allows either one of you to pause the conversation so you can re-group. Use the pause to re-orient yourself into a constructive headspace.

Stopping like this gives you time to care for yourself and reconnect with your values, goals and intentions. Additionally, reducing the number of negative experiences makes it easier to initiate and manage your anxiety during these very important tricky conversations.

Repairing the inevitable ruptures in your relationship

One of the things that makes it safe to go into tricky territory is knowing what to do when your discussion of differences goes wrong (as it inevitably will, sometimes). In this situation, some couples escalate to damaging levels of conflict; others can keep it manageable, where no harm is ultimately done.

According to leading relationship researcher Dr John Gottman, the difference is down to what he calls 'repair attempts', which have been described as the 'secret weapon of emotionally connected couples'. The Gottman Institute defines a repair attempt as 'any statement or action — verbal, physical or otherwise — meant to diffuse negativity and keep a conflict from escalating out of control'.[2]

One of the most important findings to come out of the many decades of research in Gottman's 'love lab' is that happy couples still have plenty of tension and conflict — but they are good at sorting it out and fixing any hurt that's done.

We must learn **how to make and how to receive repair attempts**. As with many aspects of relationship, what effective repair is may be very personal to your relationship culture. What works for your friends, or even your partner, won't work for you. What makes you feel loved and safe may be very different from what your partner needs. This is something that the two of you need to explore and discuss. Watch out for your expectations of what is 'normal'; what worked in your childhood is unlikely to work with your partner.

I vividly remember a couple where the man was reliably able to make his partner laugh when things got tense between them. Humour is a common way to restore good feeling and part of the relationship repair toolkit of many couples. What was remarkable in *this* relationship was that when things got difficult between them, he made her laugh by deliberately farting! Now, in many couples that would be grounds for divorce. However, for this woman it tickled her sense of humour and highlighted the absurdity of their squabbles. Not everyone's cup of tea, but it worked for them and gave me a salutary lesson in 'do whatever works for you'. Exercise 44 helps you decide at what level of size and seriousness your repair attempt needs to be.

EXERCISE 44: RESPONDING TO MINOR AND MAJOR RUPTURES

When your relationship is starting to veer off the highway, there are two main types of repair attempts.

- There are the little repair attempts that happen along the way, which don't interrupt the interaction but do keep it from going off-track. They're a bit like moving the steering wheel when you hit the rumble strip on the edge of the road. Maybe you reach out and put your hand on your partner's knee, and say 'Sorry, that came out harsher than I intended.' Or you express appreciation for how much thought your partner has put into the issue. Or you say 'Let's keep talking while we take the dog for a walk', knowing that this will diffuse the tension.
- Other times the interaction has got distressing and one or both of you is quite upset. Then you need a bigger, more substantial repair attempt. You have gone off the road and need to back up, maybe even call a tow truck, to get out of the ditch. This is a good time to take a Time Out (Chapter 4) and re-focus on your Big Picture (Chapter 5). Come back from Time Out and do your best to own your part in making the conversation feel unsafe for your partner, apologising where appropriate. Re-state your good intentions, appreciations, hopes for an outcome that works for both of you, etc. Don't neglect the non-verbal part of the repair — your body language, tone, timing and touch are all part of restoring connection.

Getting to resolution: persistence, persuasion and openness

If you believe you have spoken up in the past but got nowhere, consider the possibility that you weren't sufficiently clear, direct or persistent with your partner. Many people tell me 'I've already told them and they did nothing', yet when I enquire in detail it becomes clear that they have said one or two things either indirectly or in the heat of a moment and have given up when that didn't produce the desired result.

Many of us in the Antipodes are descended from cultures that struggle with directness. It seems rude, confrontational and aggressive. Yet if your relationship is in crisis because things are not being said or not being responded to, it is vital that you develop a way of talking about things.

For many of us it's hard to know what we want, let alone express it to our life partner. If we are brave enough to tell our partner our desires, it can feel crushing when this is not met with immediate and enthusiastic acceptance.

Remember, we are typically attracted to someone who is different from us. An inevitable result is that our partner will see things differently, will have different preferences and will organise their priorities in ways that are alien to us.

This is where we need to be **persistent**. To hold on to what we think, want or feel, and keep treating it as important and worthwhile (i.e. being Self-Differentiated). Yet, just to make the business of relationship even more challenging, we must, *at the same time*, treat our partner's perspective as being of interest and value. To be open to them and how they feel and see things (i.e. being Other-Differentiated). Persistence reflects our ability to be Differentiated in our approach to disagreement.

To recap: If you fall into the trap of trying to tell your partner they are wrong because they are different, you undermine your credibility and invite defensiveness. If you fall into the trap of appeasement, of giving in for the sake of peace, you abandon yourself and set the seeds of resentment and frustration.

If your idea is a good one, then your job is to **persuade** your partner of its merits. You will have to 'sell' them the idea in a way that shows you are **open** to them. Talk in terms that have meaning for them, that fit with their view of the world. As any good salesperson can tell you, successful persuasion involves a lot of empathy and, frequently, knowledge of what is important to the other person, of their world-view.

To be persuasive, you may need to persist past your partner's initial self-protective reflexes, past their misunderstandings of what you meant, and past their fears of losing out or surrendering their power.

You are likely to have to reach deep into yourself to understand and explain why this issue is important to you, or why it is in their interests to do it your way. This is why conflict, done well, is often a road to deepening intimacy.

Taking your time is crucial

Part of being persistent is allowing time to explore your differences. The longer I have been working with couples, the more I believe that this is a crucial factor in dealing with differences effectively. Take as much time as you need to *explore* what's going on before you try to *negotiate* a solution. Couple relationships need to function by consensus. For our decisions and choices to succeed, it needs both of us to be on board.

If you are genuinely open to, and listening to, your partner and how it is for them and what they want, you may find yourself looking for solutions that are different from those you first thought of. Creative solutions that give you *both* what you are seeking — the wonderful 'win–win' position that is quite outside the box but works well for you both.

In my experience, it takes time, as well as persistence, persuasion and openness, to create those magical moments of successful resolution.

EXERCISE 45: REVIEW AND IMPROVE YOUR BEHAVIOUR DURING A CONFLICT

Here's a checklist[3] of some behaviour that is constructive during a disagreement. You *can* use it as a prompt to give you some things to aim for. However, its main purpose is to help you review how you handled yourself *after* a conflict. Some of these prompts invite you to speculate about how your partner will rate you. If you aren't sure, you can always ask them.

Think about your last disagreement, and **rate each statement below from 0 to 10** to reflect how accurately it fits with your behaviour. 0 = not at all, 10 = totally.

____ I stayed curious about my partner's concerns and experiences.

____ I recapped what I was hearing to make sure I'd understood and my partner felt listened to.

____ I communicated clearly about what I thought and wanted and why my concerns were important to me.

___ My partner will say I was clear about what I thought and wanted and why my concerns were important to me.

___ I got clear about what the issue symbolised or meant to my partner.

___ My partner will say I was clear about what the issue meant or symbolised to me.

___ I was open regarding my fears and concerns about expressing myself clearly.

___ I believe my tone of voice and body language was warm and open, or at least neutral.

___ My partner will say my tone of voice and body language was warm and open, or at least neutral.

___ I was clear about and have acknowledged the cost to my partner of giving me what I want / doing things the way I want.

___ I made it easy for my partner to give me what I want.

___ I was genuinely open to hearing other ways of doing things, other possibilities.

___ I worked hard to create solutions that worked for both of us.

___ My partner will say they experienced me as open to other ways of doing things, other possibilities.

___ I was honest and didn't exaggerate the cost to me of doing what my partner wants.

___ I gave the conversation as much time as it needed; I didn't rush or force a conclusion.

Have a look at your scores — if an item is scored below a 5, that's a real area of weakness for you. It might be worth going back and having another go with your partner to sort that one out.

Also have a look at the overall pattern. Do you consistently think that your partner will rate your performance lower than you do? Or are you good at listening to what your partner is saying but not so good at being clear about what you think and want? These might be things you can go back to — they are likely to be areas where the issue remains unclear or unresolved between you.

PRU & FRANK

On first meeting, Frank and Pru seemed like lovely people with a lot of warm feeling between them. It was a shock to me that they had only just got back together following an incident where a Police Safety Order was issued requiring that Frank leave the home.

Unsurprisingly, both Frank and Pru grew up in what I would describe as emotionally dangerous environments. When Frank was growing up in South America, his father was largely absent, emotionally remote when at home, and had occasional outbursts of violent temper. Frank's mother had a serious drinking problem and was a 'mean drunk'. As far as Frank can remember, she was drunk most evenings and was emotionally and physically abusive to both of the kids — punching, slapping and pulling hair in her rage at their latest failing. This continued until Frank left home at 16 and moved to another city to pursue his plumbing apprenticeship.

Pru's parents were both 20 when they unexpectedly got pregnant with her. Poor, and unprepared for parenthood, they were completely overwhelmed, meaning that Pru was emotionally and physically neglected. Her father would ignore her unless she did something to annoy him, at which point he would beat her with whatever came to hand. Her mother was endlessly critical and blamed Pru for the beatings. One of her earliest memories was being embarrassed at school by playmates seeing the bruises on her arms. An only child, she became very self-reliant and capable, with very low expectations for herself.

In their previous relationships, Frank and Pru had unconsciously repeated the patterns of their own childhoods. Frank had lived with a critical, blaming older woman who had an alcohol problem; Pru was married to a controlling and abusive man (her mother blamed her for those beatings, too!).

After meeting and getting to know each other online, the early years of Frank and Pru's relationship were rosy. The warmth, tenderness and care they experienced was a revelation, and they both felt like they had turned a corner in their lives, being able to leave behind the horrors of the past. However, once they had kids, things began to regress. Their first child was colicky, leading to them both being sleep-deprived and Pru feeling like a bad mother. At the same time, Frank was in the process of growing his business and on a steep learning curve around managing staff, developing systems, etc.

With the arrival of their second child, both were overwhelmed and things went from bad to worse.

Being so 'independent', Pru had never learned how to ask for help vulnerably, so her pleas for assistance were usually expressed in the form of criticism and complaint. Likewise, Frank never talked to Pru vulnerably about the pressures on him. His angry rants about unreliable staff and impossible computer systems just added to her stress and her sense of him having no interest or care in her struggles. This was exacerbated by the reflexive defensiveness with which he met all her complaints.

It was hard to get them to acknowledge their behaviour, because each of them was deeply ashamed that they were behaving in ways that reminded them of their parents. It took many weeks and much trial-and-error learning before they were able to implement Time Out effectively.

Pru, especially, struggled with accepting that her reality was subjective and that her memory was not reliable. As we explored how invested she was in trusting her own judgement, it became clear that she had never had anyone on whom she could rely. This led to a huge upwelling of grief for her, to which Frank was able to respond very empathically.

For his part, Frank had to come to realise that what he thought was being 'calm' was simply him suppressing emotions until they burst out in rage. The irony was that the more he raged, the more he tried to keep himself calm. His big epiphany came when he realised that this was probably **exactly** what was going on for his father; then, the purpose of 'connecting with his emotions' became clear to him.

As Pru and Frank got a handle on when and how to use Time Out (sooner and more often was the key), the frequency of hurtful fights began to drop. At the same time, developing a more compassionate understanding of their own and their partner's behaviour allowed them to have a much more caring conversation about their situation. As the talk became less blaming and more intimate, each of them was surprised to recognise how wrong their assumptions about each other were.

They had to unpick several unresolved past issues, but each time they did so it became clear, in retrospect, how hard it was for both to extend trust and goodwill. The notion of acting as if your partner is there for you and persisting if you don't get the desired response was really challenging, but they got there eventually.

After 18 months of hard work, the couple still had many times when one or both got hurt, frustrated or upset, but they became skilled at using Time Out to prevent things escalating to unsafe levels of aggression. And they came to really prioritise relationship repair. Frank got good at fulsome apologies, with unflinching acknowledgement of his defensiveness, and making concrete plans about what he would do differently in future. Pru learned to stop asserting how 'right' and 'justified' her feelings were, and instead focused on asking for help in a vulnerable way and persisting without getting hostile when Frank didn't engage fully.

A surprising outcome for Pru was that as her respect for Frank increased, she found her sexual desire returning. She had thought she was 'touched out' with two pre-schoolers, but it turned out that when she was feeling well loved, she was very interested in sex. This welcome development was hugely significant to Frank, and cemented for him the value of being more interested in his inner world and more vulnerable in communicating about it.

Key points from Chapter 11

1. You are more likely to have an intimate interaction during a conflict than during a cuddle.
2. Understanding and accepting that your 'truth' is subjective, and being open to your partner's reality, are crucial to handling disagreement well.
3. Your memory is untrustworthy, especially if you are upset.
4. People who claim they are being 'rational' during disagreements are usually denying and missing out on the important information contained in their emotions.
5. Going slow and deep (looking at what's underlying the issue at hand) is a key to doing conflict well.
6. Happy and unhappy relationships have the same amount of upset; the difference is that the happy couples know how to repair quickly and effectively.
7. You may have to persist to get your partner to engage. That's annoying, but much better than ending up resentful.

Chapter 12
Power dynamics and gender roles

What is power?

In relationships, power is about the relative ease or difficulty with which you can get the relationship to work the way you want; how much influence you have over how decisions affecting you get made.

It's crucial to understand that a power imbalance in any relationship is usually only of concern to the person with less power. Your boss is probably not troubled by being able to tell you what to do (their complaints tend to be about not having *more* control over subordinates), but you may find their power over you quite oppressive. That's one of the reasons why it's likely to be the woman in a hetero couple who buys a book like this; meanwhile their spouse won't believe that there *is* a gender difference in power.

In Chapter 9, I discuss the difference between 'feeling' and 'being' vulnerable. One of the reasons men struggle to accept that a power difference exists is because they feel so vulnerable in relationships. However, traditional male strategies for dealing with feeling vulnerable (stonewalling, acting entitled, needing to be right, etc.) tend to exacerbate power differences.

I wrote this book with the expectation that you, the reader, want to be in a partnership of equals. I believe that this is an absolute bedrock value if you want a satisfying intimate relationship. Although some religious and cultural groups within our society still see commitment as necessitating the subordination of women to men, they are in the minority.

Because I work primarily with hetero couples, many of the power dynamics I observe fall along traditional gender lines — with men 'one-up' and women 'one-down'. However, I want to acknowledge that some of the same power dynamics can play out in same-sex relationships, so it is not simply a matter of gender roles. Social roles such as 'breadwinner' or 'physically powerful', 'beautiful' or 'rich', 'educated' or 'high status' can also create or foster power differences. These are what I call *structural differences*.

Structural power differences

When discussing power, 'equal' doesn't mean 'exactly the same'. Forming any kind of equal relationship is always a negotiation between different people's needs, desires and expectations. That negotiation may involve working across a 'structural power imbalance'. That is where, by virtue of some aspect of our nature, experience, opportunities or luck, one of us finds it easier to get what we want or has a greater expectation of getting what we want (entitlement). Thus, one of us has more power.

For example, you are typically on the high side of a structural power differential if you:

- are the man in a hetero couple
- are in paid employment, and your partner is not
- are more than 10 years older than your partner
- come from a financially comfortable family while your partner's family was poor
- are white, and your partner is not
- are living in your country of birth, and your partner is an immigrant
- had a tertiary education, and your partner did not
- can read and communicate easily, and your partner is dyslexic
- are able-bodied, and your partner is differently abled
- have enjoyed robust mental health, and your partner has not
- are neurotypical, and your partner has ADHD
- can earn well above the average wage, and your partner cannot
- are a 'primary' partner with a 'secondary' partner in a polyamorous relationship
- have always felt safe, while your partner has been a victim of assault (physical, sexual or emotional)
- were born in a country at peace, and your partner came from a nation at war.

It is worth stressing that more than one of these differences can be at play in a given relationship. Where the power imbalances are spread out across the people in the relationship, they can sometimes effectively cancel each other out. Multiple power differences can also mean that in some situations one person has more power, and in a different context their partner does. However, in some relationships one person is on the low side of several structural power differentials. In those cases, you must pay particular attention to issues of power and influence.

There is nothing inherently wrong with a relationship that has this kind of built-in power differential. What matters is how it is acknowledged and handled. If you're the primary breadwinner and you respond to a question about something you bought with a defensive 'I worked hard for this money', then you are exploiting the power difference.

Suppose you are on the high side of the power differential, and you deny that certain things are harder for your partner than for you. In that case, you are invalidating their experience and denying how the power difference benefits you. People are often dismissive of comments from their partners that make them uncomfortable, especially when accepting what their partner is saying requires a change of behaviour or attitude or (especially) a loss of power.

Some people fear that acknowledging a difference in power means painting themselves as oppressive or exploitative. Ironically, you are far more likely to behave in exploitative or oppressive ways if you deny the power implications of your inequalities and so ride rough-shod over your partner's experience.

On the other hand, some people on the low side of the power differential can't acknowledge it, out of shame or fear that it represents some weakness, defect or deficiency in them. In denying their reality, they unintentionally collude with structural oppression and their own insecurities. For example, the stay-at-home mother who says 'Of course he has more say in how we spend our money; he's the one who earns it' undervalues her own work and contribution.

I remember seeing this kind of internalised oppression when working with a Pasifika man and a Palagi woman. It took many sessions for them to realise that his reflexive deferral to her was not just conflict avoidance (from being raised in a home with lots of violent arguments); it was also internalised racism. He automatically assumed that she knew more and would always be more 'right' than him because she was white. The woman was appalled, but had the honesty to acknowledge how she had benefitted from his difficulty in challenging her.

In my experience, the key to managing structural power differences is a willingness to talk about the implications of the imbalance. The experience of the person with less power must be validated and given equal weight, and they must have comparable autonomy and authority to influence the relationship. This requires humility on the part of the person on the up-side of the power dynamic, plus the willingness to stop always getting things their way. It also demands courage and determination from the person on the low side.

Changing power dynamics is not easily done. It is hard for people with power and privilege to give it up, disadvantage themselves and lose the benefits they have enjoyed. It is equally challenging, especially in an intimate relationship, for the person who is being disadvantaged to step into their power and assert themselves. It's doubly tough if they must deal with a wall of denial, minimisation and defensiveness. And, it's important to stress that you don't have to. If you feel incredibly vulnerable (e.g. you are a breastfeeding mother or you've just been made redundant), you may not have the personal resources to raise the issue of power differences. It's your life, and it's okay if you want to leave things the way they are until you have more resources.

However, dealt with in the right way, structural power differences can be a place of tender and intimate sharing. When you have been treated unfairly or even cruelly by others in the past, having your experience of difference, marginalisation or oppression acknowledged and accepted by someone important to you can also be a place of great healing. Exercise 46 gives you a safe way to raise issues around a power imbalance.

EXERCISE 46: RAISING A POWER DIFFERENTIAL WITH YOUR PARTNER

Note: I've assumed here that if you want to broach the topic of a power differential, then you are the one with less power.

If you are aware that in some way your significant other has more influence over the relationship than you do, and you want to try to redress that imbalance, here is what I suggest you do. This is a blueprint for reclaiming your power.

1. As always with tricky conversations, pick a time when your partner will be available to you. You may need to schedule this. In that case, let them know it's about an aspect of your experience that is affecting your relationship, not something they are doing wrong.

2. Talk to them like they're your ally, not your oppressor. It is likely that they're oblivious to how it is for you. While this blindness is self-serving, it's best to begin by assuming it is *not* conscious or deliberate. (If you can't believe this and sincerely think that your partner is deliberately exploiting you, I would question why you would want to stay in that relationship.) Emphasise to your partner that you are not 'having a go' at them, but looking for their help with something that is not working for you.

3. Use a tone and manner that implies you know they are a decent person with good intentions towards you. Yes, it is unfair that you have to do this extra emotional work, but it is in your long-term interests to try to raise this issue in a way that will bring a concerned and caring response from your partner rather than a defensive one.

4. Begin by outlining that you will talk to them about something that is part of your personal, lived experience but is probably outside theirs. If your partner *does* have their own experiences of inequality, refer to that; it may be helpful to their understanding of what you are trying to say. Stress that their being on the high side of this power difference is not a bad thing about them. Indeed, you may celebrate that they haven't been through what you have, but note that it will limit their ability to understand the experience of inequality.

5. As you go along, check that your partner is still with you and is open to hearing more. If your significant other has shut down or is getting

defensive at any point, take a Time Out (Chapter 4). It's healthy and normal to take many conversations to work through this kind of topic.

6. Stress that you are discussing an issue much bigger and broader than your relationship. It is not your partner's fault that this imbalance exists, but it does exist and plays out in your relationship. Give one example, doing your best to avoid being blaming and instead emphasising your partner's good intentions. For example: 'I know my ADHD is difficult for you to live with, and I have been unreliable in the past. However, I have been really working on managing it better and being more reliable. I want to be more involved in planning and decision-making. I appreciate how you have had to carry a disproportionate burden of responsibility in the past, but I want to share that.'

7. See if your partner is willing to accept your experience as valid, even though it's very different to theirs. If they are, ask them what they make of it, how it makes them feel, and whether it gives them new insight into some of the ways you behave. Explicitly ask for the kind of empathic response you want. Make it as easy as possible for your partner to give you what you want.

8. If that goes well, then you can go on to give them the big picture of how the imbalance of power plays out in the relationship — now and historically. You may need to give them some more examples to make it vivid for them (or because you have remained silent about them for too long). If you are wise, you will try to show your partner how retaining greater power or control doesn't serve them in the long run — because you get resentful and withdraw or they get stressed because they carry too much responsibility, etc.

9. Ask for what you want that is different going forward. For example: 'What I'm hoping is that you will ask me how my family would approach things from fa'a Sāmoa', or 'It would mean a lot to me if you acknowledged how much work I have to do to keep our kids' social lives going.' Explore how difficult or easy it would be for them to be able to do this. It may be equally important to describe what *you* intend to do differently going forward. This is the more important part if you have tolerated an unfair situation. You are changing the rules, reclaiming your power. It's caring and courteous for you to inform your partner of this, so that they understand your intentions with the changes you make.

10. If your partner isn't willing to accept your experience, I suggest you point that out as politely as you can manage and leave the conversation there for now.
11. Think about whether anything in the way you put the issue to them might have made it hard for them to hear what you had to say.
12. Then revisit the issue within a week, stressing how important it is to have your partner accept your subjective experience and how you are looking for their help with a problem that is much bigger than this relationship. See if they have had any further thoughts about it. Maybe offer a different example and see if they can accept that experience.
13. If you persist like this and still can't get your partner to accept the notion of the structural power imbalance, then you can still try to change things. Warn them that you are going to behave differently going forward, and stress that this is something you are doing for yourself (treating yourself as worthy and important), not against them.

Treating yourself as worthwhile and important may involve developing new skills in assertion (e.g. deferring less, rocking the boat more, naming defensiveness and dismissal). Most people need help to learn these, from a book, online course or individual therapy. If your partner is aggressive or controlling, you need to be careful of your safety (see Chapter 19).

If there are good things in your relationship, by all means fight to try to keep it. However, never minimise the cost to yourself. If, in the end, you are too compromised, it may be necessary to tell your partner that this is a 'bottom line' issue. That is, if they aren't willing to change, it will mean the end of the relationship. Much couple therapy is begun by women who have woken up to their partner's male privilege but have got nowhere in getting their partner to acknowledge it, let alone change it. Those women rightly offer their partner the choice of couple therapy or separation.

The cost of male privilege

As previously mentioned, in hetero couples, men frequently don't believe that they have more power than their female partners. Indeed, aggression in men correlates strongly with them feeling powerless in the relationship.[1]

It's common for women to feel physically intimidated by, and not 100% physically safe with, male partners; but it is very rare to find the reverse (once in 30 years of practice). If you feel unsafe with your partner, you *must* listen to your intuition, act cautiously, and seek help. There are resources in Chapter 19 to help you if that's the case.

The power difference is not just about men's greater size or willingness to use physical aggression; it's also about how our society constructs masculinity.

Therapist Terry Real suggests that 'At its core, traditional masculinity rests on two pillars: the rejection of vulnerability and the delusion of dominance.'[2] Men's 'delusion of dominance' is reinforced by our current economic system. With the increasing emphasis on consumerism and material wealth, and the accompanying devaluing of unpaid work, earning potential is a greater source of power. Women are disadvantaged by lower pay rates, the impact of carrying and birthing children, and the assumption that they will do most of the childcare and other care work (e.g. for elderly relatives). While there are many good dads out there, far more men than women feel okay about having little or no involvement with their children once a relationship with the mother has ended.

Having a sense of entitlement goes along with being 'one-up'. Our society encourages men to unconsciously assume that they are entitled to deference and praise, power over others, and sexual fulfilment. Because this belief is society-wide, it is easy for men to be oblivious to it and for women to be unaware of their conformity to it. At least until a woman's resentment boils over at constantly deferring, propping up her partner's ego, being condescended to and talked over, and being cajoled for sex (or, worse, being attacked when her lack of sexual desire triggers his fears about his desirability or masculinity).

Paradoxically, an unearned sense of entitlement can place men in a disempowered position. If their partner goes along with it, it creates a falsity to the relationship that is likely to be undermined by the partner's eventual resentment. If and when their female partner refuses to accommodate their sense of entitlement, men tend to feel like they are failing, are being 'disrespected', and that they are unworthy men. When you couple this with how men often suppress and deny their dependency needs, their vulnerability to rejection and their hunger for acceptance, it starts looking worrisome for relationships.

In denying their inbuilt, human need for connection and support, men in hetero relationships often rely on their partner to attend to those needs, even as they are dismissive of them. As I discuss in Chapter 11, by being passive, and 'outsourcing' to women this essential part of their life, men end up feeling out of control; their emotional well-being is literally at the mercy of their female partners (while they still benefit from male privilege).

Over time it is increasingly difficult for those women to continue to show this mercy. Many become resentful at their double duty in caring for their own *and* their partner's emotional needs. If that doesn't do it, many women find they have had enough once there are children's needs in the mix. They lose respect for their male partner. His refusal to acknowledge and take responsibility for his inner world and its impact on their joint life comes to seem increasingly immature. As one mother of three tellingly put it: 'I do not need a fourth child on my hands.'

Many men are bewildered by being expected to be aware of and take responsibility for their own inner world. To them, having emotions that they should attend to beyond anger and lust (and maybe happiness if they get a 'win' at work or sport) is an alien notion. This may be changing; some younger, well-educated males have realised that there is more to life than 'doing' and 'winning'. However, in my experience the traditional male role expectations are still going strong in many places.

We are conditioning men to be afraid of their feelings

Traditional gender roles are not just maintained by men. Consider the woman who told her male partner 'I don't want a sissy' when he was being vulnerable. This made me reflect on how we train our boys to cut off from their feelings. In childhood, many boys will have the experience that if they show emotions, they are punished — 'punished' in the behavioural psychology sense of 'any change that occurs after a behaviour that reduces the likelihood that that behaviour will occur again'.

Sometimes the punishment is as subtle as the frown on a parent's face. Other times, the punishment is violent and brutal. As a client recently said: 'I grew up as a boy in New Zealand, and if you showed emotion, you got beaten up.' This was not because he went to one lousy school. He was from a middle-class family who moved around a bit because of his father's work — so this was his experience in four different schools in wealthy neighbourhoods.

Sometimes the punishment is confusing; a dad saying 'you'll be all right', intending to encourage but really invalidating (especially when, as happened to another client, the kid actually needed 10 stitches!).

The trouble with this approach to parenting boys is that kids are bad at *not* showing what they feel. So when we punish boys for showing feelings, they have to learn not to have them — or, more accurately, not allow themselves to *notice* they have them.

In Pavlov's famous 'conditioning' experiments, the dogs salivated at the sound of the bell because they had learned to associate the bell with food. Repetitive punishment means that many men associate having an emotion with punishment — so they understandably feel fear or anxiety the moment they experience an emotion. Having a feeling is an aversive experience for them. So when their partners criticise or shame them for being unresponsive or emotionless, they are inadvertently adding to the aversive conditioning.

To make matters worse, fear and anxiety are, of course, feelings. So what can the men do about their fear? If they can't avoid, suppress or deny it, they often project it outward as anger and blame. As I mentioned earlier, recent research (out of the University of Auckland's relationships lab)[3] stresses that men who behave aggressively usually feel disempowered.

It is easy to become frustrated with shut-down, unempathetic, entitled men. It's understandable to be appalled at the toll of emotional and physical harm they leave in their wake — especially if it's you or your children who have borne it. But although I am talking about a patriarchal structure that has a high cost on women and anyone else who doesn't fit masculine norms, I believe this way of operating doesn't serve most men well. While their hunger for dominance and avoidance of vulnerability gains many of them a certain level of power, I believe that the toll on men is also tremendous.

The cost to men is counted in loneliness, addiction, poor health, depression and suicide. In turning everything into a competition where vulnerability is a handicap and a weakness, men are denied the very thing that makes life worthwhile — love and meaningful connection with other human beings. So, as a man, I am confident that I am doing my brothers a service when I encourage them to question the benefits of male privilege.

Break the shackles of internalised oppression

When there is a traditional power imbalance in a hetero relationship, as a man working in this field I use my male privilege to challenge other men about theirs. They don't like it, but they can't dismiss me the way they might with a female therapist. From a position of caring and compassion, I confront them about the ways they wield power over others — things like:

- anger
- blame
- defensiveness, needing to be right
- stubbornness
- stonewalling, being unreachable.

I link these to their formative experiences, and highlight how these behaviours don't get them the kind of relationship they say they want.

However, I also have to challenge the women about how they collude with their oppression. As a man, I find this to be delicate work. It's tricky to avoid being *another* male telling this woman she's at fault. Yet if my female client is to become more powerful, she has to recognise how she has given away her power.

Usually, her focus will be on trying not to upset her partner. I point out that, in practice, this means letting his insecurities be the guiding force in their relationship. In my experience, challenging her partner effectively is 'good selfish'; it will lead to better outcomes for her *and* him.

When women are unthinkingly self-sacrificing and burden themselves with disproportionate amounts of mental and emotional labour, we must encourage them to consider whether this is who they want to be.

When capable women defer to their male partner's poor or impulsive judgement, they rob both of them of a chance for a better outcome.

In talking about this with Verity, she gave me a list of crucial ways in which she sees women in hetero relationships keep themselves disempowered:

- being over-emotive — talking about your feelings is not the same as being assertive
- ineffectual, repetitive criticism (a.k.a. 'nagging') — no backup or follow-through if their partner doesn't engage with their concern
- telling themself they are powerless: 'There's nothing I can do'
- getting resentful, keeping it to themself and then blowing up and behaving badly
- indirect, passive-aggressive comments (a.k.a. having a 'dig' at your partner)
- withholding sex and affection as a punishment.

In her classic book *The Dance of Anger*, Harriet Lerner talks about women traditionally having a choice of being 'nice' or 'bitchy'.[4] Her point is that neither of these is *assertive*.

The fact that 'feminism' has become a word that many women refuse to identify with (even though all it means is 'advocacy of equality of the sexes') highlights how fraught the issue of power in gender relations remains.

One way to think about a powerful, effective stance — an assertive position — is to identify what lies between 'bad selfishness' and 'bad selflessness'; the middle ground.

Finding the middle ground

Lots of relationships have one person whose behaviour is more self-centred and one whose behaviour is more self-sacrificing. Often we have learned to do this as self-protection in our formative years. This happens in same-sex relationships, too, but in hetero relationships male entitlement invites men to be (bad) selfish and women to be (bad) selfless.

It can be hard to understand the alternative — sometimes, we fear that we might become like our partner (whose behaviour hurts and frustrates us). We fear that if we're not self-sacrificing, then we're being selfish. Or, if we're not self-centred, we will be a doormat.

The table in Exercise 47 offers you a simple way to reflect on whether you are operating from a one-up or a one-down position, and suggests some attributes to aim for that define an assertive middle ground.

EXERCISE 47: WHAT IS YOUR PATTERN AROUND POWER?

The table on the following page aims to help you clarify what the **middle ground of having a solid sense of yourself** looks like across various aspects of relating. Scan down each column and work out which of the columns contains the best description of how you tend to operate in relationship with your significant other.

Do your best to be honest about how you typically operate. Not everyone will necessarily fit every attribute described here — but it gives a general idea. If you are a bit of a mixture, consider what circumstances pull you away from a 'grounded' response.

SELF-CENTRED (Entitled)	GROUNDED (Differentiated)	SELF-SACRIFICING (Oppressed)
unresponsive	empathic	overwhelmed
self-absorbed	connected	selfless
right	okay	wrong
important	good enough	unimportant
one-up	humble equal	one-down
focus on own hurts	intimate	anxiously other-focused
guarded	vulnerable	unregulated emotions
arrogant	humble	self-denigrating
aggressive	assertive	appeasing
pushing boundaries	well-boundaried	poor boundaries

Note that many 'middle ground' attributes map, not coincidentally, to the behaviours that support adult Secure Attachment (Chapter 7) and Differentiation (Chapter 6).

Love and colonialism

When one partner is part of the majority culture and the other is from a minority one, those experiences of power and freedom (or lack thereof) can also play out in their intimate relationship.

Here in Aotearoa and Australia, we are still struggling to come to terms with the impact of colonisation on Māori, First Nations and Pasifika people. Most of us in the dominant white majority are intensely uncomfortable hearing or thinking about their experiences. We want to believe that colonialism is a historical artifact rather than something that continues to play out today.

If your relationship is cross-cultural with someone from a minority culture (or vice versa), then it is likely to be important that you have a conversation about what that difference means to you.

If you come from a less-powerful culture and things have gone well for you, you may not want to reflect on this. Of course, that is your right; you may not see it as significant. But consider whether that's because you are used to underplaying its importance to protect those from the dominant culture, including your partner.

If you are from the dominant culture and have assumed that your partner's different background doesn't have implications for your relationship, I would encourage you to make sure you're right about that. There is a lot of shame, including multi-generational shame, sitting in the stories of the oppressed. It might not have happened to them, but it almost certainly happened to their parents and grandparents. Ask about that legacy, and signal your openness to hearing how it affects your partner's ability to be vulnerable, assertive or authentic.

HINE & ERIC

Hine and Eric were a pair of mid-thirties advertising executives with no children who came to see me because they felt that their relationship was going stale. Given the ticking of her biological clock, Hine, in particular, was wondering 'Is this it?' We were four sessions in, exploring the ways they were each defending themselves out of the relationship, when Hine made a passing comment about an incident at work where someone had commented that she had got a contract because she was Māori. Eric, who is Pākehā, said 'They're just jealous', and was ready to move on.

I interrupted, asking him if he knew how often that kind of thing happened and what it meant to Hine. My question was pretty exposing of Eric, as I had a fair idea from his manner and tone that he didn't. However, at that point I was more concerned with signalling to Hine that I thought this was an area worth exploring and that I was willing to take the lead in talking about it.

Eric looked suitably awkward, and defensively said to Hine, 'You've always said it's not a big deal.' Without any conscious intention, he was inviting her to keep minimising the impact of this kind of racism on her. Me gently pointing this out to him proved to be something of a turning point in the therapy and their relationship.

Doubly vulnerable as female and Māori in the cut-throat advertising world, Hine has had to be three times as good as any man to get the same rewards and respect. Not with Eric, who has always been proud and respectful of her ability and work ethic. But they met through work, and by that time she had already learned to 'never complain, just deliver'. In her experience, complaining about discrimination and unfairness led to being marginalised and rejected. She said she had learned by the time she was in high school that Pākehā and many Māori 'didn't want to know'. So she focused on success — getting in with the cool, arty crowd and excelling academically.

As I asked Hine about her experiences going right back to childhood, the energy in the room changed. As Hine let down the armour that allowed her to function in her professional and, indeed, much of her social life, she became much more vulnerable. To his credit, Eric showed appropriate concern and empathy even though the recounting of Hine's many minor and major experiences of racism and sexism was uncomfortable listening. Hine realised that, without intending to, she had hidden that part of herself from him because she was ashamed of it — seeing herself as weak if she allowed herself to feel hurt, anxious or sad because of racism or sexism.

As we spelled out the internal pressure that Hine felt to disprove stereotypes about Māori (e.g. she refused to sing or play the guitar even though, according to Eric, 'she has a beautiful voice'), I kept highlighting how much work she had been doing to protect Eric from recognising his privileged position as a white male. I stressed that I was not blaming Eric for this: 'You can't know what you aren't told or shown.'

This exploration of internalised racism, sexism and unquestioned privilege led to a deep conversation about power dynamics in their relationship. We realised that there were many places where Hine was protecting Eric — be it maintaining connections with his extended family or describing his emotional experience for him when he struggled to express himself.

Acknowledging how Hine had looked after him was humbling for Eric, but it also opened the door to him taking back a greater sense of control over his life. Hine, meanwhile, found that many of her frustrations were falling away. Eric's empathy and compassion made him particularly attractive to her. As she was able to be fully present in the relationship and talk openly about things that she had been barely conscious of, she found a renewed enthusiasm for the marriage.

The work didn't end there; other aspects of their dynamics needed addressing (Eric had very different reasons for being driven). However, those discussions went better because we put issues of power, race and privilege on the table early in the process.

Key points from Chapter 12

1. In many relationships, one person has more influence over how decisions get made. Sometimes in all circumstances, sometimes only in particular situations.

2. Often one person has more power simply because of structural differences like gender, age or ethnicity.

3. Relationships can work well across power differences if they are acknowledged and explored.

4. The person with more power often underestimates the nature and extent of their privilege and the impact it has on their partner.

5. Typically, it falls (unfairly) on the person with less power to raise the impact and costs of the power differential.

6. In our present mainstream culture, there are particular challenges for hetero men to recognise their privilege and for hetero women to assert themselves.

PART FOUR

THE MOST COMMON AREAS OF DIFFICULTY

My late mentor, Dr David Schnarch, used to say 'Couples only fight about five things.' In this section, each chapter explores one of those five issues that are frequently a source of difficulty in long-term committed relationships:

- How we set boundaries, especially about our involvement with others outside the relationship.
- Who gets to choose what we spend our time on, especially who has to do the dirty, repetitive, unglamorous work of running a household and family.
- Our sexual life — both what happens and what it means to each of us.
- How we relate to money, how it's managed and what that means.
- Working out how we want to parent, and surviving the inevitable challenges of raising a family.

Chapter 13
Boundaries

'Boundaries' is therapist jargon for 'what's okay for me and what's not okay for me'. Boundaries are a big part of how you know what matters to you, what works for you — and also the opposite: what is unimportant to you and what causes you pain and distress. They are vital to communicate to your partner.

Two kinds of boundaries in relationships

When we are in a committed relationship, there are two sets of boundaries to consider. Firstly, your personal boundaries — which are your sole responsibility and intrinsically linked to your sense of autonomy and safety in the world. Secondly, there are the boundaries we place around our relationship. Those boundaries are essential for the security and stability of the relationship. These need to work for both of us, and we are likely to start with quite different ideas about what we need and want regarding relationship boundaries.

Everyone needs a clear sense of their own boundaries, and it is totally within their rights to insist on their boundaries unilaterally . . . up to a point. You can be clear about what's okay or not for *you*, but you don't get to tell your partner what's okay for *them*. This especially applies to the boundaries around the relationship — who and what we will and won't allow in. They are a crucial part of the relationship contract, of the relationship structure that makes it defined and clear (and therefore reliable and trustworthy). In relationship, we must explore and negotiate these shared boundaries together.

Of course, if you are in a family or a polyamorous relationship, then as well as boundaries around dyads (two-person relationships), there will be boundaries around the whole family or polycule (a polyamorous relationship network), as well. I won't be getting into that, but the same general rules apply.

It ain't normal

One of the most significant differences that couples routinely have to deal with is our assumptions about what is 'normal' or 'expected' in a relationship. Typically, we assume that our expectations are 'normal' and that any deviation from or challenge to these expectations is 'wrong'. Until life shows us differently, we are oblivious to how personal, arbitrary and culturally specific our 'normal' is.

The most common way to find out that your partner has a different expectation about how to behave in a relationship is when they do something that you think is 'wrong'. For example, they tell their mother or best friend intimate details that you thought should be private between the two of you, or they spontaneously catch up with an ex-partner, or they don't come home when they said they would. You can tell that their boundary is different from yours because when you confront them about it, they are genuinely surprised and puzzled at your upset. The genuineness of their surprise is essential to knowing that this is a boundary issue, as some people do stuff that they *know* you don't like and then act surprised as a cover.

I want to stress that (a) these kinds of misunderstandings about boundaries are an ordinary and necessary part of the work of building a long-term relationship, and (b) no one person gets to dictate where the boundaries are in a relationship.

Boundaries need to be explored and negotiated

'Exploring' means talking about what a situation means to both of you, what you each see as the benefits of doing things your way, and listening to what the costs and impacts are for your partner. It often means trying to find a way to help your partner get what is important to them, in terms of boundaries, without compromising your beliefs and values.

From who we have sex with, to how we greet each other at the end of the day, to how we discipline a child or pet, a relationship offers hundreds of points of difference that need exploration and negotiation. Here are some of the typical areas that will require exploration in any relationship:

- how we talk to and treat each other
- the nature of our interactions with others: family, friends, professionals, strangers
- how we use money
- how we use our time
- how we parent
- how we manage our respective responsibilities and obligations
- how much do we plan and what for.

(I discuss many of these in other chapters, so I will not go into detail about them here.)

Learning to have these conversations in a non-judgemental and non-combative manner is key to making any relationship work. Usually, this means lots of exploration *before* negotiation. If you rush into trying to decide before exploring all the ramifications, your decision will likely need to be revised quickly.

Ideally, conversations about boundaries are an opportunity to show interest in how your partner works and what's important to them (and vice versa). Done right, they are a pathway to real intimacy and the building of trust and respect.

Boundaries and intimacy

Some people struggle to set boundaries with their loved ones — especially if they grew up in a family where others didn't respect boundaries. Often they end up feeling guilty or like they are being difficult for asserting what works for them. They don't know how to hold their own shape. In the eternal tension between autonomy and connection (see Chapter 2), they surrender too much autonomy to keep the connection, and become 'bad selfless' (see Chapter 10).

The trouble is, if we don't endure the temporary discomfort of asserting a boundary as soon as we realise there's a difference with our partner, we are likely to end up resentful. We may need to set our boundary in a more forceful and disruptive way (a.k.a. 'losing it') later on. Setting a boundary is choosing self-respect over self-sabotage. It's ensuring that we protect our limited resources of time and energy, so we don't end up burnt out.

Most importantly for relationships, boundary-setting is crucial to connecting authentically with your partner — allowing them to see and know you. Here's how it works: If I want intimacy, I have to risk the vulnerability of authenticity, of being really honest. Among other things, being authentic means saying what is and isn't okay for me. (Remember, that's what we therapist types mean when we talk about 'setting boundaries'.)

So why is it so difficult for many of us to set boundaries? Typically it is because (perhaps unconsciously) we don't believe we are good enough, important enough, loveable enough or safe enough to get what we want. As a result of those kinds of insecurities about our worth, we fear that if we set boundaries, we will be rejected or attacked.

That may have been true in the past, in your formative years or in past relationships. It may even have been a factor within your current relationship. But if you want to know and be known, to avoid burnout, and to have self-respect, then you will have to learn how to set boundaries with each other.

One key to setting boundaries effectively is to remember to talk about the positive side — what *is* okay for you, what you *do* want. The impact is vastly different when you focus on asking for what you *would* like (e.g. 'I like that you want to touch me. Would you just hold my hand or rub it more firmly, so I don't get ticklish?'), rather than what you don't want (e.g. 'Don't fiddle with my hand, it tickles me.').

If setting clean and clear boundaries is a new way of operating in the relationship, say something like this: 'I'm trying something new to help our relationship. Please bear with me if I don't do it very well.' This clearly signals your positive intention to your partner and gives them a warning that something new is coming their way.

Finally, expect that it will feel uncomfortable if you haven't been taking the risk of setting boundaries and being assertive. Still, that discomfort is minor and temporary compared with the lasting benefits of allowing yourself to be seen and known by your partner. That's what intimacy is all about.

Healthy boundaries are flexible

Some people have the opposite problem: they set boundaries readily but too rigidly. In the Attachment Grid in Chapter 7, I mentioned that people with an Avoidant Attachment style are inclined to have inflexible boundaries. Their catch-cry is 'My way or the highway!' They 'hold their own shape' like it's a matter of life and death. In their anxiety, they often slip into being 'bad selfish' without realising it. They willingly sacrifice connection to maintain their autonomy.

Having inflexible boundaries makes you hard to be around. You come across as uncaring of others, and self-centred. If you want your relationship to work, you have to tolerate the trade-off of reduced autonomy. Dr John Gottman's research has long stressed men accepting their partner's influence as a key to marital satisfaction. 'Statistically speaking, when a man is not willing to share power with his partner, there is an 81% chance that his marriage will self-destruct.'[1]

Because fear is often at the root of rigidity, it can take time for people with inflexible boundaries to learn to be more accommodating. If you're heavily invested in doing things your way and struggle to open up to other points of view, there is often an accompanying sense of doing things the 'right' way. But remember what I said about being 'right' at the start of Chapter 11. Typically that sense of 'right' comes from the way being heavily defended makes you feel safe. Big thick walls are a characteristic of fortresses, but also prisons. Being rigid keeps you isolated and alone.

If you want to be in an intimate relationship, then learning the value of 'give and take' is an important skill. It's part of learning to trust and not living so much under the unconscious influence of ancient fears.

DEANNA & CHARLIE

Charlie is a hard-working tradie who told me in our first session that he feels like he can 'never win' with his wife. Deanna is currently parenting their two pre-schoolers full-time and is frustrated by what she sees as his 'unreliability'.

Coming from a family dominated by her father's ugly and drunken bullying of her mother and with a history of sexual abuse by a neighbour (that she never told her parents about), Deanna has very understandable reasons for prioritising trust in her relationship. Her upbringing taught her 'I'm not safe' and 'I'm on my own'.

It's also understandable that Charlie keeps trying to appease her. Charlie's family all lived in fear of his strict, authoritarian mother: 'She could be brutal'. His father modelled keeping the peace by going along with whatever his wife wanted. Charlie's older brother copped the worst of their mother's wrath, and dealt with it by bullying Charlie. Charlie developed a nervous stutter and was teased at home and school — coming to believe 'I'm stupid' and 'I'm not wanted'.

Neither family talked about emotions or named what was really going on. When Deanna was distressed by witnessing the abuse from her dad to her mum, her mother would minimise, saying things like 'Don't worry, Daddy is just a bit upset.' Her mother's minimisation did nothing to help Deanna feel safe or make sense of what was going on. Charlie's family relied on cliches like 'keeping a stiff upper lip' and 'big boys don't cry' to signal clearly that his inner world was not of interest to his parents.

At the beginning of their relationship, Deanna loved Charlie's gentleness: 'He wasn't full of that macho bullshit like the other guys.' He found it hard to believe that someone as attractive and high-achieving as Deanna was interested in him. Charlie thought he was 'playing well out of my league' and, as a result, was happy to follow Deanna's lead.

Focused on getting his landscaping business going, Charlie was relieved to have a ready-made set of friends through Deanna. This arrangement worked fine when they were both working. Deanna felt secure between the high regard she was held in as an HR manager and the control she was able to exert over her and Charlie's social life.

With their mortgage well under control and Charlie's business taking off, they felt it was an excellent time to start a family. Both of them wanted the kids to have a stay-at-home mum. That fit nicely with the fact that the book-keeping (never his strong suit) was getting away on Charlie. Deanna was confident she could handle it alongside parenting.

In hindsight, this shift in responsibilities had several unintended consequences. The first was that, with Deanna becoming utterly dependent on someone else for the first time since she left home at 18, her anxiety went through the roof. The second was that, in becoming the sole breadwinner, Charlie felt an enormous pressure of responsibility, and his self-doubts began to ramp up in a way he hadn't felt since he was at school. The third was that there was a merging of their professional lives, with Deanna becoming actively involved in the business. Whereas previously they had each had the experience of going to work and being well regarded, now work was a source of tension between them.

Where Deanna had been praised in the past for her 'direct and clear' management style, this was now both triggering Charlie's insecurities about being stupid and evoking memories of his authoritarian mum. Meanwhile, as well as being financially dependent on Charlie, Deanna was also reliant on him delivering the information that allowed her to do her job. Much of her frustration centred on his unwillingness to insist that his employees keep up with their paperwork. With her HR and management background, Deanna kept trying to coach Charlie. He kept saying he would do what she suggested, but nothing changed.

As things got worse between them, Charlie kept coming home later and later. This was partly because of the financial pressure he felt, but, as he later admitted to me, there was also an element of avoiding Deanna. They called me following a fight they had when Deanna found out that Charlie 'having to work late tonight' actually involved him sitting and drinking beer with some of his employees.

When I first met them, Charlie had the most hangdog expression on his face. He was eager to accept all blame and was full of apologies for letting Deanna down. None of this appeased her: 'Because nothing changes!' Deanna's sense of self-righteousness was challenging to engage with, and, while I would never encourage someone to lie to their partner, I sympathised with Charlie's reluctance to face her wrath.

It didn't take long to work out that the shift in responsibilities had changed things in the relationship. Still, it was delicate work helping Deanna recognise that there was more in play here than 'Charlie's unreliability'. Making the connections between the lack of safety and control she experienced growing up, and her present situation, was painful for her.

It's always horrible when survivors of abuse realise that it still significantly influences their lives. Deanna was typical in wanting to 'leave that stuff behind me'. Having already done lots of therapy about it, she wanted to believe she had 'dealt with it'. My experience is that we process the impact of our upbringing in phases, and there is always more to learn and understand.

Part of the work was helping Deanna separate the individual boundary issue of 'personal safety' from the couple boundary issue of 'mutual expectations'. The former was something for her to work on for herself (and she went back to do some more individual therapy about this), while the latter was something to be discussed and negotiated **with** Charlie, not dictated to him.

Equally painful was helping Charlie recognise that by not backing himself and insisting on reasonable boundaries, he was letting down not only himself but also Deanna and the kids. In being too ready to believe that he was being 'stupid' and at fault, he left Deanna's anxieties to run unchecked. In refusing to engage with her by having the conflicts necessary to establish boundaries, both of them ended up feeling alone and unvalued.

Working out how to conflict and negotiate boundaries was difficult for them. Charlie was so reflexively deferential that it was genuinely difficult for him to think his own thoughts. He eventually found a way to be able to sit alone and write some ideas down that he could bring into discussions with Deanna. For her part, Deanna slowly realised that she was trying to manage her anxiety by controlling her environment (which mostly meant Charlie and the kids). She was smart enough to see that this would also lead to difficulties with her daughters in the future if she didn't learn to be more accepting of others' boundaries.

The issue of boundaries and responsibilities in the workplace was particularly tricky, as it is for many couples who work together in a family business. It took some effort and persistence for Charlie to stop responding to Deanna like a punishing mother, and a similar amount of work for her to stop treating him like he was deliberately trying to make her life difficult. However, once those projections were on the table, they could work out the reasonable expectations and boundaries of their respective roles. This led to Charlie being more assertive in setting boundaries with his staff, which, unsurprisingly, led to the business doing even better, relieving some of the financial anxiety he felt.

As Deanna worked out how much she had been operating in emotional isolation rather than as a team, she felt a great sense of relief. She realised that the 'unreliability' she feared in Charlie was largely a self-fulfilling prophecy driven by her insecurities. As Charlie stepped up, she started to believe again that they were a team and she didn't have to do it alone.

Key points from Chapter 13

1. Knowing what's okay and what's not okay for you is an integral part of having a healthy sense of yourself.
2. You often learn that there's a boundary issue by your partner innocently doing something you think is 'wrong'.
3. It's up to you to explain and assert your boundaries — don't expect your partner to know them automatically. Your 'normal' is not their 'normal'.
4. Your personal boundaries are yours to set, but where they impact directly on your partner and your relationship, they need to be explored and negotiated.
5. Boundaries are an essential part of intimacy — of how you come to know each other well.
6. Avoiding setting boundaries sets you up for resentment and mistreatment.
7. Rigid boundaries are often driven by fear and set you up for isolation and loneliness.

Chapter 14
What we spend our time on

Time is the great equaliser — we all have the same number of hours in the day. Your neighbour may have ten times the material assets you do, but the sun rises and sets at the same time for both of you.

Having a choice about what you spend your time on is the hallmark of affluence. By that measure, in our society, most people are affluent. While we have increasing numbers of people in poverty and whose choices are tightly circumscribed by the necessities of survival, that is not the case for the majority. Additionally, some comparatively wealthy people (such as sharemilkers or owners of start-up companies) have little choice in the day-to-day demands of their lifestyle — but in most cases, it's a lifestyle they have chosen.

Many of us don't 'feel' like we have much choice. We have structured our lives with many responsibilities that place enormous and competing demands on our time and energy. We feel trapped by our obligations and out of control over how we use our time — 'I never have enough time', 'I'm always behind', 'I can never get enough done', or 'Whatever I do, it's never enough'.

We can end up in a place where carving out space to have 'quality time' with our significant other becomes just one more chore to be ticked off the list. Isn't that sexy? Doesn't that make our partner feel desired and cherished!?

Prioritise time for your relationship

How we choose to use our time is the clearest indicator of what's important to us. You may have powerful feelings about your significant other, but if you don't put time into your relationship with them, it is hard to argue that they are your priority. You may have little choice about prioritising other things if you have to work three jobs to keep food on the table and a roof overhead. However, if you are not in a survival situation, how you use your time is a matter of choice.

Although people increasingly live in different kinds of arrangements — on their own, sole-parenting, flatting, with extended family, in a group, in retirement villages, etc. — most people still aspire to a partnership, especially if they intend to have children.

This partnership is usually the lynchpin, the central piece around which they organise their lives romantically and sexually, but also financially, socially and pragmatically. If you have a business that depends on one machine, you would be wise to take good care of the maintenance of that device so the whole business doesn't grind to a halt when it breaks down.

Yet I often see couples who have built their lives around their partnership but are putting no time or energy into caring for it. There are so many demands on your time: paid and unpaid work, parenting and caring for elderly parents, hobbies, sports, spirituality, social and community commitments, health needs, and time for yourself. The busier and more demanding your life is, the *more* vital it is that you carve out time for connecting with your partner in ways that nourish you and your relationship — not just being close, but also finding time for intimacy and connecting vulnerably. That may include sexually, but also things like sharing hopes and dreams and sorting out disagreements and misunderstandings.

How do you use 'couple time'?

If you're a busy person and something is important to you, it should be in your diary. Many people do have a notion that they need 'couple time', but often there is confusion about its purpose.

There are three broad categories of interaction that couples need to put time into:

1. PRAGMATICS AND LOGISTICS

Coordinating the functioning of the household and family. Matching up schedules. Dividing up the tasks that need doing, and making sure you both know who is doing what and when. Attending to the vital mundanities of your shared life.

Although they are essential, these kinds of interactions are not very exciting or rewarding. If your relationship has dwindled to the point where this is all you do together, you're in serious trouble.

2. CLOSENESS

Enjoying being in a relationship — relaxing together, doing mutually enjoyable activities, focusing on the positives. Closeness is usually what people are looking for when they suggest a 'date night'. Friendly, comfortable, easy sex usually fits under this category.

As discussed previously, close time means avoiding difficult topics and conflicts and keeping things reasonably superficial and comfortable. In Chapter 1, I described closeness as the payoff or reward for doing all the work involved in being in a long-term, intimate relationship. Closeness time only works if you have been doing some of the hard work of intimacy — otherwise, the closeness becomes increasingly tense and, eventually, impossible to achieve.

3. INTIMACY

Having the vulnerable and often difficult conversations and interactions that allow you to connect on a deep level. It needs to include dealing with differences (i.e. healthy conflict) as well as talking about aspirations, hopes and dreams, fears, doubts and insecurities. It also covers the kind of sex where you reveal yourself, make yourself vulnerable by asking for and showing what you are truly excited by, what interests you but makes you anxious, etc.

Remember, intimacy is not always comfortable, but when done productively it makes closeness feel easy and authentic.

The next exercise will help you work out where your time goes now, and where you might want it to go in the future.

EXERCISE 48: WHERE DOES YOUR TIME GO?

Spend at least two weeks recording how much couple time you spend on each of the following three categories: (1) Pragmatics and logistics; (2) Closeness; (3) Intimacy. If your partner is willing, get them to do the same. At the end, compare your perceptions of your time together using the questions below. If your partner isn't available to do this exercise, you can still answer the last four questions for yourself.

1. How different are our perceptions?
2. If they are different, how do we account for that difference? (Don't fight about whose perception is more accurate; instead, explore each other's reality.)
3. Does the proportion of time you spent on each category feel right?
4. If not, what would you like to spend more time on?
5. Is there a category you want to spend less time on?
6. What changes do you need to make to get the balance more how you want it?

Time use, power and boundaries

If you accept that time is a more precious resource than money, then the extent to which you feel in charge of how you use your time versus how much you feel dictated to by your partner's choices is at the heart of the power division in your relationship.

If you are in a relationship with someone who is dictatorial and tells you what you can and can't do with your time, then this power will be evident.

More common is a partner who doesn't act in partnership, who makes choices about their life that have significant consequences for yours without consulting you. As per Chapter 13, they set boundaries unilaterally, without discussion and negotiation. For example, they take on extra responsibilities at work, working longer hours and being more preoccupied with work, meaning they have less time to do chores at home and are less attentive to the kids. Or they unilaterally decide to enrol the children in an activity requiring one parent to drive them to and fro and sit there for an hour twice a week.

Typically the person who makes those unilateral decisions will have justified them by saying 'It's my career' or 'I'm the one who is in touch with what the kids need'. If you're in that position, you are fighting for your sense of autonomy or independence. As I discussed in Chapter 2, there is no question that autonomy is important — we are biologically hard-wired to have a self and a sense of control over our lives (although the importance we give to this varies widely across cultures). The problem is that it's not the only thing that's important. We are also hard-wired to connect with others, to form Attachment relationships. We have dependency needs as well as the need for autonomy. Being in a partnership involves a trade-off between these two. In an equal relationship, we have to **negotiate** partnership boundaries.

In Western society, at the moment, there is a strong emphasis on autonomy. The neo-liberal, consumerist culture we live in is based on individualism taken to quite an extreme. Of course, in Aotearoa and Australia there are many other cultures that balance things differently. Still, the importance of individual freedoms and rights predominates in public discussion. Accompanying this is a minimisation and dismissal of the obligations of the social contract (like paying taxes) that provides the stable society which allows people to enjoy those freedoms and exercise those rights.

Devaluing of the work needed to maintain connection also plays out at the individual level. The romantic myth tells us that if we find 'the right one', then everything will be easy. As I said in Chapter 13, the reality is that everything will require discussion, exploration and negotiation.

If you feel like your partner is controlling you, they might be. I have worked with many people who exert a lot of control over their partner's behaviour and choices, usually because of anxiety. Anxious people often try to control their environment rather than themselves. However, a controlling partner is not the only reason people end up *feeling* controlled. Another possibility is that you haven't accepted the reality that to get the benefits of partnership, you have to surrender some autonomy. This is just as true in business partnerships as in romantic ones. The difference is that when people set up a business partnership, they get a lawyer to draw up a very thick document that sets out how they divide responsibilities, resolve disputes, etc.

In couples where *both* people report 'being controlled' by their partner, I frequently find that neither is especially controlling in their behaviour. In those cases, 'feeling controlled' is more about not being able to handle the inevitable anxiety that arises when they run into differences with their partner (a.k.a. being Symbiotic; see

Chapters 2 and 3). If you lack the Differentiation skills to assert your autonomy while still remaining connected, you will feel controlled by your partner when they express an opinion or desire that is different from yours.

This has vast implications for how you get to use your time. If you are 'too scared' or 'can't be bothered' to assert yourself, you are giving your partner free choice about how they use their time, and you will get to do everything they don't want to do.

The traditional twentieth-century view of gender roles in Western society (which still informs the expectations of many men) took this for granted in hetero couples. Men sat at the top of the hierarchy due to their god-given superiority, decided what was important to them, and expected women to do the rest. This has left a legacy of women doing more unpaid labour and working longer hours.

Those dynamics seem to be present again in couples where the male is the primary earner. In a mirror image of our national accounts system, unpaid labour 'counts for nothing'[1] and is often devalued by *both* adults in the partnership. This is not simply a gender issue — the same dynamic occurs when the woman is the primary earner in a hetero couple or in a same-sex couple.

This privileging of paid work has enormous implications for the allocation of time. Many people have confessed to me that they stay at work to avoid responsibilities at home, knowing that their partner will pick up the slack.

Sometimes there *isn't* enough time

I routinely tell parents with pre-school-age children that the reality of this life stage is that there is never enough time or energy to go around. Unless you are a negligent parent, your children will consume an inordinate amount of your time. There will not be enough time for you to properly care for yourself and your relationship.

The same can be said for people starting up a new company, caring for sick relatives, farming animals, and doing jobs requiring crisis response — think of the demands on nurses and doctors on the frontline of our pandemic response for the past few years. (Thank you and your families for your service.)

In those circumstances, it's vital that you as a couple have an ongoing conversation about what your priorities are, and arrive at some agreement about what you are willing to let go of, do without, and where you might compromise your standards.

You might even choose to do no work on the relationship for a time. To accept things the way they are for the next six months or 'until I finish this contract', 'until I come off night shift', or 'until Mum finally passes'. That's fine if you *both* agree to this priority. Making a strategic choice about using your time and energy is very different from just neglecting the relationship.

How to discuss time

If you enter into a conversation about 'who's doing what', full of your own sense of overwhelm, inadequacy and pressure, it will be hard for you to hear how it is for your partner. There is a real danger of it becoming a competition for the 'who has the hardest life' prize — a competition that always ends badly.

As with any exploration of difference, you *must* exercise your Differentiation skills. Self-soothing your distress (Chapter 5), acknowledging the subjectivity of your experience and being open to hearing how it is for your partner (Chapters 10 and 11), owning your contribution to making things difficult (Chapter 8), etc.

It's also a place where you must be willing to examine your values and your assumptions. Are you taking for granted your partner's contribution? If they are the primary earner, do you talk about spending money (on holidays, kids' hobbies, renovations, etc.) without caring for the pressure they feel to earn the money to pay for it all? If you are the primary earner, are you reliable in your assigned roles in the non-paid part of your partnership? Have you looked at whether the division of labour is really fair?

If you are in paid employment, are money and financial security always the most important thing in your value set? How much of your investment in your paid roles is about 'caring for the family', and how much is about your sense of self, feeling worthwhile because you are doing the kind of role that our society says is valuable — because it involves money?

If you both feel overloaded, you need to be open to giving things up. The notion that you can 'have it all' is very seductive, but neither realistic nor kind to yourself. If you have too much on your plate, you need to take something off. It can be tough to see how to do that. Dropping your standards or letting go of something you thought essential is difficult. I have worked with many people who are unhappy but have an immaculately tidy home or are forging a stellar career. Usually, their partners and children are unhappy, too.

You need to do some brutal accounting that looks at *all* the costs — including the emotional toll on you and your loved ones, and the 'opportunity cost' of what else you could be doing with that time — and decide whether you can afford to do everything.

I vividly remember having a clear goal about how much I needed to earn in a month to pay off the mortgage by a specific date. The trouble was that working that hard made me a grumpy dad. Being so stressed by work, I had little emotional resilience left over to be patient with my children. That also meant I ended up fighting with Verity, who was, rightly, trying to protect our children. It took a while, and some loving challenge from my partner, before I realised that any potential future benefit of being mortgage-free sooner was not worth the present-day emotional cost to my family. So I dropped my income, became a better father, and have never regretted the extra time paying off the mortgage.

You may find it difficult to consider doing less because your sense of self is bound up with notions of success and achievement. This is typically what someone is actually talking about when they say with pride that they are 'driven' in their work. That is so commonly encouraged in our society as to be seen as 'normal' — yet it is anything but healthy.

Fairness in the division of domestic labour

In Eve Rodsky's book *Fair Play*,[2] she applies some business management principles to running a household and highlights that 'taking responsibility' for a task means taking responsibility for its conception, planning *and* execution.

Think about the task of supporting a child's sporting activity. In a traditional (sexist) family, the dad will think of this as turning up for the kid's game. Yet, for the mum, it means:

- helping your kid choose what sport
- with what club
- paying the fees
- knowing which of their friends are involved
- making sure they have the right kit
- that it's clean on the day
- that you know where you are on the team carpool and oranges roster
- making sure you are doing your bit for the club and the team
- thinking through the implications of that commitment for other obligations (other kids' sports, supporting whānau, getting enough time for your own recreation, etc.).

In hetero couples, the tradition has been for this mental and emotional work to default to the women — and for it not to have been recognised, let alone valued, by the men. Rightly, this is no longer acceptable to many women, and it is something that men need to get their heads around.

One good thing that has come out of the Covid-19 lockdowns for many couples is that some people who were then doing paid work at home have had greater insight into how demanding the non-paid work is. However, it's worrying if it took you being there all day to appreciate just how hard your partner is working. Think about why you were oblivious to this before. Did you show interest and care about their daily life? If they had tried to tell you and you weren't buying it, how come you weren't willing to take their word for it? Often, it's because the implication is that you are not pulling your weight, and no one likes to recognise that about themselves.

If you want your relationship to be one of respect and trust, it has to be **fair**. You need to get thoughtful and organised about who is doing what — recognising *all* the work that goes into your way of life, not just the obvious things.

Exercise 49 will help you start the process of making things fair.

EXERCISE 49: AGREEING ON FIRST PRINCIPLES

It doesn't matter how you organise the division of labour, so long as you *both* believe that it is fair and equitable. I suggest that you and your partner try to establish some initial principles to guide your thinking. Have a look at the list below. Discuss it together — do you agree with them all? If you disagree, how would you change things? What else would you add to make sure that your relationship is fair?

- Our time is equally valuable — we both have the same number of hours in a week.
- We need to decide what our priorities are as a team. (Meaning you need to *persuade* your partner, not act unilaterally if you disagree with their priorities.)
- Our decisions about our priorities create obligations that need to be shared out fairly.
- The person who is doing the job is the only one with access to all the information about how much time and energy it takes.

What's your approach?

When I look at the responsibilities we all have in life, there seems to be two general approaches. Some of us focus on 'what can I get away with?' while others go for 'what can I do?'. These have very different implications for how you live your life and how you operate in relationship.

1. WHAT CAN I GET AWAY WITH?

The less-bad version is the self-serving 'how little can I get away with?' It works like this: Like a truculent adolescent, I approach my commitments trying to work out how little I can do to avoid failure, punishment or approbation. This involves not investing in my responsibilities. Often there is an element of deliberately not trying for fear of failing. I usually justify this approach by seeing 'what I need to do' as a demand placed on me by someone else, rather than a responsibility that belongs to me because of my choices.

The more sinister version is 'what kind of harm and mayhem can I get away with? How much can I make others pay for my pain (typically while still plausibly denying that I am doing any such thing)?' This is the dark side that we practise, most commonly, on our families and loved ones.

Often people struggle to consciously see this in themselves and others because their family (or school or church) was so expert at denying the reality of what was happening that there is a large blind spot about this kind of behaviour. Examples of such behaviour are the parent who is shaming and then implies there's something wrong with the child when they show their hurt: 'Toughen up, ya little pussy', or the cruelly belittling teacher who then tells the parents that their child is 'overly anxious'.

If your environment featured a lot of 'getting away with it', you might not recognise it as bad; it seems ordinary and unremarkable whether you are being taken advantage of or are taking advantage of others. The tragedy is that every time you work someone over or accept being misused, you increase your disconnection and pain, making it more likely that you will make others suffer in the future.

2. WHAT CAN I DO?

This very different question reflects a very different attitude and orientation towards being in relationship. It also comes in two forms. At the simplest level, it means: I will proactively engage with my responsibilities, working out what needs doing in order to do them well, and doing that. Not because someone told me to or because I will look bad if I don't, but because I know I am defined by my choices and behaviour (*not* by my intentions or feelings), and I want to live a life of integrity and self-respect.

However, the joy of embracing the notion of 'what can I do?' is not simply the satisfaction of living up to my responsibilities, but also exploring my capacities. Approached wholeheartedly, it means investing fully in the things I have chosen for my life and discovering 'what am I capable of?' Not just working hard, but taking risks and learning new things about myself and the world. It is the continuous work of becoming more fully who I am and who I want to be.

Use Exercise 50 to help you figure out which approach you currently follow.

EXERCISE 50: EXPLORING YOUR APPROACH

Get your partner to read this section, too, then discuss which attitude you think is dominant for each of you.

If your perception is different from your partner's, make sure that you raise and explore that between you. Remember, if you want change, try to talk about what you *do* want more than what you don't.

What women can learn from men about time

Just as many men in hetero couples need to learn from their female partners about all the mental and emotional labour that goes into maintaining a home and family, women can likewise learn from men about healthy entitlement and self-care. On average, men find it much easier to prioritise the things they *want* to do alongside what they *have* to do. Ask anyone in a relationship with a surfer, a golfer or a gamer.

Some of those men are being 'bad selfish' (see Chapter 10), putting their own desires first without caring about the impact on others. However, other men are being 'good selfish' — prioritising their self-care and ability to live a life worth living in prudent and wise ways. In those cases, it is their partner's inability to care for themselves in a similar way that makes them resentful, not that the man is doing something wrong.

In our society, it seems increasingly hard for parents (and other caregivers) to learn to care for themselves as well as they do for their children. Yet children benefit so much from having happy, relaxed, satisfied caregivers. Those benefits are far more significant than a child having every desire fulfilled, or every ability extended. Your children are going to learn most from what you model. If you are modelling flogging yourself to death trying to 'get it right' or 'have it all', then that is what they will believe is normal, whereas if you are modelling a healthy balance with good boundaries and self-care, *that* will become their default setting.

Even when a couple doesn't have children, many women still reflexively play second fiddle to the desires and preferences of their partners. Then they wonder why they feel unseen and unappreciated in their relationship. Remember, being open and assertive about what's important to you (your boundaries – see Chapter 13) is crucial to being seen and known in a relationship. Treating yourself as important is the key to having your partner treat you that way.

I often hear women say 'I *told* him it was important to me', but when I enquire closely, it's something they have dropped in a conversation and never followed through on. Many women don't have the sense of entitlement they need to keep on about important things, to get angry soon enough to bring it to their partner's attention before it's too late.

For some of us, creating fairness in how we use our time is about learning to value our own time; for others, it's about learning to show love by valuing our partner's time. But for all of us, how we occupy the limited number of hours we have each week is the biggest determining factor in the shape of our life. Make sure you spend those hours in a way that has integrity for you and fits your values and priorities. There are no second chances at this life.

NIKKI & BEVAN

*Nikki thought that things would change when she returned to work after their youngest began school. Bevan had agreed he would have to do more, but she found herself doing the vast majority of the domestic labour **and** all of the mental work of running the family and caring for the kids.*

*Her attempts to raise the inequality with Bevan were met with a recitation of the things he **did** do, and then comparisons with others in his profession (law) who did none of them. In his mind, he was way better than most men he knew and she was unrealistic in her expectations. His work days were gruelling, and he felt it was unfair of Nikki to enjoy the lifestyle his work afforded them and then complain about the amount of time and energy he put into achieving it. He was particularly bitter about her insistence that the girls go to the best private schools — he and his brothers had thrived at a state-funded grammar school.*

Nikki was a valued financial controller at the local council, and they had bent their HR policy to offer her a 0.6 part-time contract when Harriet went to school. Nikki enjoyed her work and was grateful to reconnect with her professional identity and adult company. However, she felt enormous pressure to deliver, and struggled to meet her own expectations because she was so tired and fragmented.

Things reached a crisis when Harriet developed asthma which proved challenging to control and resulted in her missing quite a bit of school. Nikki inevitably fell behind at work and became increasingly anxious and distressed at not meeting her own high standards, let alone having to deal with queries and complaints from her colleagues.

Things came to a head when Bevan failed to come home early and take over the kids as arranged so that Nikki could meet an important work deadline. Enraged by his unapologetic defensiveness when he finally did arrive, Nikki physically attacked Bevan in front of their children. Of course, Nikki acting this way only made Bevan feel more justified in viewing her as unreasonable.

It was hard to get Bevan to shift from this view. Coming from a very high-performing family, he invested hugely in his professional standing and was oblivious to the powerful insecurities that drove his need for 'success'. Being 'driven' was an aspirational norm in his world, and it required quite a head-shift for him to accept that there might be a downside to this way of being.

Fortunately, he was also invested strongly in his relationship with Nikki. He was honest and brave enough to recognise that if his second wife was offering the same complaints as his first wife, maybe there was something to what they were saying.

For her part, Nikki had frightened herself badly with her assault on Bevan. Although it triggered intense shame, it also shocked her into accepting that her situation was unworkable and something had to give. She realised that she had built up a massive store of resentment against Bevan and was modelling 'bad selflessness' to her daughters.

She identified that her guilt at 'causing' the break-up of Bevan's first marriage (their relationship had begun as an affair) meant that she had been tying herself in knots trying to prove she was worth it. This was on top of already struggling with her self-worth from growing up as an 'ugly, geeky, friendless' girl.

The principle of everyone's time being of equal value was a keystone for change in their relationship. Its evident and logical fairness appealed to their very 'rational' minds. As Nikki began to talk vulnerably (rather than accusingly) about how overwhelmed she felt by all she had on her plate, Bevan started to really listen rather than be defensive.

Additionally, because of his strained relationship with his children from his first marriage, Bevan was open to re-evaluating the path he was on with his kids from this marriage.

Once they were both able to identify and manage their insecurities better, they had intimate conversations about what they wanted out of life. They realised that they had unthinkingly bought into some very shallow definitions of 'success' and how to achieve it. Nikki recognised that her obsession with private school education for her girls was an attempt to compensate for her feelings of inadequacy around their rich, privately educated friends.

Bevan started to see that he was still in an unhealthy competition with his siblings that he could never 'win', no matter how many courtroom coups he pulled off. Both of them recognised that the level of wealth they sought to attain before retirement was unnecessary, and the cost to them and their kids (in terms of stress, poor health, and missed opportunities for family time) was way too high.

It wasn't easy for Bevan to change the way he worked. He had to re-train his workplace and clients about his new boundaries. There was pushback from some partners, but others were supportive. For her part, Nikki decided that she would challenge herself by giving up paid employment for the time being; with their revised financial goals, they didn't need the money. She wanted to learn to value herself without having a professional identity to lean on.

Ironically, this meant she ended up doing **more** of the domestic labour. But it was different: firstly, she no longer felt taken for granted by Bevan; secondly, she knew that she could now rely on him to do the things he said he would; and thirdly, it felt like they were working as a team in dealing with **all** the responsibilities of the family.

Key points from Chapter 14

1. For many of us, our relationship with our partner is the lynchpin of our life, and we must put time and energy into maintaining it.
2. We need to put time into closeness and intimacy, not just the pragmatics of life.

3. We must understand our limitations, accept that we can't have it all and be willing to let go of things for which we don't have the resources.
4. Time use is a crucial boundary issue and often where we see the power dynamics of the relationship most clearly. Fairness is vital, but is often lacking in traditional hetero relationships.
5. Unpaid labour, including mental labour, needs to be counted accurately — everyone's time is of equal value.
6. Many hetero women need to learn to be 'good selfish' just as much as their male partners need to learn how to be 'good selfless'.

Chapter 15
Sex, passion, eroticism and intimacy

Although there is a lot of depiction of sex online, in movies and on TV, and in our books and social media, most people struggle to talk about sex straightforwardly. Indeed, the word is being replaced in the media with the more genteel 'intimacy' — which is a terrible shame, in my opinion. Using 'intimacy' when you mean 'sex' perpetuates very unhelpful myths about sex and intimacy (as does saying 'sex' when you mean penis-in-vagina intercourse). If you want to have an intimate sex life, you must appreciate that your sexual relationship is a mirror of the relationship as whole. What's happening around boundaries, power, parenting or finances will all have an impact on how you both show up sexually.

Earlier in the book, I gave a rough working definition of intimacy as 'sharing yourself, warts and all', a.k.a. 'making yourself vulnerable'. I have repeatedly stressed that 'into-me-see' is often uncomfortable. It depends on challenging, revealing, effortful and even scary interactions. I also said: 'Intimacy needs to include learning about yourself, growing and struggling with the less-than-ideal aspects of yourself *and* sharing that with your partner.'

Sex *can* be like that, but it often isn't, especially in long-term relationships. People who have been together for a long time tend to be the experts in having functional sex (in that both people experience pleasure, even orgasm) that is anything but intimate. Remember that the more important your partner is to you, the scarier it is for you to risk their disapproval by letting them 'into-me-see'.

So, in our long-term relationships, many of us end up avoiding any kind of sex that makes our partner feel vulnerable (e.g. being tender, soft and gentle), and also avoid any kind of sex that makes us feel vulnerable (e.g. being carnal, rough and uninhibited). That leaves us a window of comfort in which we can operate safely. Frequently, this results in sex that follows a predictable path that was fun — maybe even quite passionate — when we first utilised it, but after five, 10 or 20 years, is stale and passionless.

One of the arguments against monogamy is that humans (like all primates) are hard-wired to seek novelty. This theory goes that having sex with the same person will inevitably become boring. However, that only holds true if both people in the relationship avoid risk and refuse to grow and change. I fully accept that monogamy is not for everyone. I am delighted that it is now socially acceptable to explore other ways of organising your sexual and romantic life. However, it's important to remember that monogamy *does* work for many people and that changing partners is not the only way to introduce novelty. Changing yourselves does the same thing — with much less admin than serial monogamy or consensual non-monogamy.

A quote from musician Joni Mitchell makes a case for exploring the variety of one partner while acknowledging the challenges it entails.

I recently read an article in Esquire *magazine called 'The End of Sex,' that said something that struck me as very true. It said: 'If you want endless repetition, see a lot of different people. If you want infinite variety, stay with one.' What happens when you date is you run all your best moves and tell all your best stories — and in a way, that routine is a method for falling in love with yourself over and over.*

You can't do that with a longtime mate because he knows all that old material. With a long relationship, things die then are rekindled, and that shared process of rebirth deepens the love. It's hard work, though, and a lot of people run at the first sign of trouble.[1]

In her book *Mating in Captivity*,[2] Esther Perel talks eloquently about the importance of seeing your partner afresh and as separate from you (i.e. Differentiating from them) in maintaining the erotic energy in a relationship.

With the ageing of the baby boomer generation, there has been a lot of research into sex after 50. One astounding finding, across many studies, is that many older people are reporting good-quality sex and even 'the best sex of our lives'[3] well into their eighties. Clearly, this is not about being athletic. It's about knowing yourself, being content with who you are and who you are with, accepting your body as it is, and, most crucially, focusing on what's going on in your head, not your groin.

Understanding your erotic template and exploring the edges of it is a never-ending journey as you come to understand yourself better and better.

Intimacy requires tolerating vulnerability

Many of us are frustrated at our partner's unwillingness to open up sexually, without realising that we are so shut off verbally that what we are seeking is unreasonable and impractical. Equally, many of us are frustrated at our partner's unwillingness to open up verbally, without realising that we are so shut off physically that what we are seeking is also unreasonable and impractical.

How good are you at letting your partner know what's *really* going on with you, particularly when things aren't so good between you? Do you avoid discussing your doubts and dreams, frustrations and fears — treating your partner's interest in your inner life as a threat or criticism? Or do you avoid acknowledging your sensuality, eroticism and sexuality, treating your partner's interest in you as a threat or demand?

This is what's happening here: When I lock away my insides and avoid physical or verbal vulnerability, I become hard for my partner to read, and I am likely to come across as 'unfeeling', indifferent or hostile. This makes it unsafe for my partner to be open with me because they can't be sure how I feel, what I think or what's coming next. It is stupid to *freely* give yourself to someone who might be about to hurt you. My inability to be generous with myself invites my partner to be miserly with themself.

Looking at this through the Attachment lens (see Chapter 7), if you want intimate, passionate sex in a long-term relationship, you need to create and maintain a Secure Attachment bond. At the same time, if you're going to strengthen your Attachment and your relationship to feel safe and secure, the chemical bonding that occurs during sex, plus the limbic brain forming associations of pleasure and fun with your partner, are profound ways to achieve this.

Do you know whether you come across to your partner as an open or a guarded person in either verbal or physical terms? Do you know if your partner feels like they can 'read' you? If they can't, think about where you learned to protect yourself this way.

Lots of us have had formative experiences where we learned that it was unsafe to be open. If we had opened up, others would have used our vulnerability to hurt us. They might have laughed at, bullied, ignored, shamed, manipulated or abused us (physically, verbally or sexually). This doesn't have to be dramatic. Many of us who had nothing traumatic in our childhood nevertheless had parents who felt it was their job to 'toughen up' their children, or were just uncomfortable with expressed emotion or acknowledging sexuality. Before we could talk, we had learned to keep our feelings (especially ones perceived by our parents as 'negative') to ourselves. As a result, we did the smart thing and shut vulnerable parts of ourselves away. Protecting yourself in a disapproving, hostile, neglecting or invasive (e.g. smothering) environment is a good idea.

So, if you are like many people, you have learned that you should *never* leave yourself vulnerable. To be vulnerable is inevitably a bad thing — why would you want to leave yourself open to being hurt?

I have bad news for you. *Your partner can't really know you without you making yourself vulnerable.* Most of us want to be in a relationship where we are loved and desired for who we *truly* are. To get that kind of love, you must let yourself be known, especially your insides — the places where you can be easily hurt. That is to become vulnerable. Although most of us try to, you can't experience being open to loving and being loved without taking that risk.

How many men ruin sex for themselves

While this section does not apply to all men, I see it often enough, even in younger men, that I think the generalisation is worth making.

In a traditional upbringing, men are allowed to show two emotions — anger and lust. In the old days, the All Blacks weren't allowed to look happy even if they scored a try against South Africa. Any other display of emotion is seen as weak and met with shaming — usually mixed with a good dose of homophobia ('Ya poofta!') or misogyny ('Ya girl!').

The net result is that many men channel their complex internal life through those two narrow doors of anger and lust. Leaving the anger aside for a moment, what this means is that a lot of men think of themselves as 'horny' or 'having a high libido' when what's actually going on is that initiating sex is the only way they know to reach out for connection with their partner. So, they might actually feel anxious, lonely, confused, inadequate, satisfied, joyful or playful. But they can't admit those vulnerable feelings to themselves, let alone their partner, so the only way they feel safe expressing themselves is by communicating a desire for sex.

Further intensifying this picture is the fact that many boys learn to use masturbation for comfort and self-soothing. There's nothing inherently wrong with using sex that way, but when the vulnerable feelings are denied (to themselves, let alone to any partner), the purpose of initiating sex becomes unclear and indirect.

The result of all this is that in many hetero relationships, the man's approach to sex frequently carries a lot of extra 'baggage' in the form of unacknowledged emotional needs. His partner may not be able to articulate this, but will feel something 'off' about his initiation of sex. She is likely to sense (correctly) that the initiation is meeting some need of his own, not about desiring her as a person. This is a big part of why many women feel 'used' in their sexual relationships.

Here's a typical scenario:

- A man has an experience that leaves him feeling vulnerable. Let's say he gets told off by his boss at work.
- He can't admit to himself feeling inadequate, hurt, scared, etc., so he rants angrily about the boss.
- He also can't admit that he wants reassurance and comfort from his partner, to know that he is still acceptable and worthy in her eyes.
- Instead, he tries to initiate sex.
- His partner can sense the neediness in his approach and finds it

off-putting. This is doubly so if his anger at his boss has also leaked in her direction.

- She says 'no' to sex (perhaps using some lame excuse because she doesn't feel entitled just to say 'no' — see the following section).
- He feels rejected, and his sense of inadequacy and fear is amplified.
- He swaps to anger and becomes critical of his partner, perhaps attacking her sexuality — calling her 'frigid', etc. Or he shuts down and withdraws (i.e. sulks), blaming his hurt feelings on her sexual rejection rather than the insecurities he carries from his upbringing, which his boss's criticism has triggered.
- The woman feels unfairly treated and unsafe, and is even less likely to want to open up to him sexually in the future.

For many men, a big incentive for change is when they realise that being more self-aware and vulnerable is the path to feeling more in charge of their lives and having more frequent and passionate sex.

How many women ruin sex for themselves

Many aspects of women's position in our society, especially in the power politics of hetero relationships, make sex more difficult for women. From how women are beaten, raped and killed by men to the (still) largely unquestioned acceptance of inequality around responsibility for child-rearing and domestic labour, there are many aspects to a woman's role in our society that would put someone off sex.

However, in this section I want to focus on things that a woman has more control over. Partly as a direct mirror image of the preceding section about men, and partly because these are the things that are likely to reap the greatest reward with the least effort — it's a lot easier to work on your attitude to yourself than society's attitude to women. (I acknowledge the questionable politics of this approach — if you have the awareness and energy to fight the social issues, then you have my undying respect and appreciation.) As with the preceding section (indeed the whole book) there will be many exceptions, but these are patterns that I see occurring frequently enough to feel that making generalisations may be useful.

In a traditional view of a woman's role, her dominant feature is her selflessness. Her willingness to put the needs of others first — to support her partner, her children, her whānau and her community to be their best, and always place herself last on the priority list. Women are rightly praised for how compassionate, giving and tolerant they are — I would strongly argue that the generosity and kindness of women are the glue that holds our society together. But as with men's stoicism, the cost can be very high for individual women trapped into abandoning themselves in service of others by the straitjacket of gender-role expectations.

In hetero relationships, we see this in women having sex 'for' their partner rather than for their own pleasure. The teenage girl garnering attention by giving blowjobs at parties. The busy mother who 'lets' her partner have sex with her (or at least her body), hoping he'll be quick so she can get some sleep. Many women are having sex which does little or nothing for them personally. Worse, many are stoically enduring discomfort and pain from having penetrative sex when unaroused. Is it any wonder that they are quick to declare they are 'not interested in sex' and eager to see menopause as an opportunity to be 'done with all that'? There is nothing wrong with being uninterested in bad-quality sex. The problem lies with assuming that this is their only choice.

Most of our clients are mature adults, usually with decades of sexual experience, yet so many women we talk with cannot answer questions about what they like and want sexually. Their entire experience of their sexuality has been in service of others' pleasure (sometimes abusively so).

If they are lucky, they will have considerate lovers. They may have had plenty of pleasure along the way, but when there are challenges, when they change partners, or when their body or mind changes, these women don't know enough about who they are sexually to adapt. If they are unlucky, they will have had selfish partners, and sex will have been something they have endured as the trade-off for feeling wanted, worthwhile, 'normal', or at least temporarily safe.

Even some women who are 'into' sex can be out of touch with themselves this way. Those who use their partner's sexual interest in them to shore up their sense of attractiveness and worth can want sex more frequently than their partner, yet still not be knowledgeable about their own eroticism or confident about asserting it as equally valid.

Being 'good selfish' (see Chapter 10) is one of the keys to good sex. Knowing what works for you and what doesn't (i.e. having boundaries — Chapter 13), and being able to communicate and assert it, makes it much easier for your partner to feel confident and comfortable in their sexual relationship with you.

The assertion bit is crucial. I have worked with couples where the woman knew what worked for her but was unwilling to assert it. In the face of her partner's defensiveness, she backed off and put up with lousy sex rather than risk the conflict required to challenge the dominance of his insecurities. This avoidance lets both parties down — the woman loses the opportunity for sexual pleasure, and also loses respect for her partner. Meanwhile, her partner misses out on a chance to explore and out-grow the insecurity that fuelled his defensiveness and ends up with a disinterested sexual partner.

Another way of saying this is that you need to be Differentiated (see Chapter 6) in how you engage about sex — to know and share who you are while still being interested and caring about who your partner is.

An essential part of healthy communication around sex is being able to say what you don't like. It is vital that you look after yourself this way. However, in many hetero relationships, that is *all* the women contribute to the discussion. Being alienated from their eroticism and sexuality, they can say nothing about what they *do* like. Their partner is left to guess and to try things, and have the experience of only getting feedback about what they are doing *wrong*. The results are frequently demoralising and far from erotic.

Of course, some men have very fragile egos about their sexual 'prowess' and get hurt by any feedback, but often the men are eager to please but feel they are working in the dark. In a way that is analogous to the assumption that women will take care of men's vulnerable feelings without the men having to attend consciously, women expect men to map out a woman's eroticism and know how to arouse and please her without her having to attend consciously.

Being alienated from your own eroticism is not a reliable way to establish a mutually satisfying sexual relationship. It *can* work, especially when you are both young and your arousal is easy, but it tends to become fraught and ineffective as you age and there are more challenges to your sexual connection with yourself and each other.

Sex should never hurt (unless you're into that kind of thing)

One of the saddest pieces of misinformation out there is that it is normal for sex to be painful for women. Myths about virginity (FYI: it's a social construct — there's no hymen to 'break'), size, anal sex, etc., all normalise pain as something that women should expect as part of their sex lives.

If you believe this, you will likely ignore the warning signals of pain. Just as with the red lights on your car's dashboard, things break down if you ignore warning signals. Sadly, many women develop a pain syndrome as a direct result of this. Their body associates pain with sex, tenses up in anticipation, and the 'fight or flight' part of their nervous system kicks in. That makes it impossible for them to feel aroused, so they don't lubricate. Between the physical tension, the lack of lubrication and the sense of dread, the sex is painful. Every time this happens, it reinforces the pain pathways in the brain. Eventually, women can end up with any touch to their vulva or vagina causing intense pain.

If you aren't aroused enough, it's not the right time for penetrative sex.

That's not to say that you shouldn't use lube. You might still need to use lube in many situations even though you feel highly aroused. Following menopause or if you are on certain hormonal medications, including some contraceptives, you may not produce enough natural lubricant.

If you are having anal sex, you *must* use *lots* of lube and go slow. Anal sex requires a 'knack' of relaxing that you have to learn — but it shouldn't hurt any more than vaginal sex should. If sex is still painful, go to a doctor who is comfortable talking about sex (many aren't) and get things checked out.

By the way, intercourse shouldn't hurt for penis-owners, either. If it is, perhaps you are rushing things and your partner isn't ready, or you need to be using lube, or there is something that needs checking out by a sex-friendly doctor.

There is more than one style of desire — don't make yours (or your partner's) wrong

One thing that makes it hard for women in particular to think about and understand their own sexuality is that our society has normalised a style of desire that fits the majority of men but only a minority of women.

When I was training in sex therapy, I learned that it was normal for desire to precede arousal. We didn't question this; it seemed kind of logical. This shows why research is essential. What scientists have found is that many people get turned on (lubricate, get an erection) *well before* they have any sense of 'feeling like' sex. It takes quite a while in that state of arousal before they experience a desire for sex.

In recent years there has been some fabulous research exploring and normalising other ways of being sexual; still, it takes time for the message to get out into wider society. I strongly recommend the book *Come As You Are* by sex educator Emily Nagoski[4] (and her related TED talks) as the best introduction to this research and its practical application to people's lives. This section is essentially a summary of some of her key points.

The first thing to understand is that we have two neurological systems that think about sex. One is all about getting turned on — Nagoski calls that the 'accelerator'. The other is all about reasons *not* to have sex, turn-offs in the broadest sense — Nagoski calls that the 'brake'. We experience sexual desire when our brain believes there is more pressure on the accelerator than on the brake.

Some people have very little that presses their brake pedal and a lot that activates their accelerator. These people experience what is known as 'spontaneous desire' (meaning that it doesn't take much to trigger it). This is the dominant style for most men, and so was the focus of most attention in the early study of sex and was construed as 'normal'.

The rest of the population doesn't have that experience of desire arising 'spontaneously'. We need a lot of pressure on our accelerator and not too much on the brake before we experience 'feeling like' sex. We call this style of desire 'responsive' because it emerges in response to, rather than in anticipation of, sexual arousal. This is the style of the majority of women and some men. It's more common in men as they age because their sex hormones reduce, too — just not as dramatically as women's at menopause. In fact, most of us, of any gender, are likely to experience both types of desire over our lifetimes.

However, most of us don't know that, and this ignorance has serious consequences. If we believe what the movies are telling us — that only spontaneous desire is normal or healthy — then our responsive desire is going to seem abnormal or unhealthy. Feeling sexually broken is a great way to stamp on our sexual brake pedal. Exercise 51 gives you some pointers about how to manage having differing sexual styles in your relationship without making either of you bad or wrong.

EXERCISE 51: NEGOTIATING ACROSS SEXUAL STYLES

If you're spontaneous and they're responsive

If you mostly experience spontaneous desire and your partner is more of a responsive desire person, it's vital that you don't misinterpret their reaction to your sexual overtures.

- If you try to initiate sex, *expect the response to be hesitant and slow* as your partner tries to work out if they are open to the idea of sex. Don't interpret that slowness as reluctance or rejection. Hang in there in a friendly and relaxed way. Allow your partner space and time to work out what they want.
- If your partner isn't open to sex right now, *beware of making that a rejection of you.* It's a comment on where they are at in this moment, *not* on how much they want you or sex. Beware of thinking that 'it would be so easy' for your partner. Just because it's easy for you doesn't mean it is for them.
- Your partner requires a different route to being sexual. Explore that with them. Find out what is pressing on their brake pedal and see if you can help reduce the pressure there. Don't be churlish if it involves things that have nothing to do with sex. By all means, enquire about what pushes their accelerator — but listen carefully to what they tell you and don't just focus on the things that appeal to your sense of what's 'sexy'. Use the discussion to learn how your loved one is.wired erotically. What you find may surprise you.

If you're responsive and they're spontaneous

If you're the person whose desire is more responsive, ensure that your 'yes' is accommodating of what you need.

- Maybe there are some things you need to take off your brake pedal — 'Yes, but let me close the curtains, so I'm not worried about the neighbours', or 'Yes, but let's start in the shower, so I don't feel disgusting.'
- Likewise, practise saying 'no' in ways that make it clear you do want sex, even if now is not the right time for you. Try 'I love that you want me, but all this work I have to do is a real "brake" for me right now'.
- If you can manage it, you could suggest a time that you think might work for you. For example, 'I'm too tired tonight, but I'm missing sex, too. Let's make an early night of it tomorrow and see what happens', or 'I'm all touched out with the kids. Let's get your mum to take them on Saturday and see if I can re-find myself'.
- There may be places where it's appropriate to enlist your partner in dealing with some of your brakes. I think this is part of what's going on when women joke about their partners doing the dishes being the best foreplay.
- Make sure that you also have clear ideas about what an accelerator is for you. If you have no idea, make it a priority to find out. Note that we are not talking about 'turn-ons' in a narrow sense. Don't get trapped by conventional expectations of how sex 'should' work or what 'should' turn you on. For many, it's much more about what happens before anything overtly sexual occurs. It may be emotional states like feeling cherished or desired, safe or free. It might be feeling close, it might be feeling angry — it's your sexuality, and you need to accept and own it.

For 'responsive desire' people, there is a real art to learning how to get into sex — that's the focus of the next section.

'Wanting' sex even when you don't 'feel like it'

Please note: In this section, I am talking about how to have sex that you *want* and that you *freely choose*. If you don't want sex, that's fine. Or if you don't want sex with a particular person, that's fine too — even if you live with them. It's your body, your life, and you should *never* have sex you don't want and choose.

If you are someone whose predominant desire style is responsive, our society does not offer much of a road map for getting to being sexual. However, knowing how to do that is essential for everyone because, as I said earlier, all of us are likely to have times when our desire is more responsive than spontaneous. While it's nice to feel horny and start being sexual when already 'in the mood', in a long-term relationship there are other ways to approach sex.

These 'other ways' become increasingly important as we age, or when we are dealing with a history of sexual abuse, or experience hormonal changes or illness or injury or side effects from drugs, or any of the other things that can affect our libido and our sexual self. All of these things can get in the way of 'feeling like' or 'being in the mood for' sex — but if you *want* sex, *want* to be sexual, then not 'feeling like it' doesn't have to be an insurmountable barrier.

Wanting is about choice and preference — things that we control. '*Feeling like it*' is about emotions and physiology — things we can't directly control. One approach is to ask 'How do I bridge the gap between **how I feel** at this moment and **what I want**?'. Think about what would help you 'change gears' or 'shift wavelength' from where you are now (e.g. stressed and busy, or tired and overwhelmed) to where you want to be (i.e. in the mood for sex, receptive, even horny)? To use Nagoski's terms, this is about learning how to decrease the 'brakes' in your sex life and increase the 'accelerators'.

Even if you don't 'feel like it', you can approach sex from a place of *wanting to connect with your partner*. This may be enhanced by wanting to show appreciation for them, valuing them, or because you're feeling playful or friendly. You can also want pleasure and eroticism for their own sake or because sex makes you feel good and keeps you healthy (this is a medical fact).

There are two keys to the approach I am suggesting. The first is to accept that your brain may take longer than your body to get with the programme. So do things that you know your body likes, that you know from experience you find erotic, arousing or pleasing. Don't be alarmed if your brain is, for example, still dealing with your 'to-do list'; just gently try to focus on the sensual experience in the here and now and let your brain catch up in its own time.

The second thing is that the non-verbal language of touch and gaze is our primal language and, as such, is rich with meaning. Very often, when we don't 'feel like sex', we can still cope with the idea of a sensual experience: having our feet rubbed, lighting a scented candle, cuddling, having a shower or bath, mindfully eating or drinking something intensely flavoured.

For many people, sensual experiences help open the door to sexual ones. Other times we may need to break our state. We may need to exercise, be silly, play, or be distracted as an interim step; find something that allows us to transition out of the psychological space we were in (e.g. head full of work or that 'to-do list') and then be freed up to move towards being more sensual or sexual. There's no single answer. It may take persistent experimenting to find reliable ways for you to bridge the gap.

If you mindfully reach out to touch your partner or gaze at them with the intent to connect, wanting to be close or have pleasure or fun, you are likely to create something quite powerful. That may not immediately be a sexual feeling. One way to bridge the gap between the desire for connection and sexual arousal is to focus on sensual touch and intimate gaze. Attend to the place where your bodies are touching. Let your positive feelings for your partner and your desire for pleasure show in your face and gaze. Allow that to build the sense of connection between you.

In most cases, when you do this with an intent towards sex, with a *wanting*, it generates sexual feelings. For those who are used to 'spontaneous desire', this is a slower pathway to being sexual than they are familiar with, but it is no less satisfying once you are used to it. The trick is to maintain a sense of connection with yourself (what you want/desire) and with your partner, and move at a pace that works for you both.

If you avoid making yourself wrong for not 'feeling like' sex the moment you want it (or, worse, the moment your partner wants it); if you stay open to the idea that there may be a way to get to 'feeling like it'; and if your partner gets on board with helping you make that transition, then you will likely both end up having much more of the sex you want, regardless of how often you spontaneously 'feel like it'.

In praise of planning sex

Shifting the focus away from needing to 'feel like' sex or 'be in the mood' opens the door to making plans for sex. There's a reason why most sex therapists are fans of scheduling sex. For many people, it takes organising to decrease the pressure on the brake and increase it on the accelerator. If you want a sex life that doesn't rely on the odd occasion when all the planets spontaneously come into alignment, you need to get talking and planning how to make it happen.

I first twigged about how hot planned sex could be in talking with people about their affairs. Their sex had to be planned like a military operation, often juggling three or four people's diaries. While not everyone who has an affair has great sex, some of them do, and I learned that the planning and anticipation were part of what made it hot. (Just to be clear, I do not recommend or endorse infidelity: however hot the sex is, I don't see that it is ever worth the hurt it causes. But I accept that the forbidden can be very erotic.) Then I talked to people who were into kink, and learned more about how much planning and discussion went into creating a peak sexual experience for them.

People who experience spontaneous desire are often resistant to the notion of scheduling sex. I caution you to beware of buying what the entertainment industry has been selling you about how sex 'should' be. Songs, movies and novels love to focus on being swept away by passion in the moment. And many of us *have* had experiences like this, which we cherish (as we should; they are delightful). The danger comes in believing the fantasy that this is how sex 'should' be, in normalising what is actually a product of particular circumstances that are not repeatable over the long haul. Even if you keep having new partners, sex stops being quite so passionate and exciting. Romantic comedies are not much better than porn in helping us have realistic expectations of how sex works in real life. In real life, planning is what allows us to create conditions that allow being spontaneous and in the moment.

Part of the reluctance to plan sex stems from the fact that it requires being upfront and open about your 'brakes' and 'accelerators' and showing interest and care in what your partner's are, too. Some of us struggle with the vulnerability of revealing ourselves, while others struggle with accepting and valuing the difference that our partner brings to our sex life.

Some people are reluctant to plan sex because they are anxious they won't be able to access sexual feelings at the appointed time. They fear disappointing and frustrating their partner. Others fear aggression or withdrawal when their partner is disappointed or frustrated.

If at any time you approach sex with a whole raft of expectations about what 'should' happen, you are putting a whole lot of pressure on your brake pedal. If you turn up and focus on sensuality, affection and kindness, staying connected and open to what happens, then desire is likely to follow. If it doesn't, it usually means that something else, like sleep or verbal intimacy, is more important. And that's okay, too.

EXERCISE 52: MAKING TIME FOR SEX

Here are some guidelines for planning a 'sex date'.

- Discuss and agree on a time that looks optimal for both of you to feel like sex.
- In your planning, consider things like time of day (some people love sex first thing; others prefer it at the day's end), energy levels, the ability to put aside other pressures, privacy. You may need to do quite a bit of negotiating to arrive at a time that works for both of you.
- You are planning to create an environment that makes sex easier and more likely, *not* planning precisely what will happen (unless *both* of you are into that).
- Discuss how to minimise 'brakes' and maximise 'accelerators' in the lead-up to your date. Make sure you follow through on any plans.
- For many people, the emotional tone in the relationship is crucial to 'feeling like' sex. Pay particular attention to being warm, friendly, playful and supportive in the lead-up to your 'sex date'.

- Make sure that you build a positive sense of anticipation about your plan for sex. If you focus on your fears about it 'going wrong', 'not being in the mood' or 'disappointing my partner', you are likely to make those fears come true.
- Think and talk about how you want it to be. Sex is a language — what sort of conversation do you want to have with your partner?
- You may need to negotiate boundaries about how you talk about it (e.g. if your partner wants to tell you in explicit detail 'what I want to do to you' but you experience that as pressure to perform).
- Make sure you do have positive thoughts and conversations, building up a sense of anticipation.
- Keep intimacy and connection your priority ahead of 'having sex'.
- If it turns out to be not the right time on the day, that is okay. **Do not have sex you don't want**. Do what works for you to connect, be close or have fun together. And try again another time.

Penis-owners and the pressure to perform

Performance pressure can be an issue for people of all genders, so this section could apply to women and others struggling to get aroused or reach orgasm. However, I am addressing this section to men as our society strongly emphasises performance in all aspects of a man's life, and sex is no exception.

In the sexual arena, this often leads to a focus on erectile function and how long you can last during intercourse before you reach orgasm. Coupled with a rigid, heteronormative emphasis on penis-in-vagina intercourse and the expectation that men should take the lead during sex, many men operate in a highly anxiety-producing environment. That's a lot of pressure on their brake pedals!

The answer is to shift the emphasis from 'performance' (it turns out that sex is not a sport or a piece of theatre) to fun, sensual pleasure and connection. Exercise 53 will help you do this.

EXERCISE 53: MANAGING ERECTILE DYSFUNCTION OR RAPID EJACULATION

If you struggle with erectile problems, rapid or delayed ejaculation, then anxiety and worry likely dominate your sex life. 'Will it happen again?' 'Will I be okay this time?' 'Will my partner be disappointed / hurt / angry?'

If you approach sex with that as the *focus* of your thoughts and feelings, the sex isn't likely to go well. Anxiety thrives on attention, and the more it grows, the worse your sexual function will get, and the less pleasant your sex life will be. Here are some suggestions for how to learn to focus differently.

By yourself

- When you masturbate, enjoy the journey — don't hurry to the destination. Many men have learned to 'bang one out', to get to orgasm as quickly as possible. Instead, enjoy the sensual pleasure of stroking yourself, getting or being turned on.
- Don't take it too seriously — literally, play with yourself and enjoy finding out what is fun, what is sensually pleasurable.
- Notice that your erection is not the same hardness at different points in time. If you play for more than a couple of minutes, it will get harder and softer depending on where your mind is at (intensely erotic, mildly erotic, distracted, anxious, etc.).
- Notice also that how quickly you reach orgasm can vary quite widely.

With a partner

- You don't need an erection or one that lasts a particular length of time to have great sex with a partner. If you focus on fun and pleasure, caring and connection, you are both guaranteed a good time.
- Focusing anxiously on intercourse and orgasm is actually a passion-killer (and will make you come across as a self-centred lover). Suppose instead that you focus on giving and receiving sensual pleasure, having fun together and being connected with your partner. In that case, you can both have a delightful sexual experience without you

ever having an erection or an orgasm (or even if you come quickly).

- If you take time to find ways to pleasure your partner using your fingers, tongue, toys or anything else you want to get creative with, that's likely to be intensely erotic. Your partner will have a good time and will likely see you as a considerate lover. Spending plenty of time on non-intercourse sex also takes the pressure off you to 'perform'.

- If you decide to have intercourse, concentrate on enjoying it rather than worrying about it. Attend to the pleasurable sensations, and focus on your partner's pleasure. If your partner is female, emphasise using your pelvic bone to pleasure her clitoris (despite what porn shows you, your penis going in and out is *not* usually the most intense stimulation for a woman).

- Stay connected with your partner, not caught up in anxiety or embarrassment. If your erection is less hard, try a position with your partner on top, rocking back and forth rather than up and down. See if you can relax back into enjoying yourself (you will probably get harder again if you do).

- If you orgasm more quickly than you want to, don't collapse into embarrassment. Your fingers and your tongue are still working fine. Stay connected to your partner — see if they are interested in more sex of a different kind (especially if they haven't had an orgasm yet). Even if they don't want more sex, make sure you stay connected with them emotionally.

When the pressure to 'perform' is real

I do want to acknowledge that many men (and even more women) have had a lot of pressure placed on them by partners to 'perform' sexually. If you have a partner who is so insecure about their own attractiveness or worth that they take your sexual functioning as a comment on them, that is likely to increase your anxiety. Talk about pressure on your brake pedal!

It's important that you don't take responsibility for your partner's insecurity. In particular, it is not okay for someone to criticise you or shame you for something over which you have no voluntary control. Don't let their insecurities dictate your understanding of your sexuality!

Invite them into cooperating to make sex work for you both.

If they insist on focusing on you as having 'the problem', tell them to sort themselves out. If they won't recognise and take responsibility for the insecurities that they are projecting on to you, think hard about why you want to stay with someone who is unwilling to 'own their stuff' like that.

Reconnecting sexually

If your sex life has been a source of difficulty and upset, it is easy to get into a pattern of avoidance; for some couples, that can mean years without a sexual connection. The length of time since you last had sex creates enormous pressure to get it 'right' if you risk trying again. That is not sexy. This kind of history is another good reason to plan a sexual encounter. Exercise 54 gives you a template for how to re-approach sex when there is a lot of tension and anxiety about it.

EXERCISE 54: HOW TO HAVE INTIMATE SEX WHEN IT'S ALL BEEN GOING WRONG

If you are anxious about sex because it's gone wrong in the past, here are some ideas to explore to try to reconnect sexually. Note that many of these ideas involve **talking intimately** rather than being sexual. Often there's a backlog of hurt that needs to be cleared up before you can open up to each other. If you already know that's the case, make time to have those conversations *before* making a 'sex date'.

- If it isn't happening without planning, make a date to be sexually intimate.
- Discuss with your partner what conditions would make you feel more like being sexual. Try to set up a situation with maximum pressure on your accelerator and minimum pressure on your brake (e.g. well-rested, sober, private, what location, naked or clothed to start with, etc.).
- Remember, intimacy often involves learning about *yourself* and struggling with *your* anxieties and dilemmas in your partner's presence. Focus on the 'intimacy' part rather than the 'sex'. Ensure

that you are being intimate (i.e. open and vulnerable) in what you say and do. In this context, desire and passion flow from connected intimacy.

- Make sure your touch, gaze and actions are in line with what you want to do, and who and how you want to be.
- If you are having a whole lot of thoughts that are 'getting in the way of sex' and taking you out of being in the moment with your partner, share them rather than risk becoming disconnected.
- On the other hand, if you 'just want to get on with it', consider that you might be avoiding your insecurities. Maybe you need to connect with and talk about what's going on at a deeper level.
- You have to start from where you are. So if you feel anxious about having sex, about it all going wrong (again), about your partner's frustration or lack of engagement, etc., then **talk about it**. That's intimacy.
- Remember to frame things in terms of what is going on in *you*, primarily how your anxieties and insecurities are operating, *not* in terms of what your partner is or isn't doing.
- Remember to also talk about your positive feelings and hopes for the relationship, especially that you want to show love and care through touch and sex.
- Real intimacy (including talking vulnerably and openly about your struggles) will likely draw your partner towards you, even if what you say seems negative.
- Keep in mind that having a good sex life is a goal for both of you. If you don't believe this, you need to check it out with your partner. If they are clear that it is a goal for them, look at which of your anxieties is making this hard for you to accept.
- Keep your focus on that goal of 'a good sex life' or 'a strong sexual connection', and calmly deal with obstacles that crop up. Deal with them and persevere, showing who you are and how you feel towards your partner through touch, talk, gaze and sex.
- If you have started being sexual, the same rules still need to apply *throughout* the encounter. If you are caught up in your head worrying: *talk about it!* This will probably mean you need to stop being actively sexual and talk. Then try to get back into the sex if you can.
- Give yourself (and your partner) permission for things not to be

romantic, 'natural', smooth or easy. Intimacy is often challenging, awkward and imperfect. It won't be this bad forever.

- If it all does go wrong, don't panic. Afterwards, think about where it went wrong — notably how your anxieties and insecurities contributed. Then have an intimate talk with your partner about what you could do differently next time. And arrange a next time . . .

ELLIE & DAVE

This couple came to see me shortly after their twenty-fifth anniversary. In their early fifties, with one son away at university, they impressed as vigorous and youthful. They co-owned a very successful building supplies business. They worked well together, with a clear division of roles and an appreciation of each other's strengths based on their backgrounds (Dave in building, Ellie in management). They enjoyed socialising together and shared a love of running, both of them still casually competing. They reported no problems in their relationship other than that their sex life had dwindled to almost nothing over the past 20 years.

Their son leaving home was the final straw for Dave. He had attributed Ellie's lack of interest in sex to her role as a mother and had quietly hoped for a renaissance in their sex life once the son was out of the home. When she continued to decline his invitations, he became increasingly despairing: 'I don't want to go on like this for another 25 years. I'm too young to give up on having a sex life.'

Ellie contacted me after Dave told her he had found himself looking at escort websites. He was distressed and angry — this was not something he thought was acceptable. The thought that he might go elsewhere for sex frightened Ellie, and she initially sought help for herself. 'I love him and find him attractive, but I just don't have any interest. That's not right. I think there's something wrong with me.' She had had her hormones checked, tried taking various supplements and even using Viagra (having read that it 'may work in women, too' — which is rarely the case). But nothing helped.

I suggested that I meet with them both because, even if there is a problem with one partner, in a long-term relationship the solutions inevitably involve both of them. Also, it's rare for 'the problem' in a couple's sex life to be situated in just one person.

It was clear from the outset that Dave was ambivalent about seeing me. On the one hand, he was desperate for things to change in their sex life; on the other, he did not like talking about feelings and other intimate subjects. Vulnerability was not his long suit. Given how eager he was to stress that the difficulties all lay with Ellie, I got the impression that taking on **any** responsibility would, to him, feel like he was being blamed.

I got Dave's interest when, without him mentioning it, I talked about how powerless he must feel. I then helped him understand that locating the problem solely in Ellie meant he was defining it as something he couldn't control. I then discussed the relationship between verbal and sexual intimacy (see the section earlier on intimacy requiring tolerating vulnerability). Although he was still dubious, the fact that I was also talking about Ellie needing to learn more about tolerating physical intimacy meant that Dave wasn't going to reject my ideas out of hand.

Given how attractive they were, it was not surprising to learn that they both saw themselves as being quite 'successful' in their early experiences of sexual relationships. Both began dating in high school and had no difficulty attracting partners. Before meeting Ellie, Dave had had many short-term relationships. There were quite a few casual hookups, and his longest dating relationship was less than a year. Ellie's experience was similar, though with fewer hookups and one relationship that lasted three years, including six months of living together.

The differences emerged when I explored what sex meant to them in those early years. To his credit, Dave was honest about the competitive nature of his approach to sex. He talked about the 'thrill of the hunt' and 'scoring', and was proud of having been seen as a bit of a 'stud'. Dave readily shared a story about having a woman hit on him because her girlfriend told her he was 'a good fuck'. He was unequivocal that he enjoyed pleasing his partners and found sex very rewarding.

Ellie also talked about the power of feeling like 'I could have any guy in the room I wanted'. However, when I asked her directly whether she had sex primarily for her own pleasure or to please the men she was with, she went silent for a moment. She asked me what I meant. I asked if she usually found the sex itself rewarding — did she experience a lot of pleasure, did she reach orgasm? Ellie said, 'I hadn't really thought about it. But, yeah, sex was what I did to get a guy, but I always followed their lead. I had some pretty mediocre sex. Some of them were good at pleasing me, but I usually didn't come. Part of the reason I moved in with Jason [her previous partner] was that he was the first guy who I came with regularly. He was really into giving oral.'

Dave was looking pretty uncomfortable at this point. I suggested that it was understandable if he was feeling a bit anxious about what Ellie would say about sex with him. I highlighted that this is an example of the kind of verbal intimacy that might not be his long suit. I encouraged him to hang in there and try to remember that Ellie is talking about herself and her experience, not about him: he couldn't be expected to know if she didn't tell him.

Despite all that, Ellie clearly felt the need to reassure Dave, saying that the sex with him was great at the beginning. She thought they had 'good chemistry' and enjoyed it. However, she sheepishly admitted that she used to fake orgasms with him at times, as she felt a lot of pressure from him to come. Dave struggled not to take that personally and started to get angry. I interrupted and suggested that he reflect on what he feared it said about him. With a bit of help, he talked about feeling like a 'bad lover' and that it made him sound 'selfish'.

I pointed out that the situation was not the fault of either of them individually, but more about the interaction of their respective insecurities. Tentatively, I shared my impression that Ellie seemed driven to be pleasing and accommodating in order to feel wanted or important. On the other hand, Dave seemed to need to 'do well' and 'get it right' to be able to enjoy himself.

This change of perspective — suddenly diving into their innermost selves — caused a bit of whiplash, but I was accurate enough with my guesses to pique their interest. I asked Ellie to think about her upbringing and see if there were possible explanations for her needing to be wanted or fearing being unwanted. She immediately responded that she was adopted, and her parents always stressed how desperately wanted she and her brother were. However, on closer enquiry it became clear that she had always had a bit of a struggle to feel like she belonged. When we replaced 'having sex to feel wanted' with 'having sex to feel like you belong', it was a moment of profound recognition for her.

It took a lot more work for Dave to make the connection with his insecurities and how they influenced him day to day. However, it became clear that, in the face of his father's frequent absence (for work) and both his parents' limited ability to offer praise, he struggled to feel 'good enough'. Dave got the most attention and approval for winning — in sports when he was younger, and making money as an adult. Although initially dubious, Dave came to accept that 'being driven' was not a good thing for him. His fear of failure, of not being good enough, drove him to do things that got in the way of their intimate connection.

At their next appointment, the energy between them was visibly different, and Dave was also more open and friendly towards me, saying 'there must be something to your mumbo jumbo'. They reported that Ellie had initiated sex the weekend after our session and, in Dave's words, 'fucked my brains out'. For her part, Ellie said that the whole notion of having sex out of insecurity had really bugged her, and she got really curious about and turned on by the thought of having sex for her own pleasure.

Although she was nervous about what would happen, she approached Dave quite directly and 'took charge' of how the sex happened. Dave was surprised by what he called Ellie's 'dom vibe', but was happy to go along; he said that it was a 'bit of a relief' to be told what to do instead of having to guess.

This episode was a turning point for them. They still had a lot of work to do to understand their insecurities, self-protective behaviour, and how these played out around their sex life. Still, Ellie's determined action meant that they had a taste of how things could be different.

In trying to work out what she wanted, Ellie started reading erotic fiction. She found that as well as being a good source of ideas about things she might like to explore, it also worked well to get her in the mood. She enjoyed developing a better sense of herself sexually and was full of praise for how accommodating Dave was of her desires.

However, it wasn't all plain sailing. Ellie being less pleasing and accommodating wasn't just confined to the bedroom, which meant some changes in their broader relationship. She wasn't willing to put up with Dave's emotional withdrawal or irritation if she tried to engage him in intimate conversation. Ellie was more inclined to initiate conflict with him, and they had more fights. The upside was that they were usually able to sort things out, and, more importantly, she was no longer walking around being resentful. That removed a major 'brake' on her interest in connecting with Dave sexually, and she made sure that Dave knew that.

While Dave **intellectually** got the link between being more vulnerable and having more sex, it was difficult for him to change the habits of a lifetime. He had to work hard to accept that Ellie being more of a 'responsive desire' person did not mean that she didn't want him. It took many sessions of me saying the same thing in different ways before he understood at a **gut level** how much he was imposing the meaning of 'rejection' on to the simple fact of Ellie getting to 'feeling like sex' by a different route than him.

Doing a daily connection practice was something that Dave initially did reluctantly, but over time he came to value it. With a deliberate nod to his experience of training for marathons, we discussed it as their 'intimacy training regimen' and the need to 'build the necessary emotional muscles to be able to tolerate long-term intimacy'.

As they both became more aware of and able to manage their insecurities consciously, they reported that their lovemaking was changing, slowing down and becoming more tender and intense. At our last session, Dave could say with a big grin: 'I'm keen on 25 more years of this!'

Key points from Chapter 15

1. Tolerating the vulnerability of intimacy and pushing yourself to keep growing are the keys to sustaining passion in a long-term relationship.
2. 'Responsive' desire is an equally valid way to get to sex as the 'spontaneous' desire that our society normalises and idealises.
3. Many men ruin sex by using it to meet emotional needs that they refuse to admit to themselves.
4. Many women ruin sex by not knowing what they want, or not being 'good selfish' enough about getting it.
5. Sex should *never* be painful (unless you're into that kind of kink).
6. Like a good meal, good sex is often carefully planned.
7. Knowing what the accelerators and brakes of your desire are is crucial to the effective planning of your sex life.
8. Sex is a language, a means of expression and connection, *not* a performance or a competition. Think less about what you want to do 'to' your partner and more about how you want to communicate 'with' them.
9. Using intercourse or orgasm as a measure of 'success' frequently gets in the way of enjoying the moment.

Chapter 16
Money and its meanings

Money matters

Money is the principal way our Western culture measures importance and worth — this has significant ramifications for how you deal with it in your relationship.

Nowadays, most relationships are between two financially independent people. That is, most people have had a job and supported themselves living away from home before they move in with a partner. (This pattern may change as the high cost of housing creates a shift back to an older practice of people living with their parents longer, sometimes until they partner up.)

Although not everyone does it this way, most people seem to progress through dating to living together and then, if they wish, formalising the relationship with a marriage ceremony. Theoretically, this graduated approach to commitment offers a lot of opportunity for exploring how we deal with issues of money, worth, financial security and financial freedom. In practice, because there is a lot of vulnerability associated with money, many people avoid talking about it, which means they drift into arrangements without exploring or negotiating them adequately.

Two people who are both living independently and earning are going to have separate finances. The early negotiations about who pays for what will mostly involve joint activities. In this scenario it is pretty easy to maintain a sense of independence and worth. However, if one of you is much wealthier, then the negotiations about how you view money and wealth will have to begin early. Do you let your wealthier partner pay for a meal or holiday you couldn't afford? How do you feel about giving an expensive gift when you know your partner can't respond in kind? Do you know what issues it raises for them if you do?

Usually, the decision to live together is where things get interesting.

- If you are both from similar social classes and at similar stages of development (e.g. both early in your careers and renting), then it may be reasonably straightforward to 'split things down the middle' and share expenses evenly.
- However, it is often not 'equitable' to split things 50:50; for example, if you are from different backgrounds (e.g. working class vs middle class), at different stages in your working lives or have very different earning power (lawyer vs sales assistant). If there is a significant disparity in wealth (e.g. one of you owns your own home and the other has always rented), then that will affect what's equitable in your spending as well. How you decide what is fair and reasonable will depend greatly on your beliefs about finances, worth, fairness, and even politics.

Sorting out this transition to living together can be even more challenging for people who go from dating straight to marriage. If they do a marriage preparation course, they should be all right. The good courses include conversations about beliefs and values about money, sex, children and child-rearing, etc. If they haven't done that homework, people who haven't lived together often have no experience exploring and negotiating differences over significant issues. They are frequently operating within a belief system that thinks that the marriage ceremony is the end-point rather than the beginning of the process of forming a relationship.

Talking about money is intimate

Many of us have lost sight of the fact that money isn't real. Money is a tool we use in our society to facilitate the exchange of goods and services. Increasingly in Antipodean culture, money (and its accumulation into wealth) is seen as the sole determinant of worth, rather than one measure of value among many. While there are attempts (like feminist economics or triple-bottom-line accounting) to reduce the harm caused by this singular focus on money and material wealth, it is still the dominant force in politics and decision-making at most levels of society.

What does this have to do with relationships? Well, many, if not most, people struggle with a sense of worth. We have insecurities that tell us 'I'm not good enough' or 'I'm not important'. Given the way our society equates money with value, it is tough to talk about money without running into your fears about your worth. If you also have insecurities about safety ('I'm not safe' or 'I'm on my own, I can't rely on anyone else'), you will likely also expect other people to be unfair or uncaring of you.

In those cases, talking about money will make you feel vulnerable and raise issues of identity, worth, trust, security and equity that you may not be consciously tracking. If you can hold a Differentiated stance (see Chapter 6) in this conversation, it is an opportunity to deepen your understanding of yourself and your partner. That requires you to explore what the discussion of money brings up for you and, at the same time, be interested in what it brings up for your partner.

However, if you cannot tolerate the vulnerability, you will be defensive, reactive or simply avoidant, and you will lose this opportunity for intimacy.

Is it my money, your money or our money?

This question may be redundant if you view yourselves as two independent people: I have my money, you have yours, and we contract to deal with shared expenses. Once you start to consider yourselves as a unit or a family, then this question becomes very important.

When you see the two of you as a unit and think in terms of 'our' life — then the issue of how this unit makes financial decisions becomes essential. If you are both in the same waka (boat), who gets to steer?

For most of the twentieth century, there was no discussion. Women were economically dependent on men, first their father and then their husband. In the 1980s in Aotearoa, banks were still asking single women to find a male relative to co-sign their mortgage (and being asked for a larger deposit!).[1] The freedom of choice that comes with economic independence was a centrepiece of second-wave feminism for good reason.

By the time I began practising in the mid-1990s, there was quite a strong norm that if we are a family, all the work counts, and all money is ours, with joint decision-making about how we spend it. In the intervening 30 years, as our society has become increasingly individualistic and less socialistic, it has become common to hear women who aren't in paid work talk about 'his money'. It feels like our current culture is eroding the gains of the previous generation.

There is no question that many people in paid employment work hard for the money they earn. Increasingly so, as workers' rights are eroded and working conditions have become increasingly inhumane. However, the argument that 'I worked hard for it; therefore it's mine' typically fails to consider the unpaid work that the partner does to keep the collective lifestyle afloat. The equivalent is a stay-at-home parent who insists these are my children, not yours, because I have worked hard to raise them, and you have done little or nothing (except earning money).

It is also increasingly common for middle-class women to take their partner's earning power for granted. They lay out plans for significant spending (e.g. buying new furniture or renovating the house) with no awareness or concern for the implications for their primary breadwinner partner. Often these are the same women complaining of feeling neglected because their partner devotes too much of his time and energy to work!

Even in hetero couples where both people are in full-time paid work, the gender pay gap means that men are likely to earn more and be much more protective of their careers. Male entitlement leads them to expect their women partners to make the compromises (like changing jobs to move to be with their partner, or forgoing promotion to ensure they have enough time and energy for the family).

Look deeply into what money means to you

Men often strongly identify with their paid work. Because this is so 'normal', the underlying insecurities about their self-worth often remain unspoken and unacknowledged. Guys will insist that they have to work the way they do for the family's financial well-being, even when their partner says she would rather have less materially: 'It would be better if the kids saw more of you than if they had a bach.'

Elsewhere (e.g. Chapter 10) I have discussed the need to surrender some autonomy to benefit from being in a partnership. Nowhere is this more necessary than around how we organise our finances. Control over how money is earned, spent and accumulated is frequently the clearest illustration of how we manage power in our relationships.

In hetero couples, for every autocratic man there is a woman who has surrendered her autonomy, who equates being cared for with being ignorant of her financial realities.

If you struggle to put food on the table and keep a roof over your head, there may be no discussion about how much you work. You will work as much as you can to try to improve your situation. However, if you are not in a survival situation, how much you earn becomes about values and priorities. Some people believe that they 'need' to have $50 million dollars in productive assets before they can retire. Others are happy to rent all their lives and never own property.

If your sense of yourself is dependent on *what you do* (as opposed to *who you are*), your approach to work is going to be off-kilter. The chances are you will have been rewarded all your life — at school, on the sports field, at church, at work and in business — if you operate this way. If 'success' is essential for you to feel okay about yourself, then you're probably going to be 'successful'. Our society sees 'being driven' as a virtue rather than a sign that someone is being controlled by their insecurities. We borrow the term 'driven' from animal husbandry: and from the point of view of the cow or sheep, 'being driven' means being chased by a wolf.

If you work this way, you will struggle with allowing your partner to influence your choices about how you work. I have lost count of the number of people (mostly, but not exclusively, men) who have arrived in my office asserting that they have to work the crazy hours they do, only to acknowledge six months or so later that they *don't* have to. It would not be the end of their job, business, or their family's financial security if they worked 50 hours instead of 70. This shift only seems possible once the person realises how much their insecurities have been dictating their choices.

The other side of the dynamic is people (mostly, but not exclusively, women) who also struggle to believe in their own worth. But instead of compensating by 'proving' themselves through achievement, these people treat themselves as a junior in the partnership. Their lack of financial power and external validation makes it hard for them to back themselves in disagreements over how money is earned and spent. Their insecurities about their worth and importance invite them to back down, and put up with having less say in major decisions that affect them. Even women who see themselves as feminists can feel disempowered and worthless in the face of current social norms around the central importance of paid work.

If you are a stay-at-home parent, this position can be very disempowering. It may have been a joint decision for you to do this, but you are still the one who is in the financially dependent position. It can be hard to assert yourself when your partner can withdraw their financial support anytime. Managing the imbalance requires you both to discuss the issue thoroughly and structure things to preserve the power and autonomy of the person who is not earning.

Another significant factor in your approach to money is how it was regarded in your family as you grew up. If you were poor and your peers shamed you for your old clothes and lack of lunch, that might have a big impact on your ability to spend money now. Likewise, if your family was comfortably middle-class, had skiing and overseas holidays, a bach and a boat, you might struggle to recognise the necessity for saving.

So, as with everything in this book, you need to go deep; examine your insecurities and how they come into play around the earning and spending of money. It may be difficult to identify your insecurities if your ways of protecting yourself fit with social norms (e.g. the 'successful' man and the 'pleasing' woman).

There are people, usually men, who use money to exert control. The relationship is not then a partnership; it is a hierarchy. If your partner has complete control over your spending and aggressively interrogates you about every last dollar, raising doubts about your competence and care, this is a sign that you are in an emotionally dangerous relationship.

Money is a great place to learn to deal with difference

Even when you have a handle on how your insecurities and learning history affect your beliefs and attitudes around money, it's likely that you and your spouse will still have differences about money (like everything else).

I am fond of saying that, ideally, every couple needs a 'spender' and a 'saver'. The 'spender' is more focused on the present and enjoying life right now. 'Who knows what tomorrow will bring?' is their catch-cry. The 'saver' focuses more on the future and securing long-term security. Like good Scouts, their catch cry is 'Be prepared!'. Both of these people have good points worthy of consideration and respect.

If a spender were left unchecked, they might leave the family unprepared for future situations. Even though Aotearoa's universal superannuation system is pretty good by world standards, living on a pension is still difficult. On the other hand, if a saver is left unchecked, they might squeeze all the fun out of life, living so carefully that there is little opportunity to enjoy the journey. Having a lot of money in retirement is no good to you if you have been miserable for the previous 30 years and no longer know how to enjoy yourself.

Your insecurities are in play if the spender labels the saver as 'mean', 'miserly' and 'a scrooge', or the saver labels the spender as 'reckless', 'foolish' and 'dangerous'. In trying to bolster their sense of self by asserting that their way is 'right', reactive people make it difficult to arrive at a decision where both partners feel comfortable with the outcome.

Money is my favourite example where a couple must learn to value and appreciate what their partner brings to the relationship. Imagine each person recognising that their partner's different perspective has the potential to enrich their life. They listen, try to take in the way their partner sees things and orders their priorities. It is likely then that, with time, they will arrive at a decision that both can invest in and support.

An excellent place to examine this is looking at spending without consultation. Most couples will have a threshold of discretionary spending. The amount will vary depending on the couple's financial circumstances, but the principle remains the same: I can choose to spend up to a certain amount without consulting my partner. Beyond that amount, I need to consult before I spend. This is the embodiment of finding the balance between autonomy and partnership.

Ignorance is not bliss

One of the reasons to be in an ongoing relationship with another person (or people) is the division of labour. You are sure to have different strengths, and it makes sense for the person who is good at something to be the one to do it.

If your partner is better than you with money, then by all means let them have the lion's share of the work of managing it. But, just as with parenting, don't sign off completely. Don't let yourself be totally disabled or ignorant of what is happening. Not only is that unfair to your partner, who is likely to end up shouldering all the responsibility for important decisions, but it also leaves you disempowered in your own life.

Remember, money is power — so you need to know how your power works in general terms. You don't have to be the one reconciling the bank statements to understand why it is better to pay off the mortgage faster than buy shares with the money you inherited from Aunt Mabel.

Placing yourself in an ignorant, helpless role around money makes it hard for your partner to respect you and trust that you can be there for them if they become incapacitated. Understanding the thinking behind your overall financial strategy and being an active participant in it marks the distinction between being *dependent on* your partner and *interdependent with* your partner. This sense of interdependency builds respect and trust, a sense of shared responsibility and journey and being in this together.

On the other hand, if you are the person who is more confident or knowledgeable about finances, make sure that your insecurities don't push you into maintaining control over the relationship by keeping your partner ignorant. Not trusting your partner to have input into major financial decisions is usually a sign of disrespect and condescension — attitudes that will undermine the long-term security and joy in the relationship.

Dealing with inequality

There are many situations where partners start living together with very different financial conditions. A common one is where it is a second marriage for one or both people. When you arrive at a point of commitment to your new partner and already have assets and dependents, it is even more vital that the two of you have an intimate talk about money.

Many avoid 'pre-nuptial' agreements because they feel unromantic, even pessimistic. We are newly in love and determined to make this relationship work. The last thing we want to do is plan for the relationship ending. Yet having an explicit conversation and contract about what we each believe is fair and appropriate is a loving thing to do for yourself and each other. This is doubly true if you have children together. Bitter disputes over finances can poison your children's lives. If you love your kids, plan ahead so that they never have to endure that nightmare.

There may be a lot of emotion — from shame about your relative poverty, to pain from losses inflicted by a past break-up. So make sure you explore those aspects thoroughly before you make practical decisions. For example: if I felt 'taken to the cleaners' by my ex's lawyers, my approach to joint finances may be very fearful and self-protective. That may push me to want arrangements that are unfair to you.

Roughly speaking, you have three years in Aotearoa (two years in Australia) from the time you start living together before you're considered to be in a 'de facto' marriage. So there is time to explore this issue — but not an infinite amount. If your situation is anything other than a simple 'we both have an equal share in all money and assets', you must explore what you think is equitable in how you arrange your finances. As with our use of time, 'equitable' doesn't mean 'the same'. What's important is that you honestly explore the issues, manage your reactivity in the process, and arrive at a plan that you *both* feel is fair.

Exercise 55 will help you talk about money with your partner.

EXERCISE 55: TALKING ABOUT MONEY

Here are some suggested questions for you and your partner to answer and discuss. Be as honest as you can. Don't push for sameness; expect that you will have different answers. Take your time to explore what money means to you individually. Only then, start talking about your joint structures and plans.

- Growing up, what were your family's financial circumstances? How was money viewed and talked about in the home? What are the core lessons you learned about money and wealth?
- What's the rest of your history with money like before this relationship? How has it affected you?
- Do you have full access to each other's financial information? Can you access all the money if one of you was suddenly in a coma? If not, is there a clear understanding of why not? Was this a genuinely mutual decision?
- What are your expectations about spending without consultation? What's the threshold figure for consultation before you spend, and why do you want it there?
- What is your personal approach to planning and saving for retirement? How much are you willing to sacrifice now to create a better future?
- What kind of lifestyle do you lead? What does it take to support that lifestyle? What trade-offs are you making? Have you seriously examined the alternatives?
- If you began the relationship with different financial resources, do you have a written contract about dividing your assets should the relationship end? If not, what stops you from being upfront about this?

These are just suggestions — talk about whatever else seems significant to you about money, finances, wealth and power in your relationship.

ROSA & MIKE

Growing up as the third child in a Catholic family in Latin America, Rosa learned to be pleasing and obedient. After she qualified as a Special Needs teacher, she went travelling and met Mike early on. He was at the end of his travels, so Rosa changed her plans and came to New Zealand, which she loved. She also liked that Mike seemed close to his family — he worked in the family supermarket business. After two years of commuter relationship, with each of them visiting the other, Rosa found a job here and decided to move to New Zealand to see if the relationship had a future.

Although it was hard at the start knowing no one in New Zealand, she felt valued at work, and Mike went out of his way to help her connect with the women in his social circle, which made her feel cared for by him. As Rosa began to make friends among Mike's friends and at her school, she believed that a future together was possible.

After three years of living together, they were married in her hometown. Some of Mike's family and friends flew over for the occasion. They talked a lot about the future — plans for children and for Mike to go into business for himself.

Both of those things happened at about the same time. Shortly after their son was born, Mike spotted an opportunity to buy a food business that supplied supermarkets. They had been renting and saving and had enough saved to persuade the bank to loan on the company, with his parents providing security.

Fast-forward five years: their family went as planned, and they now had another boy and a girl. However, other things did not go as planned. They are still renting, now from Mike's parents, as they couldn't afford market rent for a 'decent' house big enough for the five of them. Mike was working longer hours to try to 'get ahead', and Rosa was increasingly distressed at how alone and isolated she was. Rosa ended up being seen by Maternal Mental Health and, as well as beginning a course of anti-depressants, was referred for couple therapy.

Rosa started to find language to describe her concerns in her individual therapy with the Maternal Mental Health psychologist. She had really wanted a home of their own. Not being a business-minded person, she had taken at face value Mike's reassurances that putting all their money into a business was 'smarter' and 'going to get us where we want to be sooner'.

'Where we want to be' was Mike having time for the family. Rosa's father was a science teacher who had been very family-oriented. Rosa had been explicit with Mike that this was what she wanted, and he had said he did, too. The fact that she saw less of Mike now than before they had children felt like a complete betrayal of their agreement.

In talking with Mike, it was clear that he was struggling. He kept trying to put a positive spin on his business situation, but it was apparent that he had no real plan to turn things around. There was an air of desperation about him. The pragmatics of the situation were bad enough: not only did he and Rosa stand to lose all their savings, but his parents would also lose a lot of money if the business failed. Additionally, he felt responsible to his employees.

On top of that, Mike was struggling with a massive burden of shame. Growing up in a business-oriented family and having studied commerce, it was unbearable to admit that he had made a serious mistake. Coming from a culture that measured 'success' solely by your financial standing, and emphasised individual reward for individual effort, he had no frame of reference to see his situation as anything other than a personal failure. He was staring into the face of becoming one of those 'losers' he had been so contemptuous of in the not-so-distant past.

Alarmingly, but not surprisingly, when I asked directly, I discovered that he was seriously contemplating suicide, thinking that if he could make it look enough like an accident his family would be 'better off without me'. This revelation triggered the crisis that had been slowly building. I got Mike to agree that he would come clean with his parents about both his financial situation and his suicidality. Rosa had had a big enough shock that she made sure he followed through.

Fortunately, his parents could help and did so without shaming him. They were able to supply both extra capital and expertise (through their contacts) to help turn the business around.

With the immediate crisis averted and Mike also doing individual therapy, their work with me became a rather lengthy debrief about how they ended up in this mess, to prevent a recurrence.

We explored the notion of values and what it means to live by them. Both of them had 'family' as their number one value, but it was clear that Mike had seen that mainly in terms of his role of providing financially for his family. Moreover, he had used that notion of 'providing' to cloak the way that his fear that he was 'not good enough' drove him to prove his worth by being financially successful. Meanwhile, Rosa realised that her notion of 'family' cast her in a subordinate role, unthinkingly deferring to the man of the house and not trusting her own judgement about finances and priorities.

With a bit of prompting, Mike acknowledged that in hindsight, they would have been better off if they had followed Rosa's plan of buying a house and him staying in the supermarket business. He was even able to apologise for how dismissive and condescending he'd been towards her opinions.

Mike continued to need to work hard on the business. However, with the help of his business mentor, he put strict boundaries in place so that he could get home each night and help with bathing and bedtime. He still had to bring work home on weekends, but did that on Saturday evenings so that Rosa had time to go out and socialise while he babysat the kids.

Rosa realised that she could not afford to 'be a passenger in my own life'. She took a greater interest in the business and discovered, to their mutual pleasure, that some of her skills and insight in handling difficult kids were relevant to managing the staff in the business. Rather than feeling left out and jealous of the business, she became invested, involved and even excited by it.

Key points from Chapter 16

1. At the start of their relationship, couples often 'drift' into financial arrangements without thinking through the implications for power in the relationship.
2. Our (crazy) culture associates money with our sense of worth. That makes it a place where people can get very reactive.
3. Many people use their paid work to prop up their sense of self and are highly defensive if questioned about the way they work.
4. If you associate value with money, it's common for unpaid work to be under-valued (or even unvalued).
5. Many people are resigned to being 'worthless' because they earn less, and act as if they, therefore, deserve less say in their relationship.
6. Every couple needs a 'spender' and a 'saver'.
7. Don't allow yourself to be ignorant about your financial situation, even if finances are not your strong suit.
8. Plan for the future, including the possibility of separation. Make sure to explore thoroughly, so your plans seem equitable to you both.

Chapter 17
Parenting as a team

In this chapter, I'm not going to talk about how to parent children, but instead focus on applying the skills discussed so far to being a *good parenting team*. This chapter is for those who want children, so skip it if that's not your choice.

You can't overestimate the impact of kids

Having kids changes everything. Research suggests that for most people (especially women), the arrival of children leads to a drop in overall satisfaction with their relationship.[1] This same study indicates that the cause of this decline in satisfaction is 'role conflicts and restriction of freedom'. Other research suggests that this effect may be softened if the relationship is functioning well before the children arrive.[2]

There is no question that the responsibilities and practicalities of having a child place new stressors on parents, sometimes extremely so. For example, sleep deprivation is a common technique used to break people down for interrogation and frequently causes psychosis. Although the CIA doesn't accept this, you can argue it's a form of torture,[3] and many parents of young children would agree.

So, if you are planning on having a family, make sure you have some very grounded and detailed conversations about how you are going to manage the likely changes and challenges. It is vital that partners who aren't going to be pregnant enter fully into imagining what their new life will look like. Beware of minimising or dismissing when your partner is trying to plan for the challenges they can foresee.

Pregnancy is the area where sex differences in hetero relationships are most acute. Even in same-sex relationships, the experience of the pregnant person and their partner are worlds apart. In our society, there is enormous responsibility placed on a person who is even intending to get pregnant — they must abstain from intoxicants, watch what they eat, track their menstrual cycle, etc. Not everybody does this, of course, but the expectation is there. Many women begin to feel that 'my body is no longer my own' even before they are pregnant. This 'giving over' of a woman's body to conception and pregnancy can be the beginning of an alienation of selfhood.

In the same way that it's crucial that men don't lose sight of family well-being as the purpose for their paid work (see Chapter 16), it's vital that women stay connected with the purpose of their health regimen. It's a choice they are making to fulfil their wish to have a child, not an end in itself. Staying connected with values and purpose are essential strategies for making our way through challenging situations.

Where a shared decision to have a child creates pressure or burden for the woman, it is an opportunity for their partner to step in and show empathy and support. If your partner is pregnant, you can't throw up *for* them, but you *can* fetch a damp cloth and a glass of water.

Sadly, the birth process can also change things markedly. While most people have uncomplicated births, you can't guarantee it will go that way. A problematic labour, traumatic delivery, or complications for your newborn can set your family off down an unexpected and challenging pathway.

If during birth your vagina, perineum or pelvic floor become damaged, that can significantly affect your relationship with your own sexuality and your sex life. Many women don't get the support they need in those circumstances. If this has happened to your partner, it's a time to be 'good selfless' (see Chapter 10), to focus more on what is happening for her and what these changes mean to her than on the implications for your sex life. If there are ongoing physical issues like incontinence or pain, be interested, and be proactive in making sure she gets the help she needs. It's vital that you both realise that challenges in your sex life can lead to a constructive change in that sex life if you work through it together as a team. Often the extra communication a couple has to do to adapt to a health challenge can lead to more intimate and relaxed sex in the long run (see Chapter 15).

Lack of support is also an issue for many women with post-natal depression. Although it is more recognised nowadays, it is still not being picked up for many new mothers. And even when it is recognised, the help available seems to vary wildly from place to place. It is an enormous challenge for a couple when their new life as a family begins with a medical or psychological crisis instead of joy and celebration. Although challenging, it is also an opportunity to strengthen your connection.

If your spouse is struggling with depression or anxiety, this is a time for you to engage. People who are overwhelmed need someone to be there with them and, sometimes, to function for them. Someone to set up an appointment with the maternal mental health service. To keep track of their medications and make sure any new prescription is filled before they run out. To take the baby and make sure they get some sleep. If there is not a strong sense of team at this crucial moment, it can leave scars that will require much work to heal down the track. However, if your partner is in need and she discovers that you have her back, that you can be relied on, this builds a foundation of trust and respect that can make your relationship almost bullet-proof going forward.

Very often, before they have children, couples can rub along quite well despite significant differences in values. Imagine a typical hetero couple. Because they have so much fun when they play together, she tolerates his disorganisation and unreliability, while he tolerates her need for control and predictability. The situation is manageable because they have enough time apart and the freedom to do things their way. However, the limitations and demands of child-rearing often highlight and exacerbate their differences. Suddenly, they *must* make a lot more joint decisions about how they are living, about their values and priorities.

This is a time to invest wholeheartedly in the type of conflict resolution strategies that have featured in earlier chapters (especially Chapters 10 and 11). To learn how to slow down and go deep when you realise you have a difference of opinion. If you have avoided these kinds of intimate conversation until now, this change will be challenging. It may help if you remind yourself that resolving conflicts over values and priorities is a necessary part of the work of building a family. That the decisions you are making now are providing the foundation for the culture that your children will grow up in. That's something that is worth working for.

One place where the issue of 'family culture' can suddenly take on a whole new dimension is relationships with wider whānau (extended family). A classic example is when your remote in-laws suddenly want to be very involved in your life, or at least the lives of your children. From their point of view, your kids belong to their tribe. This can bring acute attention to differences in family culture and expectations that were previously easy to skim over. It is common for one person to feel trapped between the expectations of their family of origin and those of their partner's.

It's essential for your relationship that you discuss these cultural differences and work out a team approach — what your shared boundaries will be regarding the involvement of the extended family. An example might be how do we celebrate birthdays? Do we do them the way your family did it, or the way my family did it? Perhaps we do some blend, or maybe we develop our own rituals. Exactly what you decide to do isn't important. What *is* important that you take time to express and explore what birthdays mean to each of you. What did you like or not like about the way your family did them? Keep talking until you find a way to do birthdays that works for both of you.

You can't overestimate the impact of not being able to have kids

If you want children, *not* being able to have them also significantly affects your relationship. Infertility rates are rising worldwide, meaning that increasing numbers of couples are struggling to conceive the children they desire.

In dealing with infertility, couples have to work through a lot. Sex that was a source of pleasure, fun and connection slowly becomes a focus of tension. As the pressure to conceive increases, sex becomes more regimented, its timing dictated by ovulation rather than emotion or desire. Each month there is fresh sadness as a period arrives. For many people this pattern is exacerbated by the excitement of a pregnancy followed by the grief of a miscarriage. Sometimes repeatedly. Sex and conception can become associated with disappointment and loss. You are likely to each deal with that stress quite differently.

Ensure that you find ways to reach out across the divide and connect about this shared journey. If you are inclined to shut it out and ignore it, make an effort to tell your partner that this is what you are doing. If you tend to process things by talking them over repeatedly, make sure there is space for your spouse. Assume that they have their own reaction, even if they are not showing it, and signal clearly that you have interest and emotional energy to hear how it is for them.

Partners can differ in their determination to conceive, creating another layer of tension around the whole process. One person can feel consumed and fixated, while their partner feels marginalised and abandoned. If you are heading towards this type of polarisation, it's pivotal that you catch yourselves. Take time to explore differences and reconnect by showing interest and empathy for your partner's position, even if it's very different from your own.

Eventually, if they don't fall pregnant, then the couple faces working through the medical options. This is a time to pause and take stock. There is nothing remotely romantic or sexy about IVF or related technologies. Many people find the process invasive and dehumanising. You need to be clear about why you want to go forward. For some couples, it is a straightforward decision. They are united in their desire for children at all costs and they will fire ahead. For others, it's time to take stock and consider the pros and cons.

Again, it is crucial that you *work as a team*. It's important to take the time to determine how far you are willing to go and how long you are willing to try. The skills and approaches suggested in Chapter 11 on doing conflict well will likely be necessary if that conversation is to stay productive.

If, after all your efforts, you don't get the family you wanted, then you may want to read the final chapter in this book, about grief. Infertility is an example of the 'infinite loss' discussed in the last section of that chapter. For some people who keenly want children but are unable to do so, the grief never ends. You are likely to grieve in different ways, and it's vital that you find a means to 'grieve together' so that this ongoing loss doesn't drive you apart.

Expect that it will take time to adjust

Given the complexity and intensity of what's going on when we have children, and the fact that most of us receive *no* training in parenting, we must have realistic expectations about how long it takes to feel competent as a parent, let alone a smoothly functioning team.

Some of the ways we have coped with our insecurities will no longer fit with family life. Using alcohol or other drugs, relentless self-sacrifice, success at work or sport, or compulsive exercise or spending are all strategies that are unlikely to make you a strong part of a parenting team. Even habits that were unremarkable pre-kids — like all-night gaming sessions or spontaneous girls' weekends — abruptly become impossible indulgences.

A new mother rarely has any option but to accept this change wholesale. She frequently loses respect for her partner when they refuse to accept the demands of their new responsibilities and instead carry on with old ways that don't support the family. This points to the importance of being self-aware enough to recognise which of the coping strategies you rely on are not going to fit with having kids. Having identified them, you need to determine what you are going to put in their place.

Ideally, you would do all this work before you have kids, but often we don't realise how much we rely on things until we have to stop doing them. We need to have compassion for ourselves, and accept that we are fallible and insecure. And, at the same time, exert a wholesome discipline on ourselves to make sure that our behaviour supports our goal of having a family. If you are struggling to kick a habit that doesn't fit with being a parent, don't be defensive about it. Share your struggle with your partner. Talk about why it's so hard to change. Use them as an ally, a coach, to help you work out what you can replace it with. A problem shared is a problem halved, so let your teammate share the burden with you.

Sex is something that we often form habits around that are totally upended by having children. From the hormonal and physical changes during pregnancy to the relentless demands of caring for an infant 24 hours a day, many things affect a woman's sense of herself in the process of having children. Most women report a marked drop-off in sexual interest. This can be very challenging, especially if their partner is someone who uses sex for reassurance and comfort. There is an opportunity for men in that situation to learn new ways of being in touch with their vulnerable emotions. It can also be an opportunity to talk intimately about things like self-pleasure. You can reassure your partner that you know how to take care of yourself and stress that there is no pressure on her to be sexual before she is ready. If a woman has gone off sex, it is also a chance for the couple to explore non-sexual ways of connecting and feeling close (see Chapter 15).

The arrival of children may be the thing that exposes those habits and highlights your need to change to more life-enhancing ways of caring for yourself. I often joke that I remained an adolescent until we finally had kids in our mid-thirties. I'm referring to the gradual realisation that if I was to be the parent I aspired to be, I had to learn to manage myself better. In this way, parenthood is often the cue or incentive we need to commit to growth and self-development.

Differentiation is crucial for parenting well

Most parents are heavily invested in the well-being of their children. When both people invest strongly in the outcome of something as unpredictable and long-term as parenting, it can make reconciling differences particularly challenging.

As discussed in the previous chapter, one partner frequently focuses on the immediate and emotional needs of the family while the other focuses on the long-term and material needs. This is a case of *both* people being right and having a valid point of view. The danger arises when they cannot acknowledge, let alone value, what their partner brings to the discussion. Once again, making it work requires Differentiation skills (Chapters 2 and 6) and the management of your neurobiology and your Attachment wounds (Chapters 5 and 7).

Many parents are concerned about harming their children by exposing them to unhealthy conflicts, aggression, abuse and violence. These things are not suitable for kids to see or be around. However, conflict-avoidant parents also harm their children by offering no experience or training in dealing with conflict healthily. Children learn what they live. Ideally, you model for them that it's okay to disagree, and that you can apologise and repair when you have done something to damage the relationship. If your children learn that people can be upset with each other and still behave in decent, even loving ways, you are giving them a huge head-start in life.

The parenting styles continuum

In the diagram below, we take a simplified view of parenting and put all of the styles of being a parent on a line that runs from neglectfully relaxed to abusively controlling.

PARENTING STYLES CONTINUUM

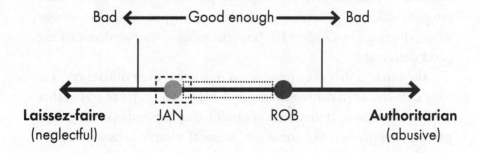

Let's accept that the extremes at either end are harmful to children. That leaves a large section of parenting styles that are 'good enough'. Most kids will probably do okay under the care of a parent whose style is inside the two thin vertical lines.

Imagine that Jan is sole-parenting, and facing a decision about where to set a boundary for her child. She's a 'good enough' parent who's towards the relaxed (laissez-faire) end of the continuum. When it comes to making decisions, the dashed rectangle around Jan shows the options she considers. She won't consider the more authoritarian end of the continuum at all. So, if there's an option up that end that might suit her child better, she's unlikely to employ it. (Please note: I am not saying that sole parents can't be good parents. I was raised by one and have the utmost respect for what they do. Jan is a 'good enough' parent in this example. However, I have frequently heard sole parents bemoan the lack of someone to share the responsibility for the endless decisions a parent has to make.)

Compare that with what happens if Jan has a partner (Rob) whose natural style is more authoritarian. If they are both involved in the parenting, and work towards an agreed strategy, then the range of options they are likely to consider is shown by the dotted rectangle. Because of their differences, they will probably have a much wider range of actions and choices available to their parenting. Remember what I discussed in Chapter 10 about the value of teamwork in making good decisions.

The catch is that they must learn to discuss their differences (i.e. have Differentiated conversations) and arrive at a course of action that satisfies them both. If they are not careful, they can end up seeing their partner's suggestions as 'wrong' or 'harmful' simply because they are outside the realm of what they personally find comfortable.

Here's how it would ideally work: We want to take the best of your ideas about parenting and the best of mine, and blend them to make a parenting culture unique to our relationship and family. This might extend to the best of your upbringing or extended family culture and the best of mine.

Beware of projecting your childhood onto your kids

Being a good parenting team is often difficult because we unconsciously use our children to resolve issues and wounds from our upbringing. For example, the man who had an abusive father who doesn't provide his kids with the safety of clear boundaries; or the woman whose parents were so busy that she came to believe she was unimportant, so she becomes over-involved in every aspect of her children's lives, undermining their confidence in themselves.

A growing industry preys on women's anxieties about being good parents, such as websites that insist the child must remain the centre of the universe and confuse over-attending with Secure Attachment. For the record, Secure Attachment is built by caregivers being *sufficiently* attuned and repairing ruptures in the relationship, *not* by there never being any ruptures.[4] Yes, your child needs a secure base and to know that they are loved and accepted and reliably cared for, physically and emotionally. However, they also need to learn to delay gratification and to tolerate the distress of not having everything exactly how they want it. The pain of frustration helps kids learn to self-regulate and persevere. As vital as it is for your child to feel secure, it is also crucial that they are allowed to develop a sense of autonomy. We can disable our children by over-functioning for them.

If you are driving yourself to meet unrealistic standards of parenting, that is no healthier than being driven to attain unrealistic standards of wealth. If you are exhausted and overwhelmed by the way you are parenting, you may need to consider whether your expectations are realistic. If your partner feels alienated and marginalised, you are probably not working well as a team. Scenarios like this should prompt you to consider whether one or more sets of insecurities are in play regarding your approach to parenting.

Another situation that evokes enormous guilt in many people is the issue of whether to be a stay-at-home parent or use childcare facilities. As usual, our society gives women completely contradictory messages about this. On the one hand, you are privileged and indulged if you stay at home; on the other, you are neglecting your children if you are in paid employment. On the one hand, you are abandoning your selfhood and identity if you stop working and focus on caring for others; on the other, you are selfish and unwomanly if you continue to pursue your career.

Of course, most couples have no choice but to put their children in childcare because they need two incomes to have any hope of being financially secure. When it's not a choice, many people experience enormous regret and guilt at what they and their children are 'missing out on'. As well as learning to discuss and acknowledge the cost of achieving their financial goals, couples under this level of financial pressure must be conscientious about negotiating roles and responsibilities in the family.

Negotiate a fair division of labour

One of the keys to harmony in the parental team is having clear and explicit agreements about responsibilities and expectations. Make sure you have read and discussed the issues about power and gender (where applicable) discussed in Chapter 12.

It is the case that there are significant biological sex differences in our experiences with children. The physical realities of pregnancy and breastfeeding and women's hormonal responses to their children invite them to be much more self-sacrificial as parents. In hetero couples, this is so ubiquitous that it has become a cultural norm. The trouble is that men's ability to be more self-focused can very easily slide into being exploitative. If a man is selfish to the point where his partner fears the child will suffer, he can rely on her to step in and do what's needed.

In taking for granted that their partner will know what the child needs, will be the one to get up in the night, will compromise their career to ensure that the children are well cared for, men directly benefit. In hetero relationships, male parents frequently retain freedoms, health, status and opportunities that are unimaginable for their partners. Not surprisingly, this leads to resentment. It's an excellent way for a man to torpedo a couple's sex life.

In her book *Fair Play*, Eve Rodsky lays out a system for structuring the division of labour in a relationship.[5] It raises some fascinating ideas about family life and the division of labour. She only has four rules; the first one, 'All time is created equal', was a focus of Chapter 14. Rodsky highlights the tendency of Western culture to see men's time as 'finite like diamonds' (and therefore precious), and women's time 'infinite like sand' (and therefore almost worthless).

In my experience, this again has a lot to do with how our society values money. If unpaid work is not valued equally with paid work, then the couple dynamic will be rooted in inequality. We can reverse the genders with a stay-at-home father and a high-flying businesswoman mother, and the result is the same.

Rodsky highlights the value of explicitly unpacking everything involved in every task required to run a family and household, both pragmatically, from conception to planning to execution, and emotionally or values-wise. Exploring and trying to explain to your partner, for example, why getting the kids to school on time is important to you (e.g. 'My dad was always dropping me off late and it gave me a reputation for slackness that dogged me right through school.').

Most couples never get to this level of detail about anything! Yet once you have kids, it is essential to lay all this stuff out to avoid misunderstandings, frustration, resentment and, ultimately, contempt.

The next couple of sections offer some structure that you can use to ensure your parenting is as effective as it can be.

Choking on your sandwich

The transition to being parents is happening later and later for many people, which is fine in and of itself. I would argue that there are pluses and minuses to having kids at any age. Verity and I had kids in our late thirties, and one consequence we hadn't anticipated was ending up as members of a 'sandwich' generation. That is, still caring for dependent children when our parents (who also had us late in life) needed increasing support.

The amount of practical and emotional work needed in that situation is mind-boggling. External stresses are a threat to making your relationship work well. It requires a *lot* of processing and communication to sort out priorities with so many crucial things on the go simultaneously.

Sadly, this is a place where I see a lot of sexism in play in hetero couples. Even more than caring for children, providing care to the elderly defaults to the woman, even when it's the man's parent who needs care! To avoid having a family life that reinforces power differences, with one person being 'bad selfless' (oppressed) and one being 'bad selfish' (entitled) (see Chapter 10), you need to work as a team about setting priorities and work out what to let go.

Being in this 'sandwich' position is often when people realise that they can't meet their financial and career goals if they are to retain their integrity, and that their family is genuinely more important than 'getting ahead' or 'success'. Others realise that they are not able to support their parents as they had expected. It doesn't matter what you decide, so long as you are both on board.

Parenting someone else's kids — how not to be wicked

There's a reason why step-parents became the stereotyped villain in fairy tales — it's a tough gig, and many people struggle with it. Stepfamilies have a lower survival rate worldwide, because of the specific stresses that step-parenting imposes on a relationship. However, you can beat the odds by understanding and accepting some fundamental realities about how step- and blended families work.

There are two key issues: loyalty conflicts and 'borrowed' authority. What I mean by **loyalty conflicts** is that if you are in a relationship with someone with children, don't *ever* force that person to choose between you and their kids. Most people will pick their kids every time. Yet it is precisely this reality that is unsettling to so many people.

Forcing a loyalty conflict is usually driven by someone allowing their insecurities to interfere with parenting. It goes like this: Especially if I haven't parented my own kids, I may have no concept of how bound to, invested in and devoted to kids it is normal to be. If I fear I am not good enough, not important, etc., then it's easy for me to get jealous, including of the time and energy you put into your kids. Your behaviour will seem like a choice *against me* rather than *for your children*.

Of course, if I do have kids of my own, the situation becomes even more complicated. My kids and how I parent them will probably differ from your kids and how you parent them. Each of us will have worked hard to get to where we are, and it is easy to fall into the trap of seeing your way of doing things as 'wrong' or, equally unhelpfully, as an indictment of how I parent.

Again, the solution is learning how to adopt a Differentiated stance (see Chapters 2 and 6), where we accept and explore our differences and work together to find solutions that work for everyone in our family. This will require you to be aware of how your anxiety around being a 'good' parent and 'getting it right' for your kids can make you overly rigid. I have seen several couples who can negotiate successfully about everything except parenting.

The other big issue for step-parenting couples is the challenge of accepting the reality that step-parents have *no authority* to discipline, control or otherwise parent the stepchild except as delegated by the biological parent. This is known as **'borrowed' authority**. That is, the only authority you have with the kids is 'borrowed' from the birth parent (or parents).

This reality leaves the step-parent in a disempowered position, and the biological parent as the meat in the sandwich. That is how the system works — so make sure you don't waste energy bucking it. *Accept it and adapt.* If you want your parenting discussions to be successful, these should show your awareness of the difficulties of your partner's role (and each role in the step-parenting system has its challenges), as well as the discomfort of your own.

The practical implication of borrowed authority is that as a step-parent, you can only exert influence indirectly. You can't parent someone else's kids as you think you should; you can only do what has the biological parent's consent. So, your only way to exert influence is by persuading the biological parent to change their approach.

This may feel like an intolerable position if you are used to being in charge — if, for example, you are a man who has lived on his own and is used to doing things your way.

To make matters worse, if you don't have children of your own (or even if you have), you also need to defer to the biological parent's expertise. They have years of practice knowing and parenting this child, so you must be humble. You are an apprentice at the feet of the master. This is not to say you don't have something to offer, and indeed many sole parents experience colossal relief at having someone with whom to share the burden of parenting. But submit your different ideas humbly and with an acceptance that you are unlikely to know the child as well as their biological parent for a long time, maybe ever.

Biological parents need to have humility as well. Your new partner offers a fresh set of eyes to look at how you parent and the dynamic you have with your child. It's *useful* if they ask you questions about why you make certain choices or set particular boundaries in your parenting. Make sure you are not arrogant or defensive if they suggest that there might be a different way to do things. Even if their suggestion doesn't fit for you, it might prompt you to consider options or directions you hadn't previously (like Jan in the parenting styles diagram).

Authority issues are all affected by how old a given child is when you start living with them. If they were six months old when you moved in, then you will know the child well and will likely act much more like a biological parent (especially if the other biological parent is uninvolved). However, remember that (unless you adopt the child) you don't have any legal standing, no matter how long you've been parenting them. This is important to be mindful of with things like separation, but also international travel.

A step-parenting expert, the late Brad Kunin, taught me a rough guide for determining how long it takes for your relationship with the kids to shift from borrowed authority to a direct connection: simply double the child's age at the time of beginning to live with you. So, if your stepson is 6 when you start living together, it's realistic to expect it will take until he is 12 before your direct relationship with him is deep enough for you to parent him directly. Of course, if your stepdaughter is 12 when you move in — then she's going to be 24 before she really listens to you!

Flowing on from this is another issue, related but separate from the 'borrowing' of authority. That's the extent of your involvement with the kids — from completely uninvolved and disengaged to 'acting like a biological parent'. This is shown in the following diagram.

A CONTINUUM OF STEP-PARENTING INVOLVEMENT

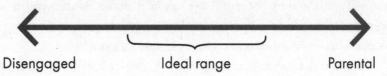

Disengaged　　　　　　Ideal range　　　　　　Parental

Where you place yourself on this continuum will be a combination of your personal preference, your partner's (the biological parent's) preference, and how connected you are with the child. Research suggests that best results are achieved somewhere in the middle. However, remember Brad Kunin's rule of thumb: the older the child at the point of living together, the further towards the disengaged end a step-parent needs to be.

In parenting, as with everything, it's vital to remember that your differences represent a resource for the family. And that you will do a better job if you harness all your strengths. You must know how to deal with differences, and have the time and energy to work through them. When you do, it's some of the most rewarding work you will ever do in your life.

BEA & JOHN

When Bea was doing her OE in her early twenties, she had a holiday romance with a Spanish guy she met in Cambodia. One of the things she liked about him was that he hung around and cared for her when she had a dose of 'Battambang Belly'. When Bea missed her second period, she realised that her tummy upset had also interfered with her contraception. She had always imagined having kids, though not on her own. However, with a marketing degree under her belt and supportive parents, she decided to keep the child, and so Lucas was five when she met John at a marketing conference.

Coming from a family of five, John had also always seen himself having kids, so he joked about getting together with Bea as 'giving me a head-start' in the family game. At 32, he was four years older than Bea and already owned his own home (with flatmates to help pay the mortgage).

Bea had stayed in touch with Lucas's father, Mateo. Once Mateo realised that she was not expecting anything of him, he showed a warm interest in Lucas, and she was pleased that he would grow up knowing who his dad was, even if they had a literally distant relationship.

To avoid adding to Lucas's confusion, she had kept other boyfriends separate from her parenting life. However, as her relationship with John deepened, she felt it was important to see how they got along. Having a parcel of nieces and nephews already, John was comfortable with meeting new kids, and they got on famously. After a few months of this, John brought up the topic of her and Lucas moving in with him, stressing that there was no rush, he would want to give his flatmates a lot of notice, but he wanted her to know that he was keen.

The timing felt good to Bea. She had been feeling increasingly stifled living in her parents' basement. While it was fantastic having them to babysit, and Lucas loved them, she felt like she wasn't getting on with her own life.

Shortly before Lucas's seventh birthday, he and Bea moved in with John. Lucas had some anxiety about leaving his grandparents and, to their credit, they went out of their way to visit frequently to help him settle.

There were also some adjustment issues for Bea and John. With this being John's house, Bea initially didn't feel like it was her home. John found it harder than he expected to accept the limitations on his life imposed by having a child. Nonetheless, they were both happy with the move, and as they sorted things out and Lucas settled in, they began to talk about their future and having kids together. Six months after moving in, Bea went off the pill, and 14 months later Stella was born, with James following along two years after.

James was two, Stella four, and Lucas 13 by the time John and Bea came to see me. Both of them were exhausted, and they were fighting a lot. The fights that really worried them were about parenting Lucas. Bea thought John had 'unrealistic expectations', and he believed she was 'too soft' and 'spoiling' him. A common source of contention was Lucas's time spent gaming on his phone, especially late at night.

John's mother 'had to run a tight ship to manage the five of us — especially us boys' (he has two brothers). A strong Catholic, she saw it as her job to keep her children 'safe from sin'. He believed that 'it didn't do me any harm', and was increasingly anxious that Lucas was 'learning bad habits' that would make him less likely to succeed in the world.

With both of their parents in high-powered jobs, Bea and her brother had a lot of freedom growing up. She remains proud of how her parents could rely on and trust her. Bea believed that for Lucas to succeed, he needed to find out for himself what worked and what didn't. Although determined to be more present in her kids' lives than her mother was, she was afraid of 'smothering' him or disabling him by undermining his self-confidence with too much criticism.

For Bea and John to have a clear run at negotiating the parenting of Lucas, they needed to recognise how much each was under the influence of, and at times compensating for, their own upbringing.

Bea already had an inkling that the amount of time she had spent in daycare and out-of-school care had had an impact. She identified strongly with an Avoidant Attachment style, and could see that some of what she had believed was 'self-sufficiency' was more about avoidance of intimacy. It was painful for her to realise that the independence and reliability she was so proud of were not age-appropriate. They represented a sense of abandonment ('I'm on my own') and feeling unimportant that she had never allowed herself to acknowledge. Her parenting tended to oscillate between unconsciously trying to compensate for this by keeping close to Lucas, and then, feeling overwhelmed by this, moving to create distance by 'giving him room to be himself'.

It was hard for John even to contemplate the possibility of any downside to how his parents had brought him up. He felt disloyal saying or even listening to anything he construed as a criticism of his mother. It took quite a bit of reassurance that reflecting on unhelpful notions you formed in your childhood was not about 'parent-blaming' or saying you had a 'bad childhood'.

Eventually, he could see that the size of the family he'd grown up in, the conventional roles (with his father a somewhat distant figure), and the high expectations his mother had of herself meant it was understandable that he had a Preoccupied Attachment style. The fact that he struggled to feel 'good enough' was more familiar to him. We explored how seeing Lucas's behaviour as a reflection on him, i.e. a 'failure', made him more anxious and aggressive in his dealings with both Lucas and Bea.

It was apparent that there were no fundamental differences in values between them, but that their respective insecurities had pushed them into increasingly polarised positions. Once they could recognise those and deal with them directly, the tone of their discussions about Lucas changed markedly. From our talks about 'good enough' parenting, they could show appreciation for what the other brought to the parenting table and felt confident that Lucas was getting the best of both of them.

Key points from Chapter 17

1. Accept that having kids changes everything, and you may need to reconsider some of your plans and goals.
2. It takes time and work to adjust to being a parent, let alone become a smoothly functioning parenting team.
3. If you also have other significant stresses, like your parents needing care, then it's even more likely that you may need to reconsider some of your plans and goals.
4. The key to being great parents is harnessing your differences, not reading all the books and blogs and getting it 'right'. Educating yourself about parenting is wise, but don't get so hung up on the theory that you don't listen to or respect your partner's perspective, even if they haven't read all the books.
5. Don't let your insecurities drive your parenting. You are very likely to harm your kids or your relationship if you do.
6. Be wary of compensating for your childhood by how you parent your kids.
7. Step-parenting and blending families presents particular challenges that you need to educate yourself about and accept.

PART FIVE

THE HARD STUFF

I n these final three chapters, I look at some tough things that can happen in relationships. I hope these chapters will offer you a way forward if you are dealing with a seriously challenging situation.

Chapter 18
Infidelity in all its forms

The foundations of a successful long-term relationship have much more to do with trust and respect than love and passion. Infidelity is such a big deal because it undermines those foundations.

Understand what the contract is

Every partnership has an agreement, a contract, at its core. In a business partnership, you lay out the contract in a thick legal document with hundreds of pages. In most intimate relationships, this contract is negotiated and established indirectly, without formally acknowledging the terms of the deal.

If you get married, then you are legally required to exchange vows, but they only need you both to say 'I, [name], take you, [partner's name], to be my legal [wife / husband / partner]', or something similar. Many ceremonies offer vows beyond this, but they are usually couched in the most general language.

This lack of specificity means that we build our relationship contract on unexamined cultural norms. There may be some discussion of values and priorities in the early stages of the relationship that helps inform our expectations. We discuss 'Do you want kids?' or 'Have you ever thought of living in the country?' We may also touch on limits and boundaries: 'My last girlfriend was a real nag', 'My last boyfriend was always off surfing with his mates', and even 'If you cheat on me, I'm gone'. Those conversations give some information about what is and isn't okay for each of you. Beyond that, we assume that our partner knows what's 'normal' and will do that.

Here's an example. Suppose I work with a group of chippies, many of whom also have long-term partners, and we all have drinks on Friday afternoon that can go on till late. In that case, I will think that's normal and believe that my partner is unreasonable and unfair when she criticises me for doing it. If my circle of friends all holiday overseas, I will be surprised when my partner objects to the cost of my plans to do the same.

Our tendency to make assumptions means that we often find out what our partner's expectations of the relationship contract are when we do something that we think is acceptable. We are surprised when they are hurt or angry about it. 'I can't believe you discussed our sex life with your friend!', 'You spent *how* much on a guitar??!' or even 'It'd be nice if you said "Hello" to me when you arrive home'. Negotiating through these instances where your expectations are different is essential to building the foundations of a long-term relationship.

What's important to get your head around is that whether or not you have explicitly talked about it, **there is a contract operating in every relationship.**

Defining infidelity

Most people think of unsanctioned sex when they hear the word 'infidelity', but I find it helpful to have a broader definition. Infidelity is simply about breaking your relationship contract.

More formally, infidelity is when you do something that you know, or believe, your partner would view as a breach of the relationship contract, usually without giving your partner a chance to object beforehand. It might be having sex with someone other than your partner. It also might be:

- Having an intense or intimate emotional relationship that your partner wouldn't be comfortable with.
- Spending money beyond an understood limit without consulting your partner.
- Hitting your kids when you have agreed that was not okay.
- Taking drugs when you had promised you wouldn't because your habit had got out of control in the past.
- Discussing your finances with your brother when you had agreed to keep your family out of it as they have a history of interfering in your decision-making.

If you have knowingly gone against your partner's expectations of how the relationship operates, you have violated the contract. In my experience, the infidelities that have been impossible to rebuild trust from have often not been sexual.

In terms of sex, these days fidelity may not mean monogamy. Increasingly, people in long-term committed relationships are experimenting with consensual non-monogamy (CNM). As a matter of interest, this frequently involves *explicit* agreements about limits and boundaries, which is a good thing.

Let's say you have a clear contract that when either of you travels away from your hometown, you are allowed to have sex with other people. The boundaries on this are (a) you will be very careful about your sexual health, using barriers like condoms and dams, and (b) that you will have no ongoing contact with any sexual partners. So the fact that you had sex with someone on your work trip last year is *not* infidelity, but the fact that you have had a 'few chats' with them via WhatsApp since then *would* be infidelity.

When the infidelity isn't hidden

In most cases, people who knowingly break their relationship contract try to hide what they are doing from their partner because they don't want to deal with their partner's objections and upset. However, there are instances where people are upfront about their actions and simply ignore their partner's protests. 'I'm going to sleep with Sam, and there's nothing you can do about it', or 'I'm going to use our money to buy that business because your fears are foolish'.

To me, this is still breaking the partnership agreement — but it's even more about violating the *whole spirit* of 'partnership'. A partnership is an arrangement between equals rooted in consensual decision-making. The kind of unilateral decision-making described above demonstrates power over another, and is a feature of a hierarchy (often a patriarchy), *not* a partnership. If you're dealing with that, you might be better off reading the following chapter than this one.

Rubbing the salt of deception into the wound of infidelity

When you want to do something but don't want to deal with your partner's reaction to it, the simple solution is to make sure they don't know about it. Let's say I start meeting with a colleague at work for coffee and lunch. Initially, I am completely upfront about it with you. It doesn't happen that often, and it's easy for me to report fully what was said because it's all so innocent.

Gradually the conversations with the colleague get more personal, more intimate. We start talking about our marriages, our hopes and dreams. At some point, I know that you would *not* be happy if you were to listen to a recording of our meetings. So I don't tell you about all the times it happens, and I mislead you by not accurately reporting the exact content of the conversation. Somewhere in there, I have crossed the line into infidelity; and to make matters worse, I have started deceiving you.

In my experience as a therapist, deception can do as much harm as infidelity, if not more. I have worked with many couples where someone has done something that breaks the contract and immediately told their partner about it. 'I got drunk at the stag do and ended up going to a brothel with a bunch of the boys', or 'I went to the casino and had a night on the pokies (when they had a history of gambling addiction)'. This behaviour is upsetting to their partner, but if it's a rare event, the couple will process it and learn from it.

If their partner finds out months later about the brothel or the casino visit, that is a much bigger deal. Most partners feel like the rug has been pulled out from under them, that they have been 'living a lie', and it makes them question everything they know and believe about their partner and their relationship.

Part of the reason why the deception is such a big deal is that it *also* breaks the contract — the part that says I will deal with you fairly and honestly, that I will give you the information you need to make wise decisions about your choices.

When couples present for therapy following infidelity that was discovered rather than confessed, I will routinely tell the contract-breaker:

Clearly, you weren't ready to be honest about what you have been doing. In many cases, that means there's more that you haven't told your partner. I'm not asking you to confirm or deny that right now. What I want to do is give you some information that comes from my long experience in these situations. In most cases, you do more harm by withholding information at this point than by whatever you have done to break the contract.

If we go forward from this point with your partner thinking they know it all, and then later they find out that there was more, that is frequently a deal-breaker. The infidelity is terrible enough — but the fact that they are here signals that they are willing to rebuild trust in you. But you can only do that based on honesty and openness.

Given how intense their reaction was to what they have found out, you may be afraid that there's no way the relationship can survive if they know any more. I'm telling you that if you withhold information at this point, it's a far more risky strategy. Now go away and think about whether there is any more you need to tell your partner about.

I also warn the partner against using my caution as an excuse to interrogate the contract-breaker endlessly, as it impairs the contract-breaker's ability to make good judgement calls. In both cases, people usually ignore my advice — the emotions in play are too powerful.

For the rest of this chapter, when I talk about infidelity the assumption is that it also involves deception, as this is nearly always the case.

Deciding whether you want to try to repair the relationship

If you are in the horrible position of having discovered an infidelity, then I believe that the question you need to answer is *not* 'Can I trust my partner?' In the short term, the answer is a clear 'no'. At this point, your partner has proved to be untrustworthy. However, that doesn't mean you need to end the relationship. It may be possible to rebuild trust.

For that to happen, you need to be able to **trust yourself**. Will you be able to look after yourself if the worst happens — if your partner breaks faith again? Will you stay sane? Will you be able to forgive yourself for taking additional emotional risks? For most people, even though it would be exquisitely painful should their partner again break the contract and deceive them, they would survive. With time, they could process it, learn the lessons they need to, and move on. In that case, they can afford to risk seeing whether rebuilding trust in the relationship is possible.

If you genuinely fear that you will have a breakdown or become suicidal; if it would render you unable to function in society if you tried to rebuild trust and were further let down and deceived, you probably need to end the relationship. The potential costs are too high. Some people who have had traumatic upbringings or abusive early relationships are not in a position to deal with the further betrayal of trust, which is completely understandable.

Why should you bother?

If your partner cheats on you, many people advise you to end the relationship immediately. 'A leopard won't change its spots' and 'Once a cheater, always a cheater', they will say. If you are the one who has broken the contract and damaged trust, you may fear that there is no way back, that the relationship is irreparably damaged.

I have worked with hundreds of couples who are processing infidelity, and in my experience it does not warrant the fatalism and cynicism of this kind of attitude. I find that working with infidelity is powerful because we can harness the massive disruption to take the relationship to a deep level of intimacy in a very short time. Much quicker than can happen under 'normal' circumstances. I'm not saying that this is easy or inevitable, and I certainly don't recommend it as a way to deepen your relationship, but it *is* possible.

The crucial thing to understand is that **you are committing to a process of exploring what's possible in this relationship, not re-committing to being together forever**. In most cases, the old relationship is dead. Typically, the old contract proves to be 'not fit for purpose', because in tolerating a lack of intimacy it allowed too much room for avoidance, self-deception and betrayal. Your task for the short- to medium-term is to determine whether you can rebuild trust and create a new relationship that maintains the good things about the old one but works better for both of you. If it helps, you can put a specific timeframe on this process. For example, 'I'll give it 12 months and see if I feel safe enough at the end of that time.'

If there have been repeated breaches of trust, then, obviously, greater caution about the prospect for change is warranted. It's important not to be naïve. There certainly are bad actors out there — people with no conscience who are selfish in the extreme. Some of these people have deceived me as successfully as they did their partners (contrary to popular opinion, psychologists are not mind-readers).

It all comes down to whether the contract-breaker is genuinely ready to take themselves on. If there are indications that this is happening (for example, they have made a much fuller, less defensive explanation than in past instances, or if the infidelity is confessed rather than discovered), then it may be worth exploring what is possible going forward. Remember, you are not committing forever; just to see what is possible if things change.

When something you feared greatly has happened, and you discover that you have survived, that life goes on, it can be very liberating. If you have betrayed not just your partner's trust but also your own integrity, it can be a powerful incentive to understand yourself — to get a profound and satisfactory answer to 'How did I end up in this situation?' By the same token, when the person who betrayed your trust can support you and be there for you as you process the pain they caused, that can be hugely healing.

So, if there has been an infidelity in your relationship, it is worth finding out whether you can turn this crap into compost and grow something new and beautiful in your relationship.

How to rebuild trust

When there has been a major breach of the relationship agreement, it is up to the contract-breaker to do what's necessary to begin the process of restoring their partner's trust. This has to happen *first*, before any other issues in the relationship are addressed. There may well be serious issues in the wider couple dynamic, including major areas of dissatisfaction for the contract-breaker — these will have to wait.

When there has been a significant infidelity, the person who has had their choices taken away by the unilateral action of the contract-breaker is left in a hugely vulnerable position if they choose to remain in the relationship. They are keeping their life bound up with someone who has proved to be untrustworthy.

To re-balance the relationship, the contract-breaker must make themselves vulnerable. Most people go into self-protective mode when you uncover their infidelity. They feel exposed, and the last thing they want to do is risk more vulnerability. It's a crucial example of the need to *be* vulnerable, even though you *feel* vulnerable (see Chapter 9). Coming from a vulnerable and caring place is what begins the work of healing.

In my decades of working with infidelity, I have developed a set of guidelines that outline the crucial tasks you need to accomplish to restore trust. The essence of these is laid out in Exercise 56. It is addressed to the contract-breaker, but can also act as a guide for partners about what to reasonably expect.

EXERCISE 56: A FORMULA FOR REBUILDING TRUST

When you have significantly hurt your partner and betrayed their trust by breaking your relationship agreement and deceiving them about it, it can be hard to know how you can rebuild that trust. Over the years, my clients have taught me there are four key elements that you need to offer your partner consistently *over a long time* (think in terms of a couple of years of doing this).

1. Intimacy

The most powerful way to reassure your partner that you have changed is not to make promises. Saying 'I won't do it again' never reassures anyone. Instead, be **self-aware** of the forces working within your psyche, especially the ones that led to you breaching trust. You also need to **share** these in a vulnerable and open way; and your sharing needs to include a clear and coherent **plan** of what you will do to prevent you from breaking the contract when those forces act on you again.

If your partner believes they know what's going on in you in-depth, they will feel confident that they know what you are going to do next.

2. Reliability

You can reinforce your partner's confidence by being reliable — someone they can lean on. One part of this is being **reliable practically**: being a person of your word, who does what they say they will, goes to where they say they are going, turns up when they said they would, etc. This extends to the small things, e.g. being reliable with household chores or coming home on time. In cases of infidelity, it can be even more vital that you don't do what you said you wouldn't do and don't go where you said you wouldn't go.

The other part is being **reliable emotionally** — being supportive of and caring to your partner. Offering support is crucial when they are upset, even angry, about the hurt you have done to them. If you want to rebuild trust, you have to tolerate facing the consequences of your choices over and over again. Your partner doesn't *want* to keep remembering or being tormented by questions, so don't treat them as being deliberately difficult when they bring their pain to you. Instead, see it as an opportunity to rebuild.

3. Empathy

Showing you care about the pain, confusion, self-doubt and anger you have caused is essential to rebuilding trust. Your partner needs to know that their distress affects you and matters to you. Being able to show this kind of **emotional empathy** consistently is the best way to make amends.

However, it is also essential to show **cognitive empathy**; to explicitly recognise that your partner's feelings make sense in the circumstances. So often, when our partner's distress triggers our own shame or embarrassment, we try to minimise or undermine the reasons why they are upset.

4. Persistence

It takes **time** to rebuild trust. You must keep doing these things repeatedly, typically long past the point when *you* think it's fair or reasonable. Your partner's pain is not yours, and only they can judge when they feel they can trust again. So if the relationship is precious to you, just keep going.

If you are the partner of someone who has broken the contract, and what is said in Exercise 56 strikes a chord with you, share it with your partner. Explain why certain bits are particularly important to you. Hopefully, this demonstrates that you aren't looking to punish your partner, but instead are seeking a way to restore trust and integrity to your relationship. It may be painful for them to do this level of self-examination and to take this degree of responsibility, but this framing up makes it clear that their pain is not your intent.

Why? Why? Why?

The most common response for a partner blindsided by infidelity is to launch into a relentless interrogation of the contract-breaker. This appears to be an attempt to regain a sense of control in their life, to try to work out what is authentic and reliable and what is not.

On one level, this is perfectly understandable and reasonable. However, people in pain often do this in unreasonable ways. For example: When I wake up at 3 a.m. with a new thought about the infidelity (or a recurrence of one I have already had many times) and angrily wake you to ask you about it, that's *not* reasonable behaviour. Understandable, but not reasonable.

Tit for tat in the suffering stakes doesn't help anyone, and having both of you sleep-deprived just makes the whole situation more volatile and dangerous. It may annoy you that *you* are the one who is awake while the person who caused this chaos in your life sleeps on untroubled. Nonetheless, save your questions until you have had time to reflect in the light of day on the best way to ask them — even if they are necessary. It's also in your interest to wait until your partner is awake and has time to offer you a considered response to an important question.

Beware of asking for details of sexual infidelity that will allow you to paint a graphic picture in your mind of what they were doing. That is *not* in your interest — it's likely to haunt you.

In my experience, two key questions need answering. One related to the infidelity, and one related to the choice to deceive. It is advantageous to separate them so that you are not confusing yourself and your partner.

The crucial question about the infidelity is something like this:

Why did you want this thing so badly that you were willing to risk our relationship (and our family)?

Often you will initially get a superficial answer to this, like 'I was drunk' or 'I was depressed', which doesn't address the question vulnerably. The in-depth answers are often about a person's insecurities or needs and yearnings that they have denied or minimised to themselves.

Someone who fears that they are unimportant might seek an affair where the third party's interest makes them feel special. They might take on a risky business deal or a time-consuming voluntary role without their partner's knowledge or consent, in the unconscious hope that succeeding there will make them feel significant and worthwhile.

Someone who has always done their duty and done what they 'should' may have a deep yearning to be freer in their choices and behaviour. They don't feel entitled to ask for what they want, but instead suddenly impulsively act on it.

Getting answers to 'What motivated you?' that make intuitive and satisfying sense is crucial to helping deceived partners settle their anxiety. Here's how it goes: If I now understand what drove you to break faith, plus I know you are aware of those drivers and are learning other ways to deal with them, then I can start to manage my anxiety better. Very often, the 'other ways' involve you becoming more open with me, talking in a more vulnerable way, which can immediately deepen the sense of intimacy and connection between us.

Once you have shared a deep answer to what motivated your infidelity, the question about the deception then becomes:

***If it was THAT important to you, why did
you not talk to me about it, or fight with me
about it, rather than go behind my back?***

In many cases, it is because your partner couldn't see any point in asking — they believed they knew the answer. However, they need to learn that asking the question would have led them to reflect more deeply on what they wanted and why they wanted it. This wouldn't be a comfortable conversation, but it might be a productive one.

I certainly have worked with couples where one person has said something like 'I want to open our relationship up to having sex with other people', or 'I want to invest all our money in this (risky) business opportunity'. While this has been disruptive and challenging to discuss, it hasn't involved breaking the contract or their partner's trust. A painful but honest conversation does much less damage than infidelity.

Dos and don'ts if your partner has broken faith with you

- Do find a way to make peace with the fact that, for now, you are in an emotionally unsafe situation.
- Don't make things worse by acting out in revenge — you likely rob yourself of choices down the line.
- Don't tell everyone you know, to shame your partner — in the long run, this will likely hurt you more than them.
- Don't accept superficial explanations — there have to be powerful motivations at work, even if your partner is oblivious to them.
- Do ask probing questions to try to find the deep explanations.
- Don't question incessantly and repetitively — that's harassment, not investigation.
- Don't ask for details about sexual activity that will allow you to make a movie in your head of what they got up to.
- Don't let your partner pathologise your understandable distress — make it clear that if they can't show empathy, the relationship doesn't have a future.
- Do be honest if you are hoping that the relationship can go

forward — many contract-breakers fear there is no hope.

- Do take the risk of extending further trust if your partner is generally a person of integrity.

Dos and don'ts if you (the contract-breaker) genuinely want to restore trust

- Don't collapse into the 'dog box'. Right now, you should be more focused on your partner's pain than your own guilt and shame.
- Don't assume it's unforgivable — believe that you can change, and give your partner reason to believe it, too.
- Do be particularly wary of withdrawal and avoidance. When you shut down because you are full of shame, you can look very callous and uncaring.
- Do take the opportunity to learn about yourself. What did you miss if you ended up in a situation that surprised you?
- Do provide deep and complex answers about your motivations.
- Do recognise that the reasons for your infidelity and your reasons for hiding it require separate explanations.
- Do be aware of and inhibit your self-protective reflexes (e.g. withdrawing or justifying). Stop adding to the hurt and pain.

KARLA & JOE

Joe grew up in a low-income family in Huntly, his father a road worker and his mum working checkout at the local supermarket. The eldest of four, he was always aware of what he couldn't do because they couldn't afford it. Joe started packing shelves at the supermarket at age 12, and was working full-time at McDonald's by 16. His work ethic made him stand out and kept winning him promotion. By the time he and Karla got together in their early twenties, he was already managing a KFC in Hamilton.

Karla was the middle of three girls who was 'always the peacemaker'. While her older sister was 'rebellious' and her younger 'withdrawn', she always tried to make things right. Her teen years were overshadowed by her parents' acrimonious divorce following her father's affair with his PA. Understandably, she had always been contemptuous of people who 'can't keep it in their pants'. Her father's business failed not long after the divorce, which forced Karla to change schools, and their standard of living plummeted. Karla did everything she could to support her mother and make life easy for her — doing well at school, helping around the house, and generally being 'Miss Goody Two-Shoes'.

She started out training to be a hairdresser, but ended up selling hair products and discovered that she had a talent for sales. When she met Joe, she was the top rep in her company and making good bonuses. They were matched up by mutual friends who thought they would appreciate each other's determination to get ahead financially. They hit it off right away and moved in together within six months. Their shared 'work hard, play hard' philosophy meant that they had the deposit for their first home together within two years.

Once the kids came along, Karla stopped working until the youngest went to school. She then started in real estate and found that she could combine this with parenting as Joe was willing to step up on the weekend days when she was her busiest (then he would disappear to his work for the evening shifts).

A dutiful wife and mother, Karla would have confidently said she would never cheat on Joe right up until she found herself in bed with Dieter.

With the kids largely off her hands, she had hoped that she and Joe would rekindle their relationship. Instead, Joe took the freedom from family responsibility as an opportunity to purchase a second KFC franchise. He was able to buy it because it was underperforming, but turning it around proved a lot more time-consuming than he had told Karla.

Although that frustrated her, she didn't realise how lonely she had become in the marriage until Dieter started paying her attention. Having 'done the right thing for 50 years', she initially felt a thrill of rebellion at encouraging what she told herself was a 'harmless flirtation' with this charming European who worked from the same real estate office.

However, after a few too many drinks at the regional conference, the flirtation became anything but harmless when she found herself following Dieter to his hotel room. What surprised her was how alive she felt the next day. Guilty, but vibrant in a way she couldn't recall since before the kids were born. Her anxiety about the consequences of her infidelity translated into a fierce determination to keep the secret from Joe. Dieter was also married, so this suited him.

However, Dieter's wife found them out and blew the whole thing open with a phone call to Joe 18 months later. Joe was devastated. He had thought things were going well between them. The fact that Karla had been happier and complaining less about how much he was working now took on a very different meaning.

When I met them, Karla's anxiety about the potential impact on the kids (both in their twenties by this point) made her appear somewhat indifferent to Joe's situation. Although she was apologetic for hurting Joe, she was resentful about how he had ignored and neglected her. There was a certain air of blaming him for putting her in that position.

For his part, Joe was bewildered. He couldn't understand how he had ended up here 'with everything I've worked for in ruins', as he saw it. Initially, he directed all his anger at Dieter and made noises about 'going around there and sorting him out'. This only made Karla angrier, because she resented the implication that she was a victim rather than a grown woman in charge of her own life.

Karla began to settle down once Joe had agreed that, for now, they did not need to tell the kids anything more specific than that they were having some counselling for their relationship. In consultation with Dieter and their manager, she decided to move to a different branch of her real estate firm, and committed to Joe that she would not be going to conferences without him in the future.

In exploring the two 'whys' of her infidelity, Karla gradually realised that she had been self-sacrificing to an unhealthy degree all her life. It was painful for her to recognise that her resentment had roots right back in her teenage years. Her feelings of 'having' to cope because her mother wasn't, and 'having' to be good (and miss out on the fun) because she couldn't bear to add to her mother's distress, defined her life at that time.

I introduced her to the idea that resentment in a partnership is a sign that you haven't looked after yourself. She recognised how readily she had let herself take a back seat to Joe's business (and the kids, but she didn't resent that).

In terms of the second 'why', it became clear that Karla believed she had tried to tell Joe about her unhappiness, and he had ignored her. However, when we looked at the things she had tried, she could see they were pretty ineffectual. We related this to her insecurity of feeling like 'I don't matter', which meant that she always expected to get nowhere.

Of course, Joe's 'I'm not good enough' was firing off in this situation.

He saw Dieter as suave and sophisticated, and it took some time before he believed that Karla truly didn't want to pursue her relationship with Dieter. Karla was clear: 'He's charming, but, honestly, he's a bit in love with himself. He's got some nice manners that make you feel special, but it's pretty superficial. One of the reasons I felt able to go on with the affair was that I was certain it would go nowhere. I would not want to live with him.'

Joe was apprehensive that Dieter was a better lover than him. Karla felt very awkward talking about her sex with Dieter, but once I assured her that it was a bad idea to get into too much detail about what they did, she could respond to Joe's anxieties. 'It wasn't what he did sexually; it was that he was interested in me and told me how I made him feel. That made me feel sexy. He also was very comfortable with me using a vibrator, which took away a lot of pressure about me coming.'

Again Karla could see that she had not looked after herself in her sex life with Joe. She had let his insecurities dominate (e.g. regarding using a vibrator, or how much warm-up there was before intercourse) to the point where it was hard for her to look forward to sex, even though she loved the closeness it brought. It was tricky to stop Joe from collapsing into feelings of failure as he listened to this. With Karla's help, I stressed that you can't know what Karla hasn't told you and that it's respectful towards Karla to allow her to take responsibility when she can now see she had many other options than cheating to make things better for her.

Once Karla recognised how much she had let herself down, she had a very different view of Joe and their relationship. She started emphasising to Joe all his good qualities and expressed a fervent desire for them to have an enjoyable future together.

For his part, Joe acknowledged that, in hindsight, he had been taking Karla for granted. He had let his insecurities about his worth hide behind 'doing well for the family' and used that excuse to avoid being in intimate relationship with Karla. He realised that the urgency he felt about 'turning around' the new business was all self-imposed, and that there was no real need for him to be working the stupid hours he had been.

They realised that they could make better use of the flexibility in their work lives. They began to take weekdays off together. Other times they would meet up for lunch, and even have 'sex dates' in the middle of the day once they realised that they both preferred that.

In their sex life and elsewhere, they discovered there was so much they *had not been talking about honestly and directly (i.e. intimately). They felt so much closer when they did. The renaissance in their relationship that Karla had hoped for finally arrived.*

Key points from Chapter 18

1. Every relationship has a contract that is usually not discussed or negotiated explicitly but is the foundation of the relationship.
2. People who break the contract because they have different assumptions about what's 'normal' don't try to hide it. That's not infidelity — that's a cue that you need to negotiate your contract in more detail.
3. Infidelity is when you do something that you know your partner will view as breaking the contract, i.e. they will be miserable, hurt or angry at you.
4. Most infidelity is hidden to avoid the consequences, which adds deception to breaking the contract. When it's discovered, the deception is often more hurtful than the original infidelity.
5. It is possible for a relationship to recover, indeed to become better than it ever was, following the revealing of an infidelity.
6. You don't have to re-commit to the relationship — but you do have to tolerate the vulnerability of finding out whether you can rebuild it, a process that usually takes months.
7. Don't act out in rage or pain by getting violent, vengeful or telling the world.
8. It is up to the person who broke the contract to take persistent action to restore trust. They must be vulnerable, reliable and empathic, and keep being like that for a long time.
9. The only worthwhile reassurance you can give is knowing what psychological forces made you be so selfish and deceitful, and having a plan for how you will handle them in the future.
10. If the contract-breaker can't be tolerant and supportive of their partner's pain and distress, they are making their own feelings more important than yours. That's a warning sign.

Chapter 19
Are you safe? (And what to do if you're not)

If you are in an unsafe relationship, one where you are intimidated or coerced, most of this book does not apply. A relationship like that is *not* an equal partnership.

I wish I didn't have to include a chapter like this in this book. But the sad fact is that for women, their intimate partner is the person most likely to abuse or kill them. That's not to say that women don't physically assault men, but men's experience of physical violence is very different. For example, following the discovery of infidelity, many people attack their partners physically. In the hetero couples I have worked with, the men on the receiving end of that violence have been pretty unperturbed by it. Some have welcomed it as their due. In contrast, the women have been shaken, intimidated and cowed.

Physical and emotional abuse is also distressingly common in same-sex relationships. And plenty of men in hetero relationships have been exploited and abused by their partners.

Threats to your safety come in many forms, both visible and invisible. The '**visible**' is about violence and intimidation (including sexual violence and coercion) that is either done to you or to people or things you love (kids, pets, your home, your possessions). It may include being slapped, punched, strangled, pushed around, pinned down, tripped, trapped or otherwise physically abused. Punching walls and breaking things is often a way that abusers try to intimidate you. It's a way to signal clearly (but deniably) 'I am willing to escalate to violence if I don't get my way'. Intimidation is as much a criminal offence as violence is.

SPECIAL WARNING: If you have been strangled, choked or smothered by your partner, you need to consider that you are at serious risk. It's really easy for someone to die that way. It's far more dangerous than being punched. The research says that if your partner has strangled you, you are in significantly greater danger of being seriously injured or killed by them in the future.[1]

While on the subject, also be wary of 'playing' with choking during sex. The ease with which strangulation can kill you is why knowledgeable people are disturbed by the prevalence of choking in porn. Many skilful kinky people who are into all kinds of pain and restraint avoid this so-called 'breath play' because it is so dangerous. If you find choking or smothering erotic, please thoroughly research the risks and be *very* careful.

The '**invisible**' threats are the emotional abuse side of things. If you are thinking something like 'My partner doesn't hit me, so it can't be an abusive relationship', I strongly encourage you not to underestimate the seriousness of emotional abuse. It is not a contest; all forms of abuse are damaging and dangerous.

Emotional abuse can take many forms, from swearing at you and calling you names, to being derogatory about you and your loved ones, to undermining your trust in yourself. In public or private, this person puts you down, attacks your intelligence, your worth, your appearance, your sexuality or sexual functioning, or your character, or compares you unfavourably with others. A classic action is blaming *you* for all the problems in the relationship, especially when *they* are the unreasonable one.

Some forms of intimidation fall into this category — emotional reactions of anger, hurt or sadness that are so extreme you will do almost anything to avoid provoking them are abusive. Your partner using threats of suicide and self-harm to control you is another form of abuse. Alongside threatening to hurt your kids, this is one of the cruellest manipulations someone can use on you. It doesn't matter if it's deliberate or a genuine expression of their distress: threatening self-harm **to get you to do what they want** is unfair and abusive. (This is not to say that people who are despairing to the point of suicide don't deserve our compassion and care — but that is a separate issue from setting boundaries against someone being coercive or manipulative.)

Accepting reality

Accepting that a person you have loved is dangerous to you (or your children) is extremely difficult to do. It's especially difficult when your partner tells you they love you or if things are great sometimes. The change to an unhealthy relationship may have happened so gradually that it's hard to see where things went off-course.

Except for genuine psychopaths (who are pretty rare), the people who will abuse you are people who feel powerless, scared and insecure. Remember, relationships get more challenging the longer they go on. In the beginning, abusers don't feel that threatened. Most people who are abusive or controlling to their partners start out gradually. This is not a conscious strategy in many cases, but it is nonetheless effective. Small comments, criticisms and complaints gradually become more frequent and aggressive. The questioning and undermining of your judgement may start out looking like normal disagreement but slowly escalates to full-blown gaslighting and domination.

To make matters worse, if you grew up in an unsafe environment, then it may be hard for you to recognise when it's happening in your adult life. An unsafe environment includes one where boundaries weren't respected, adults felt entitled to do whatever they felt like to, and in front of, the kids, or where you were psychologically or physically abused. If you come from that background, it's understandable that mistreatment by your partner doesn't set off alarm bells because it is normal for you (remember, 'normal' usually means 'whatever I grew up with').

Suppose you know that you struggle with maintaining your boundaries, that you find it hard to say what you think and want, that people take advantage of you, or that you are isolated from all support except for your intimate partner. In that case, it might be worth thinking about what's happening in your relationship.

If friends or family express concern about your partner, especially how your partner talks to or treats you, it is wise to listen to them. Maybe not if it's just one person, but if it's more than one I would encourage you to stop and consider whether they are seeing something you are not.

If you don't have any friends or family whom you are close to, think about whether that's really *your* choice. Did you end up there to appease your partner, to avoid their anger and disapproval? Isolating partners from other social support is a primary tactic of most abusive people. They want to control your perception, and can't afford you to have access to people who might encourage you to see things differently.

Then there are the understandable anxieties: 'Will I be able to house myself?', 'Will I have enough money?', 'What will happen to the kids / the pets?' If you're terrified of the practicalities of separation, consult a lawyer who specialises in separation and family court issues. If you can't afford to pay, your local Citizens Advice Bureau in Aotearoa or Community Legal Centre in Australia will typically have access to free legal advice.

Knowledge is power. Know what the stakes are before you make decisions. Finding out what's involved doesn't commit you to anything. But you can't really choose to stay if you can't choose to leave.

If you google 'am I in an abusive relationship?', you will find many lists, and even some questionnaires, highlighting the kind of behaviour that might prompt you to leave. If you have some uneasiness or questions about how your partner treats you, it is worth looking at these lists and trying to be honest about whether some apply to your relationship. Exercise 57 gives you my version of these lists.

EXERCISE 57: IS THIS RELATIONSHIP UNHEALTHY?

No checklist in a book can tell you for sure, but here are some scenarios that should make you question whether your relationship is good for you.

- You're relaxed on your own; you're anxious when you think your partner is coming home.
- You're always apologising and walking on eggshells around your partner — never knowing if the 'nice' or 'nasty' partner will turn up.
- Your relationship has periods of intense attention and affection ('love-bombing') from your partner as they try to make up for being abusive or if they sense that you are pulling away from their control.
- You don't talk about the reality of the relationship with friends or

family — you downplay how hurt or anxious you are, you hide evidence of violence like bruises or scratches.

- You have lost confidence in yourself and your judgement — maybe friends say things like 'you're not yourself' or 'you seem stressed' (and you don't want to tell them why).

If you relate to one or more of these scenarios, look at this next list of behaviours. If any of these apply, you should be worried. If *many* of them apply, you are likely in an abusive relationship.

Has your partner ever:

- Intimidated you or used others to intimidate you — i.e. you now think twice about what you say or do out of fear of the consequences?
- Been violent to you — even once? (Once is enough to intimidate you.)
- Been violent to objects (e.g. punching walls, smashing things), children or pets? (Again, once is enough.)
- Blamed *you* for their violence, aggression or their mistakes and failures?
- Made all the decisions and unilaterally decided what you can and can't do?
- Controlled what you do and who you can see — stopped you or made it hard for you to see friends or family, go to work or study, or pursue an interest or hobby?
- Controlled your access to money, transport or healthcare (including medication)?
- Denied reality (a.k.a. gaslighting) — said things didn't happen that you know did happen, or vice versa?
- Monitored your communications, allowed you no privacy either digitally or in person?
- Refused to communicate, giving you the hostile silent treatment, especially when you needed support?
- Shown intense jealousy or possessiveness — unfairly accused you of infidelity, flirting, etc.?
- Humiliated, belittled, embarrassed or shamed you — in public or private?
- Told you that you were stupid, inferior, damaged, worthless, a 'slut', a 'whore', etc.?

- Threatened or controlled your access to children or other loved ones?
- Threatened your reputation, your immigration status, or to turn others against you?
- Stalked you, checked up on you, challenged what you do with your time?
- Forced you to do sexual things you didn't want to do?
- Forced you to do other things you didn't want to do?

No list can cover all the possibilities around abusive relationships. If you're feeling uncomfortable enough about your partner's behaviour to be scanning this list, please talk to trusted friends, or call a helpline, and discuss your situation with someone who can give you an objective viewpoint about whether what you are living with is okay.

Gaslighting and messing with reality

In the 1944 movie *Gaslight*, a husband with designs on his new wife's inheritance deliberately deceives her into thinking she is going mad by altering things about the house (like the gas-powered lights), and then denying that anything has changed. These days, the term 'gaslighting' is used more widely to refer to any time someone says or does something that denies reality. 'Why are you so angry about this?' 'I'm not angry' (when they are). Or 'Where were you? I waited for ages?' 'I never said I was coming then' (when they did). Of course, in our current 'post-truth' environment, this has become the norm in politics as well.

Partners will inevitably, at times, have different experiences and inhabit separate realities. There's a lot in this book about how to negotiate across those gaps. The difference with gaslighting is that one person is genuinely open to their partner's perception, while their partner is consistently negating the other's perception, often to the point of pathologising it; for example 'You're irrational', 'You're crazy', 'You're malicious' or 'You're irrelevant'.

Most people who are gaslighting aren't plotting to steal your inheritance. It's usually more automatic. From a therapist's point of view, it often has the sophistication of a kid standing in front of a broken vase saying 'I didn't do it'. If gaslighting was part of their family culture growing up, they wouldn't even realise that they were doing anything harmful because it's 'normal'.

When you are on the receiving end of messing with reality, it doesn't really matter whether your significant other is doing it deliberately or reflexively. The impact is the same: it makes you doubt yourself, your judgement and maybe even your sanity. Your partner will, of course, try to convince you that you are over-reacting if you call them out. You might even believe that and keep making excuses for their choices.

The only way to deal with someone who messes with reality is to be self-aware. Firstly, in the sense of having a solid relationship with your intuitive sense of right and wrong. And, secondly, in the sense of having confidence that you know when you are and aren't projecting, misunderstanding or being unreasonable. Self-awareness will allow you to realise when you are being bullied or misled, and to know what's real and not. This is where having friends or whānau outside the relationship who you can trust to check your reality is so important. It will also help you keep focused on who you are and what's good for you. Organising to get your practical and emotional needs met will help you stay strong.

It's also crucial to have good boundaries. Remember, 'boundaries' means knowing what's okay for you and what's not okay. If your partner keeps negating or attacking your reality, try to find ways to say 'I'm not going to let that go on'. Things like 'It's okay if we remember things differently, but it's not okay if you call me crazy', or 'We can talk about this, but if you shout at me I'm going to leave the room'. If you are afraid to assert yourself that way, you need to think seriously about how safe it is to stay in this relationship.

Men in abusive relationships

In hetero relationships, most people who are physically assaulted and killed, controlled and emotionally abused are women. However, that is not to say it can't happen to men. And because it is rarer and contravenes our expectations, it can be hard for those men to ask for help and get taken seriously.

I have certainly worked with several couples where the woman was emotionally abusive and undermining of her male partner. Because

I am a sex therapist, I have heard many women belittle and shame their partners when they were struggling with a sexual problem. Saying things like 'You're not a real man. You can't even get it up' is abusive. And not the sort of thing a man will feel comfortable seeking support for from his mates.

Exploiting others' vulnerabilities can extend to physical abuse. For example, I saw one couple where the man was large and powerfully built and the woman was on the short side. She regularly assaulted him physically, and he was very intimidated by her. Not because he couldn't protect himself physically (he could), but because he knew that if he wasn't very careful, he could hurt her. If she called the police, he doubted that they would see him as the victim. She was quite callously exploiting this power she had over him to avoid changing her aggressive behaviour.

Whatever the genders involved, coercing people, undermining and intimidating them is **not okay**.

Having a choice

For some people, there's no doubt that they are in an abusive and controlling relationship. Their partner has beaten or raped them, threatened to kill them or their children, forced them to do things that violate their integrity, or verbally abused them regularly.

The issue for many people in unsafe relationships is 'What can I do about it?' When you have been isolated from all your family and friends, deprived of access to money, and physically or psychologically abused for the slightest show of initiative or resistance, it can be tough to believe that you have any choice in the matter. You're in an impossible situation — abused and undermined if you stay, at risk of worse abuse, even death, if you try to leave.

Likewise, if there is a big gap in power and status, it can seem hopeless to try to act against a controlling partner. A classic situation is when you are an immigrant without family support or familiarity with the social systems. Often, people who are very insecure in themselves, who see the world as a dangerous place, will choose a partner who they feel is no threat. Commonly, it's someone younger, poorer, less educated or browner than them — someone who has less structural power.

At the beginning of the relationship, the person with more power will probably feel comfortable, and the power differences may seem unimportant to you both. As I have stressed throughout this book, their insecurities will inevitably become more activated as you become more important to them over time. When that happens, they are likely to become increasingly controlling, and the power differences start to be very significant. Especially when the person with less power starts to think about leaving, and realises how dependent on their partner's wealth, status or privilege they have become.

Other people often say things like 'Why doesn't she just leave if it's that bad?', without any awareness of how impossible that can seem. So, if you're concerned about a *friend's* relationship, **please go cautiously** in how you talk to them about it; you probably don't know what they have to deal with. Don't talk to them like leaving is a simple thing.

I want to encourage you to believe that you *do* have a choice. That Women's Refuge will offer you a first step to reclaiming your life, that the police and the Family Court will keep you safe in the long run. I have to acknowledge, though, that it is not that simple. Women's Refuge does a fantastic job, and I am full of respect and appreciation for their work in saving the lives and sanity of women and children. However, other institutions have a spotty record in keeping women safe. It doesn't mean that it isn't worth trying, but often it is a long and challenging road to extract yourself from an abusive relationship.

If the abuse is subtle or has lots of cultural support, meaning that it's a norm among people you know, it can also be hard to feel like you have a choice to leave. I have certainly met women who were told by their mothers some variation of 'accepting a woman's lot': 'He doesn't beat you. He puts food in your children's mouths. What have you got to complain about?' If you grew up and live in a community (like a church) or a culture that is against divorce, it can be hard to see that as a choice.

Keeping yourself safe

If you are in an unsafe relationship, you hopefully understand that leaving is the time of greatest danger. In Aotearoa, that's when the majority of women get murdered.

If you are coming to realise that your partner is too caught up in their own feelings and perceptions of threat to be able to treat you decently, let alone with care, you must assess carefully how great the risks are. This is a time to err on the side of caution.

Listen to your gut feelings or intuition. In my internship year, I worked in a group therapy programme. I vividly remember one session where every single woman in the group described a situation where they had ignored an intuition that something wasn't right and went on to be assaulted or abused. If you have any inclination that you aren't safe, then pay attention and make your plans carefully.

If you fear for your physical safety (or that of your children or pets), you need a **safety plan**. If your partner suddenly loses it or unexpectedly comes home drunk and violent, that is not the time to try to work out what to do. You need to work things out in advance, so that you *know* what to do if there's an emergency. If you are feeling unsafe, use Exercise 58 to make that plan now.

EXERCISE 58: MAKING A SAFETY PLAN

If it's possible you might have to leave the house in a hurry, it is wise to prepare.

1. Tell people you can trust not to tell your partner about your concerns. Having more than one person who knows is safer, because one person won't always be available.
2. Have a place you can access (a friend's house you can reach on foot is ideal), and prepare a store of essential items that will allow you to continue your life. Things like money/cards, car keys, copies of your driver's licence and other ID for yourself and your children, copies of your bank details and other important documents (like a Protection Order), a backup phone with all your vital numbers stored on it, and any medicines you or your children are taking. You might also want a change of clothes and basic toiletries. If you have kids, then clothes and maybe a toy or two for them, a spare bottle and nappies if you have an infant.
3. Work out how to get out of the house safely. If you have children or

pets, decide if they are safe in the short term if you need to leave to protect yourself. If not, decide how you are going to get them out.

4. Know where you are going to go and who you are going to tell. Nowadays, many smartphones have an SOS function that automatically connects with several contacts if you activate it. Some will also take a picture from both cameras and a 10-second audio clip and send your GPS coordinates. Find out if your phone does this, and if it does, practise using it.

This is an example of one plan to consider. Your circumstances might need a different type of plan. In Aotearoa, Shine and Women's Refuge have great advice on their websites. In Australia, phoning 1-800-respect is the place to start.

If you have tried to talk with your partner about your concerns around their behaviour and just got denial, minimisation and distraction . . . If you've tried to say that things aren't okay in the relationship and you got an escalation of abuse or aggression . . . If you've tried all you know to improve things and they aren't getting better, then you are probably thinking about leaving. **Don't wait for things to get worse to make a plan.**

Don't do it alone

Deciding to leave an unhealthy relationship is difficult enough. It is doubly difficult if your judgement is being actively undermined, or of you are coping with living in fear of your safety or the safety of children or pets (or your partner!). Make sure that you have one or more safe people who you can process things with, check your thinking out, and who will keep your focus in the right place.

If you're in an abusive relationship, people who care about you will encourage you to leave — but make sure you have confidence in what they say. They need to be someone you can trust to keep you safe by not gossiping to others about your situation. They probably also need to be someone that you can trust to be fair and reasonable. If you think they are biased (e.g. because they have got out of an abusive relationship themselves and you suspect they see abuse everywhere), you won't feel able to rely on their judgement. This can leave you feeling alone in your decision-making again.

If you don't have friends or whānau who you feel confident you can trust, talk to a professional at a local counselling or violence prevention agency, a phone counselling service, or refuge or victim support agency. There are a lot of resources available so that you can be supported when you need them. Intimate partner violence and abuse are a big problem in our society, and many people will help you if you let them.

Believe you can do it and that you are allowed to

It can be hard to believe that you are entitled to end a relationship 'just' because you have become clear it is unhealthy for you. Your partner will likely tell you that you are making a mistake, being selfish, damaging the children, killing them, etc. Others in your life may also question your choice if it makes them uncomfortable in some way. If *they* have been putting up with an unhealthy or even abusive relationship, they may encourage you to do the same.

If you have kept the negative aspects of your relationship hidden from friends and family, they may be confused and question your decision to end the relationship. We do this out of misplaced shame — the shame belongs to the *abuser*; you have done nothing wrong.

It's vital that **you know and believe that you are allowed to make this decision**. Even if you're not 100% certain it's the right thing (we make most decisions without complete certainty); even if you are concerned about the impact on your kids or others in your family or community.

If it keeps coming up that your relationship is unhealthy, harmful or abusive, if your partner has made it clear that they will not change how they operate, then you are doing the right thing if you end that relationship. *Know this. Believe this.* You are entitled to a life free of constant anxiety, free of intermittent terror, free of soul-sapping criticism and complaint. Like every human on the planet, you deserve a life of dignity and respectful treatment.

You may also struggle to believe that you will cope. Maybe your partner has ground you down so far that you have no energy. Perhaps you have been told repeatedly that you are foolish, stupid or ignorant and will get everything wrong. If you have been financially dependent on your partner, you may have concerns about how you will support yourself, especially if you have been out of the paid workforce.

People *do* this. And *you* can do this. While your situation may feel impossible, know that others in as bad or worse situations have got through and found their feet. It is possible to learn or rediscover how to cope on your own, make all the choices, and support yourself financially and practically.

We are fortunate that we live in a society that has laws and systems that mostly succeed in preventing people from being left with nothing when they end a relationship. A system that encourages fairness and offers support. It's not perfect, and bad things can happen, but they happen less often than you probably fear.

More importantly, if you have been in an unhealthy, toxic or abusive relationship, you are almost certainly **more capable than you feel right now**. It's hard to overestimate how much better you will function when you are *not* under the constant stress of emotional warfare, uncertainty, anxiety and fear. You may not know it, but you are better than this. Way better.

HANNAH & PAUL

Before I see a couple for therapy, they have to separately fill out a bunch of paperwork, including some tick-box forms about issues in the relationship and ways they deal with conflict. When I got Hannah and Paul's documents, I was immediately concerned. They painted very different pictures of the relationship, especially around how they dealt with conflict.

In such cases, I will always phone the person I'm most concerned about and have a private conversation about their safety. In this case, Hannah reassured me that she felt able to speak freely in front of Paul and had no concerns for her safety. We discussed whether to mention my phone call to Paul, and Hannah said she would tell him.

When we met, I found Paul very difficult to engage. He attributed all their difficulties to Hannah's history of abuse and subsequent anxiety disorder. While he paid lip-service to the idea that 'it takes two to tango', in practice Paul always insisted that 'she started it'. He would acknowledge his ineffective self-protective behaviour, but **only** as a justified reaction to what Hannah had done. He seemed unable to tolerate the thought that sometimes he was the one who misunderstood, was over-sensitive or aggressive. As gently as I could, I kept pointing this out to Paul and spelled out that in my experience, he was unlikely to get the kind of relationship he said he wanted if he persisted in adopting such a blaming stance.

Hannah seemed only too willing to accept blame. This was very different from the description Paul offered of her 'dominating' and 'having to have things her way'. She reported feeling anxious about being unwanted, and 'broken and disgusting' as a consequence of sexual abuse she suffered from ages 9 to 11 at the hands of a friend of her parents. When she finally tried to talk to her mother about the abuse, her mother didn't believe her but the abuse stopped. We identified a life-long pattern of her appeasing and accommodating, which the abuse undoubtedly exacerbated.

Meanwhile, Paul insisted that he came from a loving family and that the ideas he had about feeling powerless and dominated by Hannah bore no relation to anything in his formative years. When pressed, he offered a relatively weak story about having difficulties with a strict teacher at intermediate school. I later learned from Hannah that his mother was a massive manipulator who was lovely only so long as you did exactly what she wanted. She also had myriad ways of guilt-tripping you about everything she had ever done for you.

Despite my best attempts to be compassionate to Paul about the level of pain and anxiety driving his defensiveness, he quickly became uncomfortable with my insistence on him taking responsibility for his behaviour, reporting feeling 'picked on' and 'blamed'. After four sessions, he refused to come back. I suggested a different style of therapy they could try, but wasn't surprised when Hannah contacted me a few weeks later asking if she could see me individually. Paul 'didn't see the point' of more therapy. I think he was happy for her to do therapy alone with me because that fit his narrative of her being the problem.

I agreed to see Hannah but warned her that, in my experience, pursuing individual therapy for relationship issues makes separation more likely (see Chapter 4). Hannah told me that the questions I had asked about her ability to speak freely in my initial phone call had stayed with her. Then, in the joint therapy, watching me struggle to get Paul to own his behaviour made her realise how much she had believed his version of events rather than her own.

When I said something to her about her 'abandoning herself', that struck a real chord.

We explored how this replicated her parents' effective abandonment of her when she told them of her sexual abuse and how that, coupled with their insistence on obedience rather than trusting her own feelings, made it very hard for her to back herself.

It took time for Hannah to realise how much, and how actively, Paul had undermined her self-belief. It was harrowing for her to acknowledge that his behaviour had been consistently self-serving and controlling of her. She struggled not to perceive this as her 'weakness' and her 'fault'. We explored ways she could try to be more assertive to see if she could change the dynamic, but it was pretty clear that Paul would rather give up the relationship than give up his defences. He hadn't beaten her, but his history of smashing objects and (once or twice) shaking her gave her genuine concern that he might go there if she wasn't careful.

It took Hannah 18 difficult and painful months before she made a move. A year and a half of trying to be more assertive and weathering Paul's anger, criticism and abuse. At the same time, she talked with trusted friends (who shared my concerns about how Paul treated her), quietly explored her legal situation, and worked out how she could make ends meet if they separated.

Her first year post-separation was very difficult, living in a two-bedroom flat with two kids half the time (Paul refused to leave the family home). Her part-time wage was not sufficient to support herself. She had to put a lot of time and effort into getting help from government agencies. At the same time, there was a massive expenditure of emotional effort dealing with Paul, who bombarded her with abusive phone calls, texts and emails under the pretence of organising access to the kids. At times it was so awful that Hannah wondered if she should have stayed. In the end, she was able to set boundaries that limited all contact with Paul to email. She had a fantastic friend screen and edit the emails, so that she only had to read the bits that contained relevant information, not all the character assassination and manipulation.

Two years later, the access patterns were reasonably stable (though Paul was still prone to changing things at the last minute). Hannah had found full-time work, her share of the marital home had allowed her a deposit on a flat of her own, and, with the mortgage being less than the rent she had been paying, she was confident of staying afloat financially. She had taken *up netball again and expanded her friendship network. Things were far from perfect, but she was able to say 'I feel like I'm coming home to myself for the first time in my life'.*

Key points from Chapter 19

1. If you feel intimidated by your partner's behaviour, that's **not okay**. Whether they are physically abusive or emotionally abusive doesn't matter. You shouldn't have to live in fear and anxiety.
2. It can be hard to accept that someone you love is harming you. It's important to realise when it's happening — use checklists, talk to trusted friends, helplines or a counsellor if you have concerns.
3. Most abusers will mess with reality ('gaslighting') and will try to cut you off from support. That's because trusting your judgement and getting help from trustworthy people are the keys to keeping yourself safe.
4. Believe that you have a choice to go. Educate yourself about the supports that are available and what your legal and financial position is.
5. Leaving is the most dangerous time. Plan for it carefully and get support.
6. Even though leaving is incredibly scary, know that you can do it, and it will be worthwhile in the long run.

Chapter 20
Major stresses, losses and grief

When the going gets tough

If we're fortunate, most of the time we live in a state of what I call 'healthy denial'. Our lives have gone well enough that we don't have to consider all the bad things that might happen to us. This is a denial of reality, but it's healthy because worrying about all the things that *might* go wrong doesn't protect us from them. Indeed, worrying about them undermines our ability to cope and adapt when challenged (as anyone with an anxiety disorder will tell you).

However, sometimes reality will puncture our 'healthy denial', and life delivers a cruel blow in the form of an unexpected loss or setback. A loved one suffers a sudden illness or accident, or suddenly dies; you get seriously injured; your job suddenly disappears; your business folds; you are caught up in a natural disaster, or a human one like a war or a sharemarket crash.

At those times, even the best relationships can struggle. Over the years, I have worked with many couples with good self-awareness, self-regulation and communication skills, shared values and love. Yet if the going gets tough enough, the pressure of their situation causes them to be distant from or even hostile to each other. All of us can be overwhelmed and pushed into limbic-system ways of relating (see Chapter 5).

What can you do when something really bad happens?

When it comes to tragedies like the loss of a loved one, the collapse of your workplace or the impact of a brain injury, the short answer to the question 'What can I do?' is 'nothing'. You can do nothing to prevent the loss and the stress and grief it entails.

So I want to emphasise that I am not suggesting that anything in this chapter can cure the pain of profound grief. I do not want to trivialise the real pain and loss that people experience by implying that you can 'attitude' it away. Instead, this chapter aims to suggest how to respond best as a team when life throws you a curveball. To assist you in letting the pressure drive you together, rather than forcing you apart.

Significant stresses and griefs are a time when the issue of identifying and expressing vulnerable emotions is vital. When the pain is enormous and intense, the temptation to avoid engaging with it directly is powerful. For example: Instead of talking about the grief of losing my child, I focus on my anger at a mistake that contributed to their death. Instead of expressing fear and vulnerability about my financial future, I spend all my energy complaining about the unfairness of my redundancy.

This focus on self-protective emotions means that what is *really* going on for you emotionally gets neglected. You're not attending to it yourself, and you're making it very hard, if not impossible, for your partner to do so. The trouble is that they are likely very aware of your vulnerable emotion and will feel confused and, possibly, frustrated that they can't engage with you around it.

If you struggle with vulnerability, you may be defensive and angry that your partner is trying to get you to connect with your pain. For many of us, it is much more comfortable to lash out in anger than to sit and accept our pain, acknowledge it, talk about it and care for the suffering it causes.

In our culture, it's common to feel good about 'doing' things. 'If there's a problem, fix it.' That attitude can be constructive in some contexts, but not when there is nothing you can do — when the solution is about *being*, not doing.

Of course, that's all talking as if the loss or setback has only happened to one of you. In long-term committed relationships, however, that's rarely the case. If you were close to your sibling, the chances are that your partner cared about them, too, and the sudden loss of your sibling to pancreatic cancer is a shock for them, too. Your redundancy may have implications for your career that don't directly affect your partner. Still, the chances are that the indirect effects will be considerable and will cause your partner their own stresses and re-appraisals.

When the loss or stress is equally shared, you will likely both be floundering. Situations like losing a child, your home to fire, your savings in a financial scam, or your health in a car accident that injures you both will place an enormous burden on your connection.

When both of you are struggling with powerful emotions, it can be hard for the relationship to operate normally. If there's a lot of self-protective behaviour floating around for both of you, things are likely to be reactive, unreasonable and, probably, unfriendly.

You need to forgive yourself and each other if you have lashed out or abandoned each other in your distress. Acknowledge that as soon as possible, apologise without justifying, and reaffirm your commitment to being there for your partner.

Get support from someone else

Sometimes your partner is not the best person to lean on. The notion that they have to be everything for you at all times is unfair to both of you. It may be appropriate, to begin with, to turn to people outside your partnership to process your grief and pain. Find friends or family with broad shoulders to listen and support you. You need people who can listen without trying to fix things, make your feelings go away, or tell you what you should do. Make sure you avoid those who get into competition with you about how bad they've had it.

Many fear 'burdening' their friends or family with their troubles. There are people who are self-involved and insist on everyone attending to and being impressed by their pain. However, you are not doing this when you are sharing your deep sorrows. You are building an intimate connection with people in your life. Rather than being burdensome, being able to 'be there' for each other is one of the essential functions of family and community. If you don't have people like that in your life, then hire a professional friend — a counsellor or therapist who can safely give you the space to feel what you are feeling and maybe come to make some peace with it, perhaps even make some sense of it. If you belong to a church, your minister or pastor may be able to be there for you. There are low-cost services in many communities, and lovely people are staffing free phone counselling services around the world. Don't hesitate to make use of them.

Having people other than your partner to lean on doesn't remove the need for the two of you to work together around your distress. Exercise 59 offers some suggestions of a pathway you can follow that may allow you to stay intimately connected in the face of a major grief or stress.

EXERCISE 59: STEPS TO GRIEVING TOGETHER

1. Acknowledge and accept the pain and distress to yourself and to each other. Some people are afraid of wallowing in this, of becoming a victim. But when something major affects your relationship, it is essential to share your experience.

2. Don't try to make it go away, or distract yourself from it with busyness or self-protective emotions like blame and judgement. Allowing life to divert you with its necessities is a different matter. Go to work and get caught up in it if you can, and if it gives you respite. But don't hide at work because home is too painful.

3. There is potential for deepening your bond if you are willing to bear witness to and share your partner's suffering. Focus on *being*, not doing; on '*being with*', not 'fixing' or 'helping'. Being vulnerable — open and honest about how you deal with your pain — is part of that. Listen for and validate the ways it's different for your partner as well as the ways it's the same.

4. Remember, your pain is proportional to your loss, to how important the thing or person was to you. Hold on to the memories and knowledge of what you had, even as you feel the pain of losing it. Don't reject the memories of joy or satisfaction just because they are now tinged with loss.

5. Over time, see if you can help each other make meaning of what has happened.

Part of grieving together is acknowledging how external stresses have sometimes made you self-protective. Whatever your situation, there will likely be sad facts about how you have operated. None of this was what you intended; it was just the best you could do with what you knew at the time. View your younger self (including your childhood self) with compassion. Do the same for your partner.

The grieving together part comes when you can both compassionately reflect on the loss of 'what might have been', the 'if only I knew then what I know now' stuff. Part of it is each of you acknowledging what you have done that was hurtful or unhelpful, emphasising the cost to your partner. For example, 'I'm sorry I've been so withdrawn; you must have felt lonely and abandoned.' Both of you doing this with compassion and empathy will likely create an atmosphere that supports connection and caring.

Sometimes people can channel grief into doing productive things. The person who loses a loved one to an accident might dedicate their life to preventing such losses for other families. The person who takes their redundancy as a challenge may start their own business and make a go of it. If you can find a productive path to channel your grief into, then by all means follow it. But for everyone who can transform their pain that way, many more are left with no way to dignify their loss as anything positive.

The temptation to blame

One of the ways we unconsciously try to deal with the arbitrary nature of life is using hindsight to pretend that we have control. For couples, the most dangerous version of this arises when we blame our partner for a situation. For example, the parents grieving over the loss of their toddler who end up saying things like 'You should have been watching her better'. The couple who lost all their savings in a sharemarket crash who get into 'You should have sought more advice before investing' or 'If you had gone back to work when I wanted you to, this wouldn't be such a big deal'.

Hopefully, it is clear that this is a doomed strategy. It's people lashing out in their pain, trying to make the world seem predictable. It's guilt and shame projected onto their partner. We must resist the temptation to blame, and instead talk about our sense of helplessness, vulnerability, anxiety, etc.

The ongoing grief of infinite loss

Some sources of grief and loss (like the death of a loved one) happen once, and then you have time to accept and adjust to the new reality. However, some (like having a child with a severe illness or disability, or never getting a foot on the property ladder no matter how hard you scrimp and save and work extra hours) are an ongoing journey that never stops. This is called 'infinite loss' or 'chronic sorrow' — which pretty well captures the essence of the journey.

Many people in this situation are so busy coping that they haven't had time to grieve — living in what I call 'survival mode'. Even if they do, our society doesn't give us much of a road map. This can be dangerous for the couple's relationship as unprocessed pain 'leaks' out in irritation, frustration, isolation and numbness, all leading to increasing distance. Couples in this situation must find a way to grieve together — to at least gain the intimacy of sharing these painful feelings safely with each other. Exercise 60 aims to help you do that.

EXERCISE 60: PROCESSING AN ONGOING GRIEF

Nothing can take away the pain of 'infinite loss', but some things can help you bear it better and work as a team to manage your challenges. From my experience with clients coping with a situation like this, I have learned some things that can help the grieving process.

1. Talk about what **has happened** and **is happening** with a trusted other (again, to start with it may not be appropriate to do this with your partner). Talk about the impact on you, your partner, your kids (if you have any), and your wider community of friends and family. Share it with another human being who cares and can be there for you.
2. Talk about what **hasn't happened**, what **won't ever happen** — the hopes, dreams and unconscious expectations that you won't ever fulfil (e.g. 'I always imagined kicking a ball around with my kid' or 'I thought by now we'd be able to have weekends away as a couple').
3. Work out what this ongoing loss **means** to you. To your view of the world, of people and of your relationship. Talk to your partner about this.

4. Try to find a place of **acceptance** — this is how your life is. It isn't 'right', 'fair' or 'normal', but it is what it is. Can you find a way to accept that (even though it's intensely painful) and make the most of it? Can you develop a new purpose and meaning for your life?
5. **Stop comparing** your insides (how you're coping, feeling) with other people's outsides (how they *seem* to be coping or feeling). It's not a contest, and there's no single 'right' way to deal with complex grief.
6. Work out what kinds of **self-care** are right for you in your situation. Beyond the basics of sleep, exercise and diet to support your physiology, what do you need to help you cope? Different people require very different things. For example, some want to talk a lot; others very little. Some wish to engage with the illness or disability (e.g. through advocacy work or professional caring); others want time away from thinking about it. Some need social time; others need alone-time.

M. Scott Peck began his famous book *The Road Less Traveled*[1] with the sentence 'Life is difficult', and Buddhism teaches that 'life is suffering'. Grief is universal. Nonetheless, some times are worse than others, and some of us have lives that are more challenging and stressful than our neighbours'. What I know is that some couples are blown apart by tragedy and struggle, and some grow stronger and closer by grieving together. If your life has turned down the hard road, I hope you find a way to bear that journey together.

TAULA & ROD

Rod and Taula were having a fabulous time on their summer vacation. Rod's family had a tradition of all going to the same camping place beside a river on the Coromandel. With a multitude of adults and older cousins on hand, they got lots of adult company and something of a respite from their three kids: Hiva (nine), Heneli (seven) and Longo (six).

No one knows why Hiva suddenly freaked out and didn't drop off the rope swing into the water hole as she had done dozens of times before. Instead, she came flying back towards the bank, fell hard and hit her head on an exposed root. From that point on, Rod and Taula's life changed.

First, there were the terrifying hours of wondering whether Hiva would live or die as she lay unconscious while the ambulance came and transported her to hospital. Then they had to endure the operation to relieve the bleeding inside her skull. When the surgeon talked about the procedure being 'a complete success', they thought everything would be all right. It wasn't until days later, when Hiva still couldn't speak properly and a nurse talked to them about rehabilitation, that they realised this would be a long haul.

Nothing prepared them for just how long that haul would be. Their life became organised around Hiva's special needs. Hiva needed physiotherapy to help her re-learn how to walk; speech and language therapy to re-learn how to talk; and an occupational therapist helped Taula structure the home and routines to give Hiva as much independence as practical. Taula had to give up her job to ensure that Hiva could attend all her rehab appointments. All their financial plans had to change, and Rod felt the pressure of being the sole breadwinner.

Initially they tried to integrate Hiva back into the local school, but in the end it became clear that she needed to go to a specialist school, complicating travel and morning and afternoon routines. Taula and Rod worried about the impact on the younger two, and Rod, in particular, stepped up to make sure they weren't missing out on the things they wanted to do. Even with good support from both families and the parents of their children's friends, it was a gruelling schedule.

When I met them 14 years later, they were at loggerheads over Hiva's long-term care. Taula was determined to go on caring for her at home and had become an activist in trying to get better support for people with traumatic brain injuries. Rod was thinking it was time to stop making Hiva's injury the centre of their life and that a community residential support home might be a better option. It was a conversation they had been having for some years by this stage, and they had become increasingly entrenched and bitter in their positions.

Taula simply could not conceive of handing the care of their daughter over to strangers, and was starting to see Rod as 'unnatural' and 'cruel' because he kept pushing for it. This hurt Rod, and he had begun talking about Taula as 'unrealistic' and 'obsessed'. Rod was keen on the change for several reasons. One was that he wanted Hiva to have a life of her own. He reported that Hiva was pushing for more independence, and he felt that 'flatting' would make her feel more normal. With the younger two leaving home, there was also an opportunity for him and Taula to start having a life together again.

From my first meeting with them, I had a sense of their strong bond of love and care, despite how estranged they felt. Hearing their story was hard — there was so much pain and grief for these very loving parents. To make it sadder, by this point a lot of this was coming out as frustration, irritation and hurt directed at each other. I began by emphasising how normal it was for humans to do that when under continued stress, and encouraged them to park the decision about Hiva's future for the time being. I suggested that for this decision to be made well, they had to get back to feeling like a team, working together by making use of their differences.

Exploring those differences, we highlighted their care for their kids and their intention to do their best for everyone in the family. I normalised having differing ideas about priorities. We also looked at the discrepancies between their respective cultures (Tongan/German and Welsh/Scots) regarding families, obligations, responsibilities, and even the meaning of 'love'. We discussed the differences between good versus bad selfishness and good versus bad selflessness. We explored where each of them might be struggling, both in their view of themselves and their view of their partner.

It did not take long for Taula and Rod to soften towards each other. They both hated how hostile things had got between them. They respected the moratorium on discussing Hiva's future, and accepted that healing their relationship was a more urgent priority. It became clear that in all the years of struggling to adapt to the next challenge that Hiva's injury threw up, they had never really talked about sadness, loss and pain. In trying to 'stay positive' and 'keep it together', their grief had largely gone unacknowledged (though it was always present).

Rod was particularly sceptical about the value of talking about it: 'How is that going to change anything?' I suggested that the grief would have an influence whether he liked it or not. His only choice was whether it was unconscious — coming out sideways through self-protective emotions like anger, blame and bitterness — or conscious, through the deliberate exploration of the vulnerable feelings of grief, sadness and loss.

It turned out that there was also guilt in there. Rod still carried a thought that if he'd been there, he could have prevented the accident (he had been at the campsite when Hiva was injured). Taula was shocked to learn that he still blamed himself, and there was a very healing moment when she held him and told him there was nothing anyone could have done.

That led to a discussion about the fundamental unfairness of their situation. They shared their sense of impotence; their inability to protect themselves and, especially, their kids from the accident's impact. They talked of how hard it was to socialise with people who had 'normal kids, normal lives and normal expectations'.

As they took stock of how much pain and grief they were carrying and how hard they had worked, there was a growing sense of reconnecting as a team. From that discussion, they each began to talk about some of the unhelpful ways they had coped. Taula recognised that her crusade to get better support for families with a dependent adult was driven by an unconscious fantasy that she could somehow make things right again, rather than accepting that they never would be. This deep reflection by Taula invited Rod to talk about how hungry he was for recognition of all the responsibility he had shouldered. Taula had always been appreciative, but in putting a 'brave face' on it he had never let her see what it had cost him, so she could never acknowledge it.

That discussion naturally segued into him re-opening the conversation about Hiva's future. This time, however, the tone was much more conciliatory and careful. Rod owned that he had been jealous of how focused on Hiva Taula had become, and that was not how he wanted to express his love for Taula (or Hiva). He was at pains to stress that he wanted to explore all the options with Hiva and for them to work together as a team to decide what was best. For her part, Taula said she was willing to explore, acknowledging that she had been too knee-jerk in her rejection of alternatives in the past.

When they finished their work with me, they hadn't yet decided about Hiva's care. They were exploring the available options, and had an understanding that until they found something that they both felt provided what they wanted for Hiva, the status quo would remain. There was a mutual understanding that Hiva needed to have some independence because, in the very long term, they expected that she would outlive them.

Their lives were still stressful and challenging, but in grieving together they reconnected intimately in a way that allowed them to go on as a team who trusted and valued each other.

Key points from Chapter 20

1. No matter how good your relationship or communication skills, under enough external pressure you are likely to become self-protective and take your stress out on each other.
2. The productive alternative is to recognise and communicate about the vulnerable emotions you are feeling, no matter how 'negative' they are.
3. When there has been a tragedy, usually there is nothing you can do about it. Being with each other is the crucial thing.
4. You may need to get support from someone other than your partner if you are both struggling.
5. Aim to reconnect by sharing your grief and learning how to be there for each other.
6. Don't fall into the trap of blaming your partner or wasting energy on blaming others.
7. When the grief is ongoing, you have to find a way to live with it. It is not fair, but it is necessary.
8. Work out what you need to do to cope — and accept that what your partner needs may be quite different.

This isn't the end . . .

Reading this book is only the beginning. Like a good relationship, this book takes work to get the best out of it. If you have made it this far, let me offer my congratulations on your dedication to the important task of learning about relationships. In my experience, determination is a significant part of making love work in the long run. Reading this far suggests that you are one of those people who is open to taking on the challenge and putting in the hard yards.

I hope that some things that were confusing or inexplicable in your life now make more sense to you. Even more, I hope that I have offered ideas and options for making yourself, your relationship and your life more of what you want. I encourage you to keep working.

In my therapy with couples, I have always given my clients a lot of handouts. They have reported coming back to them repeatedly through the years to remind themselves what they learned. It is my hope that you will be able to do the same with this book. You are likely to see quite different things in it upon reflection or on a second reading. It's taken me more than 30 years to learn what's in here, so allow yourself a bit of time to assimilate and digest.

Love is one of the great mysteries — a powerful force that shapes so much of what we do, for good and ill. We are social animals, hard-wired for connection, born into physical and emotional dependency. Yet we are all unique individuals with a hunger to control our own destiny. The clash between those innate forces is at the core of understanding why sustaining love, passion and intimacy over time is so difficult.

I have done my best to acknowledge how complex and challenging making love work is, while being clear and optimistic about how *possible* that task is. I hope I have unravelled some of the mystery for you, and that you feel better equipped to make your love work.

Notes

CHAPTER 1: HOME TRUTHS ABOUT RELATIONSHIPS

1   Helen Fisher, 'The brain in love', TED talk, 2008, <ted.com/talks/helen_fisher_the_brain_in_love>.

CHAPTER 2: PEOPLE IN RELATIONSHIPS NEED TO GROW

1   David Schnarch, *Passionate Marriage: Sex, love, and intimacy in emotionally committed relationships*, W.W. Norton & Co, New York, 1997.

2   Esther Perel, Facebook post, 1 April 2013, <facebook.com/esther.perel/posts/in-the-west-today-most-people-are-going-to-have-two-or-three-marriages-two-or-th/10151342197466711>.

3   David Schnarch, in an interview with Mary Tudor for online magazine ThirdAge.com, January 1998, <crucible4points.com/interview-with-dr-david-schnarch-for-thirdage-com>.

4   Ellyn Bader & Peter Pearson, *In Quest of the Mythical Mate: A developmental approach to diagnosis and treatment in couples therapy*, Routledge, London, 1988.

5   Throughout the book, I use capital letters to denote a specific technical term that relates to formal models of relationship theory. For example, Exploration refers to that stage within the Developmental Model of Couple Therapy, rather than to generic 'exploration'.

6   Helen Fisher, 'The brain in love', TED talk, 2008, <ted.com/talks/helen_fisher_the_brain_in_love>.

7   S. Zeki, 'The neurobiology of love', *FEBS Letters*, vol. 581, no. 14 (June 2007), pp. 2575–2579, <DOI:10.1016/j.febslet.2007.03.094>.

8   Michael E. Kerr & Murray Bowen, *Family Evaluation: The role of the family as an emotional unit that governs individual behavior and development*, W.W. Norton & Co, New York, 1988.

CHAPTER 3: WHY IT'S SO SCARY AND HARD

1   M. J. Bakermans-Kranenburg & M. H. van Ijzendoorn, 'The first 10,000 Adult Attachment Interviews: Distributions of adult attachment representations in clinical and non-clinical groups', *Attachment & Human Development*, vol. 11, no. 3 (2009), pp. 223–263, <DOI:10.1080/14616 730902814762>; K. D. Mickelson, R. C. Kessler & P. R. Shaver, 'Adult attachment in a nationally representative sample', *Journal of Personality and Social Psychology*, vol. 73, no. 5 (1997), pp. 1092–1106, <DOI:10.1037/0022-3514.73.5.1092>.

2   Universidad Complutense de Madrid, 'First direct evidence for ultra-fast responses in human amygdala to fear', *ScienceDaily*, 15 June 2016, <sciencedaily.com/releases/2016/06/160615095132.htm>.

3   Named by Daniel Goleman in his book *Emotional Intelligence: Why it can matter more than IQ*, Random House, New York, 1995.

4   Richard Pond et al., 'Social pain and the brain: How insights from neuroimaging advance the study of social rejection', in T. Dorina Papageorgiou, George I. Christopoulos & Stelios M. Smirnakis (eds), *Advanced Brain Neuroimaging Topics in Health and Disease: Methods and applications*, IntechOpen, London, 2014, <DOI:10.5772/58271>.

5   M. Schauer & T. Elbert, 'Dissociation following traumatic stress: Etiology and treatment', *Zeitschrift für Psychologie / Journal of Psychology*, vol. 218, no. 2 (2010), pp. 109–127, <DOI:10.1027/0044-3409/a000018>.

6   Joseph Wortis, *Fragments of an Analysis with Freud*, Simon & Schuster, New York, 1954.

PART TWO: THE THREE STRANDS OF RELATIONSHIP THEORY

1   Ellyn Bader & Peter Pearson, *In Quest of the Mythical Mate: A developmental approach to diagnosis and treatment in couples therapy*, Routledge, London, 1988.

CHAPTER 5: MANAGE YOUR NEUROBIOLOGY

1   H. Mason et al., 'Cardiovascular and respiratory effect of yogic slow breathing in the yoga beginner: What is the best approach?', *Evidence-Based Complementary and Alternative Medicine*, vol. 2013, article ID 743504 (2013), <DOI:10.1155/2013/743504>.

2   B. Vickhoff et al., 'Music structure determines heart rate variability of singers', *Frontiers in Psychology*, vol. 4, no. 334 (2013), <DOI:10.3389/fpsyg.2013.00334>.

3   P. Yuan et al., 'Acute cold exposure induces vagally mediated Fos expression in gastric myenteric neurons in conscious rats', *American Journal of Physiology: Gastrointestinal and liver physiology*, vol. 281, no. 2 (2001), pp. G560–G568, <DOI:10.1152/ajpgi.2001.281.2.G560>; T. M. Mäkinen et al., 'Autonomic nervous function during whole-body cold exposure before and after cold acclimation', *Aviation, Space, and Environmental Medicine*, vol. 79, no. 9 (2008), pp. 875–882, <DOI:10.3357/asem.2235.2008>.

4   Kristin Neff & Christopher Germer, *The Mindful Self-Compassion Workbook: A proven way to accept yourself, build inner strength, and thrive*, Guilford Press, New York, 2018.

5   Jill Bolte Taylor, *My Stroke of Insight: A brain scientist's personal journey*, Hodder & Stoughton, London, 2009.

CHAPTER 6: DEALING WITH DIFFERENCE

1   This chapter draws heavily on my training with and the work of Drs Ellyn Bader and Peter Pearson of the Couples Institute, and Drs David Schnarch and Ruth Morehouse of the Crucible Institute.

2   Dave Meurer, *Daze of Our Wives: A semi-helpful guide to marital bliss*, Bethany House, Ada, 2000.

3   From training materials provided by the Couples Institute.

4   Brené Brown, *Daring Greatly: How the courage to be vulnerable transforms the way we live, love, parent, and lead*, Avery, New York, 2015.

5   Adapted from a handout by the Couples Institute, <couplesinstitutecounseling.com>.

CHAPTER 7: ATTACHMENT IN ADULT RELATIONSHIPS

1   I. Bretherton, 'The origins of attachment theory: John Bowlby and Mary Ainsworth', *Developmental Psychology*, vol. 28, no. 5 (1992), pp. 759–775, <DOI:10.1037/0012-1649.28.5.759>.

2   E. Z. Tronick & A. Gianino, 'Interactive mismatch and repair: Challenges to the coping infant', *Zero to Three*, vol. 6, no. 3 (1986), pp. 1–6, <psycnet.apa.org/record/1987-15272-001>.

3   M. J. Bakermans-Kranenburg & M. H. van Ijzendoorn, 'The first 10,000 Adult Attachment Interviews: Distributions of adult attachment representations in clinical and non-clinical groups', *Attachment & Human Development*, vol. 11, no. 3 (2009), pp. 223–263, <DOI:10.1080/14616 730902814762>; K. D. Mickelson, R. C. Kessler & P. R. Shaver, 'Adult attachment in a nationally representative sample', *Journal of Personality and Social Psychology*, vol. 73, no. 5 (1997), pp. 1092–1106, <DOI:10.1037/0022-3514.73.5.1092>.

4   J. Cassidy, 'Truth, lies and intimacy: An attachment perspective', *Attachment and Human Development*, vol. 3, no. 2 (2001), pp. 121–155, <DOI:10.1080/14616730110058999>.

5   This quote is widely attributed to Heinz Kohut (see, for example, <azquotes.com/quote/728153>), but I have been unable to confirm when he first said it or which of his works it appeared in.

6   C. Kopp, 'Antecedents of self-regulation: A developmental perspective', *Developmental Psychology*, vol. 18, no. 2 (1982), pp. 199–214, <DOI:10.1037/0012-1649.18.2.199>.

7   Helen Fisher, 'The brain in love', TED talk, 2008, <ted.com/talks/helen_fisher_the_brain_in_love>.

8   Mario Mikulincer & Phillip R. Shaver, *Attachment in Adulthood: Structure, dynamics, and change*, Routledge, London, 2007.

9   J. Cassidy, 'Truth, lies and intimacy'.

10   Harriet Lerner, *The Dance of Intimacy: A woman's guide to courageous acts of change in key relationships*, Harper Perennial, New York, 1997.

CHAPTER 8: THE INFLUENCE OF YOUR INSECURITIES

1   Brené Brown, *The Gifts of Imperfection: Let go of who you think you're supposed to be and embrace who you are*, Random House, New York, 2010.

CHAPTER 11: LEARN TO DO CONFLICT WELL

1   Karla McLaren, 'Critical thinking skills for your emotions', *Karla McLaren's Blog*, n.d., <karlamclaren.com/critical-thinking-skills-for-your-emotions>.

2   Discussed in Kyle Benson, 'Repair is the secret weapon of emotionally connected couples', *The Gottman Institute Blog*, 23 February 2017,

<gottman.com/blog/repair-secret-weapon-emotionally-connected-couples>.

3   Adapted from a handout by the Couples Institute,
    <couplesinstitutecounseling.com>.

CHAPTER 12: POWER DYNAMICS AND GENDER ROLES

1   E. J. Cross et al., 'An interdependence account of sexism and power: Men's
    hostile sexism, biased perceptions of low power, and relationship aggression',
    Journal of Personality and Social Psychology, vol. 117, no. 2 (2019), pp. 338–
    363, <DOI:10.1037/pspi0000167>.

2   Terry Real, 'Working with difficult men: Where's the leverage for change?',
    Psychotherapy Networker, July/August 2019, <psychotherapynetworker.org/
    magazine/article/2385/working-with-difficult-men>.

3   N. C. Overall et al., 'When power shapes interpersonal behavior: Low
    relationship power predicts men's aggressive responses to low situational
    power', *Journal of Personality and Social Psychology*, vol. 111, no. 2 (2016),
    pp. 195–217, <DOI:10.1037/pspi0000059>.

4   Harriet Lerner, *The Dance of Anger: A woman's guide to changing the pattern of
    intimate relationships*, HarperCollins, New York, 1985.

CHAPTER 13: BOUNDARIES

1   Quoted in Zach Brittle, 'Manage conflict: Accepting influence', *The Gottman
    Institute Blog*, n.d., <gottman.com/blog/manage-conflict-accepting-influence>.

CHAPTER 14: WHAT WE SPEND OUR TIME ON

1   This is a reference to the title of Marilyn Waring's book *Counting for Nothing:
    What men value and what women are worth* (University of Toronto Press,
    Toronto, 1999). It was a foundational document in the field of feminist
    economics and lauded internationally, but largely ignored in her home
    country of Aotearoa — where she was a National Party MP in the Muldoon
    Government.

2   Eve Rodsky, *Fair Play: A game-changing solution for when you have too much to
    do (and more life to live)*, Penguin Random House, New York, 2021.

CHAPTER 15: SEX, PASSION, EROTICISM AND INTIMACY

1   Joni Mitchell, in a 1991 interview with Kristine McKenna, published in
    Kristine McKenna, *Talk to Her*, Fantagraphics, Seattle, 2004. Sighted by the
    author at <goodreads.com/quotes/1399331>.

2   Esther Perel, *Mating in Captivity: Sex, lies, and domestic bliss*, Hodder &
    Stoughton, London, 2007.

3   R. A. Clay, 'Later-life sex', *APA Monitor*, vol. 43, no. 11 (December 2012),
    p. 42, <apa.org/monitor/2012/12/later-life-sex>; Marie Claire Dorking,
    'Almost half of over 50s say they're having the best sex of their lives', *Yahoo
    Life UK*, 20 September 2021, <nz.news.yahoo.com/over-50-s-having-best-sex-
    lives-100105621.html>.

4   Emily Nagoski, *Come As You Are: The surprising new science that will transform
    your sex life*, Simon & Schuster, New York, 2015.

CHAPTER 16: MONEY AND ITS MEANINGS

1   Diana Clement, 'When single women and Māori couldn't buy a home', *The New Zealand Herald*, 8 December 2018, <nzherald.co.nz/property/when-single-women-and-maori-couldnt-buy-a-home/EPKI62DBECZQ4SJPHNNHHDFQZA>.

CHAPTER 17: PARENTING AS A TEAM

1   J. M. Twenge, W. K. Campbell & C. A. Foster, 'Parenthood and marital satisfaction: A meta-analytic review', *Journal of Marriage and Family*, vol. 65, no. 3 (August 2003), pp. 574–583, <DOI:10.1111/j.1741-3737.2003.00574>.

2   E. M. O'Connor, 'Parenthood detrimental to marriage? Not necessarily . . .', *APA Monitor*, vol. 32, no. 1 (January 2001), p. 54, <apa.org/monitor/jan01/parenthood>.

3   Kelly Bulkeley, 'Why sleep deprivation is torture', *Psychology Today Blog*, 15 December 2014, <psychologytoday.com/nz/blog/dreaming-in-the-digital-age/201412/why-sleep-deprivation-is-torture>.

4   Diana Divecha, 'Why attachment parenting is not the same as secure attachment', *Greater Good Magazine*, 2 May 2018, <greatergood.berkeley.edu/article/item/why_attachment_parenting_is_not_the_same_as_secure_attachment>.

5   Eve Rodsky, *Fair Play: A game-changing solution for when you have too much to do (and more life to live)*, Penguin Random House, New York, 2021.

CHAPTER 19: ARE YOU SAFE? (AND WHAT TO DO IF YOU'RE NOT)

1   N. Glass et al., 'Non-fatal strangulation is an important risk factor for homicide of women', *Journal of Emergency Medicine*, vol. 35, no. 3 (October 2008), pp. 329–335, <DOI:10.1016/j.jemermed.2007.02.065>; J. C. Campbell et al., 'Intimate partner homicide: Review and implications of research and policy', *Trauma, Violence, & Abuse*, vol. 8, no. 3 (July 2007), pp. 246–269, <DOI:10.1177/1524838007303505>.

CHAPTER 20: MAJOR STRESSES, LOSSES AND GRIEF

1   M. Scott Peck, *The Road Less Traveled: A new psychology of love, traditional values and spiritual growth*, Simon & Schuster, New York, 1978.

Index

Index to exercises

Main index

A

abuse *see* emotional abuse and physical
    abuse
Ainsworth, Mary 129, 130
alcohol *see* drinking
Ambivalent Attachment *see* Preoccupied
    Attachment
amygdala 36, 48–50, 56, 64
amygdala hijacks 49, 64, 86–90, 113
    see also triggers
anxiety 17, 142–43, 261, 364
Anxious Attachment *see* Preoccupied
    Attachment
approaches to responsibilities 266–68
approval from partner 18, 30, 32, 34
assertion skills 235
Attachment 129–152
    changing from Insecure 140–47
    Differentiation and 137–38
    expectations 137–38
    parenting and 318–19
    styles 129–135, 152
Attachment grid 134–35, 252
Attachment Theory 48, 123, 129,
    136–37
attitude 97–99, 110–13
attraction 33, 223, 279, 291
autonomy
    avoidant attachment 132
    boundaries 248, 250, 252
    in children 321
    finances and 302–4
    selfish/selfless 119, 191
    time use 260–62
Avoidant Attachment 131–32
    Attachment grid 135
    boundaries and 252
    boundary confusion 142
    case studies 149–152, 168–170,
        327–29
    emotional distance and 143
    independence and 118
    insecurity and 141
    relationship stress 133
    self-soothing and 144

B

Bader, Dr Ellyn 35, 159, 163
Big Picture 102–3, 199, 219, 222
blaming
    anxiety and 238
    case studies 44–47, 62–64, 80,
        204–6, 226–28, 252–55,
        361–64
    emotional abuse and 350
    fear and 238
    grief and 369
    hostility and 66
    insecurities and 157, 175–76
    justifying reactivity 53–64
    power and 239
    resentment and 194
    self-awareness and 87, 89, 102
    self-protection and 187, 191
    stopping 67
    in therapy 79
    Time Out from 71
body basics 92–95
Bolte Taylor, Dr Jill 107
Bonding stage *see* Honeymoon stage
boundaries 248–256
    case study 252–55
    confusion of 141–42, 247–330
    exploring 249–250
    flexibility 252
    gaslighting and 355
    intimacy and 250–51, 256
    normal behaviour 249–250
    setting 134–35, 250–51, 256
    sex and 273, 280
    time use 260–62
boundary confusion 141–42, 247–330
boundary setting 134–35, 250–51
Bowen, Dr Murray 39
Bowlby, John 129, 130
breathing 92–93, 100
Brown, Dr Brené 118, 167
bullying 19

C

calming yourself *see* self-soothing
Cassidy, Professor Jude 145
changing
    partner 24–25, 26, 87, 235
    your situation 24–25, 39, 91, 103, 232
    yourself 22, 24–25, 140–41, 154, 167, 177, 274
chemicals, in the body 36
childcare 321–22
childhood *see* upbringing
choking, during sex 349–350
chronic sorrow 370–71 *see also* grief
Citizens Advice Bureau 352
closeness *see also* intimacy
    intimacy and 22–24, 31, 115–16
    prioritising time for 259
    relationships and 17
co-dependency 141
colonialism 242–43
Come As You Are 282
communication 19, 190–91
Community Legal Centre 352
compliance 51
conflict *see also* Time Out
    avoiding 23, 37–38, 66–67, 73–76, 81–83, 116–17, 128, 318–19
    case studies 27–31, 125–27, 204–6, 224–27
    dealing with 18, 21, 31, 33–35, 38, 187, 207, 208–28
    emotions in 215–17, 228
    as healthy engagement 149
    intimacy and 223, 228
    memories of 212–13, 228
    misinterpretations 213–14
    repair attempts 221–22, 228
    resolution 222–27, 314
    skills to deal with 38–40, 119
    subjective views 211–14, 228
    understanding 21
connection *see also* interaction
    in conflict 217–220

intimacy and 116
rituals and 202–4
during sex 291
sex and 285–87
through disagreements 38, 40
while challenging
    misinterpretations 214–15
consensual non-monogamy (CNM) 10, 274, 334
couple therapy 76–78
Couples Institute 71, 159, 163
culture in relationships
    case studies 28–29, 125–27, 243–44, 371–74
    with children 315
    cross-cultural differences 26–27, 31, 242–43

D

de facto marriage 307
dealing with differences *see* conflict
deception 335–36
dependence, emotional
    case study 46
    hostile 37
    vulnerability 117–18, 138
Developmental Model of Couple Therapy 35, 85–152
differences *see* conflict
Differentiating stage 21, 38–41
Differentiation 114–128
    in Attachment 137–38
    case study 46
    in childhood 55
    finances and 300–301, 305–6
    parenting and 318–19, 320, 324–27
    persistence and 223
    power behaviour and 242
    sex and 280
    skills 38–41, 47
    time use 263
    vulnerability and 174
Differentiation from other 120, 123–25, 148

Differentiation of self 120–23, 142, 144, 148, 192–93
disagreeing *see* conflict
disengagement 51
Dismissive Attachment *see* Avoidant Attachment
Disorganised Attachment 133, 135, 142
dissociation 51
distance in the relationship 17, 132, 143
domestic labour 264–65, 272, 278, 311, 322–23
dominating behaviour 19, 50, 53, 351
drinking 88, 94–95
drugs 94–95 *see also* drinking

E

eating 94–95
ejaculation, rapid or delayed 290–92
emotional abuse 349, 350, 355–56 *see also* safety
emotional baggage *see* insecurities
emotional contagion 141
emotional dependence *see* dependence, emotional
emotional fusion 141
emotional style 134–35
emotional well-being 90–99, 237
emotions 106–8
    in conflict 215–17
    in males 237–39
    managing 20, 179
Empathy *see* Differentiation from other
empathy 178, 214, 313, 316, 340
enmeshment 37
erectile dysfunction 289–292
eroticism 274, 279, 280, 291
exercise 93–94
exercises *see* 'Index to exercises' on page 382
explaining actions 175–77, 183–85
Exploration stage 41–42, 47

F

Fair Play 264, 322
Family Court of New Zealand 357
Fearful-avoidant Attachment *see* Disorganised Attachment
feelings of distance 17
fight or flight response 32, 48–50
finances 299–311
    approach to 302–4
    case study 309–11
    childcare 321–22
    disputes 307
    equitable arrangements 307, 311
    expectations 96
    power, in a relationship 302–4, 311
    self-worth and 302–4, 311
    sex and 273
    shared 301–2
Fisher, Helen 139
Five Fs 50–52, 148, 176, 177, 212
food *see* eating
Freud, Sigmund 53
frustration 17

G

gaslighting 115, 215, 351, 354–55
gender roles 119, 235–240, 262, 276–280, 355–56
Gottman, Dr John 221, 252
grief 365–375
    blame for 369, 375
    case study 371–74
    effect on relationships 365–371
    getting support for 367–68, 375
    grieving together 368–69
    infertility and 316
    ongoing 370–71, 375
    sharing of 367–68, 370, 375
grounding 104–6

H

Handbook of Attachment 145
Honeymoon stage 20–21, 36–38, 121, 138
hormones 36
hostile dependence 66–73
    case studies 46, 80
    honeymoon stage 37
    reaction to vulnerability 82
Hunter, Rachel 183

I

independence 117–19 *see also* isolation, emotional
    avoidance of intimacy 128
    financial 299–300
    as opposed to isolation 22–24
    from partner's approval 34
individual therapy 78–79, 83, 122–23, 144
Individuation *see* Differentiation of self
infertility 315–16
infidelity 332–348
    case study 344–47
    deception and 335–36, 348
    defined 333–34
    dos and don'ts 343–44
    reasons for 341–43
    repairing the relationship 336–341, 348
    safety after 349
infinite loss 370–71
Insecure Attachment 48, 130–33, 135, 148
insecurities 54–56 *see also* triggers
    accepting 156–57
    case studies 29–30, 45–46, 62–64, 168–170, 252–55, 294–98, 344–47
    finances 302–4
    formation of 154–56
    identifying 157–161, 170
    impact of 134–35, 164–65

influence on behaviour 33, 67, 159
    managing 33, 54, 59–61
    parenting and 321–22
    self-protection and 170
    understanding 33, 53, 67–68, 97, 156–57
    working on 165–68
interaction 258–260 *see also* connection
interactional style 134–35
interdependence 34, 42, 60–61, 132, 306
intimacy *see also* closeness; vulnerability
    boundaries and 250–51
    case study 30
    closeness and 17, 22–24, 31, 115–16, 118–19, 128
    conflict and 18
    Insecure Attachment and 132
    as opposed to closeness 128
    prioritising time for 259
    rebuilding trust with 339–340
    as the relationship develops 47, 57
    Secure Attachment and 148–49
    self-awareness and 25–26, 185
intimidation 349, 350, 364
isolation, emotional 22–24 *see also* independence

J

justifying actions 19, 53–54, 56, 64, 175–77

K

Kohut, Heinz 137
Kunin, Brad 326, 327

L

Lerner, Harriet 240
liking oneself 18

grounding exercise 105
in team talks 199
used in conflict avoidance 117,
    209, 220, 222
when triggered 100, 101, 165
time use 257–272
approach to responsibilities
    266–68
case study 270
couple time 258–260
discussing 263–64
domestic labour 264–66
power, in a relationship 260–62
prioritising 257–58, 262–63
self-care 268–69
touch 101
triggers *see also* amygdala hijacks;
    insecurities
identifying 88–90
reacting to 53, 56, 61
strategies to avoid 90–99
strategies to cope with 67–68,
    99–109
warning signs 89–90, 110–13
trust
amygdala and 49
Attachment and 147
case study 45
exploration stage 42
honeymoon stage 37
infidelity and 336–341
reliability and 189

U

University of Auckland 238
upbringing 26–27, 54–56, 156

V

validation 57–61
case studies 45, 62–64
from parents 54
by partner 34, 64
of self 47, 65, 182–83, 195

violence 349
vulnerability *see also* intimacy
case studies 28, 47, 183–85
emotional 173–75
finances and 300–301
independence and 117–18
infidelity and 336–341
in intimacy 23, 26, 115, 128, 132,
    275
management of 134–35
men and 237–39
in relationships 138, 173–75
validation and 57–58

W

wanting (as opposed to needing)
    139–140
warning signs for triggers 89–90,
    110–13
withdrawal 51, 53
Women's Refuge 357, 359

AUTHOR PHOTOGRAPH BY ELENA BEETS

About the author

Nic Beets is a clinical psychologist and family therapist who has specialised in relationship and sex therapy throughout his three decades of practice. He has been with the same partner since he was 17, fellow psychologist Verity Thom. They have two children who have taught them much about love and priorities. Another joint project is a fortnightly column for *The New Zealand Herald* called 'Intimacy, actually', which answers reader questions on love, sex and relationships.

As well as seeing clients, Nic provides training and supervision in relationship therapy, and the Developmental Model in particular. He is the coordinator and host of the Sex Therapy Interest Group, an Australasian peer-support network for sex therapists that has been running for more than 20 years.

A keen waterman, Nic loves anything related to the sea. His current passions are SUP surfing and long-distance waka ama (outrigger canoe) racing.